GOVERNING HIGH SEAS FISHERIES

The Interplay of Global and Regional Regimes

Edited by

OLAV SCHRAM STOKKE

OXFORD
UNIVERSITY PRESS

OXFORD

UNIVERSITY PRESS

Great Clarendon Street, Oxford OX2 6DP

Oxford University Press is a department of the University of Oxford.
It furthers the University's objective of excellence in research, scholarship,
and education by publishing worldwide in

Oxford New York

Athens Auckland Bangkok Bogotá Buenos Aires
Cape Town Chennai Dar es Salaam Delhi Florence Hong Kong Istanbul
Karachi Kolkata Kuala Lumpur Madrid Melbourne Mexico City Mumbai
Nairobi Paris São Paulo Shanghai Singapore Taipei Tokyo Toronto Warsaw
and associated companies in Berlin Ibadan

Oxford is a registered trade mark of Oxford University Press
in the UK and certain other countries

Published in the United States
by Oxford University Press Inc., New York

British Library Cataloguing in Publication Data
Data available

Library of Congress Cataloging in Publication Data
Governing high seas fisheries; the interplay of global and regional regimes/
edited by Olav Schram Stokke.
p. cm.
Includes bibliographical references.
1. Fishery law and legislation. 2. Economic zones (Law of the sea)
I. Stokke, Olav Schram, 1961–
K3895.G68 2001
341.7'622—dc21 2001016286
ISBN 0-19-829949-4

1 3 5 7 9 10 8 6 4 2

Typeset by Best-set Typesetter Ltd., Hong Kong
Printed in Great Britain
on acid-free paper by
Biddles Ltd. Guildford and King's Lynn

Preface

This book on high seas fisheries management originated from a three-year international research project on 'Polar Oceans and the Law of the Sea' (POLOS, 1996–8). In addition to scholars at the Fridtjof Nansen Institute in Norway who initiated and coordinated the project, experts from four continents were involved. The views expressed by the officials who took part in the project are in their personal capacity only.

The book has been written by a group of eleven contributors, all of whom are prominent experts in their respective fields, from seven countries: Australia, Chile, Croatia, the Netherlands, Norway, the United Kingdom, and the United States. During the POLOS project, the research team met once a year at project workshops to hammer out jointly the various components of an integrated line of argument. Along with acknowledging the contributions made by workshop participants, thanks are also due to the institutions that provided venues for the workshops: in 1998, the Inter-University Centre Dubrovnik, Croatia; in 1997, the Fridtjof Nansen Institute at Polhøgda near Oslo, Norway; and in 1996, the Antarctic Cooperative Research Centre at the University of Tasmania in Hobart, Australia.

The discussion of the draft chapters prepared for the Dubrovnik Workshop benefited considerably from the anonymous reviews of individual chapters that had been prepared by external experts in the relevant subject areas. I am very grateful to David Anderson, E. D. Brown, Laurence Cordonnery, Moritaka Hayashi, Alf Håkon Hoel, Stuart Kaye, Ted McDorman, Michael Sean Sullivan, and Geir Ulfstein for conducting these reviews and generously offering advice on how the drafts could be further advanced. I would also like to thank the large number of scholars and practitioners, many of whom are acknowledged in individual chapters, who provided valuable comments on various parts of the book manuscript. Alf Håkon Hoel and Davor Vidas deserve particular thanks for examining both early and more mature drafts of the chapters with a precious blend of amiable enthusiasm and stern criticism. Arild Underdal and Oran Young, friends and colleagues at the Centre for Advanced Study in Oslo during the academic year 1999/2000 when the book was being finalized, gave helpful suggestions on the conceptual content. Willy Østreng, in his usual energetic way, was vital to the initiation of POLOS, and he remained supportive throughout the project.

By summer 1999, the chapters were assembled as a book manuscript and submitted to Oxford University Press. I am highly appreciative of OUP's Commissioning Editor of Law, John Louth, and Assistant Editor

Mick Belson, for their efficiency and patience, and am also grateful to three anonymous reviewers who provided lucid and very constructive suggestions on the submitted manuscript. I am indebted to Mary Hustad for her excellent language services, and to Maryanne Rygg and Claes Lykke Ragner for their careful copy-editing and cartographic assistance. The project has been funded by the Norwegian Research Council and by the participating institutions.

Unless otherwise stated, the book has been updated as of 1 January 2000.

Oslo   O. S. S.

Contents

List of Maps

List of Contributors

DAVID A. BALTON is Director, Office of Marine Conservation, US Department of State. Balton served on the US Delegation during the negotiation of the Convention on the Conservation and Management of Pollock Resources in the Central Bering Sea and during the United Nations Conference on Straddling Fish Stocks and Highly Migratory Fish Stocks. His publications include 'Strengthening the Law of the Sea: The New Agreement on Straddling Fish Stocks and Highly Migratory Fish Stocks' (*Ocean Development and International Law*, 1995).

ALAN BOYLE is Professor of Public International Law at the University of Edinburgh and General Editor of the *International and Comparative Law Quarterly*. He is co-author, with P. Birnie, of *International Law and the Environment* (Clarendon Press, 2nd edition, 2001). Among his many publications are the recent edited volumes *Human Rights Approaches to Environmental Protection* (with M. Anderson, 1996) and *International Law and Sustainable Development* (with D. Freestone, 1999), both published by Clarendon Press. He has acted for several governments in fisheries and law of the sea disputes.

ROBIN CHURCHILL is Professor of Law at Cardiff University. His main research interests are the international law of the sea and international environmental law, on both of which he has written widely. His publications include *EEC Fisheries Law* (Martinus Nijhoff, 1987), *International Law and Global Climate Change* (Graham & Trotman, 1991, D. Freestone co-editor), and *The Law of the Sea* (Manchester University Press, 3rd edition, 1999, A. V. Lowe co-author).

RICHARD HERR is a Reader in Political Science at the University of Tasmania in Hobart, Tasmania, Australia. He has served as Chair of two Australian national committees for Antarctic research grants over the past decade. His research interests include the evaluation of regional organization as a mechanism for resource management. He has had experience as a consultant on regional fisheries in the South Pacific and on Antarctic tourism. His publications include *Global Electronic Database of Multilateral Marine Treaties and Agreements* (Kluwer Law International, 1999) and *Asia in Antarctica* (Centre for Resource and Environmental Studies, 1994, B. W. Davis co-editor).

CHRISTOPHER C. JOYNER is Professor of International Law in the Department of Government at Georgetown University. He is co-editor of

United Nations Legal Order (Cambridge University Press, 1995) and editor of *The United Nations and International Law* (Cambridge University Press, 1997). He has written more than 300 articles in law reviews and published twelve books, among them *Antarctica and the Law of the Sea* (Martinus Nijhoff, 1992) and *Governing the Frozen Commons: The Antarctic Regime and Environmental Protection* (University of South Carolina Press, 1998). His most recent publication is *International Law in the 21st Century: Legal Rules for Global Governance* (Rowman & Littlefield, forthcoming in 2001).

GEIR HØNNELAND is a doctor of political science from the University of Oslo and Director of the Polar Programme at the Fridtjof Nansen Institute, Norway. He has published widely in academic journals on the management of natural resources and the environment in the European Arctic. He is also the author of *Centre–Periphery Relations in Russia* (Ashgate, 2001, with H. Blakkisrud), *Coercive and Discursive Compliance Mechanisms in the Management of Natural Resources* (Kluwer Academic, 2000), and *Integration vs. Autonomy: Civil–Military Relations on the Kola Peninsula* (Ashgate, 1999, with A. K. Jørgensen).

FRANCISCO ORREGO VICUÑA is Professor of International Law at the University of Chile, Member of the Institut de Droit International, Judge and Vice-President of the World Bank Administrative Tribunal, and President of the Panel of the UN Compensation Commission, among other functions. He is the author of, among other numerous publications, *The Changing International Law of High Seas Fisheries* (1999), *The Exclusive Economic Zone: Regime and Legal Nature under International Law* (1988), and *Antarctic Resources Policy* (1983), all published by Cambridge University Press.

ALEX G. OUDE ELFERINK is a Senior Research Associate at the Netherlands Institute for the Law of the Sea (NILOS) of the Faculty of Law of Utrecht University. A co-editor of the *NILOS International Organizations and the Law of the Sea Documentary Yearbook*, his current research interests include the legal regime of fisheries, the outer limits of the continental shelf, and maritime boundary delimitation, with special reference to the Arctic. He has published on a wide range of law of the sea issues, including *The Law of Maritime Boundary Delimitation: A Case Study of the Russian Federation* (Martinus Nijhoff, 1994).

OLAV SCHRAM STOKKE is Research Director at the Fridtjof Nansen Institute, Norway. A political scientist from the University of Oslo, he is co-editor of *Yearbook of International Co-operation on Environment and Development*. His research interest is international political economy, with special emphasis on regime theory applied to regional cooperation and management of natural resources and the environment. He has published extensively in these fields, including the edited volumes *Governing the Antarctic: The Effectiveness and Legitimacy of the Antarctic Treaty System* (Cambridge University Press, 1996, with D. Vidas) and *The Barents Region: Cooperation in Arctic Europe* (SAGE, 1994, with O. Tunander).

DAVOR VIDAS is Senior Research Fellow at the Fridtjof Nansen Institute, Norway. His books address Antarctic and Arctic affairs, law of the sea, and environmental law, including most recently the edited volumes *Protecting the Polar Marine Environment* (Cambridge University Press, 2000), *Implementing the Environmental Protection Regime for the Antarctic* (Kluwer Academic, 2000), and *Order for the Oceans at the Turn of the Century* (Kluwer Law International, 1999, with W. Østreng). He has been adviser to the Norwegian delegation to Antarctic Treaty meetings since 1992.

BUDISLAV VUKAS is Professor of Public International Law at the University of Zagreb Faculty of Law, and Judge at the International Tribunal for the Law of the Sea. A member of the Institut de Droit International, Professor Vukas has made substantial contributions to various fields of international law, including the law of the sea, environmental law, and human rights. He is author of 'States, Peoples and Minorities' (*Recueil des cours*, 1991) and among his many publication activities is the editorship of the five-volume series *Essays on the New Law of the Sea* (1985–96).

Abbreviations

ACFM	Advisory Committee for Fishery Management (of the International Council for the Exploration of the Sea)
AHL	allowable harvest level
Art.	Article
ASIL	American Society for International Law
ATCM	Antarctic Treaty Consultative Meeting
ATS	Antarctic Treaty System
CCAMLR	Convention on the Conservation of Antarctic Marine Living Resources
CEMP	CCAMLR Ecosystem Monitoring Program
Cmnd.	*Command Paper* (of the United Kingdom)
DWFN	distant water fishing nations
EC	European Community
EEZ	exclusive economic zone
EFTA	European Free Trade Association
EFZ	exclusive fisheries zone
EU	European Union
FAO	(United Nations) Food and Agricultural Organization
FFA	(South Pacific) Forum Fisheries Agency
Fish Stocks Agreement	Agreement for the Implementation of the Provisions of the United Nations Convention on the Law of the Sea of 10 December 1982 relating to the Conservation and Management of Straddling Fish Stocks and Highly Migratory Fish Stocks, 1995
Fish Stocks Conference	United Nations Conference on Straddling Fish Stocks and Highly Migratory Fish Stocks, 1993–5
GA	(United Nations) General Assembly
GATT	General Agreement on Tariffs and Trade
ICCAT	International Commission for the Conservation of Atlantic Tunas
ICES	International Council for the Exploration of the Sea
ICJ	International Court of Justice
ICNAF	International Convention for the Northwest Atlantic Fisheries, 1949

ILC	(United Nations) International Law Commission
ILM	*International Legal Materials*
ILR	*International Law Reports*
IMO	(United Nations) International Maritime Organization
INQ	individual national quota
IOC	(United Nations) Intergovernmental Oceanographic Commission
ISA	International Seabed Authority
ITLOS	International Tribunal for the Law of the Sea
IUCN	International Union for the Conservation of Nature and Natural Resources (now IUCN—The World Conservation Union)
IUU	illegal, unreported, and unregulated (fishing)
IWC	International Whaling Commission
LNTS	*League of Nations Treaty Series*
LOS	law of the sea
LOSB	(United Nations) *Law of the Sea Bulletin*
LOSC	(United Nations) Law of the Sea Convention, 1982
MOU	Memorandum of Understanding
NAFO	Northwest Atlantic Fisheries Organization
NASCO	North Atlantic Salmon Conservation Organization
NEAFC	North-East Atlantic Fisheries Commission
NGO	non-governmental organization
NPAFC	North Pacific Anadromous Fish Commission
NRA	NAFO Regulatory Area
OECD	Organization for Economic Co-operation and Development
OJ	*Official Journal of the European Communities*
OMFM	*Overenskomster med fremmede makter* (Norwegian Treaty Series)
para.	paragraph
PCIJ	Permanent Court of International Justice
PICES	North Pacific Marine Science Organization
Recueil des cours	*Recueil des cours de l'Académie de Droit International* (The Hague)
RGDIP	*Revue générale de droit international public*
RIAA	(United Nations) *Reports of International Arbitral Awards*
SBT	southern bluefin tuna

SCOI	Standing Committee on Observation and Inspection (under CCAMLR)
SGSSI	South Georgia and the South Sandwich Islands
TAC	total allowable catch
TIAS	*Treaties and Other International Acts Series* (United States)
UN	United Nations
UNCED	United Nations Conference on Environment and Development, 1992
UNCLOS	United Nations Conference on the Law of the Sea
UNCLOS I	First United Nations Conference on the Law of the Sea, 1958
UNCLOS II	Second United Nations Conference on the Law of the Sea, 1960
UNCLOS III	Third United Nations Conference on the Law of the Sea, 1973–82
UNCTAD	United Nations Conference on Trade and Development
UNEP	United Nations Environment Programme
UNTS	*United Nations Treaty Series*
USC	United States Code
UST	*United States Treaties and Other International Agreements*
VMS	vessel monitoring system
WTO	World Trade Organization

Introduction

OLAV SCHRAM STOKKE

The Spanish-flagged *Estai* was 28 miles . . . outside Canada's 200 mile
. . . limit on Thursday when a Canadian gunboat fired shots across its
bows, gave chase and then boarded the vessel. . . . A Spanish patrol
boat was ready to sail from the southern port of Cadiz . . . with
instructions to protect other Spanish boats in the area.[1]

I consider all this an act of organized piracy.[2]

The Spanish represent my future and the loss of it. . . . If they continue
what they're doing today, there'll be nothing left for any of us, including the Spanish.[3]

Gunboat diplomacy, of course, is not a new tactic in resource management; it has been an essential part of international fisheries relations for
centuries. The 'Cod Wars' between Iceland and the United Kingdom in
the 1970s were considerably more dramatic than the *Estai* case; they
involved naval operations on both sides, with vessel collisions and,
ultimately, severance of diplomatic relations between the two states
involved.[4] Two decades later, like the Icelanders, Canada aimed at changing high seas international law—arguing that the existing rules provide
inadequate basis for effective management of high seas fishery resources.

This book addresses the wave of international disputes that arose in the
1990s over straddling stocks, i.e. stocks that occur both within national
waters and in the high seas area beyond. Also addressed is the role that
these controversies played in strengthening the global high seas fisheries
regime. After the extension of coastal state jurisdiction in the late 1970s,
a decade of relative tranquillity ensued in international fisheries. Distant
water fishing nations tried out various cooperative modes for adapting to
the new political situation, including access agreements and industrial
joint ventures with coastal state counterparts.

However, in one region after another, the level of conflict gradually
increased again, fuelled by two processes. Inside national zones, coastal
states were often unable to prevent the development of overcapacity in the
domestic fleet; and despite their exclusive management position within 200
miles from the baselines, they failed to introduce and effectively enforce
adequate conservation measures. Comparable to this, distant water fishing
vessels that had been expelled from coastal waters soon engaged in exploration and development of fisheries opportunities in the remaining high

seas areas. Not surprisingly, some of the richest high seas fishing grounds were found adjacent to the recently established coastal zones, thus setting the scene for international rivalry over straddling stocks.

The seizure of *Estai*, which occurred on the high seas part of the Grand Banks, was the peak of a long-standing conflict between the coastal state of Canada and the European Community. Although both were members of the Northwest Atlantic Fisheries Organization (NAFO),[5] they sharply disagreed over conservation measures that had recently been adopted by it. After heated and hectic diplomatic exchange, the two parties entered into the Agreed Minute, a bilateral agreement that settled some of the underlying issues.[6] The substance of this agreement was subsequently incorporated into the regional regime, which made some notable headway in regulatory procedure and compliance control in the North-west Atlantic.

Indeed, this showdown had all the ingredients of a classic high seas fisheries dispute: (1) a coastal state concerned about the health of a stock straddling its waters but very determined to ensure a substantial share of the stock for itself; (2) distant water fishing fleets with long traditions of harvesting in the region;[7] (3) a fish stock definitely in need of conservation; and (4) fundamental disagreement on the legitimacy of high seas fishing operations in the area. If one adds (5) an unusual preparedness on the part of the coastal state to take unilateral measures in waters beyond its undisputed jurisdiction and (6) notable interplay between this regional dispute and parallel negotiations over a United Nations Fish Stocks Agreement,[8] a rough sketch of a tableau appears that will be given sharper contours and finer details in the course of this book.

As to regional management disputes, not only will the Northwest Atlantic situation be addressed in depth but also a series of other high seas controversies. Among these disputes, the Bering Sea Doughnut Hole has been particularly prominent. Before the collapse of the pollock stock around 1990, this high seas pocket, which is squeezed between the United States and the Russian (previously Soviet) zones, set the stage for one of the largest high seas fisheries the world had seen. The lack of adequate means to manage the Doughnut Hole fishery infused the straddling stock issue with considerable political energy. Proposals put forward in the US Senate to the effect that the two coastal states should extend 'bilateral fisheries jurisdiction' beyond the 200-mile limit to cover the entire Bering Sea were seen by many as threatening the fine balance that had been established by the Law of the Sea Convention between the interests of coastal states and flag states in resource management and navigation.[9] Similarly, throughout the 1990s management of fish stocks straddling into the Sea of Okhotsk Peanut Hole, the North-East Atlantic Banana Hole, the Barents

Sea Loophole, and various zones in the Southern Ocean have been matters of grave interstate rivalry.

All of the regional case studies in this book turn on straddling stocks whereas the Fish Stocks Agreement also embraces highly migratory species, such as tuna, marlin, and swordfish. The motive for focusing on straddling stocks disputes is to ensure a level of homogeneity among the cases that will allow cross-case comparison of regional management performance. Highly migratory species, which habitually move through extensive areas of ocean space, tend to raise certain management challenges that are not encountered by the regimes portrayed in this book. The number of coastal states is often high, which renders the problem of coordination more difficult; moreover, many coastal states for highly migratory species are small, developing nations with little developed capacity for surveillance and enforcement of fishery regulations. The legal basis for regional management is also different. In the case of highly migratory species, international law mandates the adoption of multilateral conservation and management measures for the entire region, including national waters; for straddling stock, such cooperative measures may be limited to the high seas area.[10]

1 Straddling stocks: overfished and under-managed

On a world scale, the essential problem in high seas management is that there are too many vessels chasing too few fish.[11] Needless to say, the two components are causally linked. Already thirty years ago, the health of many targeted stocks was in decline, and since then the world fishing fleet has doubled in tonnage. Even more important, the harvesting and processing efficiency per vessel has grown immensely—according to some estimates by a factor of three.[12] While the degree of overcapacity may be debated, there is no doubt that today the value of vessels, labour, fuels, and other inputs to world fishing is much higher than what is required for reaching the desired level of harvesting in the most efficient manner.[13] And whereas fishing effort is up, most oceanic regions currently have catch per production surface well below historic peak levels.[14] Moreover, aggregate catch figures do not adequately portray the developments in the harvested value because there is a broad trend in world fisheries whereby harvesters are forced to move down the food chain from valuable predator species such as cod and haddock to less valuable, small pelagic species.

This trend is the dismal and somewhat paradoxical outcome of industrious efforts that had begun already in the 1950s to radically modernize harvesting operations in the world's fisheries; the key factor was the extension of the spatial reach of vessels. As a deep-blue counterpart to the 'green revolution' in agriculture, the distant water strategy launched by a few leading fishing nations had four components: (1) intensive efforts were made in fish-finding marine research and enhancement of harvesting, freezing, and processing technologies; (2) a rapid build-up occurred of diverse fishing capacity, including a wide range of trawlers, purse seiners, and longliners; (3) infrastructures with global reach were established, comprising processing mother ships, land bases, and an array of service, freezer, and transport vessels that linked distant water operations and domestic consumers; and (4) massive governmental subsidies were granted to enhance the relative competitiveness of national industries, a feature highly prominent even today.[15]

Nations such as Japan, the Soviet Union, Poland, and the Republic of Korea took leading roles in this development, largely explained by the conjunction of serious food security concerns and lack of good alternatives. Early government-sponsored fisheries development schemes were closely related to rapid industrialization processes that tended to concentrate the expanding, protein-hungry populations into non-food-producing urban areas. In the United States, by contrast, the growing prosperity and a strong preference for meat placed limits on the economic viability of distant water fishing operations for species other than tuna.[16] In western Europe, important markets, such as the British, were slowed down by scepticism towards frozen fish, which rendered more proximate fishing grounds more attractive.[17]

The overall increase in fishery pressure that followed from the build-up of distant water activity soon led to lower yields that in turn spurred the search for new harvesting areas and the development of even more efficient gear. Competition between the distant water fishing fleets grew more intense; the dynamics of scarcity, rivalry, and technology improvements accelerated even more with the extension of coastal state jurisdiction. There have essentially been three modes of adaptation that the distant water fishing nations embraced to meet these new challenges. In the North-East Atlantic, the United Kingdom in particular chose *confrontation*. In an attempt to maintain the high seas status of its primary distant water fishing grounds, the UK fought and lost two 'Cod Wars' with Iceland before the concept of exclusive economic zone (EEZ) emerged as customary international law in the mid-1970s and was codified in the Law of the Sea Convention.[18] After being expelled from Icelandic waters, the British fishing companies largely dropped out of the distant water fishing league.[19]

Meanwhile, the centrally planned nations of eastern Europe, as well as operators of Spanish, Japanese, and Korean distant water fishing vessels, pursued much more successfully a different strategy—namely that of *co-optation*, or the engaging of economic interests in the coastal state. A variety of instruments, including access fees, development aid, collaborative research, chartering arrangements, and industrial joint ventures, were employed.[20] While such instruments are today still important for access to the zones of many developing countries, their overall significance for world distant water fishing activity was drastically curtailed during the 1980s by the phasing out of foreign harvesting in North Pacific waters governed by the United States and the Soviet Union. Those waters had been the most important settings for the co-optation strategy.

These overall developments, and comparable experiences in other regions, induced distant water fishing operators to intensify the search for remaining high seas options. This strategy of *avoiding* coastal state jurisdiction has been closely connected with technological advances because the development of new fisheries far from the coast usually exploits species that are of relatively low value or inhabit very deep waters previously inaccessible for technological or economic reasons; this places a higher premium on cost-efficient operations.[21]

The emergence of distant water fishing in various high seas areas during the 1980s was therefore directly related to stricter access policies on the part of coastal states. Harvesting in the Doughnut Hole had been negligible before the Americanization of the US zone off Alaska.[22] When the Doughnut Hole fishery dried up, the fleets that had operated there shifted their attention to the Sea of Okhotsk Peanut Hole, targeting pollock that straddle from Russian national waters. Similarly, the increased presence of Spanish vessels in the Northwest Atlantic in the mid-1980s, from traditional trawlers to large factory trawlers, was associated with the preceding phase-out of those vessels from waters off Namibia.[23] The more recent pressure on the Barents Sea Loophole, which began in the early 1990s, was partly caused by vessels being sold inexpensively by Canadian fishing companies—a result of the simultaneous collapse of several groundfish stocks in the Northwest Atlantic and the closure of the traditional fishery for Northern cod.

In short, the 'enclosure of the oceans' did not eliminate the high seas fisheries management challenge, but rather it lessened and moved the management problem further away from the coast. When the Law of the Sea Convention was adopted, the share of commercial marine living resources beyond 200 miles was generally estimated at only a few per cent. Today, much suggests that the figure may be somewhere around 5 per cent; the high seas share of world catches is believed to be still higher, at 10 per cent,[24] because expensive access arrangements, reduced quotas, and steadily more intrusive monitoring and enforcement measures have made operators of distant water fishing fleets more aware of the attractiveness of living resources found beyond national control.[25]

2 International responses

Some controversies, including those surrounding high seas fisheries, were left open by the Law of the Sea Convention. Relevant provisions broadly confirm the duty to cooperate on the high seas management of straddling stocks, a duty already provided for in the Geneva Conventions, without further specification of rights and obligations.[26] In this respect, Article 63 provides the following:

Where the same stock or stocks of associated species occur both within the exclusive economic zone and in an area beyond and adjacent to the zone, the coastal State and the States fishing for such stocks in the adjacent area shall seek, either directly or through appropriate subregional or regional organizations, to agree upon the measures necessary for the conservation of these stocks in the adjacent area.[27]

In accordance with this loose framework, straddling stocks issues throughout the 1980s were handled either within existing regional management regimes or by regularized or ad hoc diplomatic exchange between coastal states and distant water users. By the end of the 1980s, however, mounting tensions and declining stocks in several areas suggested that the regional approach on its own would prove to be inadequate.

Spurred by its problems in the Grand Banks and joined by several Latin American countries, Canada succeeded in placing high seas fisheries on the agenda of the United Nations Conference on Environment and Development (UNCED). At the Conference, there was clear determination among those negotiating on behalf of long-distance fishing interests that the matter should be addressed without further coastal state encroachment on high seas freedoms.[28] The largely distributive negotiations between those two blocs of interests were subsequently played out in a series of international conferences, the most prominent of which was the United Nations Conference on Straddling Fish Stocks and Highly Migratory Fish Stocks, held in New York between April 1993 and August 1995.

2.1 From Cancun to New York

The Food and Agriculture Organization of the United Nations (FAO) took on a significant role in the process that led up to the Fish Stocks Agreement.[29] A few months prior to the UNCED Conference, certain principles for management of high seas fisheries were set forth in the 1992 Cancun Declaration. On the basis of the Declaration, the FAO was instructed to take lead responsibility in drafting a Code of Conduct for Responsible Fisheries; the code was finalized in 1995.[30] Among the steps taken to implement the Code, a voluntary International Plan of Action for the Management of Fishing Capacity urged states to develop national plans aimed at obtaining a better balance between fishing capacity and available resources.[31] The FAO also contributed to the drafting of the Agenda 21 chapter on sustainable development of the oceans. Adopted during the UNCED Conference, Agenda 21 placed special emphasis on challenges associated with high seas management. Among the steps that were urged was that the states should take effective action to deter their nationals from reflagging vessels in order to escape regulatory measures applicable to high seas fishing. The Compliance Agreement, which was approved unanimously by the FAO Conference in 1993, was drawn up in response to that request.[32]

2.2 Negotiating the Fish Stocks Agreement

The UNCED Conference also called for the convening of an international conference to promote effective implementation of the Law of the Sea Convention with regard to straddling stocks and highly migratory species.[33] This appeal was subsequently echoed by the UN General Assembly.[34] In the course of six sessions, a number of controversial matters were addressed and resolved. While thorough discussion of the Fish Stocks Agreement is given elsewhere in this book, a brief introductory outline of some of the most difficult issues during the negotiations will be useful here.[35]

Not surprisingly, the *form* of the instrument was an issue of contention, distant water fishing nations preferring non-binding guidelines. What tipped the balance was the eventual preference among influential states that had mixed interests for achieving a binding treaty; in the case of the USA, strong lobbying by environmentalist groups played an important role.[36] Another matter of controversy was the spatial *scope* of the agreement. Distant water fishing nations insisted that new obligations on their part regarding the high seas must be balanced by similar duties on coastal states regarding waters under national jurisdiction.[37] In the end, whereas the Agreement generally applies to the high seas, certain basic principles of management were also given application within the coastal zones. One of these principles, the precautionary approach to management laid out in the Agreement as part of the UNCED legacy, remained controversial until consensus emerged that the application of this approach would not create a moratorium on fishing whenever there is scientific uncertainty.[38]

The notion that there should be *compatibility* between conservation measures applied inside and outside of national waters received wide support. However, whereas coastal states interpreted compatibility to imply that rules pertaining to the EEZ should be extended to adjacent high seas areas, distant water fishing nations emphasized the implications of existing high seas measures for coastal state management.[39] Both views influenced the elaboration of the concept contained in the Fish Stocks Agreement: states are required to 'take into account' both EEZ regulations and previously agreed multilateral high seas standards when establishing compatible straddling stocks measures. On the other hand, only existing EEZ regulations are reinforced by the explicit obligation to 'ensure that measures established . . . for the high seas do not undermine the effectiveness of such measures'.[40]

Among the major contributions of the Agreement is the specification of the duty to cooperate on high seas management problems; accordingly, the position and role of regional management regimes loomed large in the negotiations.[41] Distant water fishing nations were eager to ensure that empowerment of decision-making bodies under such regimes would be accompanied by openness to non-coastal states. Many coastal states favoured restricted access to regional management bodies and also argued that the authority of the latter be delimited to a share of the stock that corresponded to the stock's occurrence in international waters.

Regarding measures to improve *enforcement* of conservation and management measures, the FAO Compliance Agreement facilitated negotiations over the flag state component in this issue. Accordingly, the Conference could concentrate on port state measures and especially on the difficult matter of a framework procedure permitting, in a way acceptable to both coastal and distant water fishing nations, non-flag states to board, inspect, and under certain conditions even to detain fishing vessels on the high seas.[42] Obtaining acceptance from distant water fishing nations for such modification of the traditional primacy of the flag state in high seas enforcement required, among other things, that agreement was reached on a system for settling disputes among the involved parties.[43]

3 Governing high seas fisheries: outline of the book

A number of analyses of the UN Fish Stocks Agreement, or the high seas problematique more generally, are already in print.[44] Also in print is a substantial set of regional case studies that deal with the management of specific high seas disputes.[45] In this book, the focus is shifted from specific regimes to the interplay of various global and regional regimes set up to manage high seas fisheries. This attention to linkages between regimes is prompted by the fact that, in the 1990s, straddling stocks management came into main focus simultaneously in a large number of regions, which led to a rapid elaboration of international rules in this area.

3.1 Regime interplay and effective governance

'Governance' derives from the Greek *kybernetes* and is etymologically linked to navigation and helmsmen. At the interstate level, such hierarchic connotations are rather misleading. Those responsible for creating and operating international governance systems, or regimes, are also the ones to be governed, i.e. states, jealously guarding their sovereignty.[46] Generally, regimes are social institutions that define practices, assign roles, and guide the interaction of occupants of such roles within a given issue area.[47] They comprise a substantive component of rights and rules and usually an operational component that supports the establishment and implementation of such rules.[48]

Substantive rights and rules are often differentiated across participants. For instance, in the regime for management of Barents Sea fisheries, the two coastal states acknowledge disparate entitlements to the shared stocks, which is reflected in fixed divisions of annual quotas.[49] Similarly for operational rules, the regional regime for the management of Antarctic affairs makes a clear distinction between consultative and non-consultative parties to the 1959 Antarctic Treaty in that the latter are relegated formally to the role of observers in decision-making.[50] Only rarely, if ever, can a regime be properly described by reference to a single legal source. Instead, the characteristic pattern of differentiation is typically upheld by a network of legal instruments and customary rules. When the regime governing fisheries in the Northwest Atlantic is addressed, at least two major sources must be examined: the accord by which NAFO was established that covers both the high seas and Canadian waters but confines multilateral decision-making to the former area; and the elements of the Law of the Sea Convention that codify customary law regarding resource management in the EEZ and the high seas, respectively. Relations between these various sources could be labelled intra-regime linkages, and a high level of normative coherence is a *sine qua non*.

'Inter-regime linkages' refers to the *interplay* among distinguishable, institutional arrangements;[51] the term implies that aspects of one regime influence the material contents or the operation or consequences of another. Such interplay can be deliberately triggered by actors for reasons of expediency, but it may also simply result from functional connections among the activities involved.[52] Diffusive interplay is one type, visible when specific features of one international regime serve as models for another regime, for example by helping define basic principles or other substantive or operational regime elements.[53] The proliferation in current environmental and resource regimes of principles such as ecosystem management, precautionary measures, or sustainable development, identically or similarly phrased, seems to provide evidence of such diffusion.

A second type of regime interaction can be termed political interplay, and refers to situations when interests or capabilities defined within one regime influence the operation of another. It is quite common that states engaged in global-level resource management negotiations assume positions that reflect their interests in regional management settings: Canada's assumption of a leadership role during the Fish Stocks Conference was closely related to the frustrations Canada had experienced within NAFO. Another version of political interplay between regimes is evident when a state mobilizes its position within one regime to gain increased leverage in another. The EEZ regime, which allows the coastal state to set the conditions for foreign access to national waters, is frequently used by coastal states to induce distant water fishing nations to accept stricter management rules for adjacent high seas areas.

A third type of interplay that is relevant to regime effectiveness, normative interplay, occurs when the rules upheld in one regime either conflict with or reinforce those established under another. Illustrations may be found in the relationship between certain regimes that aim at, respectively, conservation of living resources and liberal trade practices. For instance, US rules prohibiting imports of tuna not harvested in conformity with US rules for by-catch protection of dolphin were challenged by Mexico as violating the General Agreement on Tarriffs and Trade.[54]

The fourth type of regime interconnection addressed here is operational interplay. This type of interplay denotes efforts by regime participants to coordinate activities under separate regimes to avoid normative conflict or wasteful duplication of work. The role of the International Council for the Exploration of the Sea in providing scientific advice to a range of regional fisheries management bodies is a case in point. The need for coordination across international regimes becomes steadily more urgent with the proliferation in many issue areas of cooperative processes at subregional and regional, as well as global, levels.

As will be demonstrated in this book, instances of these four types of interplay have contributed significantly to the changes in the international law of high seas fisheries that have occurred during the 1990s. Of particular interest is the question whether such regime interplay enhances the effectiveness of regional management regimes, and, if so, in what way and under what circumstances. The effectiveness of an international regime is defined here as its impact on the problems that gave rise to its formation. Throughout this book, the applied standard of effectiveness is whether the regime provides adequate means for meeting three major management tasks: (1) to generate adequate and reasonably consensual scientific knowledge about the state and dynamics of the stocks in question to guide decisions on fishery pressure; (2) to adopt, while taking heed of existing knowledge, legitimate and appropriate conservation and management measures regulating economic activities; and (3) to create and maintain a system to promote compliance with those measures among those engaged in resource use in the area.

3.2 High seas fisheries in international law

Part I of the book opens with a chapter by Francisco Orrego Vicuña which highlights the gradual reconceptualization that has occurred of a cornerstone principle in international fisheries law—freedom of the high seas. Already in the 1950s, it was clear that this principle could not be held to imply unrestrained fishing. Later on, the vagueness of the obligation to pay 'due regard' to the interest of other participants was seen as irreconcilable with effective management; the development of new zonal concepts thus provided the means for introducing conservation authority while at the same time retaining some of the rights enjoyed on the high seas by distant water fishing nations, including access to a resource surplus. Such accommodation of the often competing concerns of coastal and distant water fishing nations has also marked the more recent evolution of international law for high seas fisheries. The core of this chapter is a comprehensive assessment of the substantive and operational contributions of the UN Fish Stocks Agreement.

The remaining chapters in Part I evaluate features of the emerging global regime for high seas fisheries that are particularly crucial to the achievement of effective management. In Chapter 2, Budislav Vukas and Davor Vidas canvass the means available for addressing harvesting activities by vessels flying flags of convenience—i.e. vessels registered by states that are non-parties to regional management regimes and lack the willingness or capacity effectively to assert jurisdiction and control over these vessels. The lenient requirements for entry that mark such registers allow vessels to move in and out of the registers on the basis of short-term expediency—a practice that can severely frustrate regional management efforts. Chapter 2 first reviews a long-standing, yet largely futile, search in international law for an adequate definition of the 'genuine link' that must exist between a state and ships flying its flag; it then focuses more closely on recent trends in dealing with flags of convenience in international fisheries management.

In Chapter 3, Alan Boyle draws attention to another major challenge of contemporary international law—the provision of adequate procedures for settling fisheries disputes among states. The evolution of the dispute settlement system laid down in the Law of the Sea Convention is reviewed, in particular the flexibility provided regarding the method and procedure for resolving differences and the significant exceptions from compulsory jurisdiction maintained in international law—notably matters related to research and resource management in the EEZ. Those exceptions imply that the way in which a claim is formulated and a case is characterized can be decisive for whether it falls inside or outside the scope of compulsory jurisdiction. Particular attention is paid to implications of the Fish Stocks Agreement for the scope of the compulsory settlement system under the Law of the Sea Convention, including disputes concerning the interpretation and application of *other* fisheries agreements.

Chapter 4, by Geir Hønneland, evaluates and compares the FAO Compliance Agreement and the Fish Stocks Agreement in terms of whether they provide means likely to generate adherence among fishermen to conservation and management measures adopted for waters beyond undisputed national jurisdiction. Hønneland's framework for analysis of fisherman compliance, which is drawn predominantly from sociology and political science, includes not only traditional coercive mechanisms such as surveillance and sanctions, but also discursive means such as level of fisherman participation in decision-making.

3.3 Regional approaches to straddling stocks management

Part II of this book provides a series of in-depth case studies of regional attempts to cope with straddling stocks management. In line with the preceding chapters, the issue of effective management looms large, and two questions guide the analysis: do the regimes reviewed provide parties with adequate means to cope with the problem of fisheries management? And what has been the significance of interplay with other global or regional regimes with regard to the ability of parties to deal successfully with the high seas management challenge?

In Chapter 5, David Balton lays out the evolution of a governance system for the pollock fishery in the Bering Sea Doughnut Hole. A series of scientific symposia, involving representatives from both coastal and distant water fishing nations, was organized with a view to determining the occurrence and interrelations between stocks found in the Doughnut Hole and national zones. Negotiations on an interim moratorium on fishing had begun in 1991 and involved the coastal states, Japan, Poland, China, and the Republic of Korea. Little progress was made, however, until after the pollock had virtually disappeared from the area during the following year. In 1994 a multilateral agreement was finally concluded containing a number of innovative provisions that have subsequently reappeared in only slightly modified form in other international instruments.

An interesting contrast to the Doughnut Hole is offered in Chapter 6, where Alex Oude Elferink portrays developments in the Sea of Okhotsk Peanut Hole, so named because of the shape of this high seas enclave that is completely surrounded by the Russian exclusive economic zone. Again, pollock is the key species and here too high seas operations are a fairly recent phenomenon involving largely the same distant water fishing nations as in the Doughnut Hole. Despite several rounds of negotiations after the entry of foreign fishing fleets into these waters in 1991, no multilateral agreement has been reached. The regime that is at present governing pollock fisheries in the area is based on a set of bilateral accords between the coastal state and the various distant water fishing nations; the main feature of this regime is that harvesting is directed inside the Russian EEZ.

Whereas both the Doughnut and the Peanut Holes are fairly recent fishing grounds, the Grand Banks, addressed in Chapter 7 by Christopher Joyner, have been exploited by ocean-going fleets at least since the sixteenth century. While most of the harvest occurs inside Canada's EEZ, high seas catches taken on the 'nose' and 'tail' of the banks by fleets from Spain, Germany, the Soviet Union, and others grew rapidly in the 1980s. Today, the fishing pressure has been greatly reduced because of severe declines in many of the stocks. A moratorium is still in place regarding the historically most valuable stock—Northern cod. Under NAFO, a Scientific Council assists in the coordination of data collection and with the provision of scientific advice. Although the NAFO Commission may set national quotas and determine technical measures, the regulatory work has greatly been complicated by a long-standing allocation dispute between Canada and the European Community. The groundfish collapse that hit the region around 1990 can be partly attributed to the EC's repeated use of the NAFO objection procedure throughout the 1980s and its subsequent allocation of unilateral quotas for several species.[55] Another point of controversy discussed in the chapter is the adequacy of compliance control activities in the Northwest Atlantic.

Recent efforts to cope with straddling stock problems in the North-East Atlantic are assessed by Robin Churchill in Chapter 8. For years, stocks that feed commercial fisheries in this region were confined to waters under national jurisdiction, a fact that has rendered the North-East Atlantic Fisheries Commission (NEAFC) a rather dormant organization.[56] In the mid-1990s, however, the Norwegian spring-spawning herring roughly resumed its traditional migratory pattern of wintering off Iceland, making it again possible to fish the herring in a large high seas area in the Norwegian Sea—the Banana Hole. Today the largest catches are taken by Norway, Russia, Iceland, and the European Community. As most of the fishing occurs within national waters, the management tasks assigned to NEAFC are quite moderate. A fairly simple multilateral structure has been set up among the user states that comprises a set of agreements, negotiated annually since 1996, on quota allocation and reciprocal access to national zones. The chapter also analyses the management of oceanic redfish and mackerel. Unlike its north-western counterpart, the NEAFC Convention did not initially establish a scheme for compliance control; the main enforcement instrument in the case of herring and mackerel is the fact that most of the fishing operations occur inside national zones.

High seas fishery for cod in the Barents Sea Loophole, a piece of international waters surrounded by the EEZs of Norway and Russia, is the topic of Chapter 9, written by the present author. The hub of the regime for management of this resource is the bilateral Norwegian–Russian Fisheries Commission. Based on scientific advice that is generated under the auspices of ICES, the Commission establishes quotas and operational restrictions for the entire stock. The share of the stock fishable in the Loophole varies but has in some years been sufficiently high to attract large fleets of distant water fishing vessels. In 1991, the first trawlers appeared in the Loophole area; as in the Peanut Hole, reciprocal access arrangements have been actively used by the coastal states to cope with undesired high seas activities. Iceland, however, which has dominated the high seas activities in this region, was not brought into this structure until 1999.

In Chapter 10, Richard Herr discusses how a regime that is based on the Convention on the Conservation of Antarctic Marine Living Resources (CCAMLR),[57] a component of the broader Antarctic Treaty System, has been used in an effort to tackle the advent of a large multinational fishery for Patagonian toothfish in the Southern Ocean. Toothfish stocks straddle several zones of different jurisdictional status in this region. These include high seas waters within and beyond the CCAMLR area, undisputed coastal zones, and claimed maritime zones south of 60 degrees south latitude that are only recognized by a small group of Antarctic 'claimant states'. A series of conservation measures have been adopted, reflecting the advanced state of the Antarctic cooperation in putting into practice such principles as ecosystem conservation and precautionary management. A salient impediment to effective conservation measures is, however, the considerable activity of fishing vessels flying flags of non-member states.

3.4 Managing straddling stocks: the role of regime interplay

The Conclusions to this book draw together the threads of these chapters by providing a comparative analysis of the regional case studies in Part II and their interplay with each other and with the global developments laid out in Part I. The purpose is to enable firmer assertions with regard to the causal pathways that influence the ability of states to govern the high seas harvesting of straddling stocks.

While all the cases studied in this book feature stocks that straddle coastal zones and high seas areas, the political and legal contexts surrounding the management challenges are very different. For example, whereas some of the stocks, such as the North-East Atlantic cod and herring, have been reasonably healthy throughout much of the 1990s, the Doughnut Hole pollock collapsed during the negotiation of a regional regime. Although some of the stocks have been monitored closely for decades by international scientific organizations, rather little is known about the Patagonian toothfish now being harvested with considerable vigour in the Southern Ocean. In some, but not all cases, coastal states are able to grant quotas in their EEZs to other user states if the latter agree to restrain their harvesting activities on the high seas. Some controversies, like the one involving Norway and Iceland in the Barents Sea, juxtapose two nations that are closely knit together by both history and cultural similarity; in contrast, the conflict over management of Greenland halibut, or 'turbot' as it is called locally, in the Grand Banks is just the most recent in a decade-long series of diplomatic clashes between Canada and the European Community.

Variations such as the above, and the fact that global negotiations under the UN have been held alongside a range of regional level efforts to manage straddling stocks, make high seas fisheries a particularly promising area for analytical and empirical enquiry into the role of regime interplay in accounting for success and failure in international resource management.

Notes

1. *Reuter News* (10 Mar. 1995).
2. Emma Bonino, European Union Commissioner in charge of fisheries, cited ibid. 9 Mar. 1995.
3. Roy Stone, spokesman for the (Canadian) Fishermen, Food and Allied Workers Union, cited ibid. 12 Mar. 1995.
4. For a thorough discussion of background and course, see J. T. Thór, *British Trawlers and Iceland 1919–1976* (Gothenburg: Department of Economic History of the University of Göteborg, 1995).
5. Convention on Future Multilateral Cooperation in the Northwest Atlantic Fisheries (1978); *OJ* L378 (1978). This case is discussed by Joyner, Ch. 7 below.
6. Reproduced in 34 *ILM* 1260.
7. Spanish fishermen were among the first to exploit the riches off Newfoundland from around 1500 and have maintained a continuous presence in these waters since; K. M. Sullivan, 'Conflict in the Management of a Northwest Atlantic Transboundary Cod Stock', *Marine Policy*, 13 (1989), 118.
8. Agreement for the Implementation of the Provisions of the United Nations Convention on the Law of the Sea of 10 Dec. 1982 relating to the Conservation and Management of Straddling Fish Stocks and Highly Migratory Fish Stocks (1995); 34 *ILM* 1547. Entry into force requires thirty ratifications or accessions; as of 22 Sept. 2000, twenty-seven out of fifty-nine signatories had ratified or acceded to the Agreement; (www.un.org/Depts/los/los164st.htm).
9. E. L. Miles and W. T. Burke, 'Pressures on the United Nations Convention on the Law of the Sea of 1982 Arising from New Fisheries Conflicts: The Problem of Straddling Stocks', *Ocean Development and International Law*, 20 (1989), 343; also Balton, Ch. 5 below.
10. United Nations Convention on the Law of the Sea (1982), UN Doc. A/CONF.62/122; compare Art. 63 (2), and Art. 64. This distinction is reiterated in the Fish Stocks Agreement, Art. 7 (1).
11. S. Nandan, Chairman of the UN Conference on Straddling Fish Stocks and Highly Migratory Fish Stocks, cited in 'An Agreement on High Seas Fishing: An Update' (New York: United Nations Department of Public Information, 1995).
12. For an interesting discussion of 'technology coefficients', relevant to considerations about vessel replacement in a situation of overcapacity, see J. Fitzpatrick and C. Newton, 'Assessment of the World's Fishing Fleet 1991–1997' (www.greenpeace.org/~oceans/).
13. C. D. Stone, 'Too Many Fishing Boats, Too Few Fish: Can Trade Laws Trim Subsidies and Restore the Balance in Global Fisheries?', *Ecology Law Quarterly*, 24 (1997), 505.
14. On the development of estimates for surface-related catch figures, see 'Review of the State of World Fishery Resources: Marine Fisheries', *FAO Fisheries Circular*, 920 (1997), s. A.

15. For a discussion that is critical of a much-cited 1992 FAO study often interpreted as reporting world subsidies in fisheries at US$54 billion, see M. Milazzo, 'Subsidies in World Fisheries: A Reexamination', *World Bank Technical Paper: Fisheries Series*, 406 (1998); also Stone, 'Too Many Fishing Boats, Too Few Fish'.

16. G. Borgström, *Revolusjon i verdens fiskerier*, trans. T. Hoff (original, *Revolution i världsfisket*, 1966) (Oslo: Gyldendal, 1968).

17. R. Robinson, *Trawling: The Rise and Fall of the British Trawl Fishery* (University of Exeter Press, 1996), at 217–18.

18. In the first of these disputes, in 1972–3, as many as sixty-nine British and fifteen German vessels had their trawls cut; this roughly equalled the number of trawlers these countries had in the area; whereas in the second dispute, between 1975–6, there were thirty-five rammings; Thór, *British Trawlers and Iceland*. For a detailed account of the emergence of EEZs, see W. T. Burke, *The New International Law of Fisheries: UNCLOS 1982 and Beyond* (Oxford: Clarendon Press, 1994).

19. Robinson, *Trawling*.

20. For an analysis of the Japanese approach, see O. S. Stokke, 'Transnational Fishing: Japan's Changing Strategy', *Marine Policy*, 15 (1991), 231.

21. Fitzpatrick and Newton, 'Assessment of the World's Fishing Fleet'.

22. T. Sasaki and Y. Taku, 'Past Progress and Present Condition of the Japanese Pollock Fishery in the Aleutian Basin', document submitted to the Annual Meeting of the International North Pacific Fishery Commission, Vancouver, 1987.

23. M. S. Sullivan, 'The Case in International Law for Canada's Extension of Fisheries Jurisdiction beyond 200 Miles', *Ocean Development and International Law*, 28 (1997), 203, at 213. The underlying condition, however, was the exclusion of most of Spain's fleet from European Community waters.

24. See the paragraph 'National Fisheries Governance' in *The State of World Fisheries and Aquaculture 1998* (Rome: Food and Agriculture Organization), part 2 (www.fao.org/docrep/w9900e/w9900e00.htm).

25. S. Nandan and B. Rosenne (eds.), *United Nations Convention on the Law of the Sea 1982: A Commentary*, iii (The Hague: Martinus Nijhoff, 1995), 38.

26. Convention on the Law of the Sea, Arts. 63 and 116–20; Convention on the High Seas (1958), 450 *UNTS* 82; Convention on Fishing and Conservation of the Living Resources of the High Seas (1958), 559 *UNTS* 285.

27. Convention on the Law of the Sea, Art. 63 (2).

28. J. A. de Yturriaga, *The International Regime of Fisheries: From UNCLOS 1982 to the Presential Sea* (The Hague: Martinus Nijhoff, 1997), 182–201.

29. C. A. de Fontaubert, 'The Politics of Negotiation at the United Nations Conference on Straddling Fish Stocks and Highly Migratory Fish Stocks', *Ocean and Coastal Management*, 29 (1995), 79. For an overview of FAO activities related to high seas fishing, see S. H. Marashi, 'Summary Information on the Role of International Fishery and Other Bodies with Regard to the Conservation and Management of Living Resources of the High Seas', *FAO Fisheries Circular*, 908 (1996).

30. Food and Agriculture Organization, Code of Conduct for Responsible Fisheries (1995) (www.fao.org/fi/agreem/codecond/ficonde.asp). The Code is not restricted in scope to high seas areas.

31. The Plan of Action, adopted in Feb. 1999, is online at www.fao.org/fi/ipa/capace.asp.

32. Food and Agriculture Organization, Agreement to Promote Compliance with International Conservation and Management Measures by Fishing Vessels on the High Seas (1993); 33 *ILM* 368.

33. Report of the United Nations Conference on Environment and Development, i: Resolutions adopted by the Conference, chapter 17, UN Doc. A/CONF.151/26/Rev. 1 (vol. i).

34. UN Doc. A/Res/47/192.

35. A comprehensive analysis of the Fish Stocks Agreement is given in Part I of this book. Useful day-to-day summaries of the negotiations are provided in 'The United Nations Conference on Straddling Fish Stocks and Highly Migratory Fish Stocks', *Earth Negotiations Bulletin*, 7 (www.iisd.ca/fish.html).

36. D. A. Balton, 'Strengthening the Law of the Sea: The New Agreement on Straddling Fish Stocks and Highly Migratory Fish Stocks', *Ocean Development and International Law*, 27 (1996), 125, at 134.

37. de Fontaubert, 'The Politics of Negotiation', 81.

38. D. H. Anderson, 'The Straddling Stocks Agreement of 1995: An Initial Assessment', *International and Comparative Law Quarterly*, 45 (1996), 463, at 469.

39. Balton, 'Strengthening the Law of the Sea', 137.

40. Fish Stocks Agreement, Art. 7 (2) (a), (b), and (c).

41. Anderson, 'The Straddling Stocks Agreement of 1995', 470.

42. Vukas and Vidas, Ch. 2 below; also M. Hayashi, 'Enforcement by Non-flag States on the High Seas under the 1995 Agreement on Straddling and Highly Migratory Fish Stocks', *Georgetown International Environmental Law Review*, 9 (1996), 1.

43. Boyle, Ch. 3 below.

44. On the Fish Stocks Agreement, see in particular Anderson, 'The Straddling Stocks Agreement of 1995', Balton, 'Strengthening the Law of the Sea', P. G. G. Davies and C. Redgwell, 'The International Legal Regulation of Straddling Fish Stocks', *British Yearbook of International Law* (1997), 199, and M. Hayashi, 'The 1995 Agreement on the Conservation and Management of Straddling and Highly Migratory Fish Stocks: Significance for the Law of the Sea Convention', *Ocean and Coastal Management*, 29 (1995), 51. For recent, more general discussions of the straddling stock management challenge, see e.g. P. Birnie, 'Are Twentieth Century Marine Conservation Conventions Adaptable to Twenty-First Century Goals and Principles? Part I', *International Journal of Marine and Coastal Law*, 12 (1997), 307; and E. Hey, 'Global Fisheries Regulations in the First Half of the 1990s', *International Journal of Marine and Coastal Law*, 11 (1996), 459.

45. See e.g. W. T. Burke, 'Fishing in the Bering Sea Donut: Straddling Stocks and the New International Law of Fisheries', *Ecology Law Quarterly*, 16 (1989), 285; E. Meltzer, 'Global Overview of Straddling and Highly Migratory Fish Stocks: The Nonsuitable Nature of High Seas Fisheries', *Ocean Development and Inter-*

national Law, 25 (1994), 255; Sullivan, 'The Case in International Law for Canada's Extension of Fisheries Jurisdiction beyond 200 Miles'; R. R. Churchill, 'The Barents Sea Loophole Agreement: A "Coastal State" Solution to a Straddling Stock Problem', *International Journal of Marine and Coastal Law*, 14 (1999), 467.

46. O. S. Stokke, 'Regimes as Governance Systems', in O. R. Young (ed.), *Global Governance: Drawing Insights from the Environmental Experience* (Cambridge, Mass.: MIT Press, 1997), 27.

47. O. R. Young, *International Cooperation: Building Regimes for Natural Resources and the Environment* (Ithaca, NY: Cornell University Press, 1989). On the emergence of this broader notion of institutions, not confined to formal organizations, see R. Wallis, 'Institutions', in A. Kuper and J. Kuper (eds.), *Social Science Encyclopedia* (London: Routledge & Kegan Paul, 1985), 399.

48. O. S. Stokke and D. Vidas, 'The Effectiveness and Legitimacy of International Regimes', in Stokke and Vidas (eds.), *Governing the Antarctic: The Effectiveness and Legitimacy of the Antarctic Treaty System* (Cambridge University Press, 1996), 13.

49. O. S. Stokke, L. G. Anderson, and N. Mirovitskaya, 'The Barents Sea Fisheries', in O. R. Young (ed.), *The Effectiveness of International Regimes: Causal Connections and Behavioral Mechanisms* (Cambridge, Mass.: MIT Press, 1999), 91.

50. See in general Stokke and Vidas (eds.), *Governing the Antarctic*; sometimes, as in the case of the Antarctic, the fact that decisions are usually reached by consensus rather than voting tends to temper the significance of such differentiation.

51. O. R. Young, 'Institutional Linkages in International Society: Polar Perspectives', *Global Governance*, 2 (1996), 1, at 2.

52. O. R. Young (ed.), 'Science Plan for the Project on the Institutional Dimensions of Global Environmental Change' (Bonn: The International Human Dimensions Programme on Global Environmental Change—IHDP, 1999).

53. A more comprehensive discussion of various types of interplay is given in the Conclusions.

54. See the panel report in 30 *ILM* 1598; subsequent developments on the issue are discussed by T. J. Schoenbaum, 'International Trade and Protection of the Environment: The Continuing Search for Reconciliation', *American Journal of International Law*, 91 (1997), 268.

55. Other prominent causes are lower water temperatures and a sustained over-estimation of the stock biomass throughout the 1980s; 'Review of the State of World Fishery Resources: Marine Fisheries', *FAO Fisheries Circular*, 920 (1996), s. Bl.

56. Convention on Future Multilateral Cooperation in North-East Atlantic Fisheries (1980); *OJ* L227 (1981).

57. Convention on the Conservation of Antarctic Marine Living Resources (1980); 19 *ILM* 837.

PART I

High Seas Fisheries in International Law

1

The International Law of High Seas Fisheries: From Freedom of Fishing to Sustainable Use

FRANCISCO ORREGO VICUÑA

This chapter discusses the law of high seas fisheries as it has evolved throughout time and the prevailing legal principles in each period and their practical results in terms of effective management and conservation of the living resources of the sea. From the concept of freedom of the high seas to the detailed provisions introduced by the 1982 Convention on Law of the Sea[1] and later by the Agreement relating to straddling fish stocks and highly migratory fish stocks,[2] a number of new legal perspectives have emerged with a view to ensuring the conservation of species and controlling their over-exploitation. Principles of environmental law and ecosystem management, the strengthening of international cooperation, and the new roles assigned to flag states, coastal states, and port states all play prominent roles in the development of this legal framework.

1 High seas fishing in a historical legal context: from unrestricted freedom to the prevalence of conservation standards

Contemporary developments in the conservation and management of high seas fisheries are the outcome of a long historical evolution. This evolution has largely been related to the principle of the freedom of the high seas, the cornerstone of the political and legal order of the oceans. Through the years, different views and interpretations regarding the meaning and extent of this principle have led to changes in its function. These changes reflect the economic and political situation as well as the state of scientific knowledge in any given period.

The original understanding of the principle of freedom of the high seas was that it sought only to prohibit the interference of states in the high seas. There were two consequences of this interpretation of the principle. The first was the freedom of utilization of the high seas; the second was 'les désordres, les destructions, les gaspillages'.[3] The negative aspect of the latter consequence explains the emphasis placed on the need for measures to conserve key resources such as fisheries. As this need became increasingly understood, a number of changes relating particularly to fisheries regulation and management were introduced into the original formulation. As a result, the legal extent of the principle could no longer be conceived in absolute terms but would also be subject to the rights of other states and participants to undertake fishing activities.

The evolution of the legal concepts relating to fishing on the high seas occurred simultaneously with corresponding changes in circumstances and interests. In this respect, it is possible to recognize three distinct periods. First there was the conceptual development that led from unrestricted freedom of fishing to reasonable use whereby a measure of restraint was introduced as warranted by the interests of other participants in a given activity of exploitation of ocean resources. However, when it became clear that this approach was largely ineffective and could not alone ensure the appropriate conservation of resources,[4] regulation was introduced, thus making the transition to the next period.[5]

This second period was initially identified with the development of national claims to maritime areas, a trend which in part reflected the interest of coastal states in gaining exclusive access to given resources or activities to the exclusion of third parties.[6] But this development was also a means of introducing conservation authority in areas which until then had been subject to an increased depletion of resources because of the lack of a regulatory authority under international law as understood at the time.[7]

The particular concern for lack of regulation also found expression in the concept of exploitation of ocean resources in the general interest of the international community and not exclusively in the interest of individual nations, thus opening the third and latest period in the conceptual changes in international law. While this concept has not always been clearly defined, it has nevertheless permeated many of the solutions found under international law to conflicts involving competing interests of coastal states and distant water fishing states. This is indeed the case of the regime of the exclusive economic zone (EEZ) in which exclusive rights of the coastal state are combined with the right of access of other states to a part of the total allowable catch not exploited by the former.[8] Similarly, this concept also underlies a number of recent developments that specifically relate to fishing on the high seas. While conservation is the driving force behind these approaches, they simultaneously ensure a certain balance of interests between coastal states and distant water fishing states.

These conceptual developments found expression in both customary international law and specialized conventions. For example, while the Arbitration Tribunal upheld the freedom of the high seas in the Bering Sea Fur Seals Arbitration,[9] the need for preventing over-exploitation through conservation was also recognized, regulation of which was to be negotiated by the participants in the fishery.[10] Furthermore, in the 1974 Fisheries Jurisdiction cases, the International Court of Justice upheld the rights of fishing in the high seas, but in so doing the Court also emphasized the obligation of reasonable use in relation to conservation and the preferential rights of coastal states in the allocation of high seas stocks in such areas. The obligation to undertake negotiations in good faith so as to reach an equitable solution, the meaning of the duty to cooperate, and the role of scientific information were also underlined by the decision.[11]

The 1958 Convention on Fishing and Conservation of the Living Resources of the High Seas[12] marked a significant stage in the development of international law in that certain key concepts would thereafter be retained in major international conventions. In fact, for the first time under a major international convention, freedom of fishing in the high seas was recognized as being subject to treaty obligations as well as to the interests and rights of other states as provided for under any such convention and relating to the conservation of living resources.[13] However, these modest principles were not coupled with appropriate measures by which they could be effected.[14]

A further, more recent dimension that has been added reflects not only the nature of the changes that have occurred but also the concern of the international community for the environment.[15] Conservation of fisheries and other marine resources is no longer solely a question of economic efficiency but one of rational and effective management of fisheries and other resources that touches on the preservation of broad, fragile ecosystems. Indeed, as conservation needs have become more urgent worldwide and increasingly related to major environmental issues, developments in international law in this field have taken on a very different aspect. The question is no longer whether coastal states could or should claim new maritime areas for the exercise of given forms of jurisdiction, effectively further eroding the area of the high seas, but rather whether in view of the nature of the problems, pertinent solutions should be provided by coastal states, negotiated by interested parties, or established by the international community as a whole.

Two significant implications have ensued from this development. First, the issue is no longer whether some fisheries activities should be regulated or unrestricted, but who should undertake the appropriate regulatory functions and what the extent of these should be. Secondly, the high seas could no longer be considered an area free from certain regulations, just as coastal states could no longer freely permit unregulated fishing within their maritime areas. In this new context, the principle of the freedom of the high seas is not derogated from but rather no longer tantamount to uncontrolled fishing activities.

2 The role of the United Nations Convention on the Law of the Sea in shaping a new regime for fishing in the high seas

The Third United Nations Conference on the Law of the Sea made a major contribution to the development of the principles governing the conservation and management of living resources.[16] These principles referred mainly to fisheries within the exclusive economic zone,[17] but new approaches that were adopted were also to prove meaningful for the question of high seas fisheries.[18] Furthermore, the Convention on the Law of the Sea laid down special regimes for certain species that migrate in various ways, thus also regulating high seas fisheries of such species under the Convention and related arrangements.[19] Furthermore, specific provisions on high seas fisheries were built into the Convention.[20] The full implication of the Convention on the Law of the Sea comes into light when the provisions relating to the protection of the marine environment are also taken into account.[21] A number of principles which today are frequently encountered in international environmental law[22] emerged from this Convention in the context of marine environmental protection.

The sovereign rights that the coastal state was granted in respect of the living resources in the exclusive economic zone did not amount to an unqualified right[23] since coastal state authority was subject to specific obligations, the most important of which concerned the conservation and management of the living resources.[24] Questions concerning the determination of the total allowable catch, the harvesting capacity, and fishing access by other states were incorporated into the new regime of the exclusive economic zone.[25] The issue of conservation is now prominent and the access of other states is in fact thereby made conditional on the success of conservation and the availability of resources.[26] In this regard it is interesting to note that the historical situation has been reversed in light of these provisions; previously, open access prevailed and conservation had a secondary role in the structure of fishing arrangements.[27]

Total allowable catch is the basic concept on which the new organization of fisheries under national jurisdiction is based.[28] Although the determination of allowable catch falls within the discretionary powers of the coastal state, this state is under a specific obligation to ensure that the maintenance of the living resources of the exclusive economic zone is not endangered by over-exploitation,[29] and that proper conservation and management measures are adopted.[30] Only when all of the above has been achieved will the objective of optimum utilization come into play and allow for the eventual access of foreign fishing.[31]

In adopting the species approach, the Convention introduced another important concept into fisheries conservation and management.[32] While coastal species are subject to the rules of the exclusive economic zone and sedentary species to the rules of the continental shelf regime, a number of other situations have led to significant innovations. Anadromous species, in particular salmon, provide a first major instance where the regime governing their exploitation has been dramatically changed. Article 66 of the Law of the Sea Convention recognized the primary interest and responsibility of the state of origin in anadromous stocks, thereby radically changing the basic concept of the law of the sea in this matter. In reality, the jurisdiction of the state of origin prevailed not only in the adjacent waters but also throughout the migratory range of salmon in the high seas. This regime further provides that as a general rule salmon fisheries 'shall be conducted only' in the waters landward of the outer limit of the exclusive economic zone.[33] This means in practice that the fishing of salmon is now generally prohibited in the high seas.[34] While there are some exceptions to this prohibition that are justified by the need to avoid economic dislocation for other states, in regional practice these are not applied. Responsibility for the management of catadromous species is assigned to the coastal state in whose waters they spend the greater part of the life cycle.[35]

Another important innovation of the Convention regarding the principles that had prevailed historically in respect of high seas fisheries is found in the regime governing marine mammals.[36] Article 65 of the Convention on the Law of the Sea safeguards the right of a coastal state or the competence of an international organization to prohibit, limit, or regulate the exploitation of marine mammals more strictly than provided for under the rules applicable to fisheries in the exclusive economic zone, a provision that was also made specifically applicable to the high seas.[37] In actual fact, the meaning of this provision is that while conservation principles will naturally apply to whaling in the exclusive economic zone, there shall be no obligation as to optimum utilization or other forms of third states' participation in this respect.[38] Since this approach also applies to whaling on the high seas, it follows that freedom of exploitation is no longer the prevailing principle of international law in this context.

The species approach adopted by the Convention on the Law of the Sea dealt with two other questions that were prominent among the new issues relating to high seas fisheries, namely the regime applicable to straddling stocks[39] and to highly migratory species.[40] To the extent that these stocks straddle the exclusive economic zone of two or more coastal states, the basic principle of the coastal states' sovereign rights embodied in Article 56 of the Convention also governs this matter and remains unchanged, without prejudice to conservation agreements. However, in the case of stocks straddling the exclusive economic zone and an area of the high seas adjacent and beyond this zone, the respective coastal state and the states that fish in the adjacent high seas area shall seek to agree on the necessary conservation measures, either directly or by means of the appropriate organizations. Various proposals to recognize the 'special interest' of coastal states in relation to straddling stocks in the adjacent high seas areas were made during the negotiations of this article, but they were not successful.[41] Coastal state authority to extend conservation measures to the high seas was also the subject of specific proposals, but these proposals were also unsuccessful.[42] It should be noted, however, that Article 116 of the Convention subjects the right of high seas fishing to the rights and duties as well as to the interests of coastal states, provided for among other cases in Article 63 (2), that is, in connection with the straddling stocks regime.[43]

The issues underlying the discussion on highly migratory species were still more difficult to resolve since the interests involved were more extensive and the historical experience manifested a strong confrontational attitude between coastal states and distant water fishing nations.[44] For a coastal state in whose waters these species abound, the position is that fishing in the exclusive economic zone is subject to that state's sovereign rights in accordance with the general principles of the Convention, without prejudice to forms of cooperation which may be agreed.[45] On the other hand, some countries engaged in the distant fishing of these species, in particular the fishing of tuna, were of the opinion that they should be treated as an exception to the coastal state's sovereign rights in the exclusive economic zone, wherein only a special international regime of cooperation should apply.[46]

These differences of opinion explain the somewhat vague nature of Article 64 of the Convention, which provides for cooperation with respect to the species listed in order to ensure conservation and the promotion of the objective of optimum utilization throughout the entire region, both within and outside the exclusive economic zone.[47] In spite of the general language, Article 64 clearly indicates some important changes in the principles and concepts governing this regime. First, the provision emphasizes conservation even in the high seas, thereby strengthening the conceptual evolution that was already beginning to predominate over the traditional, unrestricted freedom of fishing. Next, by providing for cooperation in conservation and optimum utilization throughout the entire region concerned, the Article in fact deals with such resources in terms of ecosystem approaches, which is also a new development in the law of high seas fisheries. It was on the basis of these new principles and concepts that the detailed regime governing highly migratory species was later to be negotiated and approved. The situation regarding fishing of these species in the high seas was more vague, but Article 116 makes the right of fishing in the high seas subject to Article 64 and other provisions that refer to the rights and duties as well as to the interests of coastal states, following a similar approach to that relating to straddling stocks examined above. While there have been a number of interpretations of these legal cross-references,[48] the fact remains that fishing in the high seas without regard to conservation would be inconsistent with the rights and interests of coastal states and therefore incompatible with the regime established under the Convention.

The Convention on the Law of the Sea dealt with the broader issue of conservation and management of the living resources of the high seas under Articles 116–20. Here again the obligation of conservation of living resources of the high seas become prominent because the very right to fish is conditioned by it. This obligation thereby further strengthens the concepts that had already been determined in the 1958 Convention on Fishing and Conservation on the High Seas. A general obligation concerning the adoption of conservation measures in respect of nationals or cooperation with other states necessary to this effect is also provided for, including the concept of allowable catch for living resources of the high seas. Transparency in information and non-discrimination are other important requirements of the high seas fisheries regime.

The fact that the Convention on the Law of the Sea has approached the question of fisheries within the view of conservation and sustainability of resources is in itself a major achievement with regard to the environment. This is still more so when the specific environmental obligations under the Convention are examined. The general obligation to protect and preserve the marine environment follows as a consequence of the above recognition, in respect of both areas under national jurisdiction and areas of the high seas. The Convention has provided for the following significant links with the ecosystem management approach: (1) marine protected areas, (2) a preventive approach to marine pollution, (3) introduction of the precautionary principle even if at the time this was conceived in a different language, (4) an assessment of environmental impacts, and (5) integrated regimes applicable to waste management and pollution control.[49] Environmental monitoring and the international communication of findings, together with other procedures concerning improved implementation of the obligations, have also found specific application in the Convention's provisions.

3 New legal perspectives for conservation and management of high seas fisheries

Important as these developments were to the evolution of the law of high seas fisheries, they were not sufficiently comprehensive to dispose of high seas fisheries problems. The decade following the signing of the Convention on the Law of the Sea was characterized by increasing activity in high seas fisheries which laid the ground for a number of actual and potential disputes between coastal states and distant water fishing states. The most prominent of these disputes, discussed elsewhere within this book, provided the background for the testing of the general provisions that the Convention had devised regarding this matter. Important issues of interpretation arose that involved the roles of coastal states and other interests in the adoption of conservation measures in the high seas, while an extensive international and regional practice provided insight and possible answers to issues where solutions still had to be found. The growing pressure on high seas fisheries and the global scope of the problems of overexploitation would have profound implications for the conservation and management regimes required if the new problems and the kind of issues that needed to be addressed in this context were to be dealt with successfully.

Discussions held at the United Nations Conference on Environment and Development and the Technical Consultation on High Seas Fishing that was organized by the FAO and followed in 1992, were quite illustrative in this regard.[50] Defining responsible fishing practices was a first major new approach towards marine fisheries generally and high seas fisheries in particular.[51] While keeping with the concepts embodied in the Convention on the Law of the Sea, the concepts of sustainable development and utilization of high seas fisheries resources in harmony with the environment were introduced as an added approach to management. An important aspect of the new fisheries management is prevention of overcapacity. This question would no longer be solely associated with the control of nationals in the high seas but now also linked with the development of management regimes applicable to all fishing vessels in a given area.

Clearly, the implications of this development would be of consequence for international fishing bodies.[52] Issues relating to membership, new entrants to the fishery, non-contracting parties, compliance and enforcement, the role of particularly affected coastal states, decision-making, and the settlement of disputes would all have to be carefully considered. Essential questions were now arising around the new reality of high seas fisheries: To what extent would the provisions of the Convention on the Law of the Sea be able to deal with these new issues? To what extent would these new provisions need to be further developed, or to what extent would alternative arrangements need to be considered?

A first major approach to the question of whether the Convention on the Law of the Sea could provide an answer to these emerging problems was rather unfruitful. Distant water fishing nations held the view that the Convention had only provided for two basic situations: coastal state jurisdiction in the exclusive economic zone and freedom of fisheries beyond.[53] No coastal state competence, jurisdiction, or rights could be allowed beyond the 200-mile limit, irrespective of the arguments or conditions involved. It followed that any new problems relating to high seas fisheries would have to be dealt with under the traditional principles of high seas freedom and at the very most an enhanced effort at cooperation would have to be made. The practical result of this narrow interpretation was that if concerned states failed to agree in their negotiations on conservation measures for straddling or other relevant stocks in the adjacent high seas areas, the coastal state would end up powerless because distant water fishing states could continue operating irrespective of the existing problems. At most, dispute settlement mechanisms could be resorted to, but even these are not always readily available.[54] This situation would certainly be an open invitation to certain fishing states to make demands that would ensure the ineffectiveness of such negotiations.

The second major approach sought an interpretation of the Convention on the Law of the Sea that highlighted the role of coastal states in the management and conservation of high seas fisheries resources whenever efforts at negotiation and cooperation failed to adequately materialize. Many different points of view intervened in this line of thinking, ranging from the coastal state's expression of interest in exercising actual or potential jurisdiction to new claims of comprehensive national jurisdiction. A common denominator was the view that if negotiations with distant water fishing nations failed, the coastal state would not stand by as a helpless observer of events that caused damage to some of its crucial interests.[55]

The premise for this second interpretation was that conservation be ensured as the main objective of the fisheries regime established under the Convention on the Law of the Sea, either by means of negotiation and solutions agreed between the parties involved, or by the exercise of coastal state authority.[56] Authority, rights, superior rights, preferential rights, and jurisdiction have all been used to convey a policy assigning priority to conservation of high seas fisheries resources when other options were not available.[57] Irrespective of the expression used, to the extent that there is an exercise of jurisdiction there is also the corresponding problem of enforcement.[58] While enforcement in respect of nationals is not disputed, the fundamental issue concerns, of course, enforcement over foreign fishing vessels in the high seas adjacent area. Except in very exceptional circumstances, international law has thus far not authorized the exercise or enforcement of jurisdictional powers over foreign vessels in the high seas.[59]

A third approach attempted to balance these concerns by conceiving new rules on the matter as inextricably linked to the implementation of the Law of the Sea Convention. However, shortcomings in the Convention's provisions implied that any interpretation inevitably called for further development and clarification of the law. An important study prepared at the time by the United Nations Division for Ocean Affairs and the Law of the Sea rightly identified the duty to cooperate in the conservation and management of high seas fisheries resources as the cornerstone for any accommodation under the overall framework of the Convention.[60] The nature of interests and rights and how to accommodate these in high seas fisheries regimes was a prominent problem in the context of cooperation.

In spite of the fact that this approach could help settle a number of issues, there were many other questions that could not be dealt with under an interpretation of the Law of the Sea Convention and required an additional rule-making effort. This was the essential task of the United Nations Conference on Straddling Fish Stocks and Highly Migratory Fish Stocks, during the six sessions held in the period April 1993–August 1995,[61] which led to the adoption of the Agreement on the matter by consensus on 4 August 1995; it was opened for signature on 4 December 1995.[62]

4 The emerging principles of international environmental law and their implementation in fisheries conservation and management

The Agreement relating to the conservation and management of straddling fish stocks and highly migratory fish stocks has further developed the process of legal evolution, particularly by introducing conservation and management principles and approaches that are directly related to the new principles of international environmental law.[63] To the extent that some of these principles were also embodied in the Convention, they also apply to conservation in the EEZ under Article 61 and related provisions of that Convention.

A first major contribution is found in respect of the principle of sustainable development which has become the guiding element for contemporary regimes dealing with aspects of development that have a direct or indirect bearing on the environment. The objective of the Agreement as set out in Article 2 is quite explicit on this matter in purporting 'to ensure the long-term conservation and sustainable use of straddling fish stocks and highly migratory fish stocks through effective implementation of the Convention'.[64] Article 5 of the Agreement sets out the general principles of conservation and management, and, together with the related provisions of Articles 6 and 7, the Article has considerably advanced the 'conventional international standards for fisheries management'.[65] The adoption of measures to ensure the long-term sustainability of resources and to promote the objective of optimum utilization is the overall mandate established under this provision, an objective that is supplemented by the requirement of basing measures on the best scientific evidence available and the need to ensure the maintenance or restoration of stocks at levels capable of producing the maximum sustainable yield.[66] Other general principles established under Article 5 are also closely related to the guiding principle of sustainable development, with particular reference to ecosystem considerations.

A second major contribution of the Agreement to the development of international law in respect of high seas fisheries concerns the principle of preventive action, which may be considered as already embodied in the Convention on the Law of the Sea in terms of the obligation to preserve the environment. Under this principle action should 'be taken at an early stage and, if possible, before damage has actually occurred'.[67] Preventive action in the context of the protection of the marine environment is included as a general principle directing states to minimize pollution, waste, and discards.[68] However, the principle is also envisaged by the Agreement in terms of requiring that measures be taken to prevent or eliminate overfishing and excess fishing capacity and to ensure that levels of fishing do not exceed those commensurate with the sustainable use of fishery resources.[69] This general principle is of particular importance since it addresses the core problem of conservation in marine fisheries, namely the question of overfishing which has haunted the law of the sea for the best part of the twentieth century.

A third major contribution of the Agreement relates to the precautionary principle, which, although having emerged somewhat recently in international environmental law, has occupied a central place in the discussion on international regimes for environmental protection.[70] Because the precautionary principle has found important application in relation to the pollution of the marine environment, there was a natural inclination to argue in favour of its extension in similar terms to the question of fisheries management, or for that matter to the requirements of environmental impact assessment. However, since scientific uncertainty is common in fisheries management, a straightforward application of the precautionary principle would have resulted in the impossibility of proceeding with any activity relating to marine fisheries. It is on these grounds that the concept of the 'precautionary approach' surfaced with a view to providing a more flexible tool for the specific needs of fisheries management.[71] The application of the precautionary approach has been dealt with under Article 6 of the Agreement, which is considered one of the most innovative provisions of this instrument.[72] In fact, this is the first global agreement to deal comprehensively with the precautionary approach for high seas fisheries and to this extent it establishes a most significant precedent that will by far exceed the matter of straddling fish stocks and highly migratory fish stocks. The specific objectives of this approach are to protect the living marine resources and preserve the marine environment, thereby combining elements of both the precautionary principle and the precautionary approach. The key element in the implementation of the precautionary approach is given by the mandate whereby states apply the guidelines set out in annex II, determine stock-specific reference points, and take action if these reference points are exceeded.[73] On the basis of these criteria, states shall ensure that reference points are not exceeded when they are approached, and, in the event that reference points are exceeded, take the immediate action necessary to restore the stocks.[74]

The Agreement makes yet another significant contribution in relying on the principle of informed decision-making to perfect the regime governing high seas fisheries. This principle has been recognized as an essential element related to the effectiveness of international regimes on environmental protection.[75] Two general principles embodied in the Agreement refer to the question of data and scientific research. Under the first of these principles, states shall collect and make available complete and accurate data concerning fishing activities and information from national and international research programmes; among other items this includes such data that relate to vessel position, catches, and fishing effort.[76] Under the second principle, there is an obligation to promote and conduct scientific research and to develop technologies appropriate in the support of fishery conservation and management.[77] These principles are expounded in considerable detail in Article 14 of the Agreement and constitute one of the mechanisms established for international cooperation.[78] Annex I of the Agreement defines the standard requirements for the collection and sharing of data.[79]

By introducing these new principles and approaches, the Agreement has made a very significant contribution to the development of international environmental law relevant to high seas fisheries. In this respect the Agreement can be considered a unique instrument that relates international law to the present concerns and approaches to environmental realities, thereby consolidating the latest stage in the evolution of the law governing high seas fisheries.

5 Ecosystem management: one area of biological unity, two jurisdictional systems

Possibly the greatest challenge of international law as applied to high seas fisheries was how to introduce the concept of ecosystem management within a context involving different national jurisdictions and international arrangements. Scientific realities underlying the high seas fisheries of straddling stocks and highly migratory stocks and their relationship with fisheries under national jurisdiction were well known and not generally disputed at the time of the negotiations leading to the Fish Stocks Agreement and related events.[80] However, the legal consequences of such realities were quite a different question, and the views of states and other entities were again sharply divided, ranging from the argument for the need to extend national measures into the high seas to the other extreme of demanding the opening up of areas under national jurisdiction to international administration or extensive foreign participation.[81] Finding a common ground to achieve a standing compromise and ultimate solution to these issues was one of the most difficult tasks confronted by the Conference.[82]

Three elements were successfully developed and combined to reach an acceptable solution: (1) the relationship between the Agreement and the 1982 Convention on the Law of the Sea, (2) the careful definition of the geographical ambit of application of the Agreement, and (3) the compatibility of conservation and management measures. The aggregate of these approaches and provisions allowed for the introduction of ecosystem management in the fisheries of straddling fish stocks and highly migratory fish stocks, not under a nationalized administration of the high seas or under an international regime interfering with national jurisdiction, but in terms of allowing the supplementary role of both coastal states and distant water fishing states. This understanding possibly marks the beginning of a new stage in the evolution of the applicable law.

The very fact that the Agreement was concluded in implementation of the provisions of the Convention has a specific legal connotation. In spite of the fact that the Agreement has been kept as a separate legal instrument and is not a protocol to the Convention nor is it otherwise required to be a party to the Convention, its links with the latter are so specific that the application and interpretation of the Agreement cannot be undertaken independently from the 1982 Convention. Article 4 quite explicitly provides that nothing in the Agreement shall prejudice the rights, jurisdiction, and duties of states under the Convention and that it 'shall be interpreted and applied in the context of and in a manner consistent with the Convention'.[83] It has been pointed out that the Conference 'in fact repeatedly rejected proposals that would have conflicted with the

Convention, such as provisions that would have given coastal states fishery jurisdiction beyond 200 miles, or that would have undermined the exclusive fishery jurisdiction of coastal states within 200 miles'.[84] As a result of Article 4 of the Agreement and related provisions, it is quite true that unilateral measures by the coastal state over high seas fisheries have largely been curtailed without prejudice to the influence of states in the establishment of regional and subregional organizations and arrangements and other situations which have led to conservation measures. But it is also equally true that international or foreign interference with fisheries under national jurisdiction has successfully been prevented since the sovereign rights of coastal states in the exclusive economic zone will remain unaltered. Moreover, the Agreement cannot be interpreted in a manner contrary to or inconsistent with such provisions. Discretional fisheries decisions by the coastal state are not affected by the Agreement, either generally or in determining total allowable catches; nor can these decisions be subject to compulsory dispute settlement in the light of Article 297 (3) of the Convention and Article 32 of the Agreement.

These very thoughts were at the heart of the definition of the ambit of application of the Agreement. In referring to the areas of application of the Agreement, Article 3 first sets out the general rule and then provides for specific exceptions and conditions. The general rule is that the Agreement 'applies to the conservation and management of straddling fish stocks and highly migratory fish stocks beyond areas under national jurisdiction'.[85] The first exception concerns the application of the precautionary approach set out in Article 6, which relates to the conservation and management of stocks within areas under national jurisdiction; a parallel exception provides for the application of Article 7 on compatibility of conservation and management measures to such areas under national jurisdiction. In both cases this application is 'subject to the different legal regimes that apply within areas under national jurisdiction and in areas beyond national jurisdiction as provided for in the Convention'.[86] The sovereign rights of the coastal state are thereby duly safeguarded because no measure that is contrary to its jurisdictional powers in the exclusive economic zone or derogates therefrom could qualify to be applied within areas of national jurisdiction. It should also be noted that the very provisions of the Convention applicable to the exclusive economic zone are now provided with a more specific meaning under the terms of the Agreement.

A third exception provides for the application in areas of national jurisdiction of the general principles of Article 5.[87] The conditions set out by the Agreement for the operation of this exception are still more strict because such application by a coastal state is done '[i]n the exercise of its sovereign rights for the purpose of exploring and exploiting, conserving and managing straddling fish stocks and highly migratory fish stocks within areas under national jurisdiction'. This condition not only follows the language of Article 56 of the Convention in relation to the sovereign rights of the coastal state in the exclusive economic zone, but it also recognizes that such sovereign rights are exercised in respect of highly migratory species, thereby clarifying the meaning of the Convention on a point that had been much debated and bringing the ensuing national practice into a precise legal definition.

The conclusion that may be reached as to the meaning of Article 3 is that it is basically designed to be applied to areas of the high seas and that the exceptions to this rule are qualified and conditioned in such a manner that they must fully observe coastal state sovereign rights within the exclusive economic zone in order to become applicable. To this extent such exceptions are compatible with the mandate of the Conference and the provisions of the Convention on the Law of the Sea and cannot lead to any derogation of the jurisdictional powers assigned to the coastal state or its discretionary management of fisheries under national jurisdiction in the terms of the Convention. In addition, as noted above, it must also be kept in mind that the coastal state's discretionary powers are excepted from the compulsory settlement of disputes. A single area of biological unity and distribution of stocks, subject to different jurisdictional regimes conceived in a supplementary manner as to fisheries conservation and management, is what the Agreement in essence seeks to achieve.

The third basic element of the solution established by the Agreement in connection with ecosystem management and the legal interaction between areas under national jurisdiction and the high seas relates to the question of compatibility of conservation and management measures. In this respect, the controversy of major negotiating groups has been conveniently summarized by one author: 'Should high seas rules be made or altered to conform to pre-existing EEZ rules (which could be viewed as an extension of coastal state control beyond 200 miles)? Should coastal states establish EEZ rules compatible with high seas rules adopted multilaterally (which could be seen as an infringement on coastal state jurisdiction)? Posed this way, the questions were nearly unanswerable.'[88]

The final text of the Agreement sets out to solve the issue of compatibility in Article 7, which begins with an overall safeguard of the respective interests. Under this safeguard such a solution is without prejudice to the sovereign rights of the coastal state for exploring and exploiting, conserving, and managing the living marine resources within areas under national jurisdiction as provided for in the Convention on the Law of the Sea.[89] Next, the Article also safeguards the right of all states for their nationals to engage in fishing on the high seas, also in accordance with the Convention. Articles 116–19 of the Convention on the Law of the Sea shall accordingly govern this matter, which also includes the relevant interests of the coastal state and the requirements of conservation in the high seas. Based on this safeguard, the Agreement reiterates the distinction made by the Convention in Articles 63 and 64. With respect to straddling fish stocks, the relevant coastal states and the states whose nationals fish in the high seas shall seek to agree on the measures necessary for conservation in the adjacent high seas area; with respect to highly migratory fish stocks, they shall cooperate with a view to ensuring conservation and promotion of the objective of optimum utilization throughout the region, both within and beyond the areas under national jurisdiction.[90] As in the Convention, in the case of straddling fish stocks measures relate to the adjacent high seas area, and cooperation is not absolutely mandatory. In the case of highly migratory fish stocks, measures relate to the region as a whole and cooperation becomes mandatory. However, it must be recalled in this last respect that the ensuing problems of interpretation of Article 64 were solved in practice in favour of coastal state jurisdiction.[91]

The principle of compatibility is established in Article 7 (2) of the Agreement in the following terms: 'Conservation and management measures established for the high seas and those adopted for areas under national jurisdiction shall be compatible in order to ensure conservation and management of the straddling fish stocks and highly migratory fish stocks in their entirety.'[92] It is clear from the wording of this provision that the question is not that of high seas measures being applied under national jurisdiction, or of national measures being applied in the high seas, but quite simply that one and the other, adopted under their respective jurisdictional authority, will ensure compatibility by relying on similar standards of management that will not unbalance the system as a whole.[93]

The Agreement then provides that coastal states and states fishing in the high seas 'have a duty to cooperate' for the purpose of achieving compatible measures. The nature and extent of compatibility and the associated cooperation is further clarified in the listing in paragraph 2 of precisely what states shall take into account in determining conservation and management measures for the high seas, and, to the extent of Article 3, in areas under national jurisdiction. Scientific realities are paramount among such factors in that states shall take into account the biological unity and other biological characteristics of the stocks, the relationship between the distribution of stocks, the particularities of fisheries and geography of the region, and the extent to which stocks occur and are fished under national jurisdiction.[94] Similarly, consideration must be given to the respective dependence of the coastal states and the state fishing on the high seas on the stocks concerned, a criterion that in many instances will point towards the prevalence of coastal states interests.[95]

The key factors of compatibility, however, refer to the relationship between the measures adopted for each of the two basic jurisdictional areas. First and foremost, the measures adopted by the coastal state in the exclusive economic zone in accordance with Article 61 of the Convention in respect of the same stocks shall be taken into account.[96] This means that high seas measures cannot ignore the conservation efforts of the coastal state under national jurisdiction; in the light of compatibility, they must apply similar standards. Moreover, states must ensure—not merely take into account—that measures established for the same stocks in the high seas 'do not undermine the effectiveness' of the measures adopted by the coastal state; this particular element is directly related to the early formulations that measures in the high seas should be no less stringent than those under national jurisdiction. The conservation policy of the coastal state will thus be the prevailing element of any high seas regime.

The states concerned must also take into account those measures previously established for the high seas in accordance with the Convention by the coastal state and the states fishing in the high seas or by a subregional or regional fisheries organization or arrangement as the case may be.[97] It must be noted that these measures established for the high seas require the participation of the coastal state in their adoption, either because of direct cooperation between the states concerned or because of its participation in regional or subregional arrangements or organizations. This is an important difference from measures adopted under Article 61 of the Convention, which are adopted solely under the discretionary rights of the coastal state in the exclusive economic zone.

Three overall conclusions can be reached in respect of the solution found to the question of compatibility under the Agreement. First, the sovereign rights of the coastal state in the exclusive economic zone are fully safeguarded. The application of Article 7 under national jurisdiction is at all times subject to the prevalence of the coastal state's rights and in no circumstances could this be interpreted or enforced in a manner contrary to the Convention on the Law of the Sea. This does not in any way affect the obligation of the coastal state to adopt conservation measures under the terms of Article 61 of the Convention. A second conclusion relates to the influence of the coastal state concerning measures adopted for high seas fisheries. If the coastal state has enacted adequate conservation measures for the exclusive economic zone, as may well be the case, it will have a strong position in the negotiations that require that measures established for the high seas be no less stringent. Compatibility in this context will be to the advantage of the coastal state. The third conclusion concerns the opposite situation, a situation in which the coastal state lacks conservation measures within its exclusive economic zone. In this case the coastal state will not be able to require stringent measures for the high seas if it has not made a comparable effort under national jurisdiction, and will have to adapt its policies in light of the compatibility required by the Agreement.

Based on these criteria, the Agreement has also approached the difficult problem of fishing in enclosed and semi-enclosed seas and other high seas areas closely linked to the interests of neighbouring coastal states.

6 The development of international cooperation for high seas conservation and management

Once the basic principles of high seas fisheries conservation and management had been agreed to, there was still the question of how to put the principles into practice. To the extent that action is required to this effect in areas under national jurisdiction, the coastal state shall have clear authority to enact the appropriate rules and measures. In the high seas, however, the exercise of flag state jurisdiction is not enough to ensure this objective, although the flag state will maintain an active role. Various mechanisms to develop international cooperation in this respect have been devised under the Agreement, thereby also significantly developing international law in its new phase of evolution.

It has been rightly observed that the duty to cooperate under the Convention was not followed by a duty to join or establish regional organizations,[98] or for that matter to bring conservation measures into practice. This legal loophole is what the Agreement basically purports to close by defining with greater precision the duty to cooperate and by providing various mechanisms in order to give effect to such duty. To this end, the Agreement first commits coastal states and states fishing on the high seas to pursue cooperation in respect of the stocks concerned 'in accordance with the Convention'.[99] The cooperation envisaged is to be pursued either directly or through appropriate subregional or regional fisheries management organizations or arrangements, taking into account the specific characteristics of the subregion or region.

Article 8 of the Agreement further links cooperation to the objective of ensuring 'effective conservation and management of such stocks'. This objective is of fundamental importance in the establishment of organizations and arrangements and in defining the extent of the obligations under the Agreement for states parties and non-parties alike. As explained by one author, if a significant number of fishing vessels register in states that do not become members of the organization, or if members do not supervise their fishing vessels or do not observe the measures adopted, the whole effort to prevent overfishing and ensure conservation will have failed.[100]

The first requirement of the Agreement in order to achieve cooperation is that states shall without delay enter into good faith consultations with a view to establishing appropriate arrangements for conservation and management.[101] It should be noted in this respect that states are not under any obligation to undertake such consultations or take other measures in every conceivable situation, but only when conservation problems have become evident or are likely to affect the state of the stocks concerned. The general duty to cooperate is now related to specific mechanisms and no longer left in a state of uncertainty. To this end, where a regional or subregional organization or arrangement is in existence and has the competence to establish conservation and management measures, states shall give effect to their duty to cooperate by becoming members of the organization or participants in the arrangement, or by agreeing to apply the measures so established.[102] If such mechanisms are not in existence, states shall then cooperate in the establishment of an organization or enter into the appropriate arrangement, and they shall participate in its work.[103]

Membership and participation in the mechanisms of cooperation became crucial questions in light of the objective of ensuring effective conservation and management of high seas fisheries. It is in this connection that the Agreement introduces important innovations in the law of high seas fisheries and closes the loopholes that still remained in the Convention on the Law of the Sea. The first question relates to which states are entitled to become members of regional organizations or to participate in the alternative arrangements. The Agreement has provided for the participation of states 'having a real interest' in the fisheries; it has further provided that the terms of participation in the organizations or arrangements shall not preclude such states from membership or participation, nor shall those terms be applied in a discriminatory manner against any state having a real interest.[104] Participation was thus only open to states that met the condition of a real interest but at the same time there was assurance that no such state would be excluded if willing to participate. The change introduced requiring a real interest is particularly relevant because such interest can only mean the conduct of actual fishing operations of significance in the region concerned, or, as expressed by one author, such organizations must accept as members 'all states with a legitimate stake in the fishery concerned'.[105] The fact of having fished in the past or the intention to do so in the future is not enough to qualify for membership or participation under the real interest criteria, although it must be noted that the particular meaning of this provision has already become subject to differing views in regional negotiations of fisheries arrangements.

But apart from the problem of formal participation, which cannot ultimately be imposed on sovereign states,[106] the essential issue is the consequence of non-participation, and here the Agreement has again profoundly innovated on the law of high seas fisheries. As the Conference Chairman commented, '[t]he Agreement is crafted in such a way that the end result is that no one can fish in the high seas area covered by a regional organisation except through the regional organisation or by observing the conservation and management rules established by the organisation'.[107] The Agreement has in fact provided that only those states which are members of an organization or participants in an arrangement, or otherwise agreeing to apply the measures adopted under those mechanisms, 'shall have access to the fishery resources to which those measures apply'.[108] If a state entitled to participate because of its fisheries activities in the region refuses to do so, then the consequence will be that it may be lawfully excluded from such fisheries. Whether this solution amounts to a denial of the freedom of such states to fish in the high seas, as it has been argued,[109] is debatable because the freedom to fish does not mean that fishing must be unregulated or done in a manner contrary to conservation and rational management. The whole evolution of the law of high seas fisheries had been pointing in this direction,[110] and the Agreement has only made explicit what was already well advanced in international law.

The Agreement having identified which states are entitled to become members or participants in the respective mechanisms and the consequences of not doing so, the question still remains of new entrants into the fishery. This has also been a difficult matter to settle in the past because on the one hand there is a need to respect the freedom of high seas fishing, and on the other hand to ensure the effectiveness of the arrangements made by the original participants. The Agreement sets out the criteria to be taken into account for determining the nature and extent of participatory rights for new entrants.[111] The most important criteria to consider are the status of the stocks concerned and the existing levels of fishing effort; if the stock is overfished or there is no surplus available, obviously new entrants will not be allowed into the fishery but they may be considered for the allocation of future fishing rights. The interests, fishing patterns, and practices of new and existing members, as well as their contributions to conservation and management and the provision of data or scientific research, are also to be taken into account. Additional criteria include the needs of coastal fishing communities and of coastal states which are overwhelmingly dependent on the exploitation of marine resources, and the interests of developing countries in the region or subregion.

The situations described above involve the membership or participation of states in the regional organizations or arrangements either *ab initio* or as new entrants. But there is still the case where states which are parties to the Agreement have refused to become members or participants in the mechanisms of cooperation. As a result of this concern, the Agreement has also provided for various obligations and measures that aim at the prevention of activities that may reduce the effectiveness of the system of conservation and management devised. The first step is that non-members or non-participants, or states which do not otherwise agree to apply the conservation and management measures established, are not discharged from the obligation to cooperate to this effect in accordance with both the Convention and the Agreement.[112] A second step is that states in this situation shall not authorize vessels flying their flag to engage in fishing operations for the stocks subject to conservation under the organization or arrangement in place.[113] This very thought had already been included in the 1993 Agreement to Promote Compliance with international conservation and management measures by fishing vessels on the high seas[114] and in the 1995 Code of Conduct for Responsible Fisheries.[115] The third step envisaged by the Agreement is to make its provisions applicable to other fishing entities, which is intended to cover the particular legal situation of Taiwan.[116] The fourth relevant step envisaged by the Agreement is to provide for the exchange of information between states members and participants regarding the activities of other states not members or participants which are engaged in fishing operations. On the basis of this exchange of information, measures shall be taken which are consistent with both the Agreement and international law in order to deter activities that undermine the effectiveness of the measures adopted.[117] Where those other states are also parties to the Agreement, this provision goes further than the one envisaged in the 1993 FAO Compliance Agreement for a similar situation since the latter only allows for the activity to be drawn to the attention of the flag state concerned and eventually of the FAO.[118] This provision of the Agreement can be related to the status of an objective regime, with important precedents found in the Convention on the Central Bering Sea[119] and in the 1959 Antarctic Treaty.[120]

Finally, the Agreement has also taken into account the situation of non-parties, which is of course different from all of the above because these other states are not legally bound by the provisions of the Agreement. The Agreement provides in this respect that states as parties shall encourage non-parties to become parties to the Agreement and to adopt laws and regulations consistent with its provisions. In addition, deterrence of activities that undermine the effective implementation of the Agreement can be undertaken by states parties in a manner consistent with the Agreement and international law.[121]

Various other provisions of the Agreement reflect the need for change in the approach to high seas fisheries conservation and management. It is to be noted in this respect that important requirements are introduced regarding the establishment of regional and subregional fisheries organizations, including the question of transparency in decision-making and the obligation to make available and exchange scientific information. The functions of these organizations have taken into account the severe criticism that had emerged in connection with the traditional type of fisheries commissions.

The provisions of the Agreement on enforcement and compliance have also introduced important trends relating to high seas fisheries conservation and management. These include the extension of port state jurisdiction for fisheries purposes, but, as is the case with other matters, room has also been given to different interpretations of the Agreement.[122] New trends are also found in the case of the arrangements envisaged for the settlement of disputes in respect of high seas fisheries. These will be examined in separate chapters, as will the influence that the Agreement has already had in recent regional developments.[123]

7 Freedom of fishing and conservation in the high seas: the need for mutual accommodation

The long historical evolution that has characterized the law of high seas fisheries shows a close linkage between scientific knowledge and the kind of regulatory regime envisaged to cope with the problems that have emerged at different points in time. Unrestricted freedom of fishing gave place to early forms of international cooperation when it became universally accepted that the living resources of the high seas were exhaustible. Ecosystem management is again the outcome of scientific evidence.

What type of regulatory regime is best for solving the mounting problems of over-exploitation and depletion of resources is still an open question. While unrestricted freedom of fishing and loose forms of international cooperation have failed as effective regulatory mechanisms, new forms of international cooperation have emerged in the most recent stage of the legal evolution discussed. These new forms are characterized by a greater role of the coastal state, the strengthening of regional and subregional mechanisms, and the enactment of compulsory standards applicable to all fisheries in the regulated area. How effective this approach will be in practice is still to be assessed as the new mechanisms are put into place. In any event, regulatory measures which are adopted in the light of scientific knowledge and that emphasize compliance are unquestionably an improvement on the early attempts to find appropriate solutions.

Precisely because all of this evolution tends to attain a balance between two legitimate values such as fisheries development and conservation, the emphasis on regulatory elements that has strongly come to the fore should not result in law or in practice in the demise of the freedom of high seas fisheries as some have feared.[124] This freedom cannot any longer be conceived as absolute or unrestricted as in the past, but this does not mean that it should be replaced by overwhelming international regulations that, as experience has shown in many matters, would not ensure the effectiveness of either value since they may go beyond what is needed to bring about realistic solutions. As a result of this evolution, the freedom of fisheries is a specifically qualified freedom,[125] and this should be perfected to the extent required by effective conservation.[126] However, at no point should the balance attained be reversed; this would not be to the advantage of states' interests nor to those of the international community, present or future. The thought of banning high seas fisheries altogether in the interests of conservation does not seem to be, in the light of the above discussion, a realistic or appropriate solution except in the context of specific species or temporary situations.

The effectiveness of international arrangements that pursue the desired objectives of fisheries development and conservation is also important from another point of view. Unless these central values are satisfied by means of such arrangements, the option of unilateral coastal state action might reappear as a viable alternative as it was the solution already found for the 200-mile area brought under national jurisdiction. In this context, future extensions of coastal state authority cannot be ruled out if the international arrangements fail,[127] a situation which would be particularly troublesome if the Fish Stocks Agreement ended up in failure or in a situation comparable to that of the 1958 Convention. The oceans would again become a major source of contention, dispute, and confrontation with serious jurisdictional implications.

An additional and novel option that can simultaneously be considered, and which does not involve highly regulatory mechanisms, coastal state extension of jurisdiction, or mere traditional arrangements of international cooperation, is the introduction of market economy mechanisms in the management of high seas fisheries.[128] Mechanisms such as individual transferable quotas prevent the adverse effects of unrestricted open access, require the intervention of governmental or international authority basically for the allocation of quotas, supervision of the market, and enforcement of rights, and as a result allow for both fisheries development and conservation since there will be a specific interest in ensuring the availability of resources on a sustainable basis. Should the present approach to international cooperation not be as successful as is desirable, this other option offers an alternative that thus far has had limited application but positive results. This option, of course, mainly addresses the question of efficiency in fisheries operations and management, but it does not by itself solve the problems related to the allocation of initial fishing rights, cooperation, and compliance.

The changing international law of high seas fisheries that has here been discussed is the best example of how divergent interests have come to be accommodated within a common framework of understanding and convenience throughout a long historical evolution. Such acccommodation is now in process regarding the interests in both development and conservation, with the added advantages that accommodation today can be reached in a matter of a few years and not centuries, and, above all, with the advantage that development and conservation are mutually supportive values and objectives. In the light of the innovations and improvements experienced by international law in this field in the past twenty-five years, it may be expected that the way ahead will be still more constructive and that positive solutions will be found to the many problems pending, although regional conflicts and issues of acceptability of the new international rules still cast a shadow over the long-term prospects of the oceans. The basic framework to this effect is now in place, and it should be expected that its gradual implementation will provide further evidence of the positive trends upon which the international law of high seas fisheries is increasingly based.

Notes

1. United Nations Convention on the Law of the Sea (1982), UN Doc. A/CONF.62/122; 21 *ILM* 1261; hereinafter Convention on the Law of the Sea.
2. UN Doc. A/CONF.164/37 (1995); hereinafter Fish Stocks Agreement; 34 *ILM* 1542; see in general F. Orrego Vicuña, *The Changing International Law of High Seas Fisheries* (Cambridge University Press, 1999).
3. United Nations, 'Memorandum on the Regime of the High Seas, prepared by the Secretariat', UN Doc. A/CN.4/32, *Yearbook of the International Law Commission (1950)*, ii. 69, para. 11.
4. F. Orrego Vicuña, 'The "Presential Sea": Defining Coastal States' Special Interests in High Seas Fisheries and Other Activities', *German Yearbook of International Law*, 35 (1992), 264, 292.
5. P. W. Birnie and A. E. Boyle, *International Law and the Environment* (Oxford: Clarendon Press, 1992), 425.
6. Ibid. 507.
7. W. T. Burke, *The New International Law of Fisheries* (Oxford: Clarendon Press, 1994), 95.
8. D. Attard, *The Exclusive Economic Zone in International Law* (Oxford University Press, 1987); B. Kwiatkowska, *The 200 Mile Exclusive Economic Zone in the New Law of the Sea* (Dordrecht: Kluwer Law International, 1989); F. Orrego Vicuña, *The Exclusive Economic Zone: Regime and Legal Nature under International Law* (Cambridge University Press, 1989).
9. *Bering Sea Fur Seals Arbitration* (1893); Moore, *International Arbitration Awards*, 1, 755.
10. Birnie and Boyle, *International Law and the Environment*, 494.
11. Ibid. 118.
12. Convention on Fishing and Conservation of the Living Resources of the High Seas (1958), 559 *UNTS* 285; hereinafter 1958 Convention.
13. Birnie and Boyle, *International Law and the Environment*, 503.
14. Ibid. 505–7.
15. E. Brown Weiss (ed.), *Environmental Change and International Law: New Challenges and Dimensions* (Tokyo: United Nations University Press, 1992); Birnie and Boyle, *International Law and the Environment*; P. Sands, *Principles of International Environmental Law* (Manchester University Press, 1995).
16. R.-J. Dupuy and D. Vignes (eds.), *A Handbook on the New Law of the Sea* (Dordrecht: Martinus Nijhoff, 1991); R. R. Churchill and A. V. Lowe, *The Law of the Sea* (Manchester University Press, 1988); E. D. Brown, *The International Law of the Sea* (Aldershot: Dartmouth, 1994).
17. M. Dahmani, *The Fisheries Regime of the Exclusive Economic Zone* (Dordrecht: Martinus Nijhoff, 1987).
18. J. Carroz, 'Les Problèmes de la pêche à la Conférence sur le droit de la mer et dans la pratique des états', *Revue générale de droit international public*, 3 (1980), 705.
19. Burke, *The New International Law of Fisheries*, 131–41; Birnie and Boyle, *International Law and the Environment*, 530–8.

20. Convention on the Law of the Sea, Arts. 116–20.
21. IUCN, *The Law of the Sea: Priorities and Responsibilities in Implementing the Convention* (Gland: IUCN—The World Conservation Union, 1995).
22. Sands, *Principles of International Environmental Law.*
23. W. T. Burke, '1982 Convention on the Law of the Sea Provisions on Conditions of Access to Fisheries Subject to National Jurisdiction', *FAO Fisheries Report*, 293 (1983), 23.
24. B. Kwiatkowska, 'Conservation and Optimum Utilization of Living Resources', in T. A. Clingan (ed.), *The Law of the Sea: What Lies Ahead?* (Honolulu: Law of the Sea Institute, 1988), 245.
25. Burke, *The New International Law of Fisheries*, 43.
26. W. R. Edeson: 'Types of Agreements for Exploitation of EEZ Fisheries', in E. D. Brown and R. R. Churchill (eds.), *The UN Convention on the Law of the Sea: Impact and Implementation* (Honolulu: Law of the Sea Institute, 1987), 157; G. Moore, 'Coastal State Requirements for Foreign Fishing', *FAO Legislative Study*, 21 (1993), Rev. 4.
27. D. M. Johnston, *The International Law of Fisheries: A Framework for Policy-Oriented Inquiries* (New Haven: Yale University Press, 1965); W. T. Burke, 'Importance of the 1982 UN Convention on the Law of the Sea and its Future Developments', *Ocean Development and International Law*, 27 (1996), 1.
28. J. P. Troadec, 'Introduction à l'aménagement des pêcheries: intérêt, difficultés et principales méthodes', *FAO Fisheries Technical Paper*, 224 (1982); O. Flaaten, 'Limited Entry into Fisheries: Why and How', in G. Ulfstein, P. Andersen, and R. Churchill (eds.), *The Regulation of Fisheries: Legal, Economic, and Social Aspects* (Strasbourg: Council of Europe, 1987), 89.
29. Convention on the Law of the Sea, Art. 61 (2).
30. Ibid.
31. Ibid., Art. 62 (1). On Arts. 61 and 62 of the Convention on the Law of the Sea, see generally United Nations, *The Law of the Sea: Conservation and Utilization of the Living Resources of the Exclusive Economic Zone. Legislative History of Arts. 61 and 62 of the United Nations Convention on the Law of the Sea* (New York: United Nations, Division for Ocean Affairs and the Law of the Sea, Office of Legal Affairs, 1995).
32. Burke, *The New International Law of Fisheries*, ch. 3; E. Hey, *The Regime for the Exploitation of Transboundary Marine Fisheries Resources* (Dordrecht: Martinus Nijhoff, 1989), ch. 5.
33. Convention on the Law of the Sea, Art. 66 (3) (a).
34. Burke, *The New International Law of Fisheries*, 168–9.
35. Convention on the Law of the Sea, Art. 67 (1).
36. P. Birnie, *International Regulation of Whaling* (New York: Oceana Publications, 1985).
37. Convention on the Law of the Sea, Art. 120.
38. Birnie and Boyle, *International Law and the Environment*, 533.
39. Hey, *The Regime for the Exploitation of Transboundary Marine Fisheries Resources*; B. Applebaum, 'The Straddling Stocks Problem: The Northwest Atlantic Situation, International Law, and Options for Coastal State Action', in A. H. A. Soons (ed.), *Implementation of the Law of the Sea Convention through*

International Institutions: Proceedings of the 23rd Annual Conference of the Law of the Sea Institute (Honolulu: The Law of the Sea Institute, University of Hawaii, 1990), 282; E. L. Miles and W. T. Burke, 'Pressures on the United Nations Convention on the Law of the Sea of 1982 Arising from New Fisheries Conflicts: The Problem of Straddling Stocks', *Ocean Development and International Law*, 20 (1989), 343.

40. Burke, *The New International Law of Fisheries*, ch. 5; W. T. Burke, 'Highly Migratory Species in the New Law of the Sea', *Ocean Development and International Law*, 14 (1984), 273; G. Munro, 'Extended Jurisdiction and the Management of Pacific Highly Migratory Species', *Ocean Development and International Law*, 21 (1990), 289.

41. United Nations, *The Law of the Sea: The Regime for High Seas Fisheries* (New York: United Nations, Division for Ocean Affairs and the Law of the Sea, Office of Legal Affairs, 1992), 23.

42. Australia, Canada, Cape Verde, Iceland, Philippines, São Tomé and Príncipe, Senegal, and Sierra Leone, 'Amendments to Article 63, paragraph 2', Doc. A/CONF.162/L.114, *Official Records of the UNCLOS*, xvi (New York: United Nations, 13 Apr. 1982).

43. Convention on the Law of the Sea, Art. 116 (b).

44. Burke, *The New International Law of Fisheries*, 200–4.

45. United Nations, *The Law of the Sea: The Regime for High Seas Fisheries*, 19–21.

46. W. T. Burke, 'Impacts of the UN Convention on the Law of the Sea on Tuna Regulation', *FAO Legislative Study*, 26 (1982).

47. Convention on the Law of the Sea, Art. 64 (1).

48. Burke, *The New International Law of Fisheries*, 220–5.

49. L. A. Kimball, 'The United Nations Convention on the Law of the Sea: A Framework for Marine Conservation', in IUCN, *The Law of the Sea*, 17.

50. United Nations Conference on Straddling Fish Stocks and Highly Migratory Fish Stocks (1993), *Report of the Technical Consultation on High Seas Fishing and the Papers Presented at the Technical Consultation on High Seas Fishing*, A/CONF.164/INF/2 (Geneva: United Nations, 14 May 1993).

51. Ibid. 11–13.

52. Ibid. 15–18; see also the paper on 'International Fishery Bodies: Considerations for High Seas Management', ibid. 70–80; M. Savini, 'Summary Information on the Role of International Fishery Bodies with Regard to the Conservation and Management of Living Resources of the High Seas', *FAO Fisheries Circular*, 835, Rev. 1 (1991).

53. International Law Association, International Committee on the Exclusive Economic Zone, 'Principles Applicable to Living Resources Occurring Both within and without the Exclusive Economic Zone or in Zones of Overlapping Claims', Report of the Committee by Professor Rainer Lagoni, *Report of the Sixty-Fifth Conference* (Cairo) (London: International Law Association, 1992), 254, para. 49, 271.

54. Boyle, Ch. 3 below.

55. W. Burke, 'Fishing in the Bering Sea Donut: Straddling Stocks and the New International Law of Fisheries', *Ecology Law Quarterly*, 16 (1989), 285; Miles and Burke, 'Pressures on the United Nations Convention on the Law of the

Sea of 1982', 343; B. Kwiatkowska, 'Creeping Jurisdiction beyond 200 Miles in the Light of the 1982 Law of the Sea Convention and State Practice', *Ocean Development and International Law*, 22 (1991), 153.

56. Applebaum, 'The Straddling Stocks Problem', 282.

57. International Law Association, *Report of the Sixty-Fifth Conference*, para. 44, 269–70.

58. Ibid., para. 45, 270.

59. Burke, 'Fishing in the Bering Sea Donut', 303.

60. United Nations, *The Law of the Sea: The Regime for High Seas Fisheries*.

61. International Law Association, *Report of the Sixty-Fifth Conference*, para. 7.

62. Fish Stocks Agreement; supra n. 2.

63. On the principles and trends of international environmental law, see generally Sands, *Principles of International Environmental Law*; Weiss, *Environmental Change and International Law*; Birnie and Boyle, *International Law and the Environment*; A. Kiss and D. Shelton, *International Environmental Law* (New York: Transnational Publishers, 1991).

64. Fish Stocks Agreement, Art. 2.

65. D. H. Anderson, 'The Straddling Stocks Agreement of 1995: An Initial Assessment', *International and Comparative Law Quarterly*, 45 (1996), 463, 469; also generally P. G. G. Davies and C. Redgwell, 'The International Legal Regulation of Straddling Fish Stocks', *British Yearbook of International Law*, 67 (1997), 199.

66. Fish Stocks Agreement, Art. 5 (b).

67. Sands, *Principles of International Environmental Law*, 195.

68. Fish Stocks Agreement, Art. 5 (f).

69. Ibid., Art. 5 (h).

70. Sands, *Principles of International Environmental Law*, 208–13; L. Gundling, 'The Status in International Law of the Principle of Precautionary Action', *International Journal of Estuarine and Coastal Law*, 5 (1990), 23; D. Freestone and E. Hey (eds.), *The Precautionary Principle and International Law: The Challenge of Implementation* (The Hague: Kluwer Law International, 1995).

71. Sands, *Principles of International Environmental Law*, 270–1; S. M. Garcia, 'The Precautionary Principle: Its Implications in Capture Fisheries Management', *Ocean and Coastal Management*, 22 (1994), 99.

72. S. N. Nandan, 'The United Nations Conference on Straddling Fish Stocks and Highly Migratory Fish Stocks and its Potential Impact on Pacific Island Tuna Fisheries', statement made at the *Conference on Achieving Goals for Sustainable Living in the Aquatic Continent* (Hawaii: mimeo, 19–23 Sept. 1995), 3.

73. Fish Stocks Agreement, Art. 6 (3) (b); FAO, 'Reference Points for Fisheries Management: Their Potential Application to Straddling and Highly Migratory Resources', Doc. A/CONF. 164/INF/9 (1994).

74. Fish Stocks Agreement, Art. 6 (4).

75. D. Hunter, 'Background Paper for the Expert Group Workshop on International Environmental Law Aiming at Sustainable Development' (Washington: mimeo, 13–15 Nov. 1995), paras. 46–50.

76. Fish Stocks Agreement, Art. 5 (j).

77. Ibid., Art. 5 (k).

78. Ibid., Art. 14.
79. Ibid., annex I on 'Standard Requirements for the Collection and Sharing of Data'.
80. K. Sherman, 'Large Marine Ecosystems as Global Units for Management: An Ecological Perspective', ICES CM 1990/L:24 (Copenhagen: International Council for the Exploration of the Sea, 1990).
81. A. Couve, 'Negociaciones sobre la pesca en alta mar', in *Conference on 'Los intereses pesqueros de Chile en alta mar'* (Santiago: mimeo, 27 May 1996), 5.
82. M. Hayashi, 'The Role of the United Nations in Managing the World's Fisheries', in G. H. Blake *et al.* (eds.), *The Peaceful Management of Transboundary Resources* (London: Graham & Trotman, 1995), 373, 379.
83. Fish Stocks Agreement, Art. 4.
84. D. A. Balton, 'Strengthening the Law of the Sea: The New Agreement on Straddling Fish Stocks and Highly Migratory Fish Stocks', *Ocean Development and International Law*, 27 (1996), 125, at 135.
85. Fish Stocks Agreement, Art. 3 (1).
86. Ibid.
87. Ibid., Art. 3 (2).
88. Balton, 'Strengthening the Law of the Sea', 137.
89. Fish Stocks Agreement, Art. 7 (1).
90. Ibid., Art. 7 (1) (a) and (b).
91. United States Aide-Memoire (22 May 1991), in 19 *LOSB* 21.
92. Fish Stocks Agreement, Art. 7 (2).
93. Nandan, 'The United Nations Conference on Straddling Fish Stocks and Highly Migratory Fish Stocks', 4.
94. Fish Stocks Agreement, Art. 7 (2) (d).
95. Ibid., Art. 7 (2) (e).
96. Ibid., Art. 7 (2) (a).
97. Ibid., Art. 7 (2) (b) and (c).
98. M. Hayashi, 'The 1995 Agreement on the Conservation and Management of Straddling and Highly Migratory Fish Stocks: Significance for the Law of the Sea Convention', *Ocean and Coastal Management*, 29 (1995), 51, 58.
99. Fish Stocks Agreement, Art. 8 (1).
100. Balton, 'Strengthening the Law of the Sea', 138.
101. Fish Stocks Agreement, Art. 8 (2).
102. Ibid., Art. 8 (3).
103. Ibid., Art. 8 (5).
104. Ibid., Art. 8 (3); A. Tahindro, 'Conservation and Management of Transboundary Fish Stocks: Comments in Light of the Adoption of the 1995 Agreement for the Conservation and Management of Straddling Fish Stocks and Highly Migratory Fish Stocks', *Ocean Development and International Law*, 28 (1997), 1, 21.
105. Balton, 'Strengthening the Law of the Sea', 139.
106. Ibid. 140.
107. Nandan, 'The United Nations Conference on Straddling Fish Stocks and Highly Migratory Fish Stocks', 4.
108. Fish Stocks Agreement, Art. 8 (4).

109. Hayashi, 'The 1995 Agreement', 58.
110. See generally above, s. 1.
111. Fish Stocks Agreement, Art. 11.
112. Ibid., Art. 17 (1).
113. Ibid., Art. 17 (2).
114. FAO, Agreement to Promote Compliance with International Conservation and Management Measures by Fishing Vessels on the High Seas, Art. III (1) (a); 33 *ILM* 968; hereinafter FAO Compliance Agreement.
115. FAO, Code of Conduct for Responsible Fisheries (1995), Art. 6 (11); Doc. C 95/20-Rev. 1.
116. Fish Stocks Agreement, Art. 1 (3).
117. Ibid., Art. 17 (4).
118. FAO Compliance Agreement, Art. VI (8) (b).
119. Convention on the Conservation and Management of Pollock Resources in the Central Bering Sea (1994); 34 *ILM* 67, Art. XII (3).
120. Antarctic Treaty (1959), Art. X; 402 *UNTS* 71.
121. Fish Stocks Agreement, Art. 33 (1) and (2).
122. See for example the interpretative declaration which shall be made by the European Community and its member states upon ratification of the Agreement; *OJ* L189 (1998), at 41.
123. Vukas and Vidas (Ch. 2), Hønneland (Ch. 4), and Boyle (Ch. 3), below.
124. A. Del Vecchio, 'La libertà di pesca in alto mare: un principio ancora valido?', *Diritto marittimo*, 2 (1995), 328.
125. Anderson, 'The Straddling Stocks Agreement of 1995', 475.
126. Burke, *The New International Law of Fisheries*, 350.
127. Ibid. 350; W. S. Ball, 'The Old Grey *Mare*, National Enclosure of the Oceans', *Ocean Development and International Law*, 27 (1996), 97.
128. P. H. Pearse, 'Fishery Rights, Regulations and Revenues', *Marine Policy*, 5 (1981), 135; P. H. Pearse, 'From Open Access to Private Property: Recent Innovations in Fishing Rights as Instruments of Fishing Policy', in A. Couper and E. Gold (eds.), *The Marine Environment and Sustainable Development: Law, Policy and Science* (Honolulu: Law of the Sea Institute, 1991), 178; P. A. Neher, R. Arnason, and N. Mollett (eds.), *Rights-Based Fishing* (Dordrecht: Kluwer Law International, 1989).

2

Flags of Convenience and High Seas Fishing: The Emergence of a Legal Framework

BUDISLAV VUKAS AND DAVOR VIDAS

The use of 'flags of convenience' is not new to international law.[1] It is considered to be detrimental to the safety of international navigation, it hinders the application of relevant international standards as well as protection to seafarers. Various attempts have been made over the years to prevent or reduce the use of 'flags of convenience', albeit these have not always been very successful.

While the flags of convenience problem has various aspects, our primary interest here is the more recent manifestation associated with unauthorized fishing in areas of the high seas that are governed by regional fisheries conservation and management arrangements. In this context, reflagging into the register of a state not party to a specific regional fisheries agreement can be a means of deliberately avoiding the application of conservation measures adopted under that agreement and thus jeopardizing the effectiveness of such measures. The practice of reflagging has created serious problems for many regional fisheries conservation and management arrangements.

During the 1990s, certain legal aspects emerged that, seen in the light of earlier solutions in the law of the sea, offered some innovative approaches to dealing with the flags of convenience problem—now specifically related to the conservation and management of international fisheries. The international fisheries law expanded rapidly, particularly in the post-UNCED period, and two important global agreements were adopted: the 1993 FAO Compliance Agreement[2] and the 1995 UN Fish Stocks Agreement.[3] This international regulation at the global level has in many respects been influenced by regional developments, which have in turn stimulated the development and use of new methods for law enforcement and control of foreign fishing vessels at both regional and global levels.

This chapter aims to provide an overview of that development. Commencing with the law of the sea search for the 'genuine link' as a means of dealing with the problem of flags of convenience, the focus is then shifted to recent developments in the law of the sea that, in the context of international fisheries regulation, have employed various new approaches to the flags of convenience problem.

1 Overview of the problem

The legal connection between a ship and the flag state has traditionally been called 'the nationality of the ship'. The flag state accepts responsibility for a ship having its nationality, it acquires authority over the ship registered in its registry and flying its flag, as well as granting protection to such a ship.[4]

1.1 *Flags of convenience in international law: the appearance and evolution*

Because the term 'nationality' has been used to determine the status of subjects of law, i.e. individuals and corporations, the use of the same expression for ships, i.e. objects of law, has been considered inappropriate.[5] This difference is not relevant here. In both cases, the internal legal order of a state determines the characteristics that are considered relevant in defining the exclusive link to 'nationality', such as place of birth, nationality of the parents, seat of the corporation, or nationality of the shipowners. However, the intention of international law has been to restrict the states' absolute freedom in granting their nationality to ships. At the 1896 Venice session, the Institute of International Law adopted the 'Regulations relative for the use of national flags for merchant ships', wherein certain conditions for the registration of ships were determined.[6] The ownership of the ship was to be controlled by the nationals of the state of registry, and the corporations were to have their seat in that state (Articles 2 and 3 of the Regulations). Thus, although the term 'genuine link' was not specifically used, the Institute actually required the existence of a genuine link between the ship and the state of registration, i.e. the flag state.

The Regulations adopted by the Institute of International Law aimed at limiting the freedom of states in respect of their granting nationality to ships. However, in the *Muscat Dhow* and some other cases it was stated that each state retained the right to determine the conditions by which it accorded a ship the right to fly its flag.[7]

Up to the Second World War, a consistent practice regarding granting nationality to ships was developed in almost all states. Before a ship could be granted the nationality of a state, certain conditions had to be satisfied, most of which were related to the nationality of shipowners, the nationality of the crew, and in some states even the place of the construction of the ship.[8] At the same time, however, the first instances of granting a flag to ships not possessing a 'genuine link' with the state of registry were also being observed. Shipowners had their particular reasons for desiring their vessels to be registered in specific states.[9] Moreover, the basis of acceptance by these states for the registration of ships with which they had no substantial links was almost exclusively of a financial nature.

One of the initial reasons for pursuing a flag of 'convenience' was that land-locked states did not have the right to sail ships under their own flag prior to the 1921 Barcelona Declaration Recognizing the Right of a Flag of States Having no Sea-Coast.[10] Consequently, ships belonging to nationals of these states had to find an 'authorized' flag state.

At the beginning of the Second World War, many ships owned by US companies sailed under the flags of Panama and Honduras. United States companies found this advantageous because at that time US neutrality laws limited commerce with belligerent states. Even today a foreign flag can protect the merchant fleet of states that are victims of aggression, for example Kuwaiti ships in 1990 and Croatian ships in 1991 ('flags of refuge').

Since the early 1950s, economic and financial circumstances have contributed to the expansion of the fleet sailing under 'flags of convenience'. Today some 30 per cent of the world tonnage of merchant ships sails under a flag of convenience. Among the main reasons for this are evasion of national taxation, avoidance of employing a national crew of the state concerned, and circumvention of international rules and standards (especially those of the International Maritime Organization and the International Labour Organization).[11]

By the end of the 1990s, reflagging had become a serious problem: in 1997, a new increase in the level of reflagging was noted. During the period 1994–7, over 2,000 vessels had been reflagged, amounting to almost 10 per cent of the total merchant fleet.[12]

1.2 *Flags of convenience in a new context: high seas fishing*

More recently, flags of convenience have been used within a new context, the international regulation of fisheries, and in a particular area, that of the high seas, often in areas covered by regional fisheries management and conservation arrangements. With the advent of the exclusive economic zone in the law of the sea, the pressure on high seas fishing has increased rapidly. By the late 1980s, the marine fisheries faced a deep crisis: the state of the marine fish stock indicated that problems had become far more urgent than at the time of negotiation of the 1982 UN Convention on the Law of the Sea (LOS Convention).[13] By 1994, when the LOS Convention entered into force, the Food and Agriculture Organization (FAO) estimated that 70 per cent of the world's marine fisheries were fully exploited, over-exploited, or in a recovery stage.[14]

The LOS Convention has, however, provided a framework for the elaboration of new fisheries agreements on a *regional* basis. Simultaneously, with the conclusion of a number of regional fisheries management arrangements, a new problem has arisen—how to ensure the effectiveness of such regional arrangements under international law from the illegal fishing activities of non-member states. The vessels involved in illegal, unreported, and unregulated (IUU) fishing often fly flags of convenience, or employ reflagging, as a means of deliberately avoiding fisheries conservation and management measures based on regional arrangements applicable on the high seas. This manifestation of the 'flag of convenience' problem is associated with a particular motive, the avoidance of international law requirements for compliance with conservation and management measures adopted under regional arrangements.

This problem has been encountered by many regional fisheries conservation and management arrangements from the mid-1980s and throughout the 1990s. For instance, in the period from 1985 to 1993, an annual average of thirty to forty fishing vessels of non-contracting parties were sighted in the regulatory area of the Northwest Atlantic Fisheries Organization (NAFO).[15] Many of the vessels sailed under a flag of convenience, initially flags of Panama and Honduras.[16] Upon NAFO's deliverance of diplomatic démarches to these countries, some of the same vessels were deregistered, and soon continued with IUU fishing in the NAFO regulatory area under the flag of Belize.[17]

This problem, involving the same flags, has been a cause of concern for the International Commission for the Conservation of Atlantic Tunas (ICCAT). In 1996, ICCAT invited Belize, Honduras, and Panama to cooperate with its conservation and management measures; at the same time, ICCAT recommended to its members the adoption of trade measures against import of Atlantic bluefin tuna and its products from these countries.[18]

The last regional arrangement to be broached was that established under the Convention on the Conservation of Antarctic Marine Living Resources (CCAMLR).[19] Vessels under a flag of convenience were to have a severe impact upon the overall effectiveness of CCAMLR. While the reported catch of Patagonian toothfish (Dissostichus eleginoides) in the 1996–7 season in the entire CCAMLR area amounted to approximately 10,000 metric tons,[20] the unreported catch in the Indian Ocean sector of the CCAMLR area was estimated to be between 107,000 and 115,000 metric tons.[21] Over 100 vessels were observed to be involved in IUU fishing for Patagonian toothfish in the CCAMLR area, and the total wholesale value of this catch has been estimated in the 'order of half a billion dollars (A$)'.[22] About half of these vessels sailed under various 'flags of convenience', flying mainly the flags of Belize, Namibia, and Panama, but also of Vanuatu and Portugal, while flags of the Faroe Islands, Guinea-Bissau, Honduras, Malta, the Marshall Islands, and Taiwan were also sighted, although in smaller numbers.[23] The entire threat posed to CCAMLR was perceived by its members as grave enough to constitute 'the most serious challenge in its existence',[24] with the potential of undermining collaboration within CCAMLR as well as the conservation policy developed since the establishment of CCAMLR.[25]

The problem of reflagged vessels has also been reported in the case of the North Atlantic Salmon Conservation Organization (NASCO), the North Pacific Anadromous Fish Commission (NPAFC) for illegal fishing for salmon on the high seas of the North Pacific Ocean by vessels of non-member countries, and the North-East Atlantic Fisheries Commission (NEAFC).[26]

In international law, the entire problem of reflagging can be (and has been) approached from two essentially different perspectives. One is to adopt rules in order to prevent the act of reflagging itself by requiring a 'genuine link' between the vessel and the state whose flag it flies. The other approach is to impose additional duties on the flag state in respect of its vessels, be these reflagged or not, fishing on the high seas, and if this fails, non-flag states could be entitled to exert a certain degree of control and enforcement over vessels that undermine the effectiveness of conservation measures on the high seas. In the following sections of this chapter, the development of international law in this field will be examined and in the process both perspectives will be reviewed.[27]

2 The law of the sea and the flags of convenience: long-standing search for a 'genuine link'

Article 28 of the 1956 International Law Commission (ILC) Draft, as well as Article 4 of the Convention on the High Seas, confirmed the right of every state to sail ships under its own flag. However, this non-controversial right of all states has created a plethora of problems regarding the *conditions* under which the right is given to fly the flag of a state.

In his 1950 report to the ILC, its special rapporteur for the Law of the Sea, J. P. A. François, accepted the right of every state to determine the conditions for granting its nationality to ships. However, he considered that the legislation of no state should differ considerably from the principles adopted by the majority of states, which may even be regarded as 'forming in this respect an element of international law'. Accordingly, he was in favour of bringing closer the laws of different states. Yet, as he doubted that a unification of such rules would be possible, he allowed for the Commission to conclude that a rule on the question of nationality

not be included in the draft articles on the law of the sea.[28] Notwithstanding these doubts and the opposition of two of ILC's members (G.
Amado and R. J. Alfaro), the Commission decided to try to determine the
general principles that might allow a certain degree of uniformity in the
matter.[29]

In his second report (1951), François listed principles that he found the
majority of states took into account in determining the nationality of
ships. He then suggested that the Commission proclaim these as the basis
of international law in this respect. His conclusions concerning the generally accepted principles were influenced by the 1896 Regulations
adopted by the Institute of International Law (mentioned earlier in this
chapter). The main principle proposed by François was that the ownership of the vessel had to be controlled by individuals or companies that
had a close link with the state of registry. In addition to this, François
insisted that the master of the ship should posses the nationality of the
flag state.[30]

The proposal of J. P. A. François was discussed thoroughly in the
Commission; his suggestion concerning the ownership of the vessel
was accepted, but the nationality of the master was not considered as
relevant.[31] As a result of these discussions, the Provisional Articles
Concerning the Régime of the High Seas contained the following draft
article on the right to flag:

Each State may fix the conditions for the registration of ships in its territory and
the right to fly its flag. Nevertheless, for purposes of recognition of its national
character by other States, a ship must either:

1. Be the property of the State concerned; or
2. Be more than half owned by;
    (a) Nationals of or persons legally domiciled in the territory of the State con-
        cerned and actually resident there; or
    (b) A partnership in which the majority of the partners with personal liability
        are nationals of or persons legally domiciled in the territory of the State
        concerned and actually resident there; or
    (c) A joint stock company formed under the laws of the State concerned and
        having its registered office in the territory of that State. (Article 5)[32]

In their replies to the draft Articles, several governments commented on
Article 5.[33] The decisive proposal proved to be the one suggested by the
Netherlands, which, instead of listing the elements confirming national
character, proposed to mention only a general principle requiring 'a
genuine connection between the State and the ship'. This proposal was so
appealing to the members of the Commission that they unanimously
decided to redraft the Article on nationality 'on the basis of a general principle', even before hearing the report of a subcommittee that they had
established in order to prepare a text of Article 5.[34]

This change of the Commission's attitude marks a point of no return in the efforts to ensure a close link between flag states and their ships. The notion/general principle of a 'genuine link' proved to be vague and useless as a standard. The Commission also made another hasty decision; it decided to integrate Article 4 (Status of ships) with Article 5 (Right to a flag), and thus Article 29 (1) of the Commission's 1956 draft read:

Each State shall fix conditions for the grant of its nationality to ships, for the registration of ships in its territory, and for the right to fly its flag. Ships have the nationality of the State whose flag they are entitled to fly. Nevertheless, for purposes of recognition of the national character of the ship by other States, there must exist a genuine link between the State and the ship.[35]

2.1 The 1958 Geneva Convention on the High Seas

At the First United Nations Conference on the Law of the Sea (UNCLOS I) held in Geneva in 1958, Article 29 (1) of the Commission's draft underwent some changes and became Article 5 (1) of the Convention on the High Seas. Unfortunately, the first two sentences of the ILC proposal were not changed. Although we do not share all the critical comments and doubts of Meijers,[36] we do agree that the drafting of this text leaves much to be desired.

The regular relationship in the first sentence ought to read as follows: registration is inseparably linked to the acquirement of nationality, and the right to fly the flag is the consequence of having satisfied all the conditions connected to the registration and the grant of the nationality of the flag state. Therefore, if a second sentence had been necessary, this should have been formulated differently. Rather than stating that 'Ships have the nationality of the State whose flag they are entitled to fly', it might have been stated that 'the right to fly a flag of a state is based on the grant of its nationality to that ship'.

The only part in the ILC draft Article 29 (1) that underwent alteration was the final sentence. The existence of the 'genuine link' as a condition for the 'recognition of the national character of the ship by other States' was no longer mentioned. The omission of the recognition of the national character by third states has been viewed as opening the door for states maintaining an 'open registry'.[37] Contrary to the ILC draft, a 'genuine link' was partially defined in Article 5 (1) of the High Seas Convention: 'There must exist a genuine link between the State and the ship; in particular, the State must effectively exercise its jurisdiction and control in administrative, technical and social matters over ships flying its flag.' In addition to these elements of the genuine link, the Convention imposes further duties on the flag state. In accordance with Article 5 (2), the flag state must issue to ships to which it has granted the right to fly its flag documents to that effect; and for these ships, the flag state must take the required measures necessary to ensure safety at sea. Under Article 10 (1), such measures should be taken with regard to, *inter alia*, the use of signals, the maintenance of communications, and the prevention of collisions; the manning of ships and labour conditions for crews, taking into account the applicable international labour standards; and the construction, equipment, and seaworthiness of ships. In adopting such measures, Article 10 (2) requires states to conform to generally accepted international standards and to take any steps necessary to ensure observance of these standards.

The wording of these provisions on the obligations of flag states makes it clear that the duties of all states are not the same, as these duties are mostly regulated by treaties ('applicable international labour instruments') to which only the minority of states are party. On other questions, those measures which states are required to take depend upon the vague notion of 'generally accepted international standards'.[38]

2.2 The 1982 United Nations Convention on the Law of the Sea

The contents of Articles 5 and 10 of the Geneva Convention on the High Seas have been superseded by Articles 91 and 94 of the LOS Convention. Textually, the wording of Article 5 (1) of the 1958 Convention has been adopted almost without changes in Articles 91 (1) and 94 (1) of the 1982 Convention. However, whereas the 1958 Articles did not have titles, Article 91 of the LOS Convention is entitled 'Nationality of ships' and Article 94, 'Duties of the flag State'. The relevance of the titles becomes clear in the context of the content of the two articles. Contrary to Article 5 of the High Seas Convention, Article 91 of the LOS Convention does not contain any definition of the expression 'genuine link'. As in 1958, the 1982 text reads, 'There must exist a genuine link between the State and the ship.' However, the requirement of effectively exercising flag state jurisdiction and control no longer remains in the same provision; rather, it has been removed to paragraph 1 of Article 94.

What are the consequences of this change? Although the same phrases have been retained, their placement in the context of the 'duties of the flag State' changes their scope. In the 1958 Geneva Convention, the flag state duties in Article 5 were elements necessary for the *existence* of the genuine link. In the 1982 LOS Convention, however, they had become merely some of the duties of a state that had *already granted* its nationality to a ship.[39]

In this new context, these duties have been further elaborated. According to Article 94 (2), the effective exercise of the jurisdiction and control of the flag state means in particular that the state shall '(a) maintain a register of ships containing the names and particulars of ships flying its flag, except those which are excluded from generally accepted international regulations on account of their small size; and (b) assume jurisdiction under its internal law over each ship flying its flag and its master, officers and crew in respect of administrative, technical and social matters concerning the ship'. However, the non-existence of a flag state jurisdiction and control will not prevent the grant of nationality or cause its suspension or annulment.

According to Article 94 (6), where there is a non-existence of flag state jurisdiction and control, only mild remedial measures may be taken in respect of the flag state:

A State which has clear grounds to believe that proper jurisdiction and control with respect to a ship have not been exercised may report the facts to the flag State. Upon receiving such a report, the flag State shall investigate the matter and, if appropriate, take any action necessary to remedy the situation.

Finally, the contents of Article 10 of the 1958 Convention is now contained in Article 94 (3) and (5) of the LOS Convention. More precise goals covering measures necessary to ensure safety at sea have been added in paragraph 4 of this article, for example surveying by a qualified surveyor of ships, requirements concerning the qualifications of the crew, and the possession of charts, nautical publications, navigational equipment, and instruments necessary for safe navigation.

In summing up this development, it becomes apparent that every United Nations law of the sea codification conference resulted in a step backwards from the original ideas of the International Law Commission concerning a 'genuine link'. The First did not accept the Commission's proposal that a genuine link must exist 'for purposes of recognition of the national character of the ship by the States', and the Third eliminated even the requirement that effective exercise of the jurisdiction and control of the state granting nationality to the ship must exist at the moment of registration (granting of nationality).

2.3 The 1986 United Nations Convention on Conditions for Registration of Ships

The UN Convention on Conditions for Registration of Ships does not provide rules that are directly applicable to the problem of flags of convenience in the fisheries context. The Convention rather explicitly applies only to vessels 'used in international seaborne trade for the transport of goods, passengers, or both with the exception of vessels of less than 500 gross registered tons' (Articles 2 and 3).[40]

Notwithstanding the title given to the Convention, and the mention of a genuine link in the Preamble and Article 1, this Convention actually finalizes the trend of the UN Conferences on the Law of the Sea in departing from the original concept of the genuine link that was adopted by the International Law Commission. It is thus of interest to review briefly the relevant features of that Convention here.[41]

The initiative for the negotiations of the 1986 UN Convention on Registration originated in the United Nations Conference on Trade and Development. However, the various interests involved prevented the adoption of sound and clear solutions. As far as the 'genuine link' is concerned, some rules vaguely relating to the original ILC concept can be found in the 1986 Convention. For example, a state of registration is required to adopt laws and regulations that contain provisions for the participation of its nationals in the ownership of ships flying its flag; such laws and regulations should be 'sufficient' to permit the flag state effectively to exercise its jurisdiction and control over ships flying its flag (Article 8 (2)). As an alternative, the link between the state and the ship can be established by observation of 'the principle that a *satisfactory* part of the complement consisting of officers and crew of ships flying its flag be nationals or persons domiciled or lawfully in permanent residence in that State' (Article 9 (1), emphasis added). Although all the standards set in Articles 8 and 9 are vague and it is left to each particular state to choose to comply either with Article 8 or Article 9, the adoption of this solution was obviously the only possible way of reconciling the different interests present at the 1986 Conference.

However, the most significant development embodied in the 1986 Convention, as remarked by Lucchini and Voelckel, was the view that a persistent link between a ship and a state is less important than the flag state's ability to exercise administrative responsibility and control after the registration.[42] In this regard, the 1986 Convention requires that each flag state 'shall have a competent and adequate national maritime administration, which shall be subject to its jurisdiction and control' (Article 5 (1)). The duty of the flag state and its maritime administration is to ensure that ships flying its flag comply with the international rules and standards concerning, in particular, the safety of ships and persons on board and the prevention of pollution of the marine environment (Article 5 (2) and (3)).

3 Fishing under flags of convenience in the 1990s: the emergence of a global framework

The search for the elusive 'genuine link' in the law of the sea has eventually led to a 'dead end', not least where fishing vessels are concerned. The increasing number of countries offering so-called 'open registers' and the relaxed requirements and quick procedures to (re-)enter these have made it possible for fishing vessels to 'leave port under one flag, fish under another, and return home under the original'.[43] Sometimes the procedures to enter and re-enter registers require only a matter of hours.

Were any other mechanisms available in the 'traditional' law of the sea for dealing with unauthorized high seas fisheries? While the LOS Convention's 'genuine link' concept remained both vague and devoid of effective means for implementation in practice, the Convention did contain outlines of certain other concepts which could have opened for further elaboration. In conjunction with attempts to define a 'genuine link', Article 94, already examined above, lists *various duties of the flag state*. While Article 94 did impose certain duties on the flag state, it apparently has not been drafted with regard to specific requirements for fishing vessels. Article 117, moreover, defined the duty of all states to take measures for their nationals that may be necessary for the conservation of the living resources of the high seas. In combination, these provisions have enabled part of the framework to be elaborated and extended by addressing more specifically the duties, or responsibilities, of the flag state in respect of its vessels involved in high seas fishing.

One of the foundations of the law of the sea—high seas freedom—has been codified in Article 87 of the LOS Convention. Article 87 includes freedom of fishing for all states on the high seas; however, this freedom is not absolute, but rather subject to the conditions contained in the Convention's provisions on conservation and management of the living resources of the high seas.[44] Indeed, while the LOS Convention was still in its early negotiations, the International Court of Justice stated the following in 1974: '[T]he former *laissez-faire* treatment of the living resources of the sea in the high seas has been replaced by a recognition of a duty to have due regard to the rights of other States and the need of conservation for the benefit of all.'[45] In Articles 63–4 and 118, the Convention required states to *cooperate* in the conservation and management of the living resources of the high seas and in respect of straddling and highly migratory fish stocks in particular; this was not a requirement devoid of legal obligation.[46] Yet the LOS Convention stopped short of providing more concrete prescriptions on how this requirement of cooperation could be effectively related to preventing or reducing unauthorized fishing. Articles 116–20 on conservation of the living resources of the high seas remain too general in this respect. As a matter of fact, these provisions had already been proposed in the 1975 Informal Single Negotiating Text[47] and were not changed in the negotiations at UNCLOS III; their contents are basically derived from the 1958 Geneva Conventions.

Concerning control and enforcement measures *at sea*, the measures provided for by the LOS Convention included the possibility of boarding and inspecting foreign ships. The outer limit of the exclusive economic zone was defined in the Convention as the firm delimitation line between, on the one hand, regimes under the sovereignty and sovereign rights of the coastal state, and the high seas, on the other.[48] Article 73 authorizes the coastal state to undertake measures *within* its exclusive economic zone in respect of foreign ships. These include boarding and inspection, arrest, and judicial proceedings that may be necessary to ensure compliance with its laws and regulations in the exercise of the coastal state's sovereign rights *inter alia* to conserve and manage living resources in the EEZ. Beyond this, Convention provisions are very restrictive; where otherwise not agreed with the flag state in a special treaty, the right to board a ship on the *high seas* is reserved for warships encountering a foreign ship that is not entitled to complete immunity, and this in a limited number of exceptional cases only. Article 110 (1) of the LOS Convention, building on the 1958 Geneva Convention on the High Seas, includes among these exceptions piracy, slave trading, and unauthorized broadcasting, but Article 110 (1) also relates other instances to the nationality of the ship. However, any control and enforcement measures regarding foreign vessels on the high seas under the LOS Convention were not associated with fishing activity.

Although again not related in its provisions to high seas fishing, one other set of mechanisms was taken up at the LOS Convention—*port state* enforcement and control. In Article 218, the Convention established enforcement by individual port states for acts of pollution of the marine environment caused by vessels on the high seas; Article 211 (3) of the Convention provided a basis for a collaborative port state control. The LOS Convention did not, however, use the terms port state enforcement or control in respect of fisheries.

It can be seen from the above that the LOS Convention has provided a framework or frame of reference for *regional* fisheries conservation and management agreements. Elaborating on the basic premises contained in the LOS Convention, several new methods for hindering avoidance of conservation and management measures by non-party flagged vessels on the high seas have emerged in the course of the 1990s. In the early 1990s, the focus rested on *deterrence of reflagging* and aimed at minimizing the possibility for the involvement in high seas fisheries of vessels flying a flag of convenience of a state not party to a regional fisheries management agreement. Gradually, this focus has started to change. To facilitate the effectiveness of regional high seas fisheries management arrangements at the global level, various measures contained in the LOS Convention are being developed, while others are being adopted from previously existing regional agreements. This emerging global legal framework will be reviewed below.

3.1 Deterrence of reflagging: 'genuine link' déjà vu in the early 1990s

In the early 1990s, interaction between the UN Conference on Environment and Development (through its Secretariat) and the FAO focused on one major problem concerning high seas fisheries management—*reflagging*. The need for states to address this rapidly emerging problem was initially recognized through 'soft law'.

The Declaration of Cancun, adopted at the 1992 International Conference on Responsible Fishing,[49] was the first international instrument that called for deterrence of reflagging by requiring states to take 'effective action, consistent with international law' to this end (paragraph 13). However, save for broader concepts, the Cancun Declaration could not point to an effective means for deterring reflagging that already existed under international law.

A month later, Agenda 21 of UNCED responded to the call from the Cancun Declaration; chapter 17 required states 'to deter reflagging of vessels by their nationals as a means of avoiding compliance with applicable conservation and management rules for fishing activities on the high seas'.[50] In wording similar to that of the Cancun Declaration, Agenda 21 required states to take 'effective action, consistent with international law'.[51] This could still be no more than a call for *filling in lacunas* in international law, which failed to contain effective means for responding to the spreading practice of operators changing the flags of their fishing vessels to those of states not party to a regional conservation and management agreement and thus avoiding the obligation to comply with high seas fisheries measures adopted under these.

In early 1993, when an FAO Conference based on the mandate given by the Cancun Declaration was convened to negotiate a new international agreement on the subject, the initial focus of the conference was indeed the elaboration of means to deter reflagging.[52] Illustrative of the prevailing perceptions about the main purpose of this conference during its early stages were the phrases that were repeatedly used with reference to the first draft of a future agreement, namely, draft agreement on flagging and/or reflagging of fishing vessels on the high seas.[53]

The original draft for the FAO Compliance Agreement contained an article that required a party to refuse a fishing vessel the right to fly its flag 'unless [the party] is satisfied, in accordance with its own national legislation, that there exists a genuine link'.[54] Among the criteria defined in the second paragraph of this article for determining the existence of a genuine link was the nationality or the permanent residence of the beneficial owner of the vessel. The controversy over the definition of 'genuine link' was clearly on its way to entering the international fisheries law. As Moore observed:

It soon became clear . . . that consensus would not be reached on any agreement that included provisions dealing with the national registration of fishing vessels . . . It also became clear that any attempt to define more closely concepts such as genuine link that should exist between the vessel and its flag state . . . would draw the negotiations into a legal quagmire that would bog down the whole agreement initiative indefinitely.[55]

In addition to reflagging, there was also the problem of the fishing activities of newly built vessels that had not been 'reflagged', but which flew a flag of convenience.

The way further was sought in addressing the base, instead of the tip, of the 'iceberg'. Traditional rules that generally give flag states exclusive jurisdiction over their vessels on the high seas were creating a barrier to effective oversight of marine fisheries.[56] Thus, instead of directly addressing the act of reflagging, the primary focus of the draft FAO Compliance Agreement was changed to flag state responsibility in the authorization of its vessels to fish on the high seas as well as to increased transparency through the exchange of information.[57]

Further attempts to define a 'genuine link' between the fishing vessel and the state of registry as the primary tool for ensuring effectiveness of fisheries conservation measures on the high seas have since been abandoned.

3.2 Flag state responsibility

The core of the FAO Compliance Agreement lies in realizing that its objective can be reached through 'specifying flag States' responsibility in respect of fishing vessels entitled to fly their flags and operating on the high seas, including the authorization by the flag State of such operations'.[58]

The concept of 'flag state responsibility' means, in essence, placing pressure on the flag state to undertake itself those steps necessary in order to ensure that fishing vessels operating under its flag do not engage in activities that undermine the effectiveness of international conservation and management measures.[59]

The *concept* of flag state responsibility in the fisheries context does not originate in the FAO Compliance Agreement. In its rudimentary form, this concept has its origins in various bilateral agreements regarding the licensing of fishing rights that were concluded in the late 1970s and during the 1980s between certain (often developing) coastal states on the one hand and major fishing states on the other. The ultimate responsibility for the manner of performing acquired fishing rights by fishing vessels lies, in accordance with such agreements, with the respective flag state, which should ensure the compliance of vessels flying its flag according to the terms of agreement that the state has concluded.[60] This is also how, in 1984, the concept of flag state responsibility was formulated in the Strategy document of the FAO World Conference on Fisheries Management and Development.[61] The concept has thus primarily been related to *bilateral agreements* between coastal and fishing states that *grant access* to the latter to fishing in coastal states' exclusive economic zones.

In 1987, the concept of flag state responsibility was for the first time incorporated in a multilateral, though regional, agreement: the Treaty on Fisheries between the Governments of Certain Pacific Island States and the Government of the United States of America.[62] In this treaty, the concept was not limited to one phrase only. Article 4 of the Treaty contained the formulation of the basic concept of flag state responsibility and was accompanied by an elaborated set of provisions that provided the Treaty with real effect. The Multilateral Fisheries Treaty spells out in detail the *procedures* that the flag state—in this case the United States—must follow. These procedures relate to the investigation of offences against the Treaty and the laws of the Pacific Island states, the imposition of penalties, and payment to the Island states of fines that the USA collects from violators through its domestic procedures. However, also in this Treaty the concept of flag state responsibility remained linked to fisheries that were conducted under a *specific agreement* to which the flag state is a party; furthermore, the concept remained primarily applied to *zones under sovereign rights* of coastal states and the parties to the agreement in question.[63] It is true that whereas Article 1 (1) (k) specified that the Treaty area primarily comprises waters 'subject to the fisheries jurisdiction of Pacific Island parties', there are also 'other waters' within the region to which the 1987 Multilateral Fisheries Treaty applies. Nevertheless, this should be seen in the context of the background for the negotiation of this treaty. In the mid-1980s, the US policy was to negotiate international agreements in order, *inter alia*, to secure access for US fishermen to the stocks wherever the fish migrate *beyond a narrow belt* of coastal waters.[64]

The Niue Treaty on Cooperation in Fisheries Surveillance and Law Enforcement in the South Pacific Region concluded in 1992[65] was a further step in promoting the spread of the flag state responsibility concept in fisheries access agreements, although this treaty was again limited to the particular region. The Niue Treaty requires parties to 'ensure that foreign fishing agreements with flag States require the flag State to take responsibility for the compliance by its flag vessels with the terms of any such agreement and applicable laws'.[66]

The requirement formulated the same year in Agenda 21, chapter 17, was for states to 'monitor and control fishing activities by vessels flying their flags on the *high seas* to ensure compliance with applicable conservation and management rules'.[67] Agenda 21, in taking the concept of flag state responsibility in the fisheries context further, i.e. to the high seas and independent of a specific agreement to which a flag state is party, placed it within its framework of sustainability in the use of natural resources. Legally, this extension could find its basis in the more general provisions of the LOS Convention that are contained in Article 94 ('Duties of the flag State') and Articles 116–20 (part VII, section 2, 'Conservation and management of the living resources of the high seas').

The importance of the 1993 FAO Compliance Agreement was threefold: first, it introduced the concept of flag state responsibility in the fisheries context to the *global* rather than bilateral or regional level; secondly, it followed up Agenda 21 in making the concept applicable beyond zones under coastal states' sovereign rights as well as independent of a specific fisheries access agreement to which a flag state is party; and thirdly, this widening of the application of the concept was made in a provision of an international treaty, thus in a legal rather than in a programmatic document.

The basic provision of the FAO Compliance Agreement in this respect is its Article III (1) (a): 'Each Party shall take such measures as may be necessary to ensure that fishing vessels entitled to fly its flag do not engage in any activity that undermines the effectiveness of international conservation and management measures.' As implied in the treaty text of the 1993 FAO Compliance Agreement, flag state responsibility has various components, all targeted at inducing compliance control by the flag state itself (with obvious limitations, as also reflected in the treaty language). The Agreement requires a party not to allow any of its fishing vessels to be used on the high seas without that party's authorization. The flag state shall provide such authorization only if it is 'satisfied that it is able' to exercise its responsibilities effectively (Article III (3)).[68] Moreover, the flag state shall refuse to authorize any fishing vessel previously registered by another party to the Agreement (and, under certain circumstances, by a third state) that has undermined the effectiveness of international fisheries conservation and management measures on the high seas (Article III (5) (a) and (b)). However, the Agreement also contains various exceptions to these requirements and leaves a lot to the 'satisfaction' of the flag state. Perhaps the most illustrative in this respect is Article III (5) (d), which allows the flag state to authorize a fishing vessel, 'serial violator' of high seas fisheries conservation measures, if the flag state 'has determined that to grant authorization . . . would not undermine the object and purpose of this Agreement'. Also, if the ownership of the fishing vessel—'serial violator'—has subsequently changed, authorization may be granted (Article III (5) (c)). Finally, although parties are required to take enforcement measures in respect of their flag vessels, Article III (8) of the Agreement leaves much to the discretion of the flag state by using phrases such as 'where appropriate' or 'sufficient gravity'.

Another important limitation of the FAO Compliance Agreement is its scope of application. Article II (2) offers the possibility of limiting this scope significantly by allowing flag states to exempt fishing vessels of less than 24 metres in length from the Agreement. Although Article III (1) (b), in the context of flag state responsibility, nevertheless requires flag states to take 'effective measures in respect of any such fishing vessel that undermines the effectiveness of international conservation and management measures', the practical possibility for exclusion of small boats from the application of the FAO Compliance Agreement has, according to some commentators, proved crucial for certain Pacific states to withhold support for the Agreement.[69]

In many respects the 1995 UN Fish Stocks Agreement reiterates the concept of flag state responsibility as elaborated in the FAO Compliance Agreement. However, the treaty language of the Fish Stocks Agreement contains less ambiguity and allows less discretion to flag states. Moreover, there is now no option for the flag state to exclude fishing vessels under 24 metres in length.

Article 18 (1) of the Fish Stocks Agreement is, in its wording of flag state responsibility (here under the title 'Duties of the flag State'), similar to the corresponding general provision of the FAO Compliance Agreement. The differences are that Article 18 (1) is *explicitly* related to high seas fishing and that it requires compliance with *subregional and regional* conservation and management measures.

The Fish Stocks Agreement requires the flag state to take a series of concrete measures (including control by means of licensing and the establishment of regulations, national records, and reporting requirements) and to ensure compliance and enforcement regarding vessels flying its flag.[70]

3.3 Information gathering and exchange

Responsibility of the flag state remains at its own discretion in the absence of any mechanism of *verification*. In this regard, Moore notes that the first essential component of fisheries enforcement is the acquisition and collation of information about fishing activities as a prerequisite for later inducement of compliance by fishing vessel operators.[71] The same author also observes that the lack of reliable information on fishing operations on the high seas has been a major obstacle to the proper management of the high seas fisheries resources.[72]

Together with flag state responsibility, the Preamble of the FAO Compliance Agreement highlights another means for reaching the Agreement's objective: 'increased transparency through the exchange of information on high seas fishing.' As a constituent element of flag state responsibility, the Agreement also requires the gathering and providing of relevant information. Information requirements have both a database aspect and a compliance control aspect—and both are present in the FAO Compliance Agreement. Neither, however, is an innovation of that Agreement.

Information requirements have been especially elaborated through regional cooperation in the South Pacific.[73] The underlying reasoning for this is *cost-effectiveness* in enforcement, which is necessary when such a vast region has limited physical enforcement capabilities and limited funds. In such a situation, various mechanisms for collating and verifying information (for example by means of aerial surveillance and ultimately a computer nexus of information on foreign fishing vessels operating in the region) appear to be far less costly than traditional systems that involve *physical* inspection of vessels at sea.[74] Thus, the main functions of the South Pacific Forum Fisheries Agency (FFA), an organization established in 1979,[75] include accumulating detailed and up-to-date information on fisheries in the region, as well as developing and maintaining a communications network for the dissemination of information to member countries.

In addition to self-reporting by fishing vessels to a regional register, the *exchange* of information between parties to a regional fisheries agreement plays an important role in compliance control. Early examples of the requirement for information exchange are contained in the 1978 NAFO Convention and in the 1980 CCAMLR.[76] More recently, Article V of the 1992 Niue Treaty, which particularly focused on compliance control, requires each party to provide information directly to both FFA and other parties on, *inter alia*, the location and movement of foreign fishing vessels, the licensing of these vessels, and fisheries surveillance and law enforcement activities.

To a large extent the 1993 FAO Compliance Agreement builds on the above-mentioned regional, mainly South Pacific, precedents; now, however, *global* requirements applicable on the high seas are provided for.[77] The Agreement places the requirement of gathering and disseminating information about fishing vessels and their activities upon the vessels' respective flag states.

As a constituent part of flag state responsibility, the flag state is required to ensure ready identification by proper marking of a fishing vessel en-

titled to fly that state's flag and also to ensure that the flagged vessel provides the flag state with relevant information on the vessel's operations,
'in particular information pertaining to the area of its fishing operations
and to its catches and landings'.[78] To enable access to information, the flag
state shall maintain a record of fishing vessels entitled to fly its flag and
authorized to be used for fishing on the high seas.[79]

The system of exchange of information, as provided for by Article VI
of the FAO Compliance Agreement, aims at the creation of a *database* on
high seas fishing operations for the dissemination of information at the
global level. Regarding fishing vessels that have been entered into the
domestic register, the flag state shall supply the FAO with the relevant
information, including among other data the name of the vessel, the
registration number, any previous name, any previous flag, and basic
information about owner and vessel. The FAO will then circulate the
information to all the parties to the Agreement as well as to any global,
regional, or subregional fisheries organization (Article VI (4)).

Information gathered and disseminated in the manner described above
should facilitate the inducement and control of compliance. In this conjunction, the flag state is required to report to the FAO the activities of any
vessels flying its flag whose operations undermine the effectiveness of
international conservation and management measures.[80] When non-flag
states have 'reasonable grounds to believe that a fishing vessel . . . has
engaged in any activity that undermines the effectiveness of international
conservation and management measures', these must inform the flag state
concerned and 'may, as appropriate' inform the FAO.[81] However, the FAO
shall not circulate such information before the flag state has had the
opportunity to comment on the allegations.[82]

Article VIII (3) of the FAO Compliance Agreement also requires parties
to exchange information, either directly or through the FAO, on activities
of fishing vessels flying flags of non-parties to the Agreement undermining the effectiveness of international conservation and management
measures.

Overall, it can be said that the FAO Compliance Agreement is weak
regarding the requirement for any direct, physical enforcement measures;
the Agreement relies instead largely on the creation of a database register of vessels authorized to fish on the high seas and on the circulation of
relevant information about high seas fisheries. With this information
available to coastal states, the Agreement requires that the flag state act
to fulfil its flag state responsibility.

Compared with the FAO Compliance Agreement, the 1995 Fish Stocks
Agreement does not add much regarding the gathering and exchange of
information as such. However, the significant feature of the 1995 Agreement is that it places information requirements in the context of part VI

of the Agreement ('Compliance and Enforcement'), and the Agreement thus strengthens these requirements by making an explicit link between information and enforcement.[83]

Whereas the FAO Compliance Agreement only initiated vessel *monitoring, control,* and *surveillance* systems, the Fish Stocks Agreement elaborated this aspect considerably.[84] The 1995 Agreement requires the flag state to ensure that the measures it imposes on vessels flying its flag are compatible with any agreed subregional, regional, or global systems of monitoring, control, and surveillance already in effect (Article 18 (4)).

Again, member states of FFA have adopted an early example of a regionally elaborated surveillance system based on the provisions of the 1992 Niue Treaty. Moreover, as will be seen below,[85] CCAMLR, NAFO, and ICCAT have also in recent years strengthened their monitoring, control, and surveillance requirements.

The vessel monitoring system (VMS) is a combination of communications and computer technology that has recently been introduced for improving compliance by means of a surveillance system. VMS enables cost-effective and efficient identification of potential IUU fishing activity and the quick distribution of information to surveillance and enforcement officers. The system was first introduced by the Forum Fisheries Agency for the South Pacific region[86] and appears especially attractive for use in other regions consisting of vast areas and having limited physical control capabilities; not least, VMS is an interesting model for surveillance of fishing activity in *high seas* areas covered by fisheries conservation and management arrangements. Both CCAMLR (as of 1 March 1999, and not later than 31 December 2000)[87] and NAFO (as of 1 January 2001)[88] have (or will have) introduced VMS requirements for their parties for satellite surveillance of fishing activity within their respective scopes. ICCAT had previously 'encouraged' satellite tracking systems by flag states and instructed its Secretary-General to request cooperation in using this system from non-parties whose vessels were fishing tuna in the ICCAT area.[89]

3.4 Duty to cooperate: requirements being specified

In the course of the 1990s, more precise content was given to the requirement of cooperation among states in the conservation and management of straddling and highly migratory fish stocks, as earlier only outlined in the LOS Convention. In cases where vessels flying flags of non-member states were involved in high seas fisheries, the means were elaborated for requiring more *active involvement* of such states in high seas fishery management.

Referring to the provisions of the LOS Convention, the 1992 Cancun Declaration required states to 'cooperate on bilateral, regional and multi-lateral levels to establish, reinforce and implement effective means and mechanisms to ensure responsible fishing on the high seas' (paragraph 11), as well as to *balance* the freedom to fish on the high seas 'with the obligation to cooperate with other States to ensure conservation and ra-tional management of the living resources' (paragraph 12).

The importance of Agenda 21 for high seas fisheries management was actually underscored in the linking of the problem of reflagging with the emphasis on the concept of sustainable development. In chapter 17, where major problems of high seas fisheries management are listed, there is a reference *inter alia* to the lack of sufficient cooperation among states (para-graph 17.45), and cooperation at the bilateral, subregional, regional, and global levels is regarded as 'essential, particularly for highly migratory species and straddling stocks' (ibid.). With regard to the context of high seas fishing under flags of states non-members to regional arrangements (often flags of convenience), Agenda 21 contains an important require-ment: 'States with an interest in a high seas fishery regulated by an exist-ing subregional and/or regional high seas fisheries organization of which they are not members should be encouraged to join that organization, where appropriate.'[90]

The 1993 FAO Compliance Agreement shows, as one author has noted, 'a trend towards giving a more effective content to the general obligation of cooperation'.[91] In its Preamble, the 1993 Agreement does call upon states not participating in global, regional, or subregional fisheries organ-izations or agreements to 'join or, as appropriate, to *enter into under-standings*' with these (emphasis added). However, save for the flag state responsibility and information exchange requirements, as discussed above, the FAO Compliance Agreement did not contain any further elaboration of duty to cooperate.

The 1995 UN Fish Stocks Agreement makes a significant step forward in *explicating the way* in which fishing states and coastal states shall give effect to their duty to cooperate in conservation and management of high seas living resources, i.e. straddling and highly migratory fish stocks. In fact, the duty to cooperate forms the basis of the Fish Stocks Agreement, where, in the function of the Agreement's objectives of long-term conser-vation and sustainable use, this duty has been spelled out through spe-cific requirements of a global international treaty.[92]

While a wider discussion of duty to cooperate under the 1995 Agree-ment is provided elsewhere in this book,[93] it is of primary interest here to look at how high seas fishing by states non-members of regional arrange-ments has been addressed by the Agreement. Two provisions are crucial in this respect.

Article 8 (3) of the Fish Stocks Agreement specifies how states whose vessels are involved in high seas fishing in areas covered by regional arrangements of which they are not members are to give effect to their duty to cooperate. These states can either become members/parties to the respective arrangements, or they can agree to apply the conservation and management measures adopted under these arrangements. A consequence is linked to these requests; as provided in Article 8 (4) of the Agreement, only states that act accordingly 'shall have access to the fishery resources' to which the measures under a respective regional arrangement apply.[94]

It has been noted that the 1995 Agreement 'will assist the ongoing process of clarifying the point that the freedom of fishing, as first articulated in conventional form in 1958, is a specifically qualified freedom'.[95] In this context, the entire process following the 1958 Geneva Convention, the decisions of the International Court of Justice in the late 1960s and in the 1970s, and the 1982 LOS Convention and its follow-up, led finally to its conclusion in the 1995 Fish Stocks Agreement. When high seas fishing contravenes internationally agreed conservation measures, the alternatives are cooperation or exclusion. Scovazzi comments on the underlying idea in the following observation:

as regards fisheries, the high seas are no longer the province of *laissez-faire*. It is an area governed by the principle of sustainable development, which can lead to the exclusion of those States which persistently undermine the conservation and management measures agreed upon by the others.[96]

In consequence, the following was concisely expressed by one author: 'Only those who play by rules may fish.'[97] The detail of 'rules of the game' will, however, become legally binding only for parties to the 1995 Agreement when this enters into force. The Agreement still lacks several ratifications for its entry into force; once the Agreement is in force, it will indeed be of importance that major fishing states, not least those providing for flags of convenience, also ratify it.[98] It should, however, be added that the 1995 Agreement goes far with respect to non-parties to the Agreement, and provides in Article 33 (2) that parties shall take measures to 'deter the activities of vessels flying the flag of non-parties which undermine the effective implementation of this Agreement'.

The requirements in the fulfilment of the duty to cooperate have more recently also been explicated at the *regional* level. Recalling the ongoing UN Conference (at that time) on Straddling and Highly Migratory Fish Stocks, ICCAT adopted a resolution in late 1994 whereby the Executive Secretary 'shall contact all non-Contracting Parties known to be fishing in the Convention Area . . . to urge them to become Contracting Parties or

"Cooperating Parties" '.[99] ICCAT has repeatedly required such cooperation from Belize, Honduras, and Panama.

Another interesting regional example in this respect is CCAMLR's fairly
broad interpretation of the concept of duty to cooperate. In late 1997, the
Commission decided to invite Mauritius and Namibia to participate in
its meetings and to accede to the CCAMLR Convention.[100] The reason for
CCAMLR's decision was not based solely or primarily on IUU high seas
fishing itself, at least not in the case of Mauritius, but rather on the fact
that those two countries had actually been, though perhaps unwittingly,
assisting in this activity by providing port or landing facilities for illegal
catches of Patagonian toothfish.[101]

3.5 *Control and enforcement by non-flag states on the high seas*[102]

When the flag state is neither successful at taking, nor even willing to take,
responsibility for fishing vessels under its flag engaged in high seas
fishing, and when international cooperation is not effective in securing
implementation of conservation and management measures on the high
seas,[103] international law allows for a certain degree of control and enforcement by non-flag states. The 1990s witnessed a significant development
in this respect with regard to both the scope of control and enforcement
measures by non-flag states on the *high seas* and the introduction of these
in their *ports*.

As has been mentioned above, while boarding and inspection on high
seas is provided for in certain cases by the LOS Convention, the elaboration of new procedures regarding foreign fishing vessels on the high seas
is only nominally related to the LOS Convention rules on boarding and
inspection.[104] The major difference is that, with the 1995 UN Fish Stocks
Agreement, these measures of control and enforcement in respect of IUU
fishing also became legalized at the *global* level in the area of the high seas,
rather than only in zones under sovereign rights, as was the case in earlier
global instruments.

Any acts of interference with a foreign ship on the high seas, beyond
the few exceptions expressly provided in the LOS Convention, were
deemed legal under the Convention only if 'derived from powers conferred by treaty' (Article 110 (1)).[105] This *lex specialis* clause has enabled
the introduction into international fisheries law of means for control and
enforcement of foreign fishing vessels on the high seas (for example such
as boarding and inspection, and reporting) through bilateral and *regional*
treaties.

While there were examples of bilateral, and even regional, treaties that
allowed the seizure and arrest of foreign vessels,[106] regional treaties mainly provided only for boarding and inspection; the 1978 NAFO

Convention is a well-known example containing such a provision (Article 18). More recently, the 1994 Convention on the Conservation and Management of Pollock Resources in the Central Bering Sea under certain circumstances permitted the boarding state to _continue_ the boarding until the flag state carried out its responsibilities (Article XI). Balton observes that Article XI (6) and (7) of the Bering Sea Doughnut Hole Convention constitutes the most ground-breaking and precedent-setting provisions for enforcement action.[107] However, any further action, especially such as the right to prosecute the offender, remains reserved for the flag state.

Pursuant to Article XI (6) of the Bering Sea Doughnut Hole Convention, each party consents _in advance_ to boarding and inspection of its vessel by another party in the Doughnut Hole. As in other regional agreements, this is indeed limited to the area of application of the agreement and to the parties to the regional agreement.

Whereas the provisions on boarding and inspection of the 1995 Fish Stocks Agreement (Articles 21 and 22) are in many respects modelled after the Bering Sea Doughnut Hole Convention,[108] there is a significant difference. Article 21 (1) of the Fish Stocks Agreement contains a concept novel for any _global_ agreement. State parties to the Fish Stocks Agreement that are members to a regional organization or arrangement are authorized to board and inspect fishing vessels flying the flag of any other state party to the Fish Stocks Agreement, _regardless_ of whether this state is a member of the regional organization or arrangement in question. This in effect means that a state party to the Fish Stocks Agreement may become bound to apply conservation measures adopted under a regional agreement to which it is _not a party_. This provision is wider than any regional agreement can regulate and has rightly been labelled a 'unique and far-reaching exception to the flag state principle'[109] and the 'beginning of a new era in high seas fisheries enforcement'.[110]

3.6 Control and enforcement by port states

The LOS Convention itself did not relate control and enforcement by port state to fisheries and high seas living resources management. Port state _enforcement_, through _individual_ port state jurisdiction that undertakes investigations and institutes proceedings, was originally envisaged in Article 218 of the Convention as a complementary means—when flag state enforcement fails—for preventing and reducing vessel-source marine pollution, primarily from discharges on the high seas in violation of the applicable international rules and standards. Moreover, the LOS Convention, largely prompted by the _Amoco Cadiz_ spill in 1978, provided the basis for a _collaborative_ port state _control_. In accordance with Article 211 (3) of the Convention, two or more states may harmonize their policy

by entering into cooperative arrangements to 'establish particular requirements for the prevention, reduction and control of pollution of the marine
environment as a condition for the entry of foreign vessels into their ports
or internal waters'.[111]

As a response to increased flagging out by European and North
American shipowners in favour of flags of convenience since the late
1970s (and thus the increased threat of sub-standard ships), the concept
of port state control has received widespread support. Various regional
'memoranda of understanding' have started to require a more systematic
and comprehensive policy of ship inspection in ports and exchange of
information among participating states. Subsequent to the 1982 Paris
Memorandum of Understanding (MOU) on Port State Control, similar
MOUs were adopted during the 1990s for regions such as Latin America,
Asia-Pacific, the Caribbean, the Mediterranean, the Indian Ocean, and—
most recently—West and Central Africa.[112] As a result, a recent UN report
concludes that 'most of the world's oceans will soon be covered by a
global network of regional port State control agreements'.[113]

The developments of the 1990s have also expanded these concepts of
control and enforcement by introducing them into the field of fisheries
regulation—as yet another set of mechanisms available for preventing or
reducing unauthorized high seas fishing by vessels flying flags of states
non-members to regional arrangements, including indeed 'flags of convenience'. The first steps to introduce port state control regarding high
seas fisheries were taken at the regional level. In 1989, the Pacific Island
states members of FFA adopted the Convention for the Prohibition of
Fishing with Long Drift-Nets in the South Pacific.[114] This Convention provided for restrictions both on access to ports and the use of service facilities in the ports of parties for vessels involved in drift-net fishing (Article
3 (2) (d)). These and similar rules were, however, limited in both their
territorial scope and content.

Proposals made in the negotiations of the 1993 FAO Compliance Agreement advocating 'an extensive form of port state jurisdiction, modelled
on the provisions in the LOS Convention for vessel source pollution'
failed in securing consensus.[115] The end-result, as contained in Article V
(2) of the Compliance Agreement, is quite limited. In the absence of any
special agreement, 'where it has reasonable grounds for believing that the
fishing vessel has been used for an activity that undermines the effectiveness of international conservation and management measures', the
port state is entitled to undertake only one action: promptly to notify the
flag state of the contravention. For any investigatory measures in respect
of the fishing vessel to be undertaken by the port state beyond this action,
the Compliance Agreement requires the conclusion of a special agreement to this effect. Notwithstanding the limitations of this provision,

its importance remains in the 'globalization' of the concept of port state enforcement—or at least a degree of it—in high seas fishing.

Discussions at the UN Fish Stocks Conference (1993–5) showed that a high measure of controversy still existed over the 'import' of port state jurisdiction into the field of fisheries; various criticisms expressed at the Conference considered this as going beyond the LOS Convention framework and contrary to well-established international practice. On the other hand, those favouring the introduction of port state jurisdiction pointed to the sovereignty of the coastal state over its ports as a well-established principle under general international law, conferring on the port state the right to prohibit access to its ports.[116]

Several important fishing nations, including Iceland, Norway, and the United States, had already adopted domestic legislation authorizing *refusal of access* to their ports for fishing vessels suspected of having on board fish caught in a manner that contravened internationally agreed conservation measures on the high seas. A noteworthy development at the regional level concerning port states was the adoption in 1994 by certain Pacific Island states of the Arrangement on Regional Fisheries; the Arrangement provided that parties may inspect documents and catch on board vessels entering their ports and, when inspection discloses reasonable grounds for suspicion of violation of the Arrangement, parties 'may *detain* the vessel for such reasonable period as is necessary' to enable the flag state to take control over its vessel (Article 16; emphasis added).[117] At the third session of the Fish Stocks Conference (March 1994), a clause with almost identical wording that would also enable the port state to detain a foreign vessel was included in the Revised Negotiating Text for the Fish Stocks Agreement.[118] Whereas later drafts retained the port state entitlement to inspect documents and catch, and the provision on port state has become more consolidated in the drafts, any further mention of detention of ships was excluded.[119]

Commenting on the outcomes of the fourth session of the Conference (August 1994), Barston argued the following: 'It would have been preferable to have kept the port state concepts within the UNCLOS/IMO context of the Paris Memorandum, and Article 211 (pollution) . . . which would have avoided misapplication of the port state concept.'[120] Other commentators who were less critical expressed concern and the need for strict interpretation in order to 'prevent the possible abuse of the provision' on port state.[121]

The final outcome, as contained in Article 23 of the Fish Stocks Agreement, is labelled quite neutrally 'Measures taken by a port State', especially if compared with the titles of the proposed provisions in the 1994 draft ('Part VI: Port State Enforcement') and the April 1995 draft ('Boarding and inspection by port States').

The underlying principle, formulated in Article 23 (1), is 'the right and the duty' of a port state to take non-discriminatory measures in accordance with international law, in order to 'promote the effectiveness of subregional, regional and global conservation and management measures'.

In specifying the measures that the port state in the exercise of its powers may take with vessels which voluntarily enter its ports, paragraph 2 lists, '*inter alia*', the inspection of documents, fishing gear, and catch on board. Whereas the measures listed are quite limited, the inclusion of the words '*inter alia*' had already given rise to different interpretations. According to some commentators, in the case of inaction by the flag state, '*inter alia*' could be interpreted to include detention, arrest, or continued boarding.[122] Other commentators, while admitting that it is not clear what other actions can be undertaken, argue that it is 'evident, however, that it *excludes the detention* of vessels since the reference to that effect in the original draft was subsequently deleted after strong objections'.[123]

If it has been *established* through inspection that the catch has been taken in a manner that undermines the effectiveness of internationally agreed conservation and management measures on the high seas, Article 23 (3) allows the port state to prohibit landings and trans-shipment.

In comparing this provision of the 1995 Agreement with the LOS Convention concept of port state enforcement (Article 218), Hayashi notes that under the Fish Stocks Agreement 'the port state power is much limited in that the institution of proceedings is not mentioned'.[124] On the other hand, in contrast to the LOS Convention where there is no requirement for the port state actually to utilize the enforcement jurisdiction because the provisions of Article 218 are permissive rather than mandatory,[125] it is both the right and *the duty* of the port state under the 1995 Agreement to take measures accordingly.

The real importance of the port state provisions of the Fish Stocks Agreement is well highlighted by the observation of another author:

Once the concept of port state enforcement is accepted for fisheries activities, then the expansion of the scope to cover *regional* measures can be considered almost inevitable since in the field of fisheries few universally accepted, global regulations exist, most of them being adopted at the regional level.[126]

This is precisely what characterized developments in the late 1990s. At its 1997 meeting, ICCAT modified its existing port inspection scheme after the Commission, having found this type of enforcement to be 'the most fundamental and effective tool for monitoring and inspection', agreed that most of ICCAT's recommendations could only be enforced during offloading.[127] Moreover, in September 1997, NAFO adopted a 'Scheme to Promote Compliance by Non-contracting Party Vessels with the

Conservation and Enforcement Measures Established by NAFO'. In accordance with this Scheme, a non-party vessel that has been sighted engaging in fishing activity in the NAFO regulatory area is *presumed* to be undermining the NAFO Conservation and Enforcement Measures.[128] If such a sighted vessel enters the port of any state party to the NAFO Convention, it must be inspected. If the vessel is found to have species on board to which NAFO conservation measures apply, *all* parties to NAFO will prohibit landings in their ports and trans-shipment in their waters. Only a few months after NAFO's adoption of its Scheme, CCAMLR adopted an almost identical Scheme for its own regulatory area.[129]

Anderson characterizes this development as a 'concerted exercise of port state powers'.[130] There is indeed a clear parallel with the development of various regional MOUs in the field of marine pollution—a common, regional policy of ship inspections accompanied by a systematic exchange of information and collective banning of entry into ports (i.e. landings and trans-shipment) of participating states as a consequence of violating internationally agreed measures.

The problem of 'third parties' becomes even more obvious at the regional level. In the case of CCAMLR, where the majority of gateway (and thus catch landing) ports to the Southern Ocean are in the territory of CCAMLR parties,[131] there are still third states such as Mauritius and Namibia that also provide port or landing facilities for toothfish catches. Thus, with CCAMLR's recent adoption of measures relating to port state control in ports of its parties, the illegal catch will, of course, be mainly channelled to the nearest accessible ports of non-parties. As mentioned above, the CCAMLR Commission has already invited Mauritius and Namibia to cease providing port or landing facilities for vessels that have carried out unregulated fishing in the Convention Area. It is of importance in this context that these two states had already ratified/acceded to the 1995 Fish Stocks Agreement,[132] under which it is equally 'the right and the duty' of the port state to take measures to promote the effectiveness of internationally agreed conservation measures for high seas fisheries.

4 Conclusion

The 1998 UN Secretary-General's annual report on oceans and the law of the sea stated that the *'primary responsibility* for the enforcement of international rules and standards rests with the flag State'.[133] Not only was this the case when the LOS Convention was adopted in 1982, but this remains largely the case today.

However, two words in this UN Secretary-General's statement require qualification in the context of high seas fisheries. Whereas 'responsibility' of the flag state was used in a rather general nature in 1982, the notion of flag state responsibility has today acquired a far more precise content. The discretion of the flag states in interpreting the extent of their responsibility is significantly diminished by the provisions of recent international agreements that specify the flag states' various duties in respect of their ships involved in high seas fishing.

'Primacy' in enforcement is, as it was in 1982, attributed to the flag state. However, this primacy is not nearly as exclusive today as it was at the time of adoption of the LOS Convention. Enforcement and control by port states are becoming increasingly accepted in global and regional international agreements. Other forms of control and enforcement by non-flag states at sea, such as boarding and inspection, have also rapidly spread in international fisheries law at both regional and—with the 1995 Fish Stocks Agreement—global levels.

We are currently witnessing a changing balance between inherent jurisdiction of the flag state in control and enforcement over its fishing vessels on the one hand, and action that may be taken by a non-flag state in support of internationally agreed measures on the other. In 1982, the primacy of legal boundaries such as the 200-mile limit of the exclusive economic zone was far more pronounced in respect of the control of fishing vessels at sea than it was at the end of the 1990s. Natural boundaries, such as those determined by straddling fish stocks and their coverage by internationally agreed conservation measures, are increasingly being recognized in the sphere of policy and law, with consequent implications on control and enforcement regarding fishing vessels. Where claims to exploitation in high seas fishing come into conflict with obligations towards conservation and management, the balance swings increasingly in the favour of conservation.[134] Consequently, various means have been introduced to counterbalance flag states' exclusive jurisdiction regarding control of and enforcement on their fishing vessels engaged in high seas fishing.

Rather than being a futile search for a 'genuine link' between the flag state and a fishing vessel flying its flag, these newly introduced means are crucial in increasing the effectiveness of regional fisheries conservation and management agreements faced with non-party fishing vessels engaged in high seas fishing contrary to conservation measures applicable there, whether or not these vessels operate under a 'flag of convenience'.

This treaty law development still evidences significant limitations. At the global level, neither the 1993 FAO Compliance Agreement nor the 1995 Fish Stocks Agreement has entered into force. Once in force, these agreements will in principle become legally binding for their parties only; regional fisheries management and conservation agreements are even further limited in the scope of their parties and application area.

Nonetheless, it has been shown in this chapter how, in a relatively short period, the various recent international agreements have contributed both to the formation of new concepts and to the development of concepts only rudimentarily provided for by the LOS Convention. Today, the international community is becoming equipped with a wide selection of mechanisms that offer, first, an elaborated content of flag state duties and responsibilities regarding high seas fishing by vessels flying its flag, and secondly—when the former fails—provisions that enable non-flag states to undertake measures of control and enforcement of foreign fishing vessels both at sea and in ports. From this point forward, the development of a consistent state practice will indeed be of crucial importance in overcoming inherent limitations of international treaty law.

In the context of international fisheries regulation, we subscribe to the conclusions reached in the 1998 FAO study, that regional fisheries arrangements 'provide the only realistic mechanism for the enhanced international cooperation' in the conservation and management of straddling and highly migratory fish stocks.[135] Many solutions adopted at the global level have to a significant extent been influenced by regional developments and, in turn, several regional arrangements, such as those under CCAMLR, ICCAT, and NAFO, have recently started to follow up with various regionally agreed measures. However, the same FAO review suggests that, overall, only 'very few bodies have started to implement the conservation and management measures provided for in the post-1982 fishery instruments'.[136]

Notes

1. For a comprehensive study, see B. Boczek, *Flags of Convenience: An International Legal Study* (Cambridge, Mass.: Harvard University Press, 1962).
2. Agreement to Promote Compliance with International Conservation and Management Measures by Fishing Vessels on the High Seas (1993); 33 *ILM* 969.
3. Agreement for the Implementation of the Provisions of the United Nations Convention on the Law of the Sea of 10 December 1982 relating to the Conservation and Management of Straddling Fish Stocks and Highly Migratory Fish Stocks (1995); 34 *ILM* 1547.
4. D. D. Caron, 'Ships, Nationality and Status', in R. Bernhardt (ed.), *Encyclopedia of Public International Law*, Instalment 11 (Amsterdam: Elsevier Science, 1989), 289.
5. Report of the International Law Commission Covering the Work of its Eighth Session (UN Doc. A/3159), Art. 29 *Commentary*, para. 1, in *International Law Commission*, ii (1956) 278–9; also L. Lucchini and M. Voelckel, *Le Droit de la mer*, ii (Paris: editions Pedone, 1996), 43.
6. 'Règles relatives à l'usage du pavillon national pour les navires de commerce', Institut de Droit International, *Tableau général des résolutions (1873–1956)*, ed. H. Wehberg (Bâle: Editions juridiques et sociologiques SA, 1957), 128–30.
7. Caron, 'Ships, Nationality and Status', 290.
8. Lucchini and Voelckel, *Le Droit de la mer*, 63.
9. For a thorough discussion, see Boczek, *Flags of Convenience*.
10. *LNTS*, vii.
11. J. S. Ignarski, 'Flags of Convenience', in R. Bernhardt (ed.), *Encyclopedia of Public International Law*, ii (Amsterdam: Elsevier Science, 1995), 404–5.
12. 'Review of Measures Taken by Regional Marine Fisheries Bodies to Address Contemporary Fishery Issues', *FAO Fisheries Circular*, 940 (1998), 74 (quoting unpublished paper by A. Smith, 'An Analysis of the Lloyds Maritime Information Service Database' (1998), 2).
13. UN Doc. A/CONF.164/7, of 4 May 1993; also Introduction to this book.
14. 'Review of the State of World Marine Fishery Resources', *FAO Fisheries Technical Paper*, 335 (1994), 136.
15. On NAFO management of high seas fisheries, see Joyner, Ch. 7 below.
16. *NAFO Annual Report* (1994), 18. Several other flags were involved in IUU high seas fishing in NAFO area in 1994–5, including the Cayman Islands, Sierra Leone, St Vincent and the Grenadines; *NAFO Annual Report* (1995), 19. Also, vessels flying flags of New Zealand, the USA, and Venezuela have been sighted.
17. *NAFO Annual Report* (1994), 18. However, as Burke observed, NAFO had experienced reflagging problems when their usual states of registry had accepted restrictions pursuant to decisions of NAFO, and vessels responded by reflagging in order to avoid such restrictions; W. T. Burke, *The New*

International Law of Fisheries: UNCLOS 1982 and Beyond (Oxford: Clarendon Press, 1994), 306–7.

18. ICCAT, *Report for Biennial Period, 1996–97*, part I; recommendations were adopted by the Commission at its 10th special meeting (San Sebastian, Nov. 1996), and entered into force on 4 Aug. 1997.

19. The Convention was signed in 1980 and entered into force in 1982; 19 *ILM* 837.

20. Catch of Patagonian toothfish alone comprised 97% of the entire finfish catch in the 1996–7 season.

21. CCAMLR, *Report of the CCAMLR Observer to ATCM XXII*, Doc. XXII ATCM/IP21 (Apr. 1998), paras. 3 and 6.

22. CCAMLR, *Report of the Sixteenth Meeting of the Commission* (Hobart: CCAMLR, 1997), para. 5.31.

23. Ibid., paras. 5.1 to 5.45; also, for an overview of vessels and flags involved, see G. Album, 'The Patagonian Toothfish and Norwegian Interest', *Norges Naturvernforbund Report*, 3 (Oslo: Norwegian Society for the Conservation of Nature/Friends of the Earth Norway, 1997), appendix.

24. Comment of New Zealand in CCAMLR, *Report of the Sixteenth Meeting*, para. 5.12; similarly Norway, ibid., para. 5.5.

25. See remarks by the CCAMLR Chairman in CCAMLR, *Report of the Sixteenth Meeting*, para. 1.3; and comments made by the European Union, ibid., para. 5.2. Also, see para. 8 in CCAMLR, *Report of the CCAMLR Observer to ATCM XXII*. For a broader discussion of the Patagonian toothfish problem, see Herr, Ch. 10 below.

26. UN Doc. A/CONF.164/INF/5 (8 July 1993), para. 111; and *FAO Fisheries Circular*, 940 (1998), 88–9.

27. This study is limited to examining development through international law of the sea and fisheries agreements and does not explore the possible impact of various other measures, such as *domestic trade limitations*. Recent reports can be found on measures of this nature, such as the 'U.S. Effort to Shut Illegally Caught Toothfish out of its Market', *Antarctica Project Newsletter*, 8/1 (Mar. 1999), 2. Neither do we explore the possible impact of legal measures on the *fishers' perception* of the probability of being caught operating illegally and their compliance in general. Hønneland, Ch. 4 below, deals with this theme.

28. UN Doc. A/CN.4/17, in *Yearbook of the International Law Commission* (1950), ii. 38.

29. 64th meeting of the Commission, paras. 26–38, ibid. (1950), i. 190–1; Report of the International Law Commission Concerning its Second Session (UN Doc. A/1316), para. 85, ibid. (1950), ii. 383.

30. UN Doc. A/CN.4/42, ibid. (1951), ii. 75–7.

31. 121st meeting of the Commission, paras. 10–127, ibid. (1951), i. 327–34; 284th meeting, paras. 63–77; 285th meeting, paras. 1–26; 320th meeting, paras. 41–67, ibid. (1955), i. 12–13, 14, 61–4, and 223–4.

32. Report of the International Law Commission Covering the Work of its Seventh Session (UN Doc. A/2934), ibid. (1955), ii. 22.

33. UN Doc. A/CN.4/97, Add. 1, ibid. (1956), ii. 14–16.

34. 341st meeting of the Commission, paras. 9–41, ibid. (1956), i. 36–8.
35. Ibid. 278.
36. H. Meijers, *The Nationality of Ships* (The Hague: Martinus Nijhoff, 1967), 127 ff.
37. V. Brajković and E. Palua, 'Državna pripadnost brodova i suvremena nastojanja oko unifikacije kriterija za njeno podjeljivanje', *Jugoslovenska revija za medjunarodno pravo*, 26 (1979), 234.
38. B. Vukas, 'Generally Accepted International Rules and Standards', in A. H. A. Soons (ed.), *Implementation of the Law of the Sea Convention through International Institutions* (Honolulu: The Law of the Sea Institute, University of Hawaii, 1990), 405–27.
39. G. Hafner, 'Neke primjedbe uz "stvarnu vezu" izmedju države i broda u suvremenom pravu mora', *Zbornik Pravnog fakulteta u Zagrebu*, 35 (1985), 575.
40. In addition, the 1986 Convention is not in force, nor is it expected to come into force in the foreseeable future. In 2000, fourteen years after its adoption, only eleven states have ratified this Convention, which will only enter into force when ratification is received from not less than forty states with a combined tonnage of at least 25% of world tonnage (Art. 19 (1)); 26 *ILM* 1236.
41. For a more comprehensive comment, see H. W. Wefers Bettink, 'Open Registry, the Genuine Link and the 1986 Convention on Registration Conditions for Ships', *Netherlands Yearbook of International Law*, 18 (1987), 70.
42. Lucchini and Voelckel, *Le Droit de la mer*, 70–1. As will be seen later in this chapter, analogous reasoning was to a large extent present in the drafting of the 1993 FAO Compliance Agreement.
43. P. Birnie, 'Reflagging of Fishing Vessels on the High Seas', *Review of European Community and International Environmental Law*, 2 (1993), 270.
44. Art. 116 of the LOS Convention lists several limiting categories for the freedom of high seas fishing.
45. *Fisheries Jurisdiction (United Kingdom v. Iceland)*, Judgment, *ICJ Reports* (1974), 32. On the balancing of high seas freedom with requirements for conservation, see Orrego, Ch. 1 above.
46. For an elaboration on the obligation to cooperate in the conservation and management of high seas fisheries resources, see UN Doc. A/CONF.164/INF/5, paras. 66–70 and 80–6.
47. UN Doc. A/CONF.62/WP.8, part II.
48. This, of course, is without prejudice to the regime of the continental shelf, which—if configuration of the seabed allows—can extend to submarine areas beyond the outer limit of the exclusive economic zone; Art. 76 of the LOS Convention. Sovereign rights of the coastal state, under the continental shelf regime, also comprise exploration and exploitation of living organisms belonging to sedentary species (Art. 77 (4)).
49. The Conference, convened by the Government of Mexico in collaboration with FAO, was held in Cancun, Mexico, 6–8 May 1992; for Cancun Declaration, see UN Doc. A/CONF.151/15, annex; also UN Doc. A/CONF.164/INF/2, annex 2, text reprinted in J.-P. Lévy and G. Schram (eds.), *United Nations Conference on Straddling Fish Stocks and Highly Migratory Fish Stocks: Selected Documents* (The Hague: Martinus Nijhoff, 1996), 363–6.

50. Agenda 21, ch. 17, para. 17.52, in Report of the United Nations Conference on Environment and Development (Rio de Janeiro, 3–14 June 1992), UN Doc. A/CONF.151/26, ii (13 Aug. 1992).
51. Ibid.
52. The Cancun Declaration requested the FAO to prepare an international Code of Conduct on Responsible Fishing, which was eventually finalized in late 1995. The so-called FAO Compliance Agreement which in 1993 resulted from the 27th session of the FAO Conference also forms an integral part of the Code of Conduct (FAO Conference resolution 15/93, para. 3).
53. Para. 22 of the Report on the Organizational Session of the United Nations Conference on Straddling Fish Stocks and Highly Migratory Fish Stocks (held 19–23 Apr. 1993), UN Doc. A/CONF.164/9 (2 June 1993); see also draft agreement title as used by Birnie in 'Reflagging of Fishing Vessels', 270.
54. Art. IV of the draft, 'Allocation of Flag'; FAO Doc. COFI/93/10 (Jan. 1993), annex 2.
55. G. Moore, 'The Food and Agriculture Organisation of the United Nations Compliance Agreement', International Journal of Marine and Coastal Law, 10 (1995), 413.
56. D. A. Balton, 'Strengthening the Law of the Sea: The New Agreement on Straddling Fish Stocks and Highly Migratory Fish Stocks', Ocean Development and International Law, 27 (1996), 132.
57. Moore, 'FAO Compliance Agreement', 413; Balton, 'Strengthening the Law of the Sea', 132.
58. Preamble of the FAO Compliance Agreement.
59. Art. III (1) (a) of the FAO Compliance Agreement; the concept is discussed by G. Moore, 'Enforcement without Force: New Techniques in Compliance Control for Foreign Fishing Operations Based on Regional Cooperation', Ocean Development and International Law, 24 (1993), 199.
60. There is nothing revolutionary in this requirement; it is no more than specification, in the context of fisheries access agreements, of the basic principle of the law of international treaties, as codified in Art. 26 of the 1969 Vienna Convention on the Law of Treaties: pacta sunt servanda.
61. Para. xvii of the Strategy for Fisheries Management and Development, in Report of the FAO World Conference on Fisheries Management and Development, Rome, 27 June–6 July 1984 (1984).
62. 26 ILM 1053.
63. Pacific Island states that were original signatories of the Treaty include Australia, the Cook Islands, Fiji, the Federated States of Micronesia, Kiribati, the Marshall Islands, Nauru, New Zealand, Papua New Guinea, the Solomon Islands, Tuvalu, and Western Samoa. Four more states belong today to the group of Pacific Island states, members of the Forum Fisheries Agency: Niue, Palau, Tonga, and Vanuatu.
64. US President's Letter of Transmittal of the 1987 Multilateral Fisheries Treaty to the US Senate, 18 June 1987; 26 ILM 1051.

65. Niue Treaty on Cooperation in Fisheries Surveillance and Law Enforcement in the South Pacific Region (1992); 32 *ILM* 138.
66. Ibid., Art. IV (5).
67. Agenda 21, ch. 17, para. 17.51; emphasis added.
68. Conservation Measure 119/XVII ('Licensing and Inspection Obligations of Contracting Parties with Regard to their Flag Vessels Operating in the Convention Area'), adopted by the CCAMLR Commission in Nov. 1998, paraphrases in para. 2 this provision of the 1993 FAO Compliance Agreement; text of the Measure in *Schedule of Conservation Measures in Force, 1998/99* (Hobart: CCAMLR, 1998), 20.
69. D. H. Anderson, 'The Straddling Stocks Agreement of 1995: An Initial Assessment', *International and Comparative Law Quarterly*, 45 (1996), 471. On the position of some of these states, such as the Solomon Islands and Western Samoa, see R. Barston, 'United Nations Conference on Straddling and Highly Migratory Fish Stocks', *Marine Policy*, 19 (1995), 165. Indeed, the current status of ratification of the FAO Compliance Agreement, as of 1 Jan. 2000, does not provide evidence of wide acceptance. Although several important flag states (including the United States) and the European Community have ratified the Agreement, there are thus far only fourteen ratifications/acceptances altogether, and of these only four since 1997. The Agreement, however, requires twenty-five ratifications before it can enter into force.
70. Arts. 18 and 19 of the Fish Stocks Agreement contain detailed provisions to this effect.
71. Moore, 'Enforcement without Force', 198.
72. Moore, 'FAO Compliance Agreement', 416.
73. For a recent account of this regional cooperation, see R. A. Herr, 'Small Island States of the South Pacific: Regional Seas and Global Responsibilities', in D. Vidas and W. Østreng (eds.), *Order for the Oceans at the Turn of the Century* (The Hague: Kluwer Law International, 1999), 203.
74. See the discussion in Moore, 'Enforcement without Force', 198–200.
75. On the role of the FFA, see Herr, 'Small Island States', 206–8.
76. Arts. VI (1) (a) and (3) and XI (4) of the NAFO Convention; also Art. XX (2) of CCAMLR.
77. It has been noted, however, that the *conceptual* origin of a regional register rests with the FAO's Committee on Fisheries and the discussion at its 11th session, in 1977; Moore, 'Enforcement without Force', 199.
78. FAO Compliance Agreement, Art. III (6) and (7).
79. Ibid., Art. IV. It has been noted that many states do not register their fishing vessels in domestic registers; Birnie, 'Reflagging of Fishing Vessels', 273.
80. FAO Compliance Agreement, Art. VI (8) (a).
81. Ibid., Art. VI (8) (1) (b).
82. Ibid.
83. See also below, ss. 3.5 and 3.6.
84. For general principles, see the Fish Stocks Agreement, especially Art. 5 (1); for flag state duties, Art. 18 (3) (g).
85. See below, ss. 3.5 and 3.6.

86. For details on FFA's Vessel Monitoring System, see the Forum's website (www.ffa.int).

87. CCAMLR Conservation Measure 148/XVII ('Automated Satellite-Linked Vessel Monitoring Systems (VMS)'), in *Schedule of Conservation Measures in Force, 1998/99*, 19.

88. FC Doc. 99/1, part VI. This has been in the follow-up of a pilot project on satellite tracking in the NAFO regulatory area; *Conservation and Enforcement Measures*, NAFO/FC Doc. 98/1, 70–2.

89. ICCAT, 'Resolution on Vessel Monitoring', adopted by the Commission at its 14th regular meeting, Madrid (Nov. 1995).

90. Agenda 21, ch. 17, para. 17.60.

91. T. Scovazzi, 'The Application of the United Nations Convention on the Law of the Sea in the Field of Fisheries: Selected Questions', *Annuaire de droit maritime et océanique* (1997), 201.

92. Various obligations in giving effect to duty to cooperate in accordance with the LOS Convention are specified in Art. 5 of the Fish Stocks Agreement.

93. Orrego, Ch. 1 above.

94. Further to this, see also Art. 20 ('International Cooperation in Enforcement') of the Fish Stocks Agreement.

95. Anderson, 'The Straddling Stocks Agreement of 1995', 475.

96. Scovazzi, 'Selected Questions', 202. For a discussion in the context of high seas freedom, see Orrego, Ch. 1 above.

97. Balton, 'Strengthening the Law of the Sea', 138.

98. In accordance with Art. 40 (1), the Agreement will enter into force one month after the deposit of the thirtieth ratification/accession; as of 22 Sept. 2000, there are twenty-seven ratifications/accessions.

99. ICCAT, 'Resolution on Coordination with Non-contracting Parties', adopted at the Commission's 9th special meeting, Madrid (Nov.–Dec. 1994), para. 1.

100. CCAMLR, *Report of the Sixteenth Meeting*, para. 8.10.

101. Ibid., para. 8.10 and annex 5; also s. 3.6 below on the impact this may have for port state control under CCAMLR.

102. Only a brief overview is provided in this section because other chapters in this book deal with these means of control and enforcement in further detail; Hønneland, Ch. 4, and Balton, Ch. 5.

103. As discussed in the previous sections of this chapter; see also provisions of Arts. 19 and 20 of the Fish Stocks Agreement.

104. M. Hayashi, 'The 1995 UN Fish Stocks Agreement and the Law of the Sea', in Vidas and Østreng (eds.), *Order for the Oceans at the Turn of the Century*, at 43–4.

105. The same was provided by Art. 22 (1) of the 1958 Geneva Convention on the High Seas.

106. For a thorough discussion, see M. Hayashi, 'Enforcement by Non-flag States on the High Seas under the 1995 Agreement on Straddling and Highly Migratory Fish Stocks', *Georgetown International Environmental Law Review*, 9 (1996), 9–10.

107. Balton, Ch. 5 below.

108. Ibid.

109. Hayashi, 'The 1995 UN Fish Stocks Agreement', 43.
110. Balton, Ch. 5 below.
111. For a thorough examination of the concepts of port state enforcement and control, see G. C. Kasoulides, *Port State Control and Jurisdiction: Evolution of the Port State Regime* (Dordrecht: Martinus Nijhoff, 1993); D. Anderson, 'Port States and Environmental Protection', in A. E. Boyle and D. Freestone, *International Law and Sustainable Development* (Oxford: Clarendon Press, 1999); T. L. McDorman, 'Port State Enforcement: A Comment on Article 218 of the 1982 Law of the Sea Convention', *Journal of Maritime Law and Commerce*, 28 (1997), 305; and E. J. Molenaar, *Coastal State Jurisdiction over Vessel-Source Pollution* (The Hague: Kluwer Law International, 1998), 101–31.
112. See an overview by M. Valenzuela, 'Enforcing Rules against Vessel-Source Degradation of the Marine Environment: Coastal, Flag and Port State Jurisdiction', in Vidas and Østreng (eds.), *Order for the Oceans at the Turn of the Century*, 496.
113. *Oceans and the Law of the Sea*, Report of the Secretary-General, UN Doc. A/53/456, of Nov. 1998, para. 233. In addition to the MOUs adopted thus far, there is a work in progress for the Gulf region.
114. Adopted in Wellington, New Zealand, on 23 Nov. 1989; 29 *ILM* 1449.
115. Anderson, 'Port States and Environmental Protection'.
116. Hayashi, 'The 1995 UN Fish Stocks Agreement', 46; Anderson, 'Port States and Environmental Protection', summarizes the contested positions at the Conference.
117. Arrangement concluded between the Federated States of Micronesia, the Marshall Islands, Palau, the Solomon Islands, Kiribati, Nauru, Papua New Guinea, and Tuvalu; Anderson, 'Port States and Environmental Protection'. Anderson, ibid., considers the support for the inclusion of provisions on port state jurisdiction in the Fish Stocks Agreement given by the Pacific Island states as decisive in the ultimate adoption of the port state provision.
118. UN Doc. A/CONF.164/13/Rev. 1 (30 Mar. 1994), para. 38.
119. Draft Agreement of 23 Aug. 1994 (UN Doc. A/CONF.164/22, Art. 21) and Draft Agreement of 11 Apr. 1995 (UN Doc. A/CONF.164/22/Rev. 1, Art. 22). Drafts for Convention, of 14 and 28 July 1993, submitted by Argentina, Canada, Chile, Iceland, and New Zealand at the 2nd session of the Conference, also mentioned a possibility of detention, although in quite different wording; UN Doc. A/CONF.164/L.11, Art. 11 and UN Doc. A/CONF.164/L.11/Rev. 1, Art. 11.
120. Barston, 'United Nations Conference on Straddling and Highly Migratory Fish Stocks', 166.
121. Hayashi, 'The 1995 UN Fish Stocks Agreement', 46.
122. F. Orrego Vicuña, 'Port State Jurisdiction in Antarctica: A New Approach to Inspection, Control and Enforcement', in D. Vidas (ed.), *Implementing the Environmental Protection Regime for the Antarctic* (Dordrecht: Kluwer Academic, 2000), 45.
123. M. Hayashi, 'The Role of the United Nations in Managing the World's Fisheries', in G. H. Blake, W. J. Hildesley, M. A. Pratt, R. J. Ridley, and

C. H. Schofield (eds.), *The Peaceful Management of Transboundary Resources* (London: Graham & Trotman, 1995), 387 (emphasis added).

124. Hayashi, 'The 1995 UN Fish Stocks Agreement', 45–6.
125. McDorman, 'A Comment on Article 218', 319.
126. Hayashi, 'The 1995 UN Fish Stocks Agreement', 46.
127. Recommendation by ICCAT for a Revised ICCAT Port Inspection Scheme, adopted at the 1997 Commission meeting (effective as of 13 July 1998), in ICCAT, *Current Management Recommendations & Related Resolutions* (www.iccat.es/conserm).
128. This may be seen as a step further away from the Fish Stocks Agreement, which requires that undermining of internationally agreed measures has to be *established*.
129. Conservation Measure 118/XVI ('Scheme to Promote Compliance by Non-contracting Party Vessels with CCAMLR Conservation Measures'), in CCAMLR, *Report of the Sixteenth Meeting of the Commission*, 39. The possible benefit from the experience of NAFO was mentioned in the Commission's deliberations that year; ibid., para. 5.10 (intervention by Norway).
130. Anderson, 'Port States and Environmental Protection'.
131. Ports of Australia, Argentina, Chile, France/sub-Antarctic islands, New Zealand, South Africa, United Kingdom/Falklands.
132. Mauritius acceded to the Fish Stocks Agreement on 25 Mar. 1997 and Namibia ratified the same Agreement on 8 Apr. 1998; Status of the Agreement, as maintained by the UN Secretariat, Office of Legal Affairs, Division for Ocean Affairs and the Law of the Sea (www.un.org./Depts/los/). Namibia also ratified, on 7 Aug. 1998, the FAO Compliance Agreement; Status of the Agreement, as maintained by FAO (www.fao.org/legal/treaties/).
133. UN Doc. A/53/456 (Nov. 1998), para. 220; emphasis added.
134. See also UN Doc. A/CONF.164/INF/5, para. 121.
135. *FAO Fisheries Circular*, 940, vi and 96.
136. Ibid., vi and 96–7.

3

Problems of Compulsory Jurisdiction and the Settlement of Disputes Relating to Straddling Fish Stocks

ALAN BOYLE

1 Introduction

No single category of international disputes since 1945 has generated more litigation than the law of the sea. At least eleven disputes have been the subject of judgments in the International Court of Justice (ICJ),[1] with a further three awaiting judgment on the merits.[2] During the same period there have been eight arbitrations[3] and one conciliation award.[4] As Judge Oda has observed, the contribution of these cases, in particular those of the ICJ and PCIJ, to the formation of a comprehensive and organized body of law of the sea cannot be overestimated.[5] Nine of these twenty-three disputes were principally about fish stocks; four were disputes over fishing rights between coastal and distant water fishing states; and a further four dealt with maritime boundaries where fisheries were the principal economic interest at stake. The remaining case, an arbitration, involved onshore facilities and fish processing rights. More recently, the *Tuna-Dolphin* and *Shrimp-Turtle*[6] cases in the GATT dispute system indicate that fisheries disputes have lost none of their economic importance to states. Finally, the three cases to come before the International Tribunal for the Law of the Sea have all been fisheries or fisheries-related disputes.[7] As we shall see below, the characterization of the *Saiga Case* as a fishing dispute is a critical jurisdictional issue in the case.

The modern law of fisheries is defined principally by the 1982 UN Convention on the Law of the Sea (UNCLOS),[8] and more recently by the 1995 Agreement on the Conservation of Straddling Fish Stocks and Highly Migratory Fish Stocks.[9] These treaties have significantly extended the offshore fishing and conservation rights of coastal states when compared to the 1958 Convention on Fishing and Conservation and the *Icelandic Fisheries Cases* of 1974. They have also placed limits on high seas fishing, both in the interests of sustainable use and in order to afford greater protection to coastal states whose EEZ fishing is affected by high seas fishing activities. As other chapters of this book illustrate, there continue to be serious international fisheries disputes in many parts of the world, not all of which are necessarily amenable to negotiated solutions.

Along with improvements in the policing of fishing vessels and the need to ensure long-term sustainability of stocks, the availability of adequate compulsory procedures for resolving otherwise intractable disputes remains one of the main challenges of contemporary fisheries law.[10] The purpose of this chapter is to see how far the international community has met that challenge. It is, however, illusory to think that there is at present a satisfactory system in existence. As we shall see, there are immense problems in using existing law to ensure that disputes relating to straddling fish stocks will if necessary be resolved by an independent third party. This has implications not only for the effectiveness of international fisheries law but also for the ability of governments to negotiate settlements in the event of a dispute with other states. Moreover, without the assurance of authoritative interpretation of the two main treaties, neither of which is easy to interpret, there is inevitably a risk that state practice will fragment, that the treaties themselves will be undermined, and that rights conferred by law will in practice be eroded by uncertainty and argument.[11] It is thus far from clear that existing provision for compulsory dispute settlement can promote the sustainable management of straddling fish stocks or provide solutions for the regional disputes that are considered in the second part of this book.

2 Evolution of compulsory jurisdiction over fisheries disputes

2.1 The 1958 Geneva Conventions

The purpose of the four conventions adopted by the First UN Conference on the Law of the Sea at Geneva in 1958 was broadly to codify and develop existing customary law. Little attention was devoted to the settlement of disputes,[12] and with the exception of fisheries, there was sufficient support only for the adoption of an Optional Protocol Concerning Compulsory Settlement of Disputes.[13] This Protocol allowed any party to refer disputes arising out of the interpretation or application of the four conventions to the ICJ, unless by agreement the parties resorted to arbitration or conciliation.[14] It was not widely supported and never had more than thirty-nine parties. Despite the many law of the sea disputes that have subsequently arisen, including those referred to arbitration or adjudication by agreement or under the optional clause in the ICJ Statute, none are known to have been referred to any forum under the Protocol, which remains historically important only for two reasons. First, the relative lack of support reflected the opposition of the Soviet bloc, while in the then newly independent states of the third world, it was indicative of reluctance to accept the ICJ as a forum for compulsory jurisdiction. Secondly, the additional provision for arbitration and conciliation, albeit only by agreement, shows an early recognition of the need for a range of alternative fora to suit differing preferences. Both considerations are relevant in understanding the rather different dispute settlement provisions of the 1982 UNCLOS.

The 1958 Fisheries Convention proved to be the least successful of the Geneva Conventions, and its dispute settlement provisions have also had no practical use. Although some thirty-six states became parties to the Fisheries Convention, these never included many of the major coastal fishing states. Articles 9–12 provide for any party to submit disputes concerning the exercise of fishing rights to a special commission of five members,[15] who are intended to be experts 'specialising in legal, administrative or scientific questions relating to fisheries, depending upon the nature of the dispute to be settled'. Decisions of this Commission are by majority vote and are binding on the states party to the dispute. The enforcement powers of the UN Security Council under Article 94 (2) of the Charter apply to the Commission's decisions. A party may reapply after a reasonable period of at least two years if there have been substantial changes in the stock affecting the factual basis of the award.

The Fisheries Convention is a noteworthy precedent for later UNCLOS negotiations for two reasons. First, resort to the special commission is compulsory unless the parties agree otherwise. This was probably an essential element in a delicate balance of interests without which agreement on extending the powers of coastal states over high seas activities would probably have been impossible. The self-evident purpose of Articles 9–12 is to restrain abuse of power by coastal states and at the same time provide for some check on the unreasonable exercise of high seas fishing freedoms by other states. Secondly, the choice of a special commission of fisheries experts rather than the ICJ or general arbitration is significant. It reflects a sensible perception that courts and lawyers do not necessarily have all the expertise required for every type of law of the sea dispute. The preference in this case for a functionalist approach to the choice and composition of dispute settlement bodies again shows the need for a range of alternative fora. These two issues—the scope of compulsory settlement and the adaptation of dispute settlement institutions to different functions—were probably the most important matters that had to be resolved in drafting part XV of the UNCLOS text.

2.2 The UN Committee on Peaceful Uses of the Seabed and Ocean Floor beyond the Limits of National Jurisdiction

In 1968 the UN General Assembly established a Seabed Committee to consider proposals for revising the existing law of the sea.[16] Whether these revisions would be confined to seabed issues, as western states hoped, or deal more comprehensively with the law of the sea, as many developing states sought, was ultimately resolved in the latter's favour, resulting in the opening of the UNCLOS III negotiations in 1973. Many of the issues discussed at UNCLOS received a preliminary airing in the Seabed Committee, however, including dispute settlement. At the twenty-sixth session of that Committee, the UK made proposals for elements of a convention on the deep seabed, including the creation of a specialized tribunal with jurisdiction over interpretation, the terms of licences, and the boundaries of allocated areas.[17] The members would be lawyers or specialists in seabed operations, and the tribunal might either adjudicate or conciliate. At the twenty-eighth session, the USA put forward draft articles for a chapter on dispute settlement that expanded on the UK's position.[18] The USA proposed compulsory jurisdiction for a tribunal on matters to be agreed; it would consist of lawyers but sit with technical assessors in cases concerning navigation, pollution, fishing, and so on. The tribunal's decisions would be binding. There would be provision for urgent cases, and a procedure whereby owners or operators of detained vessels could seek prompt release. These proposals proved controversial but influential, and they formed the initial basis for discussion at the 1974 session of the Conference.[19] Their basic points—provision for compulsory jurisdiction, and a specialized tribunal—remain intact in the Convention finally agreed, despite much elaboration and many subsequent changes.

3 The UNCLOS dispute settlement scheme

The main object of the Convention's scheme for compulsory jurisdiction is to guarantee the integrity of the Treaty and to act as a restraint or moderating influence on the excessive claims and tensions likely to arise over time.[20] During the UNCLOS negotiations, it became clear that in order to achieve the widest possible consensus on dispute settlement provisions, which would be an integral part of the 1982 Convention rather than an optional extra as in 1958, considerable flexibility in the choice of procedures would be essential. Three basic elements emerged in the final agreement. First, parties to a dispute would remain free in principle to agree on whatever method of dispute settlement they preferred, and only in default of agreement would there be unilateral, binding, compulsory settlement. Secondly, states would be allowed the maximum possible choice of procedures, to accommodate both different types of dispute and the differing views of states on what they would accept.[21] This meant, in particular, that judicial settlement could not be the only or even the primary forum, as it had been in 1958. As Adede observes: 'the approach of offering states a cafeteria of modes of settlement ranging from the informal and non-binding procedures to the formal and binding procedures remained the central theme.'[22] Thus, compulsory jurisdiction would be exercisable not by the ICJ alone but by a range of fora, including a new specialist court, among which the parties would again have the right to choose. Lastly, while it was intended that the procedures available should as far as possible be comprehensive as regards parties and issues, agreement was only possible at the price of significant exclusions from compulsory jurisdiction that make that part of the system less than fully comprehensive.

What is remarkable about the system as a whole is that agreement was reached at all, given the very divergent views among different groups of states on dispute settlement issues generally. No comparable agreement had been achieved up to then in other contexts, including the 1969 Vienna Convention on the Law of Treaties, nor has anything quite so extensive been agreed since.

3.1 Freedom to choose the method of settlement

Fundamentally, the parties to UNCLOS are free to settle their disputes by any peaceful means of their choice (Articles 279–84). Nothing compels them to go to court, or to arbitrate, if they can agree on some other method. For this reason Article 283 requires all parties to a dispute to exchange views as a preliminary to any further steps, while Article 284 allows any party to invite the other to seek conciliation before invoking any other procedure. Informal resolution of any dispute is thus still possible if that is what the parties want.

Moreover, if the states concerned are parties to another agreement entailing compulsory binding settlement of the dispute, 'that procedure shall apply in lieu of the procedures provided for in [part XV of UNCLOS], unless the parties to the dispute otherwise agree' (Article 282). Thus two states that have made declarations in similar terms under Article 36 (2) of the ICJ Statute will remain subject to the compulsory jurisdiction of the ICJ even in UNCLOS cases.[23] Similarly, parties to the MARPOL Convention continue to be subject to compulsory arbitration under Article 10 of that agreement unless they can agree otherwise.

For these various reasons, the 1982 Convention's provisions on compulsory dispute settlement are essentially residual; the principle of binding compulsory settlement only applies if the parties have not been able to settle the dispute by conciliation or other agreed means.

3.2 Choice of forum for compulsory jurisdiction

There were several reasons for the failure to secure agreement on a single forum for exercising compulsory jurisdiction. Some states, including the Soviet bloc and many developing states, were reluctant either to accept the principle of judicial settlement or to allow the ICJ to be the sole or principal forum. Some of these states sought the creation of a new tribunal. Others argued that no single forum would be appropriate for the whole range of issues likely to arise and that provision should be made for specialist bodies, not necessarily composed of lawyers, to deal with the more technical matters.[24]

The eventual compromise, embodied in the so-called 'Montreux formula' of Article 287, attempted to satisfy all of these arguments by creating a new tribunal, the International Tribunal for the Law of the Sea (ITLOS), while allowing the parties to choose the most appropriate or acceptable forum from four possibilities, each of which would enjoy compulsory jurisdiction:

- the ICJ;
- the ITLOS;
- arbitration;
- special arbitration.

The composition of these bodies reflects differences in their intended functions. Whereas the ITLOS will be composed of persons of 'recognized competence in the field of the Law of the Sea',[25] and will function as an alternative to the ICJ, arbitrators appointed under annex VII need not be lawyers but must be 'experienced in maritime affairs'. Special arbitrators appointed under annex VIII similarly do not have to be lawyers but will instead be persons selected for their expertise in the four areas for which special arbitration is available: fisheries, protection of the marine environment, scientific research, or navigation. FAO, UNEP, the IOC, and IMO will maintain lists of appropriate experts in these fields. Experts appointed to sit with the ICJ, ITLOS, or an arbitral tribunal in accordance with Article 289 are also 'preferably' to be chosen from the list of special arbitrators.

It is thus possible within the UNCLOS scheme to tailor the choice of tribunal to the characteristics of each dispute and to bring in technical expertise where necessary; the Convention certainly cannot be characterized as favouring adjudication by lawyers in all cases. This has important implications for fisheries and environmental disputes and does demonstrate that these could be handled within the Convention's scheme even where they involve mainly technical, or a mix of legal and technical, issues. In such cases, resort to special arbitration, or the appointment of experts to sit with judicial or arbitral tribunals, may be the most appropriate way of ensuring that the right fisheries, scientific, or environmental expertise is applied to deciding the dispute.

While special arbitrators possess only a limited and specific jurisdiction, the Convention does not try to allocate a specific functional jurisdiction to each of the four compulsory fora.[26] Rather, as we have seen above, it leaves the choice of forum to the parties to the dispute and gives them the freedom to select whichever they deem most suitable. Fisheries disputes could thus be taken to any of the four dispute settlement options provided by the Convention, and in this respect the 1982 Convention is fundamentally different from the scheme for compulsory settlement found in the 1958 Fisheries Convention and described earlier. Where the parties cannot agree on the choice, arbitration under annex VII becomes the residual forum for the exercise of compulsory jurisdiction in all cases, including fisheries disputes.[27] Under Article 287, parties to the Convention may also make a declaration accepting in advance the compulsory jurisdiction of one or more of the four fora; this declaration will determine which body has compulsory jurisdiction only in relation to other states making the same choice. Where the parties to a dispute have declared their acceptance of different fora, or have made no declaration, arbitration is again the residual forum. In practice, very few of the parties have made such a declaration so, by default, arbitration is at present the nominal preference of most states.[28]

4 Binding compulsory settlement

In making provision for compulsory settlement of disputes an integral part of the 1982 Convention, the parties went further than had been possible in the earlier 1958 Geneva Conventions. In principle, questions of interpretation and application of the Convention are subject to compulsory jurisdiction under Article 288 (1). However, there was no consensus on bringing all of the Convention's provisions within compulsory jurisdiction. The most significant exclusion involves the exercise of jurisdiction over fisheries or marine scientific research in the exclusive economic zone.[29] States also have the option of excluding disputes concerning equitable delimitation of their territorial sea, EEZ or continental shelf boundaries, or historic bays and titles.[30] In general terms, questions of *entitlement* to maritime zones fall within compulsory jurisdiction, whereas equitable *delimitation* can be excluded.

The effect of these various exclusions is to categorize and separate different kinds of dispute, some of which will lead to binding compulsory settlement, others of which will not. With the exception of seabed disputes, for which a special tribunal is created with exclusive jurisdiction,[31] these categorizations do not have a functional basis. The excluded matters are not treated differently because some other way of dealing with them is more appropriate, although in some cases it may be, but because they concern subjects which proved politically sensitive and where many of the rules are open-textured and flexible, such as delimitation based on equitable principles. The reluctance of some states to commit themselves to binding settlement in these cases was strong and understandable, particularly with regard to fisheries and boundaries, but it does seriously diminish the overall integrity of the Convention.

4.1 *Exclusion of EEZ fisheries disputes*

EEZ disputes in general present the most complex problems for compulsory jurisdiction under the 1982 Convention. The practical effect of Article 297 is that there will usually be binding compulsory settlement for those EEZ disputes that relate to navigation or protection of the environment, but not for disputes that relate to the coastal state's exercise of its discretionary powers over fishing and marine scientific research within the EEZ. To complicate matters further, some, but not all, fisheries disputes excluded from binding compulsory settlement are subject instead to non-binding compulsory conciliation. Finally, under Article 298, states have the option of excluding from compulsory settlement certain disputes concerning law enforcement in the EEZ in regard to fisheries or scientific research.

The inclusion of navigation and protection of the environment within compulsory settlement was intended to restrain coastal state claims to 'creeping jurisdiction' over shipping within the EEZ, and it reinforces a balance established by parts V and XII in favour of freedom of navigation.[32] There is no comparable restraint on coastal state claims with regard to fishing. Here, the exclusions from binding compulsory settlement are far-reaching and significant. They do little to protect the already limited claims of distant water fishing states to fish or conduct research within the EEZ of another state. Such EEZ access rights for other states as are afforded by Articles 62, 69, 70, and 246 are exercisable only by agreement, and in the case of fishing only on heavily qualified terms involving subjective judgements by the coastal state about conservation, harvesting capacity, and total allowable catch. Yet fisheries disputes arising under these articles are excluded from compulsory jurisdiction of a court or tribunal when they are concerned with the sovereign rights of coastal states over living resources in the EEZ (Article 297 (3) (a)). These sovereign rights include the determination of harvesting capacity and total allowable catch, the allocation of a surplus, and the regulation of conservation and management of EEZ stocks.[33]

Disputes concerning EEZ stocks excluded from compulsory binding settlement by Article 297 (3) (a) will in a limited range of cases be subject to compulsory conciliation. However, this is only required if the coastal state has 'manifestly' failed to ensure proper conservation and management of EEZ stocks or has 'arbitrarily' refused to determine an EEZ surplus or allocate it to any state (Article 297 (3) (b)). The terminology suggests that what is taken out of compulsory jurisdiction by Article 297 (3) (a) is not necessarily put back into compulsory conciliation by Article 297 (3) (b). Moreover, it seems reasonably clear that conciliation is intended to deal mainly with issues of third party access to the EEZ rather than with the management of straddling stocks. Even if that is not correct, it affords a remedy only in extreme cases of manifest or arbitrary abuse.

The dispute settlement provisions for the EEZ reflect the reality that the management of resources within the EEZ is very much a matter for coastal state discretion,[34] a point reinforced by Articles 297 (2) (b) and (3) (c) which respectively prohibit a conciliation commission from questioning a coastal state's decisions on access for research purposes, or from substituting its own discretion for that of the coastal state in regard to fisheries conservation, management, and third party access. Coastal states at the UNCLOS negotiations were not willing to subject their newly found EEZ rights to international accountability, and the exclusions from compulsory jurisdiction were deliberate and necessary in the interests of consensus. The UNCLOS articles leave unanswered the difficult question of whether disputes concerning straddling stocks—that is stocks that straddle both the high seas and EEZ waters, are within or outside the exclusion from compulsory binding settlement.

There is no doubt that disputes relating only to high seas fisheries and research are within the Convention's provisions on binding compulsory settlement. Thus, as regards fish, the initial question is whether the dispute involves high seas freedoms or coastal state sovereign rights in the EEZ. But what if it involves both? Most of the more intractable fisheries disputes occur because the stocks in question straddle two or more EEZs, or straddle the EEZ and the high seas.[35] As later chapters of this book show, this is particularly true in the Northwest Atlantic and the North Pacific/Bering Sea. In these areas it makes little sense to separate the question of high seas fishing from the management of fish stocks in the adjacent EEZ. Overfishing or poor management in one area will necessarily have an impact on the other, as can be observed in the Canada–Spain dispute considered in Chapter 8. Whereas Canada arguably had a good case for complaint with regard to fishing of the high seas by Spain and other EU states, and such a dispute is subject to compulsory settlement, Canada has also accepted that its own management of the Canadian EEZ has resulted in overfishing.[36] What needs to be established is whether this EEZ aspect of the dispute is also susceptible to compulsory binding settlement under the Convention.

It has been argued that Article 297 (3) (a) should be narrowly construed to exclude only disputes concerning stocks that exist wholly within the EEZ of one or more states; that is, exclusive or shared stocks.[37] If this is correct then disputes involving stocks that straddle the EEZ and the high seas would remain fully within compulsory jurisdiction, even if the dispute related to the exercise of coastal state sovereign rights. The argument in favour of this interpretation is that only then could a court deal with the stock as a whole; it cannot do so if compulsory jurisdiction applies only to the actions of states fishing the high seas but not to coastal state EEZ management of the same stock. But the same could be said of shared stocks that merely straddle several EEZs. In both cases inclusion within compulsory jurisdiction is difficult to reconcile with the explicit wording of Article 297 (3) (a), which provides that 'the coastal state shall not be obliged to accept the submission to such settlement of any dispute relating to its sovereign rights with respect to the living resources in the exclusive economic zone, or their exercise'. It is far from clear that the word 'in' can be narrowly construed so as to apply only to stocks that never venture beyond any EEZ, even if it is possible to identify fish with this characteristic. Nor is it evident that what may be a sensible and desirable interpretation of this Article in fact reflects the intention of parties to the UNCLOS negotiations. It is at least as plausible to assume that coastal states did not want there to be compulsory jurisdiction in respect of their obligations regarding straddling stocks. The conclusion may be undesirable but the interpretation is neither absurd nor unreasonable.[38] However, for reasons considered in the next two sections, it would be unwise to draw any firm conclusion on this point at present. What can be observed is that neither the text of the Convention nor the negotiating records of UNCLOS III provide definitive support for either view. Nor, as we shall see below, does the 1995 Fish Stocks Agreement fully resolve the dilemma, since it refers the issue back to the disputes settlement provisions of part XV of UNCLOS.

If disputes concerning shared or straddling stocks are indeed excluded from compulsory binding settlement then the parties are left with two options:

- make an *agreed* submission of all the issues in dispute to a tribunal of their choice;
- submit only the high seas issues to compulsory settlement.

The weakness of the former is precisely that it requires agreement, and of the latter that it fails to deal comprehensively with the dispute and is almost bound to fail for that reason. Moreover, there is manifest inequity in subjecting to compulsory jurisdiction states whose vessels fish on the high seas while at the same time denying these states the right to bring proceedings or counter-claims against a coastal state whose own actions within the EEZ may be affecting the very same straddling stock. This lack of equivalence in the due process rights of high seas and coastal states may well justify a tribunal refusing on equitable grounds to entertain claims brought by coastal states unless they are willing to agree to jurisdiction over any counter-claim made by the respondent high seas state with regard to the straddling stock in dispute.[39] The inherent inequity may be simply another manifestation of the unsatisfactory nature of the Convention's treatment of fisheries, but that is little consolation for those high seas fishing states whose interests are most affected.

4.2 Exclusion of disputes concerning maritime boundaries: fishery zones and EEZs

Here the position regarding compulsory jurisdiction is also complex, and directly relevant to fishing. Insofar as they involve questions of interpretation or application of UNCLOS, maritime boundary disputes are in principle subject to compulsory binding settlement. Thus a dispute about the *entitlement* of islands to a shelf or EEZ under Article 121 (3)[40] would be subject to compulsory settlement. However, Article 298 allows states to make a declaration opting out of one or more of the four compulsory procedures with respect to disputes that concern *equitable delimitation* of the territorial sea, EEZ, or continental shelf, or which involve historic bays or titles. Where this right to opt out is exercised, an obligation arises to submit delimitation disputes that arise after entry into force of the Convention to non-binding conciliation unless they necessarily involve disputed sovereignty over islands or land territory, in which case no compulsory process of any kind is required. Thus, the first problem is simply that some states will and others will not be subject to compulsory jurisdiction in boundary delimitation disputes, but that is no worse than the present position under general international law.

The second problem arises from the combination of Articles 297 and 298. Take a dispute involving possible EEZ claims around islands or rocks

where sovereignty is unsettled, such as Rockall, the Senkaku/Diaoyutai
Islands, or Takeshima/Tokdo. Suppose a claimant state purports to exercise fisheries jurisdiction over straddling stocks within this EEZ. How do
we categorize such a dispute? Does it relate to the exercise of sovereign
rights and law enforcement within the EEZ, which is excluded under Articles 297 and 298 from compulsory jurisdiction? Is it a maritime delimitation dispute concerning the interpretation or application of Article 74
and excluded from binding compulsory jurisdiction under Article 298 if
one of the parties has opted out under that Article? Does it necessarily
involve disputed sovereignty over land territory so that even compulsory
conciliation can be excluded? Or is it a dispute about entitlement to an
EEZ under part V and Article 121 (3) of the Convention? If it is the latter,
then it is not excluded from compulsory jurisdiction under either Article
297 or 298. Much may thus depend on how the dispute is formulated. If
it is presented as misuse of fisheries jurisdiction powers within the EEZ,
then it will surely be excluded under Article 297. But if it is an invalid
claim to an EEZ contrary to Article 121 (3), then it would appear not to
be excluded. Then suppose, instead, that the dispute is reformulated as a
claim that on equitable grounds the island or rock should be given no
weight as a base point in a delimitation under Article 74?[41] Prima facie
this appears to be caught by Article 298 (1). It is not necessary for present
purposes to answer all of these questions,[42] but they should suffice to
show that everything turns in practice not on what each case involves,
but on how the issues are characterized. Formulate them wrongly and the
case falls outside compulsory jurisdiction. Formulate the same case differently, and it falls inside. The important question for disputes concerning straddling fish stocks then becomes whether the applicant state's
characterization is decisive, or whether the forum before which the
dispute is brought can make its own characterization.

4.3 *Characterization of UNCLOS disputes in practice: the* Saiga Case

In the *Saiga Case*,[43] the first before the ITLOS, the tribunal held by a majority that the arrest of an oil tanker supplying bunker fuel to fishing vessels
in the exclusive economic zone of Guinea could *arguably* be characterized
as a fishing dispute for the purpose of jurisdiction to order prompt release
of the vessel under Article 73 of the Convention. It did so in spite of the
fact that Guinea, the arresting state, had made the arrest not for a violation of its fisheries law but for alleged violation of its customs laws. The
Convention provides for prompt release in the case of fisheries offences
but not for customs offences. At the same time it also confers no jurisdiction to apply customs laws in the EEZ or to make arrests for such offences
beyond the contiguous zone. The tribunal's characterization of the case as

a fisheries dispute is not the last word on the matter because it decided only that this characterization was plausible, not that it was correct. The minority judges held that the court had applied the wrong test and should have concluded that the dispute was not a fisheries case for the purposes of Article 73. Unlike the majority, they would have given Guinea's own characterization of its actions decisive weight. On a subsequent application for provisional measures,[44] however, the tribunal again rejected Guinea's characterization of the case, this time as an EEZ fisheries dispute excluded from compulsory jurisdiction by virtue of Articles 297 (3) and 298 (1) (b); the tribunal held instead that for the purpose of jurisdiction to prescribe provisional measures the case appeared prima facie to fall within compulsory jurisdiction under Article 297 (1).

Both decisions may illustrate no more than the tendency of courts to make interpretations fit the result they wish to reach. On this view, what constitutes a fisheries dispute will vary according to the context in which the question arises, and there is no necessary illogicality in characterizing a dispute as a fisheries case for prompt release applications but as something else when compulsory jurisdiction is in issue. Such procrustean tendencies may enable a court to do justice in the instant case, but only at some cost in integrity, consistency, and predictability.[45] Orderly relations among states are not necessarily assisted thereby, while in the context of disputes over straddling fish stocks the uncertainty regarding the proper characterization for the purposes of part XV of UNCLOS is not removed.

What does seem clear from the evidence of both the *Saiga* cases is that characterization of the issues in dispute will be decided by the court or tribunal hearing the case, rather than by the parties to the dispute. It follows that in practice, given the textual uncertainty inherent in the Convention and the Agreement, and the power of interpretation and appreciation exercisable by a court or tribunal in such cases, the question whether disputes concerning the relationship between conservation and management of straddling or highly migratory fish stocks on the high seas and within the EEZ falls fully within compulsory binding dispute settlement is essentially one to which there is no definitive answer. If a court or tribunal wants to establish that compulsory jurisdiction exists in such cases, even at the cost of some intrusion on coastal state sovereign rights, it appears possible for it to do so.

4.4 Inclusion of disputes concerning related agreements

Article 288 (2) also brings within the jurisdiction of a court or tribunal any dispute concerning interpretation or application of any other international agreement 'related to the purposes of the Convention' and submitted 'in accordance with the agreement'.[46] Quite what this article means is not free from doubt. On one view it permits the parties to other agreements to incorporate the 1982 Convention's dispute settlement regime. Only two such 'related agreements' appear at present to meet this interpretation. First, Article 30 of the Fish Stocks Agreement applies part XV *mutatis mutandis* to disputes concerning interpretation and application of that Agreement or of any subregional, regional, or global fisheries agreement relating to straddling or highly migratory fish stocks, although, as we have seen, most aspects of EEZ fisheries management are taken out of compulsory jurisdiction by Article 297 (3). Secondly, Article 2 of the 1994 Agreement on the Implementation of part XI of the 1982 UNCLOS[47] provides for the 1982 Convention and the 1994 Agreement to be read as a single instrument, and by implication would thus seem to import the compulsory dispute settlement procedures of part XI.

A broader reading of Article 288 (2) is that it covers any agreement that makes provision for binding decision by a court or tribunal. Would this cover treaties, such as the 1973/78 MARPOL Convention[48] and the 1996 Dumping Protocol,[49] that provide for compulsory arbitration, but where resort to any other forum requires agreement of the parties? If Article 288 (2) applies to other treaties only insofar as they envisage compulsory settlement, then it would cover only cases of compulsory arbitration under MARPOL or the Dumping Protocol. The problem with this interpretation is that, as we saw earlier, Article 282 provides that treaties that have their own procedure for binding dispute settlement take priority over part XV of UNCLOS unless the parties agree otherwise, so Article 288 (2) would not operate in these cases. Alternatively, if it applies to cases of agreed submission by both parties, then it would not be true to call jurisdiction under Article 288 (2) a 'compulsory procedure'. It is of course always open to the parties to a dispute arising under these earlier agreements to agree to use the 1982 Convention's procedures under Article 282. Whatever the correct interpretation, a treaty which makes no provision for compulsory binding jurisdiction is not transformed by Article 288 (2) into one that does. Article 288 thus does little or nothing to extend the scope of compulsory jurisdiction over straddling stock disputes. As we shall see below, however, the Fish Stocks Agreement adopts a very different position. Unlike Article 288, the Agreement does import compulsory jurisdiction into other related fisheries agreements and thus has a very considerable impact on the practical scope of compulsory jurisdiction in fisheries cases.[50]

4.5 Exclusion of disputes concerning related agreements

In a remarkable reading of Article 281 of UNCLOS, four of the five arbitrators in the *Southern Bluefin Tuna Arbitration* held in an award delivered in July 2000 that they had no jurisdiction to consider the merits of a dispute concerning the application of Articles 64 and 116–19 of the Convention to high seas tuna fishing in the Pacific. Notwithstanding that such a dispute otherwise falls squarely within compulsory jurisdiction, the tribunal held that this dispute, between Australia, New Zealand, and Japan, had to be settled in accordance with the 1993 Convention for the Conservation of Southern Bluefin Tuna ('SBT Convention'). The tribunal accepted that the dispute 'while centered in the 1993 Convention, also arises under the UNCLOS', but for the purposes of dispute settlement procedures it declined to separate the UNCLOS aspects of the dispute from those concerned with the SBT Convention. That Convention did not provide for compulsory binding settlement of disputes, and the clear implication of Article 282 is that if no settlement of the dispute could be reached using the 1993 Convention's procedures, part XV of UNCLOS would then apply. However, the arbitral tribunal instead took the view that the parties to the 1993 Convention had thereby agreed to exclude any further procedure under part XV of UNCLOS by virtue of Article 281 (1). In their interpretation both of the 1993 Convention and of Article 281 of UNCLOS, the arbitrators assume that UNCLOS is *not* a regime of compulsory jurisdiction once an UNCLOS dispute becomes interlocked with a dispute under another treaty. The dispute settlement procedures of that treaty will then prevail over UNCLOS compulsory jurisdiction.

This is an extraordinary reversal of the intentions underlying part XV, and it makes even more important the extension of compulsory settlement to regional fishery agreements which the 1995 Fish Stocks Agreement will affect once it enters into force (see below). Although explained by the arbitrators as providing a balance of rights and obligations for coastal and non-coastal states, in reality the award does the reverse: it leaves high seas fishing states vulnerable to creeping coastal state jurisdiction beyond the EEZ if they enter a regional fishery agreement with no provision for compulsory settlement of disputes. This is precisely the outcome UNCLOS dispute settlement was intended to deter. The result of the arbitration is that UNCLOS states parties which favour compulsory settlement of high seas fishery disputes should therefore be careful before they participate in regional fishery agreements: they will be more securely protected under UNCLOS alone. The best that can be said of this award is that UNCLOS parties should pause before opting for arbitration in preference to the more established expertise of the ICJ or ITLOS.

4.6 Compulsory and consensual jurisdiction: the reality of UNCLOS

From what we have seen so far the reality of UNCLOS is that its provision for compulsory binding settlement of disputes is less impressive and comprehensive than it might seem at first sight. The most significant areas where the commitment to compulsory settlement is unequivocal are freedom of navigation and protection of the marine environment.[51] The former is consistent with the Convention's general treatment of navigation interests and the strong lobbying of the maritime powers. The latter remains a novelty among even the most ambitious of environmental treaties, where compulsory conciliation and optional acceptance of binding adjudication are usually the most the parties are prepared to agree on.[52] However, the main reason for such a strong regime in this Convention is the need to protect navigation from excessive interference on environmental grounds by coastal states, so this novelty is perhaps also less than it seems.

Elsewhere, and especially on those issues where disputes have been most numerous—fisheries and boundaries—we can see that the fragmentation resulting from the partial exclusion of these issues leaves a largely empty shell which can be filled only if the parties agree on consensual submission of the dispute to whatever forum they choose.[53] This does not mean that there will be no cases on the Convention before international tribunals—all of the arbitrations and most of the ICJ cases that have dealt with law of the sea issues until now have been cases of consensual, not compulsory, jurisdiction. Rather, it does remind us not to exaggerate the significance of compulsory jurisdiction in the judicial settlement of disputes.

As we saw above, Article 280 emphasizes the freedom of parties to agree at any time to settle a dispute concerning the Convention by any peaceful means of their own choice, whereas Article 299 preserves the right of the parties to agree to submit to the Convention's procedures matters otherwise excluded from compulsory jurisdiction by Articles 297 or 298. In practice, because of these articles, it is quite likely that many fisheries and boundary disputes will have to be or will be more satisfactorily dealt with by consent before ITLOS or some other forum rather than under compulsory jurisdiction.[54] Article 21 of the Statute of the ITLOS should be sufficient to enable the parties to refer any dispute concerning the 1982 Convention and related agreements to the Tribunal, including those that fall wholly or partly outside the provisions on compulsory jurisdiction. Moreover, Article 22 of the Statute also allows all of the parties to treaties already in force and that concern the subject matter of the Convention to submit disputes arising under these treaties to the Tribunal by agreement. Happily this Article poses none of the interpretation difficulties which affect Article 288 (2), and there is no reason to doubt that it would cover the 1996 Dumping Protocol and the 1973/78 MARPOL Convention, as well as any fishery treaty. Both the 1995 Fish Stocks Agreement and the 1993 Agreement on Compliance by Fishing Vessels also allow the parties by agreement to refer disputes to ITLOS, the ICJ, or arbitration.[55]

5 Settlement of disputes under the Fish Stocks Agreement

The 1995 Fish Stocks Agreement represents an attempt to deal with the serious problems of overfishing of straddling EEZ and high seas stocks that emerged in the period after the adoption of the 1982 UNCLOS and the development of the 200-mile exclusive economic zone. In addition, it also provides a new global framework for the regulation and management of highly migratory fish stocks that are not the subject of this paper. The Agreement is in many respects radical in its reform of international fisheries law; it introduces obligations of sustainable use, requires the precautionary approach to be applied in the conservation and management of stocks, and places on parties a more extensive obligation of cooperation through regional fisheries bodies.[56] In effect, it amends the 1982 Convention, as well as other regional and global fisheries treaties covering straddling and highly migratory stocks. Although without prejudice to the rights, jurisdiction, and obligations of parties to UNCLOS, the Agreement is to be interpreted and applied 'in the context of and in a manner consistent with the Convention'.[57]

One of the principal purposes of the Fish Stocks Agreement is to 'ensure that the measures taken for conservation and management in the EEZs and in the adjacent high seas areas are compatible and coherent, in order to take into account the biological unity of the stocks and the supporting ecosystem'.[58] Article 7 thus requires coastal states and states whose nationals fish adjacent high seas areas to seek to agree on measures necessary for the conservation of stocks in the adjacent high seas area, and to cooperate to ensure compatibility between the measures adopted for high seas areas and those adopted for areas under national jurisdiction. The Article lists various matters that are to be taken into account in determining compatibility. States are also required to ensure that high seas measures do not undermine the effectiveness of conservation and management within the EEZ. The chairman of the conference, Ambassador Satya Nandan, pointed out that 'the collective interest of the international community must [also] be taken into account if sustainable use of high seas resources was to be secured'.[59]

The Chairman also stressed the importance of making provision for compulsory binding dispute settlement, consistent with the 1982 UNCLOS, but flexible enough to allow the parties a range of choice.[60] Although arbitration was initially envisaged as the only forum for compulsory jurisdiction under the Fish Stocks Agreement, a US proposal to incorporate the provisions of part XV of UNCLOS was accepted. Parties to the Agreement are thus given the same wide choice of compulsory fora for dispute settlement and the freedom to select a compulsory forum for fisheries disputes different from their choice for other matters.[61] However, this solution does little to resolve the problems inherent in the UNCLOS scheme for fisheries dispute settlement, and it adds further complexity to the task of deciding which fishery disputes fall within compulsory jurisdiction. The main effect of the Agreement's dispute settlement provisions is largely to replicate the UNCLOS scheme for the benefit of states that are not parties to that Convention. What it signally does not do is to clarify the extent to which straddling stock disputes are subject to compulsory binding settlement.

5.1 Application of the 1995 Fish Stocks Agreement

The Fish Stocks Agreement as a whole applies only to straddling and highly migratory fish stocks in areas beyond national jurisdiction, i.e. on the high seas.[62] Neither term is defined, although highly migratory species are listed in annex I of the Convention. There are stocks that fall into neither of these categories, so it cannot be assumed that all fisheries disputes are potentially subject to the Agreement's provisions. In particular, the Agreement appears not to cover stocks that are exclusive to one EEZ or are shared across several EEZs, nor would it apply to stocks that are found only on the high seas. However, there are, exceptionally, certain articles which also apply to straddling stocks within the EEZ and which thus place some obligations on coastal states with regard to the management of these stocks. The essential point is that, in the conservation and management of straddling stocks within the EEZ, coastal states are required to apply the general principles of Article 5, the precautionary measures of Article 6, and to a more limited extent the compatibility with conservation measures in adjoining areas provisions of Article 7.[63] These are of course precisely the matters that are most likely to affect other states, both in adjacent EEZs and on the high seas, and therefore to generate disputes.

Under Article 1 (3) the Agreement specifically applies *mutatis mutandis* to 'other fishing entities whose vessels fish on the high seas'. This novel provision is intended to allow for Taiwanese participation in the Agreement, without having to address that country's uncertain international status.[64] It opens up the possibility of entities other than states becoming subject to the Agreement's compulsory dispute provisions to an extent not provided for in UNCLOS. UNCLOS does permit entities that are not states to appear before the Seabed Disputes Chamber, or, with the consent of other parties to a dispute, in litigation before the ITLOS, but it does not envisage them becoming subject to the compulsory settlement provisions of part XV.[65] This omission is potentially rectified by the Agreement.

5.2 *Dispute avoidance*

Parties to the Fish Stocks Agreement have the same freedom to settle disputes by any agreed means as they enjoy under UNCLOS. Unilateral compulsory settlement is therefore again a residual measure of last resort. The Agreement goes further, however, in obliging parties to cooperate to prevent disputes from arising. Article 28 thus requires them to strengthen or agree on 'efficient and expeditious decision-making procedures' within fisheries management bodies. The Agreement as a whole tries to enhance the role and effectiveness of these bodies, and this article is a frank admission that if they did work better there would be fewer disputes for other fora to settle. Another novel provision seeks to encourage informal settlement of disputes concerning 'matters of a technical nature' by an ad hoc expert panel whose role is to try to resolve matters expeditiously without recourse to binding procedures.[66] The parties themselves are expected to establish the panel. Much effort has thus been devoted to minimizing the need for formal dispute settlement, and to avoiding the expense, delay, and complexity of international litigation. This is undoubtedly the correct approach, but it assumes that the applicable rules of international law are clear enough to provide the necessary guidance. In fisheries disputes that may not be the case.

5.3 *Importation of the UNCLOS dispute settlement provisions*

Article 30 provides simply that part XV of UNCLOS applies *mutatis mutandis* to any dispute concerning interpretation or application of the Fish Stocks Agreement, whether or not the parties to that dispute are also parties to UNCLOS. In effect part XV is incorporated into the Agreement by reference, without any significant alteration beyond what is necessary to permit non-parties to UNCLOS to nominate conciliators, arbitrators, and experts, and to designate a preferred forum for compulsory settlement.

There will thus be compulsory settlement for fisheries disputes under the Agreement in largely the same circumstances as already apply under UNCLOS. This means of course that disputes concerning the exercise of a coastal state's sovereign rights in the EEZ will be excluded under Article 297 (3). Indeed, Article 32 of the Agreement makes this clear by stating explicitly that that Article also applies to the Agreement. Thus, although Articles 5, 6, and 7 of the Agreement are, as we have seen, applicable to coastal states, their application cannot be the subject of compulsory jurisdiction if properly characterized as involving the exercise of sovereign rights. Disputes about harvesting capacity of the coastal state, allocation of surpluses to other states, and the terms of coastal state conservation and management laws will thus be subject only to the conciliation requirements of Article 297 (3) (b).

It might be argued that Article 7 strengthens the case for putting EEZ straddling stocks within compulsory settlement. As we saw above, this Article requires coastal and high seas fishing states to make every effort to agree on compatible conservation and management measures for straddling stocks within a reasonable time. It also provides that if such measures cannot be agreed, any party may invoke the Agreement's procedures for settlement of disputes. This of course begs the question what those procedures are in such a case: as between compulsory binding adjudication or non-binding conciliation it points neither one way nor the other. It is true that the Article goes on to allow a 'court or tribunal' to prescribe provisional measures in such disputes, but this does not demonstrate that the same court or tribunal is intended to have compulsory jurisdiction to determine the merits. Moreover, although the Article does place some obligations on coastal states with regard to the management of EEZ stocks, it is principally aimed at ensuring that high seas stocks are managed in such a manner that the effectiveness of conservation and management measures in the EEZ is not undermined.[67] Given Article 7's limited impact on coastal state management of EEZ stocks, and its very different treatment of high seas fishing, it is difficult to read into it any intention to clarify the applicability of compulsory dispute settlement in regard to straddling stocks.

Despite the significant changes that the 1995 Fish Stocks Agreement makes to the substantive UNCLOS fisheries law, it remains far from clear, for the reasons set out in the previous paragraphs, that disputes concerning coastal state overfishing or inadequate management of straddling stocks within its own EEZ can usefully be the subject of any form of binding process initiated by another fishing state or entity, even if there is a serious impact on the viability of stocks in other EEZs or on the high seas beyond national jurisdiction. Conciliation appears to remain the most that may be available as of right in such cases, and then only on the limited terms described earlier.

The converse is not true as regards high seas fishing states, however. As was seen earlier, because overfishing by these states would not fall within the Article 297 exclusions, it could be the subject of a compulsory binding process. The imbalance of compulsory jurisdiction over high seas states and EEZ states that is one of the more remarkable features of part XV of the 1982 UNCLOS has been faithfully and fully reproduced in the

1995 Agreement by virtue of its lock-stock-and-barrel incorporation of part XV. The conclusion that flows from this is obvious: that the 1995 Agreement does not reform the law relating to fisheries disputes, but merely extends the existing UNCLOS scheme with all its imperfections to non-UNCLOS states.

5.4 Application to other fishery agreements

If the 1995 Agreement does nothing to change the UNCLOS dispute settlement machinery, the same cannot be said of its impact on disputes under other fishery treaties. Article 30 (2) provides that part XV of UNCLOS applies *mutatis mutandis* to any subregional, regional, or global agreement relating to straddling or highly migratory stocks, including 'any dispute concerning the conservation and management of such stocks'. On one interpretation, this merely means that all such agreements are covered by Article 288 (2) and will be subject to the jurisdiction of a court or tribunal under part XV if 'submitted to it in accordance with the agreement'. As shown earlier, this interpretation would not necessarily import compulsory jurisdiction into these agreements.[68] Article 30 (2) would on that view be limited to extending to non-UNCLOS states the benefits of Article 288 (2), whatever these may be. The alternative and better view is more far-reaching: that, as between parties to the Fish Stocks Agreement, Article 30 (2) amends existing fishery treaties and incorporates into them the disputes settlement provisions of part XV of the 1982 UNCLOS. This is closer to what Article 30 (2) actually says. Moreover, not only does Article 30 (2) not refer to Article 288, but it avoids entirely any reference to the submission of a dispute to a court or tribunal 'in accordance with' the relevant fisheries treaty.

The latter interpretation is not merely textually more convincing, it is also considerably closer to the object and purpose of the Fish Stocks Agreement and to the intent of the parties to the negotiations.[69] If the Agreement is to work effectively, it must change existing law and existing treaties, and that purpose is borne out additionally by Article 30 (5). That Article prescribes the law to be applied in all disputes arising under the Agreement *or any other fishery treaty*:

Any court or tribunal to which a dispute has been submitted under this Part shall apply the relevant provisions of the Convention, of this Agreement and of any relevant subregional, regional or global fisheries agreement, as well as generally accepted standards for the conservation and management of living resources and other rules of international law not incompatible with the Convention, with a view to ensuring the conservation of the straddling fish stocks and highly migratory fish stocks concerned.

The effect of this provision is to amend the substantive terms of other fisheries treaties insofar as they are inconsistent with the new law laid down in the Agreement. From this perspective it is far from radical to see Article 30 (2) as also importing new or stronger dispute settlement provisions into existing treaties. In these two significant ways the Agreement thus adds to the dispute settlement provisions of UNCLOS, expanding both the category of disputes subject to compulsory jurisdiction and the law to be applied in resolving these disputes.[70]

5.5 Provisional measures

The Fish Stocks Agreement does make one change to the disputes settlement articles of UNCLOS. Article 290 of the Convention allows a court or tribunal to prescribe provisional measures to protect the rights of the parties or to prevent serious harm to the marine environment.[71] It says nothing about fisheries. Article 31 of the Agreement rectifies this deficiency by allowing a court or tribunal to prescribe provisional measures to prevent damage to the fish stocks in question. There is also, as we have seen, power to order provisional measures pending agreement between coastal and high seas fishing states under Articles 7 and 16 of the Agreement.

6 Conclusion

Modern fisheries law has for some time recognized the special interest of coastal states in the management of adjacent high seas fisheries.[72] It has been slower to acknowledge a comparable interest on the part of high seas fishing states in the conservation and management of EEZ stocks by coastal states. This imbalance of rights and obligations between these two groups of states continues to be reflected in the fisheries articles of the 1982 UNCLOS and in the 1995 Agreement on Fish Stocks. Equitable utilization of common property resources does not of course mean equality of rights and obligations for all concerned. It can legitimately justify preferential rights for coastal states, as in the 1974 *Fisheries Jurisdiction Cases*. So long as high seas fishing rights remain in existence, however, the law will always have to regulate some kind of equitable, if lopsided, balance of interests between coastal and high seas fishing states.

Much of the Law of the Sea Convention is about balancing the interests of different groups of states, and maintaining that balance is one of the reasons for adopting the principle of compulsory binding dispute settlement in part XV of the Convention. Disputes about straddling fish stocks are necessarily disputes about the balance between coastal and high seas fishing states, and, more generally, about the interest of the international community in sustainable utilization of fish stocks and preservation of the marine ecosystem. Leaving aside for the moment the problem of interpreting the Convention and the Agreement and viewing the matter from this broader perspective, it is easier to see that whereas coastal states and high seas states may have unequal rights and obligations with regard to fisheries access and management, they do have an equal interest in access to dispute settlement options. Both share a need for authoritative interpretation of difficult and complex texts; in both cases compulsory dispute settlement may be required in the event of failure to reach agreement on the management of shared access to straddling stocks. To hold that only coastal states have the right to compulsory binding settlement in such cases is to stabilize and protect one side of an equitable balance while leaving the other side vulnerable to erosion and instability. Put crudely, it enables coastal states to protect and possibly expand their rights while denying the same privilege to high seas states.

The question whether disputes concerning all or part of a straddling stock fall inside or outside compulsory jurisdiction is thus more than a technical question of treaty interpretation. It poses some fundamental questions about the nature of equitable utilization as a legal principle governing use of common resources and about equitable access to justice in international law. If, as we have seen, these questions cannot be answered decisively by reference to textual analysis, the intention of the parties, or *travaux préparatoires*, but remain open for judicial resolution, then it is not difficult to suggest a clear answer. In both the interests of equitable access to justice and the effective management and sustainable use of straddling stocks, compulsory jurisdiction should apply to all aspects of such a dispute. The rights of coastal states must of course be maintained, but they should also be accountable for compliance with their obligations insofar as these affect other states or the international community as a whole. The exception for sovereign rights created by Article 297 (3) of the Convention and incorporated in the 1995 Agreement should thus be construed narrowly to cover only the exercise of coastal state discretion on matters that are purely of EEZ concern only, i.e. matters that do not affect straddling stocks, whether inside or outside the EEZ.

Alan Boyle

Notes

I am particularly grateful to David Balton, Robin Churchill, Francisco Orrego Vicuña, Donald Rothwell, and Budislav Vukas for their comments on an earlier version of this chapter, but it should not be assumed that they agree with everything. An earlier version of this chapter was first published in *International Journal of Marine and Coastal Law*, 14 (1999) and is reproduced by permission of Kluwer Law International.

1. *Corfu Channel Case (United Kingdom v. Albania)*, ICJ Reports (1949), 3; *Fisheries Case (United Kingdom v. Norway)*, ICJ Reports (1951), 116; *North Sea Continental Shelf Case (Federal Republic of Germany/Denmark; Federal Republic of Germany/the Netherlands)*, ICJ Reports (1969), 3; *Fisheries Jurisdiction Cases (United Kingdom v. Iceland; Federal Republic v. Iceland)*, ICJ Reports (1974), 3, 175; *Aegean Sea Continental Shelf Case (Greece v. Turkey)*, ICJ Reports (1978), 3; *Tunisia/Libya Continental Shelf Case*, ICJ Reports (1982), 18; *Gulf of Maine Case (Canada/United States of America)*, ICJ Reports (1984), 246; *Libya/Malta Continental Shelf Case*, ICJ Reports (1985), 13; *Land, Island and Maritime Frontier Case (El Salvador/Honduras: Nicaragua intervening)*, ICJ Reports (1992), 351; *Jan Mayen Case (Denmark v. Norway)*, ICJ Reports (1993), 38; *Fisheries Jurisdiction Case (Spain v. Canada)*, ICJ Reports (1998).
2. *Maritime Delimitation between Nicaragua and Honduras in the Caribbean Sea (Nicaragua v. Honduras)*; *Qatar/Bahrain Maritime Delimitation Case*; *Land and Maritime Boundary Case (Cameroon v. Nigeria)*.
3. *Anglo-French Continental Shelf Arbitration* (1977), 54 ILR 6; *Guinea–Guinea-Bissau Maritime Boundary Arbitration* (1985), 25 ILM 251; *Franco-Canadian Fisheries Arbitration* (1986), 90 RGDIP 151; *St. Pierre and Miquelon Arbitration* (1992), 95 ILR 645; *Dubai–Sharjah Arbitration* (1981), 91 ILR 543; *Beagle Channel Arbitration* (1977), 52 ILR 93; *Eritrea–Yemen Maritime Delimitation Arbitration* (1999) (text on PCA website); *Southern Bluefin Tuna Arbitration* (2000) (text on ICSID website).
4. *Jan Mayen Conciliation* (1981), 20 ILM 797.
5. The International Court of Justice Viewed from the Bench, *Recueil des cours* ii. 244 (1993), 9, especially at 127–55.
6. Panel Reports on US Restrictions on Imports of Tuna (1991), 30 ILM 1598 (USA–Mexico) and (1994), 33 ILM 839 (USA–EC and the Netherlands); Appellate Body Report on US Import Prohibition of Shrimp and Certain Shrimp Products (1998), 37 ILM 832. Under the revised dispute settlement procedure agreed in 1994 panel reports are automatically adopted unless the Conference of the parties decides otherwise by consensus; A. Porges, 'The New Dispute Settlement: From the GATT to the WTO', *Leiden Journal of International Law*, 8 (1995), 115.
7. *The M/V Saiga Case (St Vincent and the Grenadines v. Guinea)*, ITLOS Nos. 1 and 2 (1997/8), a fisheries dispute insofar as it involves the supply of fuel to distant water fishing vessels operating in the EEZ of the respondent state; *Southern Bluefin Tuna Case (Australia and New Zealand v. Japan)*, ITLOS Nos. 3 and 4

(1999); *The Camouco Case (Panama* v. *France)*, ITLOS No. 5 (2000), prompt release of a fishing vessel.

8. Reproduced in 21 *ILM* 1261.
9. Text reprinted in *Yearbook of International Environmental Law*, 6 (1995), 841.
10. Agenda 21, ch. 17, 'Report of the UN Conference on Environment and Development', UN Doc. A/CONF.151/26/Rev. 1, vol. 1 (1993), 238.
11. For further development of these arguments, see A. E. Boyle, 'Settlement of Disputes Relating to the Law of the Sea and the Environment', *Thesaurus Acroasium*, 26 (1997), 299; J. Charney, 'The Implications of Expanding International Dispute Settlement Systems: The 1982 Convention on the Law of the Sea', *American Journal of International Law*, 90 (1996), 69; see also D. Anderson, 'Legal Implications of the Entry into Force of the UN Convention on the Law of the Sea', *International and Comparative Law Quarterly*, 44 (1995), 313.
12. Convention on the Territorial Sea and Contiguous Zone, 516 *UNTS* 205, in force 10 Sept. 1964; Convention on the High Seas, 450 *UNTS* 82, in force 30 Sept. 1962; Convention on Fishing and Conservation of Living Resources of the High Seas, 559 *UNTS* 285, in force 20 Mar. 1966; Convention on the Continental Shelf, 499 *UNTS* 311, in force 10 June 1964.
13. Optional Protocol of Signature Concerning the Compulsory Settlement of Disputes; 450 *UNTS* 169, in force 30 Sept. 1962.
14. Art. 73 of the Draft Convention proposed by the International Law Commission required compulsory judicial settlement only in respect of the Continental Shelf; 'Report of the ILC to the General Assembly', *Yearbook of the International Law Commission* (1956), ii. 253, and compare 'Report of the Special Rapporteur', ibid. 3, at paras. 19–23.
15. Compare Art. 57 of the ILC's Draft Convention, *Yearbook of the International Law* Commission (1956), ii.
16. UN, 'Report of the Committee on the Peaceful Uses of the Seabed etc.', GAOR, 26th session, Supp. No. 21.
17. Ibid., iii. 83–91.
18. Ibid., vol. v, UN Doc. A/AC.138/97 (1973).
19. A. O. Adede, *The System for Settlement of Disputes under the UN Convention on the Law of the Sea: A Drafting History and a Commentary* (Dordrecht: Kluwer Academic, 1987), 13.
20. See generally D. Anderson, 'The International Tribunal for the Law of the Sea', in M. Evans (ed.), *Remedies in International Law: The Institutional Dilemma* (Oxford: Hart, 1998), 71; R. Churchill, 'Dispute Settlement in the Law of the Sea: The Context of the International Tribunal for the Law of the Sea and Alternatives to it', in Evans (ed.), *Remedies in International Law*, 85; J. Merrills, *International Dispute Settlement*, 2nd edn. (Cambridge: Grotius, 1991), ch. 8; R. R. Churchill and A. V. Lowe, *The Law of the Sea*, 3rd edn. (Manchester University Press, 1999), ch. 19; L. Sohn, 'Settlement of Law of the Sea Disputes', *International Journal of Marine and Coastal Law*, 10 (1995), 205; Adede, *The System for Settlement of Disputes*; J. P. A. Bernhardt, 'Compulsory Dispute Settlement in the Law of the Sea Negotiations: A Reassessment', *Virginia Journal of International Law*, 19 (1978), 69; J. Charney, 'Entry into Force of the 1982 UNCLOS',

Virginia Journal of International Law, 35 (1995), 381; G. Lehoux, 'La Troisième Conférence sur le droit de la mer et le règlement obligatoire des différends', *Canadian Yearbook of International Law*, 18 (1980), 31; S. Rosenne and A. Soons (eds.), *UN Convention on the Law of the Sea 1982: A Commentary*, v (Dordrecht: Martinus Nijhoff, 1989); P. W. Birnie, 'Dispute Settlement Procedures in the 1982 UNCLOS', in W. E. Butler (ed.), *The Law of the Sea and International Shipping: Anglo-Soviet Post UNCLOS Perspectives* (New York: Oceana, 1985), 39; M. P. Gaertner, 'The Dispute Settlement Provisions of the Convention on the Law of the Sea: Critique and Alternatives to the ITLOS', *San Diego Law Review*, 19 (1982), 577; G. Jaenicke, 'Dispute Settlement under the Convention on the Law of the Sea', *Zeitschrift für ausländisches öffentliches Recht und Völkerrecht*, 43 (1983), 813; A. L. de Mestral, 'Compulsory Dispute Settlement in the 3rd UNCLOS: A Canadian Perspective', in T. Burgenthal (ed.), *Contemporary Issues in International Law: Essays in Honor of Louis B. Sohn* (Kehl: N. P. Engel, 1984), 169; E. D. Brown, 'Dispute Settlement and the Law of the Sea: The UN Convention Regime', *Marine Policy*, 21 (1997), 17; C. Chinkin, 'Dispute Resolution and the Law of the Sea: Regional Problems and Prospects', in J. Crawford and D. Rothwell (eds.), *The Law of the Sea in the Asian Pacific Region* (Dordrecht: Martinus Nijhoff, 1995), 237; T. Treves, 'The Law of the Sea Tribunal: Its Status and Scope of Jurisdiction after November 16, 1994', *Zeitschrift für ausländisches öffentliches Recht und Völkerrecht*, 55 (1995), 421.

21. Adede, *The System for Settlement of Disputes*, 242 ff.; A. O. Adede, 'Settlement of Disputes Arising under the Law of the Sea Convention', *American Journal of International Law*, 69 (1975), 798; L. Sohn, 'Settlement of Law of the Sea Disputes', *International Journal of Marine and Coastal Law*, 10 (1995), 205.

22. Adede, *The System for Settlement of Disputes*, 247.

23. T. Treves, 'Aspects of the Relationship between the Jurisdiction of the ITLOS and the ICJ', in W. P. Heere (ed.), *Contemporary International Law Issues: Conflicts and Convergence* (Dordrecht: Martinus Nijhoff, 1996), 308. The 1958 Optional Protocol would presumably not apply in lieu of part XV, however, because of Art. 311 (1), under which the 1982 Convention prevails over the 1958 Conventions.

24. Adede, *The System for Settlement of Disputes*, 242 ff.; Sohn, 'Settlement of Law of the Sea Disputes', 205.

25. Annex VI, Art. 2.

26. The exception to this proposition is the allocation of deep seabed disputes to the Seabed Disputes Chamber of ITLOS under part XI of the Convention.

27. Arts. 287 (3) and (5).

28. As of Nov. 1999 the following states had made declarations accepting compulsory jurisdiction as follows: Argentina (ITLOS/special arbitration); Austria (ITLOS/special arbitration/ICJ); Cape Verde (ITLOS/ICJ); Chile (ITLOS/special arbitration); Croatia (ITLOS/ICJ); Egypt (arbitration); Finland (ICJ and ITLOS); Germany (ITLOS/special arbitration/ICJ); Greece (ITLOS); Italy (ICJ and ITLOS); Netherlands (ICJ); Norway (ICJ); Oman (ITLOS/ICJ); Portugal (ITLOS/ICJ/arbitration/special arbitration); Spain (ICJ); Sweden (ICJ); Tanzania (ITLOS); UK (ICJ); Ukraine (arbitration/special arbitration/

ITLOS); Uruguay (ITLOS). See Sohn, 'Settlement of Law of the Sea Disputes' and Brown, 'Dispute Settlement and the Law of the Sea'. For a fuller analysis of the complexities of Art. 287, see T. Treves, 'Aspects of the Relationship between the Jurisdiction of the ITLOS and the ICJ', in Heere (ed.), *Contemporary International Law Issues*, 305.

29. Arts. 297 (2); 297 (3); 298 (1) (b).

30. Art. 298 (1) (a).

31. Deep seabed disputes are allocated to the Seabed Disputes Chamber of ITLOS under part XI of the Convention.

32. P. W. Birnie and A. E. Boyle, *International Law and the Environment* (Oxford: Clarendon Press, 1992), ch. 7.

33. Arts. 61–70. It is assumed here that these articles of UNCLOS will apply *mutatis mutandis* to the exercise of sovereign rights within an exclusive fisheries zone.

34. Arts. 55–75, 238–62; W. T. Burke, *The New International Law of Fisheries: UNCLOS 1982 and Beyond* (Oxford: Clarendon Press, 1994), 59–80; B. Kwiatkowska, *The 200 Mile EEZ in the New Law of the Sea* (Dordrecht: Martinus Nijhoff, 1989); D. Attard, *The Exclusive Economic Zone in International Law* (Oxford University Press, 1987); F. Orrego Vicuña, *The Exclusive Economic Zone: Regime and Legal Nature under International Law* (Cambridge University Press, 1989).

35. E. Meltzer, 'Global Overview of Straddling and Highly Migratory Fish Stocks: The Non-sustainable Nature of High Seas Fisheries', *Ocean Development and International Law*, 25 (1994), 255; Burke, *The New International Law of Fisheries*; G. Ulfstein, P. Andersen, and R. Churchill, *The Regulation of Fisheries: Legal, Economic and Social Aspects* (Strasbourg: Council of Europe, 1987).

36. In 1995 Canada and the European Community concluded an 'Agreed Minute on the Conservation and Management of Fish Stocks'; 34 *ILM* 1260, and P. Davies, 'EC–Canada Fisheries Dispute', *International and Comparative Law Quarterly*, 44 (1995), 927. The dispute between Spain and Canada concerning the arrest of the trawler *Estai* on the high seas is currently before the ICJ.

37. E. D. Brown, *The International Law of the Sea*, i (Aldershot: Dartmouth, 1994), 228.

38. See the account of the negotiation of Art. 297 in Rosenne and Soons (eds.), *UN Convention on the Law of the Sea 1982: A Commentary*, v. 85–106.

39. On the basis that it is inequitable for one state to claim rights against another in litigation while refusing to accord the same rights to the other state, see *Diversion of the Waters of the Meuse* (1937), PCIJ Series A/B No. 70, p. 25, on which see B. Cheng, *General Principles of Law as Applied by International Courts and Tribunals* (London: Stevens and Sons, 1953), 142–3.

40. B. Kwiatkowska and A. H. Soons, 'Entitlement to Maritime Areas of Rocks which Cannot Sustain Human Habitation or Economic Life of their Own', *Netherlands Yearbook of International Law*, 21 (1990), 139; E. D. Brown, 'Rockall and the Limits of National Jurisdiction of the UK', *Marine Policy*, 2 (1978), 181; Brown, *The International Law of the Sea*, 150.

41. On the effect of islands in maritime delimitations, see *North Sea Continental Shelf Case*, ICJ Reports (1969), 3, para. 57; *Channel Arbitration* (1978) *Cmnd.* 7438; *Gulf of Maine Case*, ICJ Reports (1984), 246, para. 201; *Dubai–Sharjah Boundary Award* (1981), 91 *ILR* 543; *Guinea–Guinea-Bissau Arbitration* (1985); 25 *ILM* 251, para. 97; *Tunisia–Malta Continental Shelf Case*, ICJ Reports (1982), 18, para. 104; *Jan Mayen Case*, ICJ Reports (1993), 38, para. 80.

42. See further A. E. Boyle, 'UNCLOS, ITLOS and the Settlement of Maritime Boundary Disputes between Taiwan and Japan', in Taiwan Institute of International Law (ed.), *Dispute over Diayou-Senkaku* (Taipei, 1997), 143–62.

43. *The M/V Saiga Case*, ITLOS No. 1 (1997); A. V. Lowe, 'The M/V Saiga: The First Case in the International Tribunal for the Law of the Sea', *International and Comparative Law Quarterly*, 48 (1999), 187.

44. *The M/V Saiga Case*, ITLOS No. 2 (1998).

45. Lowe, 'The M/V Saiga: The First Case'.

46. On the drafting of this article, see Rosenne and Sohn (eds.), *UN Convention on the Law of the Sea 1982: A Commentary*, v. 46–8.

47. Agreement Relating to the Implementation of Part XI of the UNCLOS 1982 (1994); 33 *ILM* 1311; D. H. Anderson, 'Further Efforts to Ensure Universal Participation in the UNCLOS', *International and Comparative Law Quarterly*, 43 (1994), 886; J. Charney, 'Entry into Force of the 1982 UNCLOS', *Virginia Journal of International Law*, 35 (1995), 381.

48. IMO, *MARPOL 1973/78 Consolidated Edition* (1992).

49. Art. 16 of the 1996 Protocol which replaces the 1972 Convention provides for compulsory arbitration, or, if the parties agree, for reference to any of the procedures listed in Art. 287 (1) of UNCLOS; 36 *ILM* 7.

50. See below, s. 5.4.

51. Art. 297 (1).

52. See e.g. 1992 Framework Convention on Climate Change, Art. 14; 1992 Convention on Biological Diversity, Art. 27; 1985 Convention for the Protection of the Ozone Layer, Art. 11.

53. See also A. E. Boyle, 'Dispute Settlement and the Law of the Sea Convention: Problems of Fragmentation and Jurisdiction', *International and Comparative Law Quarterly*, 46 (1997), 37, from which parts of this chapter are drawn.

54. Ibid.

55. Art. 9, Agreement to Promote Compliance with International Conservation and Management Measures by Vessels on the High Seas. The possibility of consensual references under the 1995 Agreement on Straddling and High Migratory Fish Stocks would seem to be implicit in Arts. 27–32 of that Agreement. On the 1996 Protocol to the London Dumping Convention, see n. 49.

56. For details of the negotiation of the Agreement, see 'Structure and Process of the 1993–1995 UN Conference on Straddling Fish Stocks and Highly Migratory Fish Stocks', *FAO Fisheries Circular*, 898 (1995); D. H. Anderson, 'The Straddling Stocks Agreement of 1995: An Initial Assessment', *International and Comparative Law Quarterly*, 45 (1996), 463; D. A. Balton, 'Strengthening the Law of the Sea: The New Agreement on Straddling Fish Stocks and Highly Migratory Fish Stocks', *Ocean Development and International Law*, 27 (1996), 125;

D. Freestone, 'The Effective Conservation and Management of High Seas Living Resources: Towards a New Regime?', *Canterbury Law Review*, 5 (1995), 341; E. Hey, 'Global Fisheries Regulation in the First Half of the 1990s', *International Journal of Marine and Coastal Law*, 11 (1996), 459; D. Freestone and Z. Makuch, 'The New International Environmental Law of Fisheries: The 1995 UN Straddling Stocks Convention', *Yearbook of International Environmental Law*, 7 (1996), 3; P. G. G. Davies and C. Redgwell, 'The International Legal Regulation of Straddling Fish Stocks', *British Yearbook of International Law*, 67 (1996), 199.

57. Art. 4.
58. 'Structure and Process of the 1993–1995 UN Conference', 15.
59. Ibid. 19.
60. Ibid. 15 and 19.
61. T. Treves, 'The Settlement of Disputes According to the Straddling Stocks Agreement of 1995', in A. Boyle and D. Freestone (eds.), *International Law and Sustainable Development: Past Achievements and Future Prospects* (Oxford: Clarendon Press, 1999).
62. Art. 3.
63. See Freestone and Makuch, 'The New International Environmental Law of Fisheries'; Davies and Redgwell, 'The International Legal Regulation of Straddling Fish Stocks'; and on Art. 6, D. Freestone, 'International Fisheries Law since Rio: The Continued Rise of the Precautionary Principle', in Boyle and Freestone (eds.), *International Law and Sustainable Development*.
64. Note, however, that there is no provision for a 'fishing entity' to become a party to the Agreement. Since no treaty can bind a non-party without its consent (Vienna Convention on the Law of Treaties, Arts. 35–7) it must be assumed that 'application' of the Agreement to a fishing entity can only create rights and obligations with the consent of the entity concerned. On the present legal status of Taiwan, see J.-M. Henckaerts (ed.), *The International Legal Status of Taiwan in the New World Order: Legal and Political Considerations* (London: Kluwer Law International, 1996); see also Boyle, 'UNCLOS, ITLOS and the Settlement of Maritime Boundary Disputes'.
65. UNCLOS Arts. 187, 190, 279–87, and annex VI, Art. 20. For a fuller analysis of this issue, see Boyle, 'UNCLOS, ITLOS and the Settlement of Maritime Boundary Disputes' and Boyle, 'Dispute Settlement and the Law of the Sea Convention'.
66. Art. 29.
67. See especially Art. 7 (2). Davies and Redgwell, 'The International Legal Regulation of Straddling Fish Stocks', at 263, regard this article as 'evidence of the priority accorded coastal state interest'. Orrego, Ch. 1 above, makes the same point.
68. See s. 4.4.
69. Balton, 'Strengthening the Law of the Sea'.
70. Ibid., at 143.
71. On the application of this article, see *M/V Saiga No. 2*, ITLOS No. 2 (1998).
72. See 1958 Convention on Fishing and Conservation of the Resources of the High Seas, Arts. 6–8; *Fisheries Jurisdiction Cases*, ICJ Reports (1974), 3 and 175;

1982 UNCLOS, Art. 116 (b), and generally D. Nelson, 'Some Issues with Regard to the Development of the Legal Regime of High Seas Fisheries', in Boyle and Freestone (eds.), *International Law and Sustainable Development*; F. Orrego Vicuña, 'Coastal States' Competences over High Seas Fisheries and the Changing Role of International Law', *Zeitschrift für ausländisches öffentliches Recht und Völkerrecht*, 55 (1995), 520.

4

Recent Global Agreements on High Seas Fisheries: Potential Effects on Fisherman Compliance

GEIR HØNNELAND

1 Introduction

This chapter discusses the extent to which the evolving law of high seas fisheries, here represented by the Fish Stocks Agreement and the FAO Compliance Agreement of 1993, prepares the ground for compliance with future high seas regulations on the part of individual fishermen. Hence, there is an explicit focus on the *target group* of fisheries management, the *fishermen* (meaning in practice the *captains*), or the *vessels* under their charge. One major question is, who has the right to manage fishermen on the high seas? It has long been a firmly established rule of international law that a ship on the high seas is subject to the exclusive jurisdiction of its flag state. However, in the discussions of the United Nations Conference on Straddling Stocks and Highly Migratory Fish Stocks, one of the most controversial issues was the extent to which a fishing vessel should be subject to the enforcement of other states than the flag state when fishing in high seas regions.[1] Another, related, issue is the potential of these agreements to induce compliance with regulations when such are explicitly established for various high seas regions.

The following discussion of compliance in fisheries elaborates briefly on the elements of *research, regulation,* and *compliance control* levels of a fisheries management regime that are believed to contribute to fisherman compliance according to two leading theoretical approaches in social science studies on fisheries management. The discussion then addresses the extent to which the Fish Stocks Agreement and the FAO Compliance Agreement meet the requirements presented by models within the two theoretical perspectives on compliance in fisheries as well as the issues of enforcement and regime linkages between the agreements and other global and regional arrangements.

2 Compliance in fisheries

In one of the major social science works on compliance from recent years, Tyler singles out two basic perspectives on compliance: the *instrumental* and the *normative*.[2] In their fundamental assumptions on human behaviour, these perspectives largely concur with the two traditions that have dominated the social science debate on fisheries management, *the tragedy of the commons* and related models on the one hand, and the theories of *cooperative action* on the other.[3] The instrumental perspective primarily comprises the economic compliance literature, its line of argumentation being that individuals are driven solely by self-interest and that compliance is determined by the certainty and severity of sanctions in the event of violation. Likewise, following the logic of the tragedy of the commons,[4] *coercive measures*—i.e. the use or threat of power—are the only reliable mechanism to implement management regulations.[5]

The normative perspective emphasizes the *morality* and *internalized norms* of individuals. According to this argument, people comply with laws they consider fair, appropriate, or *legitimate*. In the rather 'scattered' cluster of *cooperative action theory* in the social science literature on fisheries management, *legitimacy* is stressed as the main factor that determines compliance. Some of these theories view coercive measures as intrinsic to any compliance system but argue that these must be supplemented by attempts to increase the legitimacy of regulations.[6] Other theorists would emphasize legitimacy as the main factor contributing to compliance, but limit their object of study to smaller compliance systems.[7] The primary compliance mechanism becomes *discursive measures*, communicative efforts to make subjects perceive behavioural prescriptions of a compliance system—or the system itself—as legitimate.

A compliance system normally consists of three subsystems: *rule-making, surveillance*, and *prosecution*.[8] The rule-making system consists of the actors, rules, and processes directed at the regulation of subjects' behaviour, i.e. at the inducement of compliance. The surveillance subsystem embraces the actors, rules, and processes that collect and analyse information regarding violations and compliance. Finally, the prosecution subsystem consists of the actors, rules, and processes governing the responses undertaken to induce compliance in subjects that are revealed as violators by the second subsystem. When eliciting compliance from fishermen in a fisheries system and states in an international regime, one important difference should be observed, namely that the *temporal* aspect applies somewhat differently to the two situations. Whereas states often choose between compliance and non-compliance *at a certain point in time* and thereafter relatively seldom change their major direction of behaviour (i.e. in a specific case), fishermen continuously face repeated choices concerning the same issue area. In an international regime, measures can be taken some time after the introduction of the regime to identify which states have and which have not complied. Responses can be directed towards states that have not complied. Within fisheries management, however, choices concerning compliance are made continuously and decisions probably change frequently from case to case. It is thus more difficult to establish at a certain time who has complied and who has not and thereafter undertake measures towards the latter. Hence, *all three subsystems of compliance are at all times directed towards the total array of targets.*

Concrete efforts can be undertaken within the different subsystems to elicit compliance. The coercive measures prescribed by the instrumental perspective will essentially be found at 'the lower end' of the compliance system, i.e. within the surveillance and, most importantly, within the prosecution subsystems.[9] Theorists would argue that fishermen will comply only if the possible gains to do so outweigh those of violation. This implies that the perceived probability of being detected in violation is sufficiently high and that sanctions are sufficiently severe to render violations unprofitable.[10] The basic coercive measure to be applied to make detection seem probable is *extensive surveillance.*[11] The level of enforcement necessary to induce compliance among fishermen will vary with the specific fisheries, the context of the fisheries, and other compliance mechanisms applied. Surveillance—or compliance control—can be performed both at sea (during the fishing activities) and on shore (when the catch is landed). Furthermore, compliance control can be in the form of *passive* and *active* surveillance. The term *passive compliance control* implies the examination of the information fishermen are obliged to submit about their activities at sea; authorities *passively* receive data from the vessels and examine whether the data give evidence of lawful or unlawful behaviour. The concept of *active compliance control* entails the physical checking by inspectors of this information, either at sea or on shore.

The discursive measures prescribed by the normative perspective include efforts at all levels of the management system to increase the legitimacy of regulations, of the actors that have produced them, and of the procedures through which this was done. Most of the cooperative action theory has focused mainly on the rule-making system, i.e. on how the participation by fishermen in the bodies that formulate the regulations can enhance the legitimacy of regulations, the enacting body, and the applied procedures. Furthermore, a growing interest has been observed in fishermen's attitudes to research institutions and procedures. It is, however, also essential to include the surveillance and prosecution subsystems in our understanding of discursive measures that result from the cooperative action tradition. While limited attention has so far been assigned in this literature to the bodies and procedures of surveillance and prosecution, the underlying logic of the cooperative action tradition would imply that compliance can also be increased by enhancing the legitimacy of the surveillance and prosecution subsystems.

3 Possible compliance-inducing elements of the agreements

The 1992 UN Conference on Environment and Development (UNCED) established a programme of conferences, among them the UN Conference on Straddling and Highly Migratory Fish Stocks. In an effort to develop an international Code of Conduct for Responsible Fisheries, shortly after the UNCED conference the FAO undertook the negotiation of a treaty aimed at countering the tendency of reflagging of vessels.[12] The Agreement to Promote Compliance with International Conservation and Management Measures by Fishing Vessels on the High Seas (FAO Compliance Agreement) was adopted in November 1993. During the negotiations of this Agreement, the initial mandate for deterring reflagging of vessels proved too narrow.[13] As will be further elaborated below, the FAO Compliance Agreement evolved to address more generally the obligations of flag states.

On the basis of the theoretical background outlined above, it follows that compliance can be induced through either *coercive* or *discursive* measures. Hence, a discussion of the possible effects on individual compliance of the evolving law of high seas fisheries should involve two basic questions:

- To what extent does the evolving law of high seas fisheries create favourable conditions for the utilization of coercive measures to elicit compliance in high seas areas?
- To what extent does the evolving law of the high seas fisheries improve the basis for legitimate regulation measures?

To be more specific, one should ask to what degree the provisions of the Fish Stocks Agreement and the FAO Compliance Agreement create conditions for a successful adaptation of coercive and discursive compliance mechanisms, respectively, within research, regulation, and control activities of management regimes of high seas fisheries. Moreover, one should investigate *which* regulations the provisions of the two agreements prescribe compliance with, or, if this is unclear, how the provisions foresee the elaboration of such rules.

For practical purposes, in comparing the two agreements, the two mechanisms employed in my model for compliance in fisheries, i.e. coercive and discursive measures, are treated separately. It should be noted that the issue here is merely the *potential* of utilizing the two mechanisms if the provisions of the mentioned agreements are implemented or lead to the introduction of practical measures. In other words, it is a discussion of the degree to which the two agreements may function as adequate *points of departure* for practical measures aimed at securing compliance with regulations only partly in effect. Moreover, it should once again be emphasized that the issue here is *individual compliance* by fishermen and not compliance by states with the agreements.

3.1 Coercive elements of the agreements

Both the Fish Stocks Agreement and the FAO Compliance Agreement refer to the LOS Convention and Agenda 21, adopted by the UNCED, in their respective preambles. It is the express intention of the Fish Stocks Agreement to contribute to the implementation of the LOS Convention.[14] The FAO Compliance Agreement refers to the fact that under international law, and also reflected in the LOS Convention, all states have the duty to take measures for their respective nationals or to cooperate with other states in taking measures that may be necessary for the conservation of the living resources on the high seas. Furthermore, the FAO Agreement recalls that Agenda 21 appeals to states to take effective action, consistent with international law, to deter reflagging of vessels by their nationals as a means of avoiding compliance with applicable conservation and management rules for fishing activities in high seas areas. The Fish Stocks Agreement aims particularly at addressing the problems in chapter 17, Programme Area C, of Agenda 21, namely that the management of high seas fisheries is inadequate in many areas and that some resources are over-utilized. Problems that are noted are unregulated fishing, over-capitalization, excessive fleet size, vessel reflagging to escape controls, insufficiently selective gear, unreliable databases, and lack of sufficient cooperation between states.

Both agreements take as their point of departure the insufficient regulation of measures, and the poorly specified responsibility on the part of states to introduce these, in high seas areas. Both agreements also look to the well-established principle of *flag state responsibility* to modify this situation. This means that all states must ensure that fishing vessels flying their respective flags do not engage in activity that undermines the effectiveness of international conservation and management measures (FAO Compliance Agreement, Article 3 (1) (a)) or jeopardize the measures of subregional and regional management bodies (see below) (Fish Stocks Agreement, Article 18 (1)). Both agreements prescribe that only vessels authorized to fish on the high seas by the flag state have the right to do so (FAO Compliance Agreement, Article 3 (2); Fish Stocks Agreement,

Article 18 (3) (b) (ii)). Furthermore, the agreements prescribe the establishment of national records of vessels that are granted such an authorization (FAO Compliance Agreement, Article 4; Fish Stocks Agreement, Article 18 (3) (c)). It should be observed that the two agreements not only repeat the existing principle of flag state authority as given in the LOS Convention, but they also further develop the responsibility of the flag state. This will be elaborated below.

The measures mentioned so far are mainly associated with the *rule-making system* of a compliance system. According to the instrumental perspective on compliance, the rule-making subsystem only provides the basis for the existence of a compliance system specifying which rules the subjects of the compliance system are supposed to comply with. Hence, in itself, the rule-making system cannot be said to have any power in eliciting compliance. In its elaboration of a *surveillance* and *prosecution subsystem*, the FAO Compliance Agreement mentions the obligation of the flag state to introduce a system of *passive control*; this obligation requires that a state ensure that all fishing vessels entitled to fly its flag shall provide that state with necessary information on the vessel's operations, including information on fishing areas and catches (FAO Compliance Agreement, Article 7). Furthermore, the FAO Compliance Agreement establishes the responsibility of the flag state to exercise *active control*— followed by sanctions in the event of violation—over its own vessels by requiring that a state take enforcement measures towards vessels flying its flag and introduce sanctions sufficiently grave to be effective in securing compliance with the requirements of the Agreement. It is further specified that sanctions shall include refusal, suspension, or withdrawal of the authorization to fish on the high seas in cases of serious violations (FAO Compliance Agreement, Article 8).

Whereas the FAO Compliance Agreement leaves the responsibility for enforcement and compliance control with the flag state, the Fish Stocks Agreement introduces interstate bodies of regulation, which is fundamentally a new step in the evolving law of high seas fisheries. Moreover, the Fish Stocks Agreement provides for a much more elaborate list of enforcement and compliance control measures. A main principle of the Agreement is that coastal states and states fishing on the high seas shall pursue cooperative management measures pertaining to these fisheries, which in turn enhances the possibility of effective enforcement of regulations. More specifically, it obliges states concerned to cooperate in the establishment of *subregional or regional fisheries management organizations or arrangements*, taking into account the characteristics of the high seas area in question to ensure effective management of the stocks (Fish Stocks Agreement, Article 8 (5)). Only states that are members of such organizations or participants in such arrangements (or that agree to apply the measures established by such) shall have access to the fishery resources to which those measures apply (Fish Stocks Agreement, Article 8 (4)).

The Fish Stocks Agreement also includes provisions for passive control measures that demand that vessels fishing in high seas areas supply their respective flag states with 'timely reporting of vessel position, catch of target and non-target species, fishing effort and other relevant fisheries data in accordance with subregional, regional and global standards for collection of such data' (Fish Stocks Agreement, Article 18 (3) (e)). Furthermore, the Agreement introduces the requirement of states to conduct *active control* towards vessels flying their own flag. Flag states must comply with 'requirements for verifying the catch of target and non-target species through such means as observer programmes, inspection schemes, unloading reports, supervision of transshipment and monitoring of landed catches and marked statistics' (Fish Stocks Agreement, Article 18 (3) (f)). Further requirements include

monitoring, control and surveillance of such vessels, their fishing operations and related activities by, *inter alia*:

(i) the implementation of national inspection schemes and subregional and regional schemes for cooperation in enforcement pursuant to Articles 21 and 22, including requirements for such vessels to permit access by duly authorized inspectors from other States;

(ii) the implementation of national observer programmes and subregional and regional observer programmes in which the flag State is a participant, including requirements for such vessels to permit access by observers from other States to carry out the functions agreed under the programmes; and

(iii) the development and implementation of vessel monitoring systems, including, as appropriate, satellite transmitter systems, in accordance with any national programmes and those which have been subregionally, regionally or globally agreed among the States concerned. (Fish Stocks Agreement, Article 18 (3) (g))

In Articles 19–21, provisions are laid down that specify how enforcement shall be conducted by flag states as well as by inspecting non-flag states in the subregional and regional organizations or arrangements. Basic procedures for boarding and inspection at sea are presented in Article 22 and procedures for boarding and inspection in ports in Article 23. Regarding international principles for fishing on the high sea, the Fish Stocks Agreement is truly innovative; as was mentioned at the beginning of this chapter, the Agreement was one of the most controversial issues during the negotiations. In the 'Enforcement of High Seas Fisheries' section of the 'Guide to the Issues', which was elaborated by the conference in 1993, primary emphasis was placed on strengthening flag state responsibility.[15]

However, two different groups of coastal states[16] submitted working papers on the issue, proposing the right of any party to agree to board and inspect a vessel flying the flag of any other party. In the Chairman's Negotiation Text, produced later in 1993, the question of high seas enforcement by non-flag states was dealt with in a section relating to regional arrangements for compliance and enforcement that implied that states could agree to allow for such measures.[17]

At the fourth session of the conference in August 1994, the revised version of the Negotiation Text (prepared in March 1994) was subjected to intensive discussions partly prompted by the recent adoption by Canada of an amendment to its Coastal Fisheries Protection Act. The amendment allowed Canadian authorities to inspect any vessel on the high seas that was covered by the regulations of the Northwest Atlantic Fisheries Organization and to arrest the vessel if a violation was disclosed. At the end of the session, the Chairman reformulated the Revised Negotiation Text into a Draft Agreement that allowed for boarding and inspection (but not detention or arrest) by non-flag states.

During the pursuant informal discussions, it was proposed by the Norwegian delegation that, upon detection by an inspecting non-flag state of a violation, the inspecting state shall immediately notify the flag state and seek its views about the incident.[18] If, according to this proposal, a flag state considers that its vessel has been arrested without that flag state's consent, it may call for immediate release of the vessel and invoke procedures for the settlement of disputes. On the other hand, if no such objection is made, the flag state's consent may be assumed. Moreover, the proposal envisioned that such enforcement measures could be taken against a vessel of any state that would become party to the Agreement, whether or not that state was a participant in the regional organization or arrangement in question. Upon further discussion, the Chairman produced a revised version of the Draft Agreement at the end of the fifth session in 1995. For the first time, a detailed article on enforcement on the high seas was included.[19] In contrast to previous drafts, this Draft Agreement set out substantive provisions on the actual contents of enforcement measures by laying down the global minimum standard to be applied irrespective of the particular standards of the region concerned.[20]

Hence, both the FAO Compliance Agreement and the Fish Stocks Agreement lay the ground for the elaboration of management regulations and procedures that contain a substantive coercive element. Both emphasize the responsibility of flag states to take certain measures in this respect. The Fish Stocks Agreement additionally obliges states to cooperate in the establishment of subregional and regional organizations or arrangements to manage high seas fisheries. Moreover, both agreements impose the obligation on flag states to conduct compliance control of their own vessels and to sanction them in the event of detected violation (of either flag state law or regulations elaborated by the subregional or regional bodies). Enforcement and compliance control measures are, however, more explicitly and elaborately stated in the Fish Stocks Agreement than in the FAO Compliance Agreement. In cases where interstate management bodies have been set up, the former also accords a compliance control responsibility with these. The coercive element of high seas fisheries management is further emphasized by measures of international cooperation, including the exchange of information on high seas fisheries (FAO Compliance Agreement, Articles 5–6; Fish Stocks Agreement, Article 20), a factor that increases the 'extensiveness' of surveillance in that violations are reported among states.

In sum, the agreements contribute to strengthening the coercive elements of international law on high seas that are related to all three subsystems of a compliance system: rule-making, surveillance, and prosecution.[21] According to the instrumental perspective of compliance, the success of a compliance system in eliciting compliance will in the end depend on whether detected violations are sanctioned severely enough to make compliant behaviour the most cost-efficient choice of behaviour for subjects. Since we are here talking about such compliance systems a priori, it remains an open question whether high seas management systems will in fact introduce sufficiently extensive surveillance and severe sanctions. The main point in this context is that the evolving law of high seas fisheries provides the legal foundation for the introduction of such coercive measures by national or regional authorities in concrete management settings.

3.2 Discursive elements of the agreements

Discursive or legitimacy-enhancing elements are more visible in the Fish Stocks Agreement than in the FAO Compliance Agreement.[22] For example, the Fish Stocks Agreement explicitly states in Article 5 (b) that management decisions shall be made on the best scientific evidence available. According to the cooperative action perspective, this provision enhances the legitimacy of regulations because decisions made on the basis of sound scientific advice are believed to be more legitimate than arbitrary regulations. The process of collection and provision of scientific information is further outlined in Article 14, which, *inter alia*, calls for scientific cooperation between states in the development of analytical techniques and stock assessment methodologies (Fish Stocks Agreement, Article 14 (2)).

Article 8 of the Fish Stocks Agreement is perhaps more deliberately intended to function as a legitimacy-enhancing measure, whereby all involved states shall be granted rights to participate in management bodies. In the cooperative action perspective on fisheries management, participation in the elaboration of regulations is a basic precondition for legitimate management solutions that in turn are assumed to contribute to increased compliance with established regulations. Although it is not specified in Article 8 that representatives of fishermen themselves shall participate in the process, state participation is probably better than no participation at all, even though this remains to be tested empirically. Furthermore, *transparency* in the management process is also, according to the cooperative action perspective, supposed to increase the legitimacy of rules. This principle is laid out as follows in the Fish Stocks Agreement:

1. States shall provide for transparency in the decision-making process and other activities of subregional and regional fisheries management organizations and arrangements.
2. Representatives from other intergovernmental organizations and representatives from non-governmental organizations concerned with straddling stocks and highly migratory stocks shall be afforded the opportunity to take part in meetings of subregional and regional fisheries management organizations and arrangements as observers or otherwise, as appropriate, in accordance with the procedures of the organization or arrangement concerned. Such procedures shall not be unduly restrictive in this respect. Such intergovernmental organizations and non-governmental organizations shall have timely access to the records and reports of such organizations and arrangements, subject to the procedural rules on access to them. (Fish Stocks Agreement, Article 12)

Surveillance probably increases the legitimacy of the Fish Stocks Agreement through the specific provisions for the performance of boarding and inspection aimed at *securing the interests of the fishermen* (Article 22):

1. The inspecting State shall ensure that its duly authorized inspectors:
(a) present credentials to the master of the vessel and produce a copy of the text of the relevant conservation and management measures or rules and regulations in force in the high seas area in question pursuant to those measures;
(b) initiate notice to the flag State at the time of the boarding and inspection;
(c) do not interfere with the master's ability to communicate with the authorities of the flag State during the boarding and inspection;
(d) provide a copy of a report on the boarding and inspection to the master and to the authorities of the flag State, noting therein any objection or statement which the master wishes to have included in the report;
(e) promptly leave the vessel following completion of the inspection if they find no evidence of a serious violation; and
(f) avoid the use of force except when and to the degree necessary to ensure the safety of the inspectors and where the inspectors are obstructed in the

execution of their duties. The degree of force used shall not exceed that reasonably required in the circumstances. (Fish Stocks Agreement, Article 22, para. 1)

In line with the normative perspective on compliance, both agreements can be said to include provisions that are believed to be perceived as legitimate by fishermen and in turn lead to increased compliance with regulations. However, such provisions are found to a larger extent in the Fish Stocks Agreement than in the FAO Compliance Agreement. The participation of all involved states and the transparency of the management process are the most prominent among these provisions; this reflects the traditional prescriptions of the cooperative action perspective on fisheries management.

The most important coercive and discursive features of the two agreements are summarized in Table 4.1.[23] Again, it must be remembered that the focus is on the *potential* of the agreements. Just as it is impossible to state in advance that the coercive elements will be sufficiently severe to secure compliance (see above), one cannot a priori declare that particular measures will be perceived as legitimate by user groups. The logic of the theoretical perspectives outlined above, however, gives an indication of the expected consequences of an implementation of the agreements.

4 Enforcement and regime linkages

The Fish Stocks Agreement is explicit in its aspiration to contribute to the implementation of the LOS Convention as well as to function as a basis for the introduction of regional and subregional arrangements in high seas areas. A brief discussion will be given here of the linkages between the Fish Stocks Agreement and the LOS Convention This will be followed by a discussion of the linkages between the Fish Stocks Agreement and the FAO Compliance Agreement on the one hand, and the two regional management arrangements which have actually materialized on the other, namely the Bering Sea Doughnut Hole Convention and the Canadian–EC Agreed Minute concerning fishery in the Grand Banks. Consistent with the rest of the chapter, the focus is on provisions that are most relevant in an enforcement and compliance context.

4.1 *The Fish Stocks Agreement and the LOS Convention*

As pointed out by Hayashi,[24] the Fish Stocks Agreement constitutes an important contribution to the LOS Convention in three particular respects. First, it facilitates the implementation of the provisions of the

Table 4.1 Main coercive and discursive/legitimacy-enhancing elements of the FAO Compliance Agreement (1993) and the Fish Stocks Agreement (1995), categorized into the main subsystems of a compliance system

Compliance subsystem	The FAO Compliance Agreement (1993)	The Fish Stocks Agreement (1995)	Type of compliance mechanism
Rule-making	• authorization of vessels by flag states (Art. 3) • national vessel records (Art. 4)	• authorization of vessels by flag states (Art. 18)	• coercive/discursive
		• national vessel records (Art. 18)	• coercive/discursive
		• the development of management regulations and procedures in subregional and regional organizations or arrangements (Art. 8)	• coercive/discursive
		• regulations to be based on best scientific data available (Art. 5)	• discursive
		• participation of all involved states in the management process (Art. 8)	• discursive
		• transparency of management process (Art. 12)	• discursive

Surveillance	• passive control: obligation of vessels to report to flag states (Art. 7), as well as exchange of such information between states (Arts. 5–6) • active control: obligation of flag states to conduct compliance control (Art. 8)	• passive control: obligation of vessels to report to flag states (Art. 18), as well as exchange of such information between states (Art. 20) • active control: obligation of flag states and possibility of non-flag states to conduct compliance control (Arts. 18–23) • provisions to secure the interests of the fishermen during boarding and inspection (Art. 22)	• coercive/discursive • coercive/discursive • discursive
Prosecution	• prosecution and sanctions by flag states (Art. 8)	• prosecution and sanctions by flag states (Arts. 18–23)	• coercive/discursive

Convention[25] by specifying the ways in which the provisions of the latter
can be implemented. Secondly, it strengthens the regime of the LOS Convention, for instance concerning the issue of collection and sharing of
information and data from high seas fishing. Thirdly, the Fish Stocks
Agreement further develops several framework rules of the Convention.
The latter point appears most important in an enforcement context.

The Fish Stocks Agreement further elaborates on the duties of the flag
state established by the LOS Convention. Most notably, the Agreement
makes the 'effective control' principle of the LOS Convention more stringent inasmuch as it permits states to authorize the use of their flag vessels
to fish on the high seas only where they are able to exercise effective
control over these vessels. The Agreement provides a series of concrete
measures in this respect, including the following: (1) control by means of
fishing licences; (2) authorizations in accordance with regionally or globally agreed procedures; (3) establishment of regulations on the flag state's
high seas fishing activities; (4) establishment of a national record of authorized fishing vessels; (5) requirements for recording and timely reporting
of vessel position, catch of target and non-target species, fishing efforts,
and other relevant fisheries data; (6) monitoring, control, and surveillance
of vessels, their operations, and market statistics; (7) regulation of activities to ensure compliance with regional or global measures.[26]

The Fish Stocks Agreement also elaborates on the principles in the LOS
Convention on enforcement against foreign vessels on the high seas and
port state jurisdiction. Under established law and the LOS Convention,
vessels on the high seas are in principle subject to the exclusive jurisdiction of their flag states. In allowing for inspection by non-flag states, the
Fish Stocks Agreement establishes an important exception to the flag state
principle. The LOS Convention introduced the principle of 'port state
enforcement', implying that a port state is empowered to undertake investigations of a foreign vessel that is voluntarily within a port or at an
offshore terminal of that state. Although this provision relates only to
international marine pollution rules and standards and not to fisheries,
the Fish Stocks Agreement does include a similar concept of port state
enforcement of foreign vessels. Hence, when a vessel that has been fishing
on the high seas is voluntarily in the port or offshore terminal of another
state, the port state is permitted to inspect documents, fishing gear, and
catch on board the vessel.[27]

4.2 Influence by established regional arrangements

The FAO Compliance Agreement and the Fish Stocks Agreement were not
influenced solely 'from above', namely by the instructions of the UNCED

and aspirations to contribute to the implementation of the LOS Convention. The negotiation of the two treaties partly overlapped in time with the negotiation and final agreement on the establishment of two regional arrangements for high seas areas, the Bering Sea Doughnut Hole Convention[28] and the Canadian–EC Agreed Minute[29] concerning fishery in the Grand Banks.[30] The enforcement measures agreed upon in these two regional arrangements clearly influenced the negotiations of the two global agreements.

Both regional arrangements are most innovative precisely in the field of enforcement. Most importantly, both arrangements allow for boarding and inspection of vessels on the high seas by non-flag states, a provision later found to be a globally applicable measure in the Fish Stocks Agreements. According to Article 11, paragraph 5 of the Bering Sea Doughnut Hole Convention, each vessel fishing for pollock in the Doughnut Hole must, upon request, accept an observer from another party on board. If a violation is detected, the boarding inspector may remain on board the fishing vessel either until officials of the flag state arrive on the scene or until the vessel is ordered out of the Doughnut Hole.[31] Interestingly, these provisions became the model for Articles 21 and 22 of the Fish Stocks Agreement.[32] It should also be observed that there are substantial linkages between the Bering Sea Doughnut Hole Convention and the two global agreements as far as the further elaboration of flag state responsibilities is concerned.[33]

The Agreed Minute between Canada and the EC increases the range of permitted non-flag state enforcement actions in the NAFO area. A pilot project was established to provide for the presence of a trained observer on all fishing vessels in the NAFO Regulatory Area. According to the agreement, 35 per cent of such fishing vessels had to be equipped with satellite tracking systems, the data from which were to be made available to all NAFO members.[34] Moreover, any state having ten or more vessels fishing in the NAFO Regulatory Area is obliged to provide an inspection vessel for NAFO purposes. If a NAFO inspector detects a 'serious violation',[35] the flag state of the vessel must itself inspect the vessel within forty-eight hours. In the meantime, the NAFO inspector has the right to remain on board to secure evidence. Moreover, vessels that have been fishing in the NAFO Regulatory Area were subject to a dockside inspection at each port of call. These same provisions are found in the Fish Stocks Agreement. As pointed out by Davies and Redgwell: 'Indeed, the provisions of NAFO, the Agreed Minute, and the negotiated settlement of the straddling stocks conflict in the Central Bering Sea were very much present in the minds of the negotiators of the 1995 Agreement.'[36]

5 Conclusion

Major advancements have been made during the last decade concerning enforcement of the international law of the high seas. General provisions in the LOS Convention have been strengthened and further developed by the two global instruments of the FAO Compliance Agreement and the Fish Stocks Agreement. In particular, new ground has been broken concerning enforcement by non-flag states on the high seas. The introduction of this principle in the Fish Stocks Agreement is in turn assumed to have been influenced by similar provisions being introduced more or less simultaneously in actual regional management arrangements, most notably provisions of the Bering Sea Doughnut Hole Convention and the Canada–EC Agreed Minute concerning fishing in the Grand Banks.

This chapter has investigated the degree to which the FAO Compliance Agreement and the Fish Stocks Agreement contain provisions that, if implemented in concrete management settings, are likely to contribute to compliance on the part of individual fishermen. The two leading perspectives within social science studies of fisheries management, *the tragedy of the commons* and *cooperative action theory*, which correspond to the more general *instrumental* and *normative* perspectives on compliance, have been applied to categorize the provisions as either *coercive* or *discursive* compliance mechanisms. There are striking similarities as well as dissimilarities between the two agreements. While both contain similar provisions for mainly coercive elements such as flag state responsibility for authorization, record-keeping, control, and prosecution, the former is much more elaborate and detailed. A more distinct difference is the introduction of enforcement measures by non-flag states in subregional and regional arrangements and the emphasis on legitimacy-enhancing elements such as participation of concerned parties and transparency of the management process of the Fish Stocks Agreement. These are absent in the FAO Compliance Agreement. Whether the various provisions will have influence on the behaviour of individual fishermen is, however, an empirical question to which the answers remain to be seen.

Notes

1. M. Hayashi, 'Enforcement by Non-flag States on the High Seas under the 1995 Agreement on Straddling Stocks and Highly Migratory Fish Stocks', *Georgetown International Environmental Law Review*, 9 (1996), 1.
2. T. R. Tyler, *Why People Obey the Law* (New Haven: Yale University Press, 1990).
3. See G. Hønneland, 'The Interaction of Research Programmes in Social Science Studies of the Commons', *Acta Sociologica*, 42 (1999), 193, for an overview of this literature.
4. G. Hardin, 'The Tragedy of the Commons', *Science*, 162 (1968), 1243.
5. *Compliance mechanisms* should be understood as the instruments at hand for public authorities to encourage compliance with behavioural prescriptions in a compliance system.
6. This is especially true for the so-called *co-management* literature, which normally views state regulation of a fisheries as a necessity but claims that legitimacy can be enhanced if fishermen have a say in the management process; see S. Jentoft and B. McCay, 'User Participation in Fisheries Management', *Marine Policy*, 19 (1995), 227; B. McCay and S. Jentoft, 'From the Bottom up: Participatory Issues in Fisheries Management', *Society and Natural Resources*, 9 (1996), 237; or S. Sen and J. R. Nielsen, 'Fisheries Co-management: A Comparative Analysis', *Marine Policy*, 20 (1996), 405 for recent overviews of this literature.
7. See e.g. J. M. Baland and J. P. Platteau, *Halting Degradation of Natural Resources: Is There a Role for Rural Communities?* (Oxford: Clarendon Press, 1996); D. W. Bromley (general ed.), *Making the Commons Work: Theory, Practice, and Policy* (San Francisco: Institute for Contemporary Studies Press, 1992); B. McCay and J. M. Acheson (eds.), *The Question of the Commons: The Culture and Ecology of Communal Resources* (Tucson: University of Arizona Press, 1987); E. Ostrom, *Governing the Commons: The Evolution of Institutions for Collective Action* (Cambridge University Press, 1990); E. Ostrom, R. Gardner, and J. Walker, *Rules, Games, and Common-Pool Resources* (Ann Arbor: University of Michigan Press, 1994); or E. Pinkerton (ed.), *Co-operative Management of Local Fisheries: New Directions for Improved Management and Community Development* (Vancouver: University of British Columbia Press, 1989).
8. These basically correspond to what R. B. Mitchell, *Intentional Oil Pollution at Sea: Environmental Policy and Treaty Compliance* (Cambridge, Mass.: MIT Press, 1994), refers to as primary rule system, compliance information system, and non-compliance response system.
9. The existence of a rule-making system is, however, taken for granted. Naturally, the terms *compliance* and *non-compliance* only bear meaning in relation to some existing set of rules.
10. Elaborations of equilibrium levels of enforcement necessary to deter fishermen from violating are found in the economic literature on compliance in fisheries, J. G. Sutinen, A. Rieser, and J. R. Gauvin, 'Measuring and Explaining Non-compliance in Federally Managed Fisheries', *Ocean Development and International Law*, 21 (1990), 335.

11. The model also includes certain preconditions concerning the *competence* and *willingness* of inspectors to reveal violations, G. Hønneland, 'A Model of Compliance in Fisheries: Theoretical Foundations and Practical Application', *Ocean and Coastal Management*, 42 (1999). This will not be pursued further in this context.

12. D. A. Balton, 'Strengthening the Law of the Sea: The New Agreement on Straddling Fish Stocks and Highly Migratory Fish Stocks', *Ocean Development and International Law*, 27 (1996), 121.

13. Ibid.

14. Cf. its full title: Agreement for the Implementation of the Provisions of the United Nations Convention on the Law of the Sea of 10 December 1982 relating to the Conservation and Management of Straddling Fish Stocks and Highly Migratory Fish Stocks.

15. Hayashi, 'Enforcement by Non-flag States'.

16. One group of South American Pacific coastal states (including Chile, Colombia, Ecuador, and Peru) and another one consisting of Argentina, Canada, Chile, Iceland, and New Zealand; ibid.

17. Ibid.

18. Ibid.

19. Ibid.

20. Cf. Balton, 'Strengthening the Law of the Sea' or Hayashi, 'Enforcement by Non-flag States' for more detailed information on the negotiation of the enforcement provisions of the agreement.

21. Vukas and Vidas, Ch. 2 above.

22. The FAO Compliance Agreement mainly contains provisions of procedures for flag state enforcement of regulations. This is not to say that it does not lay the ground for legitimate management solutions; the existence of a fair and well-functioning coercively based enforcement system is also believed to enhance legitimacy and compliance. The difference between the two agreements in this respect is, however, that the Fish Stocks Agreement—more explicitly than the FAO Compliance Agreement—takes into account some of the lessons of the normative perspective on compliance.

23. It should be noted that most coercive elements can also be characterized as discursive, or legitimacy-enhancing. The legitimacy of a management system increases when it contains certain coercive elements where the objective is a more fair distribution of costs and benefits. This is not questioned by *cooperative action* theory although it has been directed more towards pointing at such efforts as participation and influence by user groups in the management process.

24. M. Hayashi, 'The 1995 Agreement on the Conservation and Management of Straddling and Highly Migratory Fish Stocks: Significance for the Law of the Sea Convention', *Ocean and Coastal Management*, 29 (1995), 51.

25. The aspiration of the Fish Stocks Agreement to further the implementation of the LOS Convention should be obvious from its very title. The title was proposed on the basis of another 'implementing agreement' of the LOS Convention, namely the agreement regarding the implementation of part XI of the

Convention. The Chairman of the Fish Stocks Conference, Satya Nandan, had also played a prominent role here; cf. Hayashi, 'The 1995 Agreement'.

26. Fish Stocks Agreement, Art. 18 (3).
27. Ibid., Art. 23 (3).
28. Convention on the Conservation and Management of Pollock Resources in the Central Bering Sea (1994); 34 *ILM* 67.
29. Canada–European Community: Agreed Minute on the Conservation and Management of Fish Stocks (1995); 34 *ILM* 1260.
30. For a broader analysis of the Doughnut Hole Convention, see Balton, Ch. 5 below, or W. V. Dunlap, 'The Donut Hole Agreement', *International Journal of Marine and Coastal Law*, 10 (1995), 114. For a discussion of the Agreed Minute, see Joyner, Ch. 7 below, or P. G. G. Davies and C. Redgwell, 'The International Legal Regulation of Straddling Fish Stocks', *British Yearbook of International Law*, 67 (1997), 199.
31. Balton, Ch. 5 below.
32. Ibid.
33. Ibid. Admittedly, the chronology is somewhat uncertain here as the negotiations of the agreements overlapped in time.
34. Davies and Redgwell, 'The International Legal Regulation of Straddling Fish Stocks'.
35. As a 'serious violation' count a refusal to cooperate with a NAFO inspector, net size violations, interference with on-board satellite equipment, and the misreporting of catches; ibid.
36. Ibid. 257; the same point is made by Joyner, Ch. 7 below.

PART II

*Regional Approaches to Straddling
Stocks Management*

5

The Bering Sea Doughnut Hole Convention: Regional Solution, Global Implications

DAVID A. BALTON

In the course of the state visit by the President of Russia to the United States of America, the sides noted with concern that, in spite of four international conferences held to develop an international regime for the conservation and management of living marine resources of the central Bering Sea, the pollock resource in that region has suffered a precipitous decline, which could upset the balance of the Bering Sea ecosystem as a whole.[1]

1 Introduction

In 1728, when Vitus Bering first explored the sea that was to bear his name, he could scarcely have anticipated that, more than 250 years later, the leaders of the two most powerful nations on earth would be concerning themselves with the fate of a small, white fish that at that time thrived in the waters of that region. But by 1992, the tides of history, geography, law, economics, and technology had conspired to bring 'the pollock resource' to the attention of Presidents Bush and Yeltsin. Alerted to the impending depletion of the pollock stock, the two world leaders called for an immediate prohibition on pollock fishing in the central part of the Bering Sea—a high seas area known as the Doughnut Hole.

The nations whose huge factory trawl vessels were fishing for pollock in the Doughnut Hole at that time—Japan, the People's Republic of China, Poland, and the Republic of Korea—strongly resisted this call for an immediate shutdown of the fishery. The pollock fishery of the Bering Sea was then the largest single-species commercial fishery the world had ever known. Yet, the shutdown nevertheless became a reality within six months of the Bush–Yeltsin summit. The pollock resource in the Bering Sea had collapsed from overfishing.

By the end of 1992, the factory trawl vessels operating in the Doughnut Hole simply could no longer harvest a profitable quantity of pollock. Their governments agreed to bar them from fishing for pollock in the Doughnut Hole during 1993 and 1994. The moratorium on pollock fishing in the Doughnut Hole remains in effect as of this writing, and fishing will not resume unless the pollock resource stages a significant recovery.

In hopes of such a recovery, for the pollock and for their respective fishing industries, the six nations involved (the United States, the Russian Federation, Japan, the People's Republic of China, the Republic of Korea, and Poland) have brought into force a forward-looking treaty to manage the pollock fishery of the Doughnut Hole should it ever resume. This chapter reviews the background and elements of that treaty, the 1994 Convention on the Conservation and Management of Pollock Resources in the Central Bering Sea ('the Convention'). The relationship of the Convention to other developments in the international law of fisheries, particularly the Fish Stocks Agreement, will also be analysed.

2 Origins of the Convention

2.1 Geography of the Bering Sea

The Bering Sea is an arm of the North Pacific Ocean that is bounded by the Alaskan mainland to the east, by the coast of the Russian Federation (including the Kamchatka Peninsula) to the west, by the Aleutian Islands to the south, and by the Seward and Chuckchi Peninsulas (and the Bering Strait which runs between them) to the north.[2] Lying between 52 and 66 degrees north latitude and between 162 east and 157 degrees west longitude, the Bering Sea covers slightly more than 875,000 square miles. The Bering Sea has extremely wide and smooth continental shelves off both coasts. However, the continental margins at the edge of the shelves fall off steeply; this 'shelf break' is also indented by seven of the largest submarine canyons in the world.

Prior to 1977, the United States claimed a territorial sea of only 3 nautical miles, while the Soviet Union claimed a territorial sea of 12 nautical miles. Neither nation claimed jurisdiction over fisheries in any area beyond its territorial sea. This left the vast majority of the Bering Sea as a high seas area, open to fishing by vessels of any nation in an essentially unregulated condition.

Circumstances changed radically and irreversibly for fisheries in the Bering Sea in 1977. Both the United States and the Soviet Union advanced fisheries jurisdiction claims that extended 200 nautical miles from their respective shores. The new political geography of the Bering Sea resulting from these claims left more than 90 per cent of the waters under the fishery jurisdiction of one or the other of these two coastal states. Only a small pocket of approximately 50,000 square miles of high seas remained in the central part of the Bering Sea: the Doughnut Hole, so named

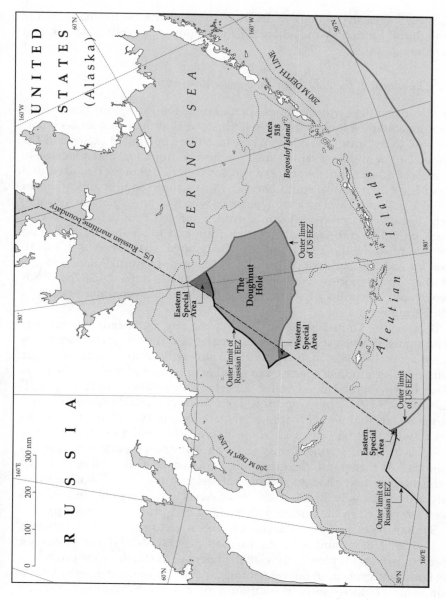

Map 5.1. The Bering Sea

because it appeared on newly drawn maps as a 'hole' surrounded by the 'doughnut' formed by the adjacent fishery zones of the Soviet Union and the United States.[3]

2.2 The advent of the Doughnut Hole pollock fishery

Within these new fishery zones surrounding the Doughnut Hole, other nations could no longer fish at will: instead they had first to seek permission to fish from the relevant coastal state. The United States and the Soviet Union initially granted such permission (for a fee) and allocated to vessels of other nations a share of surplus fishery resources that exceeded what their own vessels could harvest. Most nations sought allocations of Alaska pollock (*Theragra chalcogramma*), which is an extremely versatile fish that is often processed into surimi, a minced product used to produce imitation crab legs, scallops, shrimp, and other imitation seafood commodities. In the 1980s, pollock also gained acceptance as a substitute for cod and haddock, especially as the once-plentiful Atlantic stocks of these two species were becoming depleted. Indeed, as the 1980s progressed, the pollock fishery became the dominant economic activity in the Bering Sea.

Because the United States in 1977 lacked any significant trawler fleet with which to harvest pollock in the Bering Sea, the US government allocated several million metric tons of surplus pollock in its zone, together with other groundfish species, to a number of foreign nations. At the same time, however, the United States undertook a concerted effort to 'Americanize' its fisheries by supporting the construction of new trawlers and other vessels that would fly the US flag. Before the end of the decade, the US trawler fleet had the capacity to harvest the total allowable catch of pollock in the US zone, bringing to an end the allocations to foreign nations.[4] At that point, the economic value of the pollock fishery to the US fishing industry had an approximate retail value of US$2 billion annually. Approximately 20,000 residents of Alaska, Washington, and Oregon were employed in the business of catching and processing this resource.

Similar developments took place in the Soviet fishery zone. Although the Soviet Union (and later the Russian Federation) did not phase out foreign fishing completely, the establishment of the Soviet zone prompted a significant growth in Soviet fishing capacity in the Bering Sea, with a concomitant decrease in the amount of pollock available to foreign vessels.

While the pollock allocations remained plentiful in the US and Soviet zones, vessels from other nations did not see a need to attempt pollock fishing in the Doughnut Hole. The deeper water of the Aleutian Basin in which the Doughnut Hole is located was thought to have insufficient pollock density to support large-scale fishing operations. Moreover, the bottom trawl nets used in the shallower waters above the continental shelves would not work effectively at depths found in the Doughnut Hole.[5] The data available from the early 1980s reveal only negligible pollock harvests in the Doughnut Hole throughout 1982. Indeed, prior to 1980, there were no significant fisheries of any kind conducted in the Doughnut Hole, other than a Japanese salmon gillnet fishery regulated pursuant to a trilateral USA–Japan–Canada treaty.[6]

As foreign trawlers found themselves displaced from the US exclusive economic zone (EEZ) and to a lesser extent from the Soviet zone, they explored the Doughnut Hole to determine whether they could maintain their pollock catch in the relatively small area outside US and Soviet jurisdiction. They found that by using trawl nets suspended in mid-water they could successfully harvest pollock in the Doughnut Hole. The Doughnut Hole pollock fishery grew rapidly, from negligible levels in the early 1980s to more than 1.4 million metric tons in 1989 alone.

During the first part of that period, only vessels from Japan and Korea operated in the Doughnut Hole. Beginning in 1985, Chinese and Polish vessels joined in the Doughnut Hole fishery. The following year, Soviet vessels also began to harvest small amounts of pollock in the Doughnut Hole to supplement their pollock catches in the Soviet zone.[7]

2.3 Collapse of the pollock fishery

The combination of the growing pollock fishery in the Doughnut Hole, the newly 'Americanized' pollock fishery in the US EEZ, and the continuing pollock catches in Soviet waters comprised an enormous fishery. Table 5.1 shows catches of pollock in each of the three areas.[8]

The rapid growth of the Doughnut Hole pollock fishery in the mid-to-late 1980s quickly led to fears of overfishing. The United States and the Soviet Union raised concerns that pollock populations in the Bering Sea were interrelated, that the unregulated pollock fishery in the Doughnut Hole would undermine efforts of the two coastal states to conserve the resource, and that, if left unchecked, the dramatic increases of catch in the Doughnut Hole would ultimately harm the Bering Sea environment as a whole. Japan initially responded that pollock in the Bering Sea represented at least six separate populations and that pollock fishing in the Doughnut Hole would have no effect on the status of stocks in either coastal zone.[9]

In 1988, the United States and the Soviet Union invited scientists from the six nations involved in the fishery to a meeting in Sitka, Alaska, to discuss the state of the pollock resource. According to one account, the meeting concluded that 'available oceanographic and biological data led

Table 5.1 Catches of pollock in the Bering Sea (000 metric tons)

Year	Harvest in US zone (eastern Bering Sea and Aleutian Islands)	Harvest in Soviet zone (western Bering Sea)	Harvest in Doughnut Hole
1980	959	928	18
1981	973	891	0
1982	956	1,019	4
1983	981	971	71
1984	1,098	756	182
1985	1,179	662	363
1986	1,189	867	1,040
1987	1,237	812	1,325
1988	1,228	1,327	1,397
1989	1,230	1,029	1,448
1990	1,347	814	918
1991	1,074	504	293
1992	1,047	620	10

Source: Derived from Meltzer, 'Global Overview of Straddling and Highly Migratory Fish Stocks', 286–7.

scientists to believe that the pollock stocks in the Bering Sea are one complex and should be treated as such for management and conservation purposes'.[10] Another account of the Sitka conference reported that 'the meeting voiced fears that overfishing was taking place, and called for expanded research in the region and a coordinated international program for fishery exploitation. The calls of the scientific community went unheeded.'[11]

Further scientific analysis of the pollock populations produced a growing belief that there are actually three separate pollock stocks in the Bering Sea: one in the western part of the sea, one in the eastern part of the sea, and one in the Aleutian Basin. The Aleutian Basin stock spawns in US waters off Bogoslof Island in the south-eastern part of the Bering Sea and later migrates through other parts of the Aleutian Basin, including the Doughnut Hole and the Russian EEZ. No pollock is thought to spawn in the Doughnut Hole itself.[12]

The record high of 1.4 million metric tons of pollock harvested in the Doughnut Hole in 1989 was extraordinary—and troublesome—in two respects. First, in absolute terms, the Doughnut Hole was witnessing a massive fishery where no fishery had existed just seven years before. Second, in relative terms, the catch of pollock in the Doughnut Hole, which represented less than 20 per cent of the Aleutian Basin and less than 10 per cent of the Bering Sea as a whole, exceeded the catch taken in either the US or Soviet zones and amounted to nearly 40 per cent of the overall Bering Sea pollock harvest.

By 1990, scientific evidence began to mount, indicating that the pollock stock of the Bering Sea was suffering a precipitous decline. By 1992, the stock had completely collapsed. Reported catches of pollock in the Doughnut Hole during the first six months of 1992 were as low as 11,000 metric tons, compared to approximately 173,000 metric tons and 503,000 metric tons during the same period in 1991 and 1990, respectively.

2.4 The international law framework

The period during which the Doughnut Hole pollock fishery arose and then crashed coincided with the beginning of a new era in the international law of the sea in general and in the international law of fisheries in particular. As has been discussed in earlier chapters,[13] the 1982 United Nations Convention on the Law of the Sea ('the LOS Convention') codified the right of coastal states to establish EEZs out to 200 miles from their shores and to exercise plenary authority over fisheries within their EEZs.[14] Beyond the EEZs of all coastal states remained what was left of the high seas. The LOS Convention recognized the traditional right of all states for their vessels to fish on the high seas but made this right subject to several important qualifications.[15]

However, the LOS Convention lacks detailed rules for the conservation of fishery resources. In particular, the LOS Convention gives very little guidance for conserving and managing fish stocks, such as pollock in the Bering Sea, which 'straddle' the 200-mile line that divides EEZs from the adjacent high seas. Instead, Article 63 (2) of the LOS Convention essentially leaves conflicts over straddling stocks to be solved on a region-by-region basis.[16]

The LOS Convention created the legal conditions that led to the Doughnut Hole pollock fishery. The coastal states claimed EEZs out to 200 miles, as was their right under the LOS Convention. The coastal states increased their own capacity to harvest pollock within their respective EEZs and gradually decreased (and, in the case of the United States, ultimately phased out) allocations of pollock to foreign nations, as was their right under the LOS Convention. The foreign nations, in turn, developed a fishery in the Doughnut Hole, the only area of the Bering Sea left open to them under the LOS Convention.

Unfortunately, the creation and rapid expansion of the Doughnut Hole pollock fishery, coupled with continued harvests of pollock in each of the coastal zones, was more than the pollock resource could sustainably bear. It was at this point that the LOS Convention proved insufficient to deal with the situation. Although Article 63 (2) calls upon the coastal states and the states fishing in the Doughnut Hole to 'seek to agree' on measures necessary to conserve the pollock resource, the LOS Convention did not offer any specific guidance on the contours of such agreement or on what would happen if agreement could not be reached.

2.5 Calls for extension of coastal state jurisdiction

To address the Doughnut Hole fishery, calls arose within the United States and the Soviet Union for the extension into the Doughnut Hole of their fisheries jurisdiction, either individually or jointly. The United States had an additional concern as well: growing evidence indicating that fishing vessels operating in the Doughnut Hole regularly crossed into the US EEZ to fish illegally. In January 1988, for example, an aeroplane chartered by the Alaskan Factory Trawlers' Association videotaped seven foreign vessels fishing illegally about 38 miles inside the US EEZ adjacent to the Doughnut Hole. Four of the vessels were positively identified as Japanese.[17] The United States promptly protested to the Japanese Government and demanded an immediate investigation.

US Alaska Senator Ted Stevens soon thereafter called for the United States and the Soviet Union to extend 'bilateral fisheries jurisdiction' over the entire Bering Sea.[18] On 9 March 1988, the US House of Representatives held a hearing on the problem of illegal fishing in the Bering Sea and on efforts to address fishing in the Doughnut Hole. Congressman Young, also from Alaska, proposed that the United States work with the Soviet Union to close the Doughnut Hole to foreign fishing.

On 21 March 1988, the United States Senate unanimously adopted Resolution S.396, introduced by Senator Stevens, expressing the 'sense of the Senate on the need to stop uncontrolled fishing in the international waters of the Bering Sea'. Noting the 'massive increase in the level of fishing activity' in the Doughnut Hole, the Resolution called upon the US Secretary of State to undertake negotiations with the Soviet Union to establish a moratorium on all fishing in the Doughnut Hole and called upon all nations to observe the moratorium pending the negotiation of an agreement for the conservation and management of fishery resources in the Doughnut Hole.

Resolution S.396 stopped short of calling for an outright extension of US fisheries jurisdiction beyond the 200-mile limit in the Bering Sea. One reason why the Resolution did not go so far was that such an action could have harmed US fishery interests elsewhere. At that time, US fishing vessels were operating (and are still operating today) in several high seas areas of the Pacific and Atlantic Oceans. If coastal states in those regions had extended fisheries jurisdiction beyond 200 miles, US fishery operations could have been seriously compromised. The Soviet Union faced similar concerns with respect to its high seas fishing vessels, particularly those operating in high seas areas off South America and Africa. Moreover, the USA and the Soviet Union, as naval superpowers, did not want to give other coastal states a pretext for claiming excessive maritime jurisdiction of any kind that would interfere with the freedom of navigation enjoyed by their commercial and military vessels under the LOS Convention.

But the news from the Doughnut Hole did not improve. The nations whose fishing vessels operated there did not agree to a fishing moratorium.

3 Negotiation of the Convention[19]

Between February 1991 and February 1994, the United States, the Soviet Union (succeeded by the Russian Federation), Japan, the People's Republic of China, Poland, and the Republic of Korea held ten diplomatic conferences to negotiate the agreement that was to become the Convention. Though these conferences were held at the diplomatic level, much of the discourse at the negotiations could not be described as diplomatic. Economic concerns of considerable magnitude stood between the Bering Sea coastal states on the one hand and the 'distant water fishing nations' (or DWFNs) on the other, causing intense political pressure on the respective delegations. Still, as a result of human perseverance, ingenuity, and the undeniable realization that the pollock resource had collapsed, the negotiations ultimately produced an agreement to regulate the Doughnut Hole pollock fishery, should it ever resume.

From the outset, the United States and the Soviet Union saw the need to cooperate with each other on this matter. For one thing, given the phase-out of foreign fishing in the US EEZ, the United States had decreasing leverage with the DWFNs. That is, because US vessels were harvesting the entire allowable catch of pollock in the US zone, the United States Government could not lure foreign vessels out of the Doughnut Hole with promises of pollock allocations in its zone. More generally, neither the United States nor the Soviet Union acting alone would have as much influence over the other states as they would if they presented a united front—the two superpowers acting together.

Between mid-1987 and early 1991, the United States and the Soviet Union worked bilaterally to develop a proposal to bring the Doughnut Hole pollock fishery under control. Although, as discussed below, the

Soviets initially proposed that the United States and the Soviet Union should attempt to regulate the Doughnut Hole on a bilateral basis—without the consent of the DWFNs—the two coastal states eventually agreed that the fishery would best be regulated through a multilateral agreement that would include both themselves and the DWFNs. They also determined that the instrument should be 'free-standing' rather than tied to any existing international institution or regime.

3.1 Using the Law of the Sea Convention

Both the United States and the Soviet Union recognized that any agreement to regulate the Bering Sea pollock fishery would need to be based on the LOS Convention. They initially disagreed, however, as to *which provisions* of the LOS Convention would provide the best basis for such an agreement.

The Soviet Union advanced the view that the Bering Sea is a 'semi-enclosed sea' within the meaning of Article 122 of the LOS Convention.[20] The Soviets further asserted that Article 123[21] provided a legal basis for the two Bering Sea coastal states—on their own—'to manage the living resources of the entire Bering Sea rather than only 92 per cent of its area occupied with the territorial seas and economic zones of the USSR and USA'.[22]

The United States had never recognized the Bering Sea (or any other maritime area) as enclosed or semi-enclosed. The concern was that such recognition would lead to a proliferation of similar claims that would encroach upon maritime areas in which high seas freedoms, particularly freedoms of navigation, apply and would run counter to US national security interests. In any event, even if the Bering Sea were considered to be semi-enclosed, the United States believed that little would be gained from the perspective of fisheries management. The United States viewed Article 123 as simply not giving the coastal state(s) adjacent to a semi-enclosed sea any right to regulate fisheries in a high seas area in the semi-enclosed sea. Moreover, Article 123 imposes no obligation at all on other states to enter into any agreement; Article 123 (d) merely empowers the coastal state(s) to invite other interested states or international organizations to cooperate with them.[23]

The United States ultimately persuaded the Soviet Union that the Doughnut Hole agreement should be negotiated on the basis of other provisions of the LOS Convention, namely, those that recognize the right of the coastal state to exercise exclusive fisheries jurisdiction within its EEZ (Article 56) and those that regulate high seas fishing (Articles 116–19). The United States also urged reliance on Article 63 (2), which obligates both coastal states and high seas fishing states to 'seek to agree' on measures to conserve straddling stocks in a high seas area such as the Doughnut Hole.

During the six-nation negotiations that ensued, the coastal states drew heavily on the LOS Convention in support of their positions. They pointed out that the LOS Convention gave them the exclusive responsibility to conserve and manage the pollock resource in their respective zones, as well as the right for their vessels to harvest the total allowable catch of pollock in those areas. With increasing consternation, they insisted that the unregulated 'free-for-all' fishery in the Doughnut Hole was undermining those rights by threatening the sustainability of the Bering Sea pollock resource as a whole. The coastal states predicted that the intensity of the Doughnut Hole pollock fishery would cause the resource to collapse entirely. More broadly, they claimed that the collapse of the pollock resource would have profound and unpredictable consequences for the ecosystem at large, calling into question the commitment of the DWFNs to honour their obligations under Article 192 of the LOS Convention to protect and preserve the marine environment.

The Soviet Union and the United States noted that, under Article 63 (2) of the LOS Convention, DWFNs must seek to reach agreement with the coastal state(s) concerning the conservation of straddling stocks on the high seas, regardless of whether coastal state vessels fish for that stock on the high seas. There is no corresponding obligation on the coastal state to seek to reach agreement with DWFNs concerning the conservation of the straddling stock in the coastal state zone. Furthermore, the right of non-coastal states to fish in high seas areas such as the Doughnut Hole is subject to certain conditions, including the rights, duties, and interests of coastal states enumerated in Article 116. The freedom to fish on the high seas is also subject to the obligation to conserve, and to cooperate with other states in conserving, living marine resources of the high seas.

The coastal states added that, in the final analysis, the people who live in the fishing communities of Alaska and the Soviet Far East were more vulnerable to economic harm resulting from overfishing in the Bering Sea than any nationals of the DWFNs. Unlike the fishing fleets of the DWFNs, these communities could not move to other areas in search of other stocks once the pollock resource collapsed.

The DWFNs responded that their vessels, particularly those from Japan and the Republic of Korea, had for years fished for pollock in the Bering Sea and, indeed, had developed the technology to harvest and process pollock successfully. They regarded the displacement of their vessels from the coastal zones as unfair. They argued, at least at first, that pollock harvests in the Doughnut Hole had no significant bearing on what they viewed as separate pollock stocks occurring in the coastal zones. In any event, the coastal states bore at least as much of the responsibility for the condition of the pollock resource as the DWFNs, and they would have to bear at least as much of any conservation burden necessary to allow the resource to recover. The DWFNs would not agree to restrict or terminate the Doughnut Hole pollock fishery simply to allow the coastal states to go on fishing for pollock in their zones.

In the view of the DWFNs, the LOS Convention, by recognizing the right of coastal states to establish EEZs out to 200 miles, had already transferred to those states exclusive jurisdiction over most of the valuable fisheries grounds on the planet. No theory of justice could support any further control by coastal states over the relatively few desirable fishing grounds in the remaining high seas areas. Moreover, the United Nations Charter recognized the sovereign equality of all states, a principle that must be respected in the elaboration of any agreement to regulate the Doughnut Hole fishery. The coastal states should have no preferential rights under any such agreement.

3.2 Overcoming obstacles to agreement

The ten conferences held to negotiate the Convention were marked by generally increasing concern on the part of the coastal states about the status of the pollock resource and the larger Bering Sea ecosystem. This concern was countered by reluctant concessions on the part of the DWFNs to reduce (and ultimately suspend) the Doughnut Hole pollock fishery. Momentum toward an agreement increased as the collapse of the Aleutian Basin pollock stock became more evident. By mid-1991, all delegations acknowledged that, in the words of a joint press release, 'the pollock catch in the area has undergone a serious decline' and 'reaffirmed the need to take urgent conservation measures'. Soon thereafter, reports in the United States indicated that the stock of pollock which spawns off Bogoslof Island in the US EEZ, which migrates throughout the region, had declined by 75 per cent over two years. The United States responded by all but closing this once highly lucrative fishery for the entire 1992 season.

The DWFNs slowly agreed to take limited conservation measures with respect to their own fishing vessels, pending the conclusion of negotiations. They consented, for example, to the deployment and exchange of scientific observers and the use of automatic satellite transmitters on vessels. First Japan, and then the other DWFNs, began to gradually reduce the number of vessels operating in the Doughnut Hole. When evidence of the collapse of the pollock stock could no longer be ignored, the DWFNs finally agreed to a complete cessation of pollock fishing in the Doughnut Hole, effective at the beginning of 1993.[24] Negotiations on the text of the Convention accelerated as these interim measures took effect.

Between the fourth and fifth conferences, the Soviet Union formally dissolved. This event, which historians will undoubtedly rank among the most momentous of the twentieth century, had virtually no bearing on the negotiations. The Russian Federation simply replaced the Soviet Union, without any change in perspective or even a change in the head of delegation. As noted in the introduction to this chapter, President Yeltsin joined with President Bush on the occasion of the latter's very first summit meeting in June 1992 to issue a 'Joint Statement on the Need for Voluntary Suspension on Fishing in the Central Bering Sea' calling for an immediate 'voluntary suspension' of fishing activities in the Doughnut Hole.[25]

The last five conferences, held in rapid succession between January 1993 and February 1994, succeeded in resolving the remaining differences over the text of the Convention. The resolution of those differences, which are described in more detail in the next section of this chapter, involved agreement on a mechanism for determining the allowable harvest level of pollock in the Doughnut Hole, an approach to allocating that harvest level among the parties, and establishment of a set of obligations to ensure effective compliance by vessels with applicable conservation and management measures.

3.3 Adoption and entry into force of the Convention

The final conference, hosted by the United States in February 1994, ended with the heads of all six delegations placing their initials on a fully agreed text for the Convention. The delegations also agreed upon a Record of Discussions[26] that outlined technical matters to be addressed in the following months in preparation for the entry into force of the Convention and expressing the view that compatibility and consistency of conservation and management measures should be achieved between the Doughnut Hole and the two EEZs.

The United States, the People's Republic of China, the Republic of Korea, and Russia signed the Convention on 16 June 1994, in Washington. Japan and Poland signed later in 1994. Upon signing the Convention, the United States representative hailed it as

a state-of-the-art fisheries agreement. It is a unique, forward-looking agreement that will ensure the long-term sustainability of pollock in the Bering Sea, one of the world's most important and productive fishing grounds. . . . Today we stand at the brink of a new era in fisheries conservation and management. The depressed state of the world's fisheries stocks requires that we take bold steps to control more effectively our vessels to ensure the long-term health and well-being of fish stocks. This agreement is a step in that direction.[27]

President Clinton transmitted the Convention to the US Senate for advice and consent to ratification on 9 August 1994. The Senate promptly provided such advice and consent on 6 October 1994. After several delays, all states that had participated in the negotiations deposited instruments of ratification. The Convention entered into force on 8 December 1995.[28]

4 Elements of the Convention[29]

4.1 Scope of the Convention

Article I of the Convention limits the geographic scope of the Convention to

the high seas area of the Bering Sea beyond 200 nautical miles from the baselines from which the breadth of the territorial sea of the coastal States of the Bering Sea is measured (hereinafter referred to as 'the Convention Area'), except as otherwise provided in this Convention. Activities under this Convention, for scientific purposes, may extend beyond the Convention Area within the Bering Sea.

Accordingly, the Convention generally applies only to the Doughnut Hole, the high seas area of the Bering Sea beyond the EEZs of the coastal states. In adopting this general rule, the parties nevertheless recognized that scientific analyses of, and related research on, the pollock resource could not be limited to the Doughnut Hole, as the resource occurred not only in the Doughnut Hole, but also in both EEZs.

During the early stages of negotiations, Poland proposed that all aspects of the Convention—including any agreed conservation and management measures for pollock—apply both to the Doughnut Hole and to the EEZs of the coastal states (or at least to the portions of those EEZs in which the 'Aleutian Basin pollock stock' occurred). The coastal states responded that the Polish proposal conflicted with the Article 63 (2) of the LOS Convention, which calls upon states to seek to agree on conservation measures *for the high seas area only*.

The coastal states nevertheless accepted that, in order to achieve effective conservation, measures for pollock adopted for the high seas area would have to be compatible with measures adopted by the coastal states for managing the same stock in their respective EEZs. To this end, the Record of Discussions adopted in conjunction with the Convention recognized the necessity for compatible measures. The coastal states expressed their intention to prohibit fishing for Aleutian Basin pollock in their respective zones as long as the Convention continued to prohibit fishing for that stock in the Doughnut Hole. If conditions improved such that a Doughnut Hole fishery could resume, the coastal states would similarly open their zones for fishing on the Aleutian Basin stock 'to an appropriate level', taking into account the harvest level set for the Doughnut Hole under the Convention.

The 'biological scope' of the Convention is generally limited to pollock. The DWFNs, led by Japan, wanted the Convention to deal only with pollock, leaving questions concerning other species in the Doughnut Hole for consideration in other fora (or not at all). The United States and the Soviet Union initially sought a provision in the Convention to reaffirm the prohibition on high seas fishing for anadromous species found in other treaties.[30] They also argued in favour of a prohibition on the retention of anadromous species and herring caught incidentally in the course of pollock fishing. More broadly, the coastal states hoped that the Convention would create a forum for cooperative efforts on all species related to pollock. However, in light of the intense political pressure to wrap up negotiations quickly, the coastal states realized that the complexity of the issues raised in connection with other species would unduly prolong negotiations on the Convention.

Accordingly, Article II generally limits the Convention to a consideration of pollock only, unless the parties subsequently agree to consider additional species. As discussed below, any such agreement would require the consensus of all parties.[31] The coastal states nevertheless secured agreement on the inclusion of two statements relating to species other than pollock in the Record of Discussions:

It is the shared view of the representatives of the above-mentioned Governments that fishing operations for living marine resources other than pollock in the Convention Area, which could occur in the future, by the fishing vessels of any Party should only be conducted pursuant to specific authorization issued by the Party.

It is the shared view of the representatives of the above-mentioned Governments that there is no fishing for anadromous species in the Convention Area. It is the intention of the Parties to prohibit the retention on board their fishing vessels of anadromous species or herring that are incidentally taken in the Convention Area in the course of fishing operations for pollock.

Although the Record of Discussions is not legally binding, the second of these statements clearly represents at least a political commitment on the part of all the governments concerned to accommodate the concerns of the coastal states regarding the prohibitions on fishing for anadromous species and on retention of anadromous species and herring.

4.2 Institutions

Unlike most regional fishery agreements, the Convention does not establish a standing commission with an independent secretariat. Instead, the Convention provides for an Annual Conference of the parties, as well as a Scientific and Technical Committee to perform a variety of functions necessary to provide the Annual Conference with the scientific data and other information necessary to implement the Convention. The negotiators of the Convention believed that the limited number of nations involved and the small size of the Doughnut Hole did not necessitate the creation—and the attendant expense—of a standing commission with its own staff.

The functions of the Annual Conference appear in Article IV (1) of the Convention. The most vital of these functions are the establishment of the annual allowable harvest level ('AHL') of pollock in the Doughnut Hole, the establishment of individual national quotas ('INQs') of such pollock, and the adoption of other conservation and management measures (including enforcement measures) relating to pollock fishing in the Doughnut Hole. Article IV (3) requires the Annual Conference to take full account of the reports and recommendations of the Scientific and Technical Committee in exercising these functions.

The Scientific and Technical Committee, comprised of at least one representative of each party, derives its mandate from Article IX of the Convention. In accordance with a Plan of Work adopted by the Annual Conference, the Scientific and Technical Committee is to 'compile, exchange, and analyse information on fisheries harvests, and pollock and other living marine resources' covered by the Convention. The Committee may also make recommendations to the Annual Conference with respect to the conservation and management of pollock (including the AHL) and may investigate other scientific matters that may be referred to the Committee by the Annual Conference.

4.3 Decision-making rules

The original proposal for the Convention advanced by the United States in coordination with the Soviet Union would have given each coastal state a veto over substantive decisions to be made pursuant to the Convention, that is by the Annual Conference. The DWFNs, by contrast, initially proposed that all such decisions be made by simple majority, a formula which, in their view, recognized the sovereign equality of all states involved in the regime. However, because the simple majority formula would have enabled the four DWFNs to outvote the two coastal states in the Annual Conference, the Soviet Union and the United States found this proposal unacceptable.

As a compromise, the DWFNs proposed that the Annual Conference adopt all substantive decisions by consensus, an approach which in effect would allow any party to veto a proposed decision. This decision-making formula presented two difficulties from the perspective of the coastal states. First, it could create a deadlock within the Annual Conference and thus prevent changes in the status quo, namely unregulated fishing in the Doughnut Hole. Because the coastal states were seeking to change this status quo, they worried that a consensus-based decision-making structure would frustrate their objectives. Second, the DWFNs' proposal did not address a fundamental question: what would happen if the Annual Conference could not achieve consensus on a critical question, such as the establishment of the AHL for pollock in a given year?

The negotiators finally reached agreement on an innovative decision-making system. In accordance with Article V of the Convention, each party has one vote in the Annual Conference. All decisions on 'matters of substance'[32] require consensus among the parties; other decisions are to be taken by simple majority. However, as discussed below, the Convention also sets unique predetermined 'default' rules to prevent deadlock on the two most critical issues that the Annual Conference must address annually—the establishment of the AHL and the division of the AHL into INQs.

4.4 Conservation and management measures

Any effective regime for the conservation and management of fishery resources must answer these two basic questions: how will the total harvest levels be set, and how will the total harvest levels be divided among the participants in the regime? These two questions, which proved very difficult to answer during negotiations on the Convention, ultimately yielded themselves to resolution through the following set of provisions.

Article VII (1) of the Convention tasks the Annual Conference with the requirement to establish the AHL of pollock in the Doughnut Hole for the succeeding year, based on an assessment of the Aleutian Basin pollock biomass by the Scientific and Technical Committee. However, Article VII (2) provides a mechanism for dealing with the possibility that, despite every effort, the Annual Conference may fail to achieve consensus on this matter in a given year. In such cases, the AHL is set in accordance with part 1 of the annex to the Convention.[33]

Part 1 of the annex, in turn, provides for institutions in the United States and the Russian Federation—as 'the coastal States of the Bering Sea'—to establish jointly the biomass of Aleutian Basin pollock. If these two institutions cannot perform this task jointly, then the biomass of Aleutian Basin pollock in the known spawning area for this stock off Bogoslof Island in

Table 5.2 Relationship between pollock biomass and annual harvesting level

Aleutian Basin pollock biomass	AHL
1.67 million metric tons or more but less than 2.0 million metric tons	130,000 metric tons
2.0 million metric tons or more but less than 2.5 million metric tons	190,000 metric tons
2.5 million metric tons or more	Determined by consensus at the Annual Conference

the US EEZ is deemed to be 60 per cent of the total biomass of Aleutian Basin pollock. The United States is given sole responsibility for determining the size of the pollock biomass in the area off Bogoslof Island.[34]

Having created a guaranteed mechanism for setting the size of the Aleutian Basin pollock biomass, the Convention next creates a 'sliding scale' for AHLs dependent on the size of the biomass (assuming that the Annual Conference does not reach consensus on a different AHL). If the biomass is less than 1.67 million metric tons, the AHL is zero—no directed fishing for pollock in the Doughnut Hole is permitted.[35]

If, however, the pollock resource recovers, part 1 of the annex sets the AHL in accordance with Table 5.2 (again, assuming that the Annual Conference does not reach consensus on a different AHL).

While the numbers set forth in this table ultimately resulted from political compromise during the negotiations, they do reflect certain realities. An Aleutian Basin pollock biomass of 1.67 million metric tons corresponds, under the formula set in the Convention, to a biomass of pollock in the area off Bogoslof Island of approximately 1 million metric tons, below which US law generally prohibits a directed fishery on the Aleutian Basin pollock stock in the US EEZ. Thus, the Convention establishes the same threshold for fishing in the Doughnut Hole as US law establishes for fishing in its zone. Under the same circumstances, the Russian Federation would also prohibit fishing for pollock on the portion of the Aleutian Basin stock that occurs in its zone, as envisioned in the Record of Discussions.

Should the Aleutian Basin pollock biomass increase above 1.67 million metric tons, the table, roughly speaking, apportions approximately 30 per cent of the catch to the Doughnut Hole.[36] Pursuant to US and Russian law, the remaining 70 per cent would be harvested in the zones of the two coastal states.[37] These numbers, too, resulted from political compromise. The DWFNs had argued for a larger allocation for the Doughnut Hole, noting that in the late 1980s the catch in the Doughnut Hole represented approximately 40 per cent of the total harvest. The coastal states responded that the Doughnut Hole represents only 20 per cent of the Aleutian Basin and only 10 per cent of the Bering Sea. They complained, moreover, that the fishing patterns for pollock in the late 1980s had led directly to the collapse of the Aleutian Basin stock and thus could hardly form a legitimate basis for dividing the resource.

The negotiators next grappled with the question of how to divide any AHL greater than zero into INQs for each party. The DWFNs argued that INQs should be based on 'historical' fishing levels in the Doughnut Hole, which would have granted them as a group approximately 95 per cent of the AHL. They argued also that because vessels from Russia and the United States would be allowed to harvest pollock in the EEZs of their respective nations, those vessels should not be able to fish for pollock in the Doughnut Hole at all.

Russia and the United States responded that the Doughnut Hole pollock fishery only began in the mid-1980s and could not be considered 'historical'. They also reiterated that the unsustainable fishing patterns that had produced the collapse of the pollock resource could not be regarded as a legitimate basis for establishing INQs. Russia and the United States argued, moreover, that under traditional rules of inter-national law, as reflected in Article 116 of the LOS Convention, they had as much right for their vessels to fish in a high seas area such as the Doughnut Hole as any other nation.

The negotiators finally settled on Article VIII of the Convention, which leaves the task of establishing INQs to the Annual Conference. However, if the Annual Conference cannot achieve consensus on INQs in a given year, the provisions of part 2 of the annex to the Convention apply, under which an 'olympic' fishery would ensue: vessels from all parties would be allowed to fish for pollock in the Doughnut Hole without the creation of INQs. Instead of INQs, the Annual Conference would simply establish a starting date for the fishery and a mechanism for monitoring harvests on a 'real-time' basis, for example by requiring independent observers on each vessel to transmit prompt reports of all harvests to all parties by means of satellite communication. When the AHL was reached, the fishery would end immediately.

Because the Aleutian Basin pollock biomass has still not recovered to 1.67 million metric tons, there has never been an AHL greater than zero. The Annual Conference has not faced the question of setting INQs, nor have the provisions of part 2 of the annex ever become operative. It is nevertheless possible to speculate that these provisions of the Convention would probably favour the interests of the parties with the most techno-logically advanced vessels. The reason for this is that any party can block consensus in the Annual Conference and force the establishment of an olympic fishery in the Doughnut Hole. In such a fishery, no party or vessel would receive a guaranteed quota—rather, the entire AHL would be 'up for grabs', with the best vessels likely to catch the lion's share.

4.5 Scientific advice

As noted above, one function of the Annual Conference is to adopt appropriate conservation and management measures beyond the mere setting of the AHL and INQs.[38] The efficacy of any such measures clearly depends in large measure on the quality of the scientific advice on which they are based. The Convention provides for cooperation on scientific and technical issues related to the pollock resource, both through the activities of the Scientific and Technical Committee and otherwise.

During the negotiation of the Convention, the coastal states sought to give a mandate to the Scientific and Technical Committee to consider species in addition to pollock, in order to provide the scientific basis for measures concerning other species affected by, or related to, the Doughnut Hole pollock fishery. The coastal states noted, in this regard, the growing movement in fisheries management away from single-species regulation toward 'multispecies' or 'ecosystem' approaches. The DWFNs, by contrast, tried to limit, and to a considerable degree succeeded in limiting, the mandate of the Scientific and Technical Committee to a consideration of pollock only.

Under Article IX (1) of the Convention, the Scientific and Technical Committee can consider ('compile, exchange and analyze information on') pollock and other living marine resources covered by the Convention. However, paragraph 4 of that Article allows the Committee to make recommendations to the Annual Conference only with respect to the conservation and management of pollock. Recommendations pertaining to the conservation and management of other species would depend on an explicit request from the Annual Conference, which would have to be adopted by consensus of the parties. As long as the DWFNs continue to view the Convention as a pollock-only instrument, such a request is unlikely to materialize.

Under Article X, the parties also commit themselves to cooperate in the conduct of scientific research outside of the Scientific and Technical Committee. However, the scope of such cooperation is once again generally limited to pollock, except as may be determined by the Annual Conference. The parties agree to exchange scientific data that they develop individually, as well as the data from their respective pollock fishing operations. The accommodation of scientific observers from one party aboard fishing vessels of another party is also envisioned. Article X further provides for the possibility of trial fishing in the Doughnut Hole during years in which the AHL is zero, in accordance with specific research plans. Such trial fishing has in fact taken place each year since the entry into force of the Convention, in accordance with terms and conditions established by the Annual Conference under Article X (4).

4.6 Monitoring and enforcement: flag state responsibilities

During the course of negotiations, the coastal states insisted on the need to ensure that any vessels fishing for pollock in the Doughnut Hole both comply with the conservation and management measures of the Convention and refrain absolutely from fishing illegally in the coastal states' EEZs adjacent to the Doughnut Hole. The DWFNs eventually agreed to a series of stringent requirements for vessels designed to accommodate these concerns. Indeed, one commentator noted of the Convention that 'its unique combination of enforcement mechanisms promises to make it one of the most effective multinational fishing agreements ever reached'.[39]

Pursuant to Article XII of the Convention, each flag state must ensure that any vessel flying its flag observes the following strictures:

- To prevent 'rogue' vessels from undermining the Convention, vessels may only fish for pollock in the Doughnut Hole pursuant to specific authorization issued by the flag state.
- To allow all parties (particularly the coastal states) to know where each authorized vessel is operating at any given time, and to minimize the possibility for illegal fishing in the coastal states' EEZs, all fishing vessels must use satellite position-fixing devices, with location data to be shared with all parties on a real-time basis.
- For the same reasons, and to facilitate the monitoring of harvest levels, fishing vessels must notify all parties of their intention to enter the Doughnut Hole forty-eight hours in advance, must notify all parties of the location of any trans-shipments of fish twenty-four hours prior to trans-shipment, and must report catch data regularly.
- Flag states must investigate and penalize violations committed by their vessels and report to the Annual Conference on such actions.

4.7 Monitoring and enforcement: cooperative actions

The coastal states were not, however, satisfied that this series of requirements would prevent violations of the Convention or illegal fishing in their EEZs. They sought additional means by which they could take part in monitoring the activities of all vessels fishing in the Doughnut Hole, including the right to board and inspect vessels flying the flag of other parties that were fishing in the Doughnut Hole. They even sought the right to seize and prosecute such vessels found to be engaged in violations.

The DWFNs initially opposed most of these proposals. They argued that, under traditional concepts of international law as reflected in the LOS Convention,[40] a fishing vessel on the high seas remains under the exclusive jurisdiction of the flag state. No other state can board and inspect, or otherwise exercise jurisdiction over, a vessel on the high seas unless the flag state (or the master of the vessel) consents to such action. In particular, the DWFNs adamantly rejected any possibility that a state other than the flag state could take prosecutorial action against or impose penalties on a vessel, its captain, or its crew for violations occurring on the high seas.

However, the DWFNs were not averse to allowing the coastal states to place observers on their vessels operating in the Doughnut Hole. The practice of placing observers on vessels had become more common and was becoming accepted as a useful means of promoting adherence to conservation and management rules as well as improving collection and reporting of fishing data. The difficult issue was that of cost. Who would finance the training of observers and their transportation to the fishing vessels? Who would pay the observers' salaries? Who would bear the costs of their meals and accommodations on board the fishing vessels?

Article XI, paragraph 5 of the Convention contains the provisions relating to observers. Each vessel fishing for pollock in the Doughnut Hole must, upon request, accept an observer from another party. If such an observer is not available, the flag state must place one of its own observers aboard the vessel. The parties agree to establish a Central Bering Sea Observer Program which, among other things, will train and certify observers to work aboard these vessels. Each vessel will bear the cost of the observers' meals and accommodations; the question of who will bear other costs will be worked out later. The activities of the observers include

monitoring the implementation of conservation and management measures adopted pursuant to this Convention (e.g., measures relating to fishing activities, location thereof, incidental catch, and fishing gear) and reporting of their findings to the flag-State Party and observer's Party.[41]

The remainder of Article XI, concerning enforcement actions that may be taken by states other than the flag state, constitutes the most groundbreaking and precedent-setting aspect of the entire Convention. As noted above, traditional international law recognizes the ability of a state other than the flag state to board and inspect, or otherwise to take enforcement action with respect to, a fishing vessel on the high seas *with the consent of the flag state.* Prior to the Convention, flag states would typically only grant such consent—if they granted it at all—on a case-by-case basis. In other words, another state would have to seek such consent in an ad hoc manner each time it sought to take action with respect to a foreign fishing vessel on the high seas. The flag state retained the right to deny such consent in any given case.

Pursuant to Article XI (6) of the Convention, by contrast, each party consents *in advance* to allow officials of any other party to board and inspect its vessels in the Doughnut Hole in order to monitor for compliance with conservation and management measures adopted under the Convention. Another party desiring to board a vessel need not seek any further consent from the flag state beyond that expressed in the Convention, nor may a flag state withdraw its consent (except by withdrawing from the Convention).

These provisions of the Convention, although unusual, are not the first of their kind.[42] The provisions that follow in the Convention, outlining the steps which the 'boarding and inspecting State' may take upon the discovery of a violation, however, were truly novel for this type of international agreement. If the violation is serious, as set forth in Article XI (7) (b), and if the flag state is not in a position to assume immediate control over the vessel (i.e. the flag state does not have an enforcement vessel of its own in the immediate area), the boarding officials may remain on the vessel until officials of the flag state arrive on the scene or the flag state 'otherwise carries out its responsibility for the operation of the vessel' (e.g. by ordering the vessel out of the Doughnut Hole).

The implications of this regime are significant. Among the parties to the Convention, only the United States and possibly the Russian Federation are likely to maintain fisheries enforcement vessels in or near the Doughnut Hole. Accordingly, only the coastal states will be in a position to board and inspect fishing vessels in the Doughnut Hole on a regular basis. If a vessel from another party is found to have committed a serious violation, the right of the coastal states to have their boarding team remain on board the vessel should, in most cases, force an immediate end to the violation and, by virtue of the evidence collected by the boarding team, may lead to more vigorous prosecution.[43] As discussed more thoroughly in the following section, these provisions became the model for Articles 21 and 22 of the Fish Stocks Agreement and are a part of what appears to represent the beginning of a new era in high seas fisheries enforcement.

Taken as a whole, the Convention would appear to offer solutions to the issues raised in the course of negotiations. Through implementation of the Convention, the parties will (1) generate sufficient information about the status of the pollock resource to enable informed decisions on conservation measures, (2) establish such conservation measures for all vessels operating in the Doughnut Hole, and (3) establish an adequate system to ensure compliance with conservation measures, including surveillance and enforcement. Of course, because there has been no directed fishing for pollock in the Doughnut Hole (other than trial fishing) since the Convention entered into force, only time will tell if the Convention has truly responded to the collapse of the pollock in a responsible way.

5 Global implications

This chapter earlier highlighted the international law framework within which the Convention was negotiated, particularly the framework established by the LOS Convention. Although the LOS Convention did not enter into force until after the conclusion of negotiations on the Doughnut Hole Convention,[44] and despite the fact that none of the states participating in the Doughnut Hole negotiations had formally expressed their consent to be bound by the LOS Convention, each of those states accepted the basic fishery provisions of the LOS Convention as setting the parameters for addressing the straddling stock situation in the Bering Sea.

These basic provisions of the LOS Convention, however, did no more than set the parameters for the Doughnut Hole negotiation. They did not provide specific guidance on how to give effect to the right of all states for their nationals to fish on the high seas, as reaffirmed in Article 116 of the LOS Convention, while also making that right 'subject to the rights, duties and interests of coastal States' as required by the same article. Nor did the basic provisions of the LOS Convention specify any particular formula for allocating the straddling stock of pollock in the Bering Sea among the two coastal states and the DWFNs. In the end, the fishery provisions of the LOS Convention proved insufficient to prevent the collapse of the Bering Sea pollock resource.

In this respect, the Bering Sea crisis fitted into an unfortunate pattern that was emerging in the mid- to late 1980s. Governments were forced to recognize that, despite general acceptance of the fishery provisions of the LOS Convention, those provisions were inadequate to address, much less reverse, serious declines in the abundance of several key fish stocks around the world.

To remedy this situation, the international community decided to elaborate new global agreements for the conservation and management of ocean fisheries, particularly the Agreement to Promote Compliance with International Conservation and Management Measures by Fishing Vessels on the High Seas (the 'FAO Compliance Agreement') and the Fish Stocks Agreement. The negotiation of these agreements coincided to a significant degree with the negotiation of the Doughnut Hole Convention, both chronologically and substantively. The following sections deal with the relationship of the Doughnut Hole Convention to these two new global treaties.

5.1 Relationship to the FAO Compliance Agreement

The FAO Compliance Agreement began as an effort to deter the reflagging of fishing vessels from one state to another as a means of avoiding otherwise applicable conservation and management measures. States that were party to regional fishery agreements, whose vessels were thus obligated to abide by fishery restrictions imposed through those agreements, despaired at the growing number of vessels that were reflagging to states that were not party to the agreements. Having reflagged, those vessels would continue to fish in the same fisheries, unconstrained by the restrictions.

Agenda 21, adopted by the 1992 United Nations Conference on Environment and Development, called for action to address this phenomenon.[45] Shortly thereafter, the FAO initiated negotiations on what was to become the FAO Compliance Agreement. The negotiators of the Compliance Agreement soon realized, however, that reflagging was only part of a larger problem; too many flag states simply lacked the ability or the will to control the activities of their own vessels which were fishing on the high seas. The FAO thus decided to elaborate a broader agreement, one that expanded upon the fundamental concepts of 'flag State responsibility' derived from the LOS Convention.

Although the negotiations of the FAO Compliance Agreement began two years later than the commencement of the Doughnut Hole negotiations, they ended first. The FAO Conference formally adopted the Compliance Agreement on 24 November 1993. Except for Russia, which was not a member of the FAO, all states involved in the Doughnut Hole negotiations participated actively in the negotiation of the FAO Compliance Agreement and joined consensus at the FAO Conference on the adoption of that treaty.

Even though the FAO Compliance Agreement did not resolve a number of the key issues under consideration in the Doughnut Hole negotiations, it did contain three related provisions concerning the responsibilities of flag states for their vessels fishing on the high seas directly relevant to the Doughnut Hole:

Each Party shall take such measures as may be necessary to ensure that fishing vessels entitled to fly its flag do not engage in any activity that undermines the effectiveness of international conservation and management measures.

In particular, no Party shall allow any fishing vessel entitled to fly its flag to be used for fishing on the high seas unless it has been authorized to be so used by the appropriate authority or authorities of that Party. A fishing vessel so authorized shall fish in accordance with the conditions of that authorization.

No Party shall authorize any fishing vessel entitled to fly its flag to be used for fishing on the high seas unless the Party is satisfied that it is able, taking into account the links that exist between it and the fishing vessel concerned, to exercise effectively its responsibilities under this Agreement in respect of that fishing vessel.[46]

These three provisions represent a new vision for high seas fisheries. States could no longer allow their fishing vessels to venture out into high seas areas in the manner that the early explorers ventured out beyond the frontiers of known civilization. The FAO Compliance Agreement requires flag states actively to oversee the high seas fishing operations of their vessels. They must decide on a case-by-case basis whether to authorize any vessel flying their flag to fish on the high seas. Most importantly, flag states may not permit any such vessel to fish on the high seas at all unless they are able to prevent the vessel from undermining agreed high seas conservation rules.[47]

Prior to the FAO Compliance Agreement, none of these rules had found explicit expression in any international agreement. All three rules, however, derive directly from more general provisions of the LOS Convention that obligate states to conserve high seas living resources[48] and require that there be a 'genuine link' between a state and a vessel entitled to fly its flag.[49]

The first two of these provisions also found expression in Article XI of the Doughnut Hole Convention. That Article requires each party to 'take all necessary measures to ensure that its nationals and fishing vessels flying its flag comply with the provisions of this Convention and measures adopted pursuant thereto' and to 'ensure that its fishing vessels fish for pollock in the Convention Area only pursuant to specific authorization issued by that Party'.[50]

The third of these provisions of the FAO Compliance Agreement, which requires a flag state to ensure that it can effectively exercise responsibility over a vessel before the issuance of an authorization for that vessel to fish on the high seas, does not appear explicitly in the Doughnut Hole Convention. Other aspects of the Convention, however, are designed to meet the same concerns for effective control over fishing vessels in the Doughnut Hole. The Convention, as discussed above, requires each vessel fishing in the Doughnut Hole to use real-time satellite position-fixing devices, to notify other parties of their intention to enter the Doughnut Hole forty-eight hours prior to such entry, to give twenty-four hours' notice in advance of trans-shipments of fish, and to carry observers. These provisions, coupled with the right of all parties to the Convention to board and inspect vessels fishing in the Doughnut Hole, should prevent any vessel operating there from repeatedly violating the conservation and management measures of the Convention.

5.2 Relationship to the 1995 Fish Stocks Agreement

The relationship between the Convention and the Fish Stocks Agreement is more complex and nuanced, in part because of the broader scope and specificity of the Fish Stocks Agreement compared to the FAO Compliance Agreement.

Like the FAO Compliance Agreement, the Fish Stocks Agreement owes its origins to the 1992 United Nations Conference on Environment and Development.[51] Negotiations on the Fish Stocks Agreement began at the United Nations in the spring of 1993, after several rounds of Doughnut Hole negotiations had already taken place. The two sets of negotiations overlapped for more than one year, with the Doughnut Hole negotiations finishing first, in February 1994. Substantive negotiations on the Fish Stocks Agreement continued until August 1995; the Fish Stocks Agreement was formally opened for signature in December 1995.

As in the Doughnut Hole negotiations, the participants in the United Nations negotiations generally divided themselves into two camps—DWFNs and coastal states. Japan, the Republic of Korea, the People's Republic of China, and Poland were staunch members of the DWFN camp who strongly resisted proposals presented by the coastal state camp to impose further restrictions on high seas fishing. Russia, despite the fact that some of its vessels continued to fish on the high seas (although not as many as prior to the collapse of the Soviet Union), remained firmly in the coastal state camp and called repeatedly for tighter controls over vessels fishing in the Doughnut Hole and in the small high seas area in the centre of the Sea of Okhotsk known as the 'Peanut Hole'.[52]

Only the perspective of the United States in the United Nations Conference differed in any meaningful respect from its perspective in the Doughnut Hole negotiations. The United States found itself in *both* camps in the United Nations negotiations, trying to balance its strong interests as a coastal state with respect to the straddling stock of pollock in the Bering Sea against its interests as a DWFN with respect to highly migratory species (particularly tuna) which the sizeable US high seas fleet fishes in two oceans.

The other states participating in the Doughnut Hole negotiations appreciated the pivotal role that the United States could, and ultimately did, play in the United Nations negotiations. The United States not only 'straddled' the two camps in that negotiation but also held the unique and enviable position of an 'honest broker' with considerable clout.

At a critical juncture toward the end of the Doughnut Hole negotiations in October 1993, the pivotal position of the United States in the United Nations negotiations helped to bring about a favourable resolution of some of the key Doughnut Hole issues. The United States understood that although the four DWFNs were concerned about the prospect of new restrictions on pollock fishing in the Doughnut Hole, they were even more concerned that the United Nations negotiations would result in significant new restrictions for *all* high seas fisheries. The DWFNs essentially faced the following dilemma: unless they agreed to accommodate US concerns over fishing in the Doughnut Hole, the United States might be forced in the United Nations negotiations to 'tip' toward the coastal state camp and seek to solve its Doughnut Hole problems through a global agreement that would affect all high seas fisheries for straddling stocks and highly migratory stocks. This 'tipping' of the United States could well have produced a United Nations treaty that would distinctively disadvantage the DWFNs in many regions. The DWFNs, perhaps because they feared such an outcome, or perhaps because they also realized that the decimated Bering Sea pollock resource was no longer worth fighting so hard over, softened in their approach and hastened agreement on the Doughnut Hole Convention.

The Doughnut Hole Convention, in turn, then became a critical precedent for elaboration of the most hotly debated aspects of the Fish Stocks Agreement—Articles 21 and 22, which provide for the rights of states other than flag states to board and inspect fishing vessels on the high seas and to take certain actions to prevent the continuation of discovered violations of agreed conservation and management measures. These articles of the Fish Stocks Agreement correspond closely to the concepts of, and even to much of the actual language of, Article XI of the Convention.[53]

A number of the other elements of the Doughnut Hole Convention and the Fish Stocks Agreement correspond closely as well. Both treaties require that conservation and management measures be based on the best available scientific information, and both call for the collection and sharing of fisheries data in a timely manner. The Record of Discussions adopted in conjunction with the Doughnut Hole Convention provides for general 'compatibility' between the measures taken for the straddling stock of pollock in the high seas and those taken for the same stock in each of the EEZs, as required by Article 7 of the Fish Stocks Agreement.

The decision-making structure of the Doughnut Hole Convention, with its default rules in the event that the Annual Conference cannot reach consensus on key issues, clearly 'facilitates the adoption of conservation and management measures in a timely and effective manner', as envisioned by Article 10 (j) of the Fish Stocks Agreement.

Some tensions nevertheless exist between the two treaties. Where Article 8 (3) of the Fish Stocks Agreement gives all states with a 'real interest' in a high seas fishery the right to become a member of a regional organization or arrangement established to regulate that fishery, a state other than the six current parties to the Doughnut Hole Convention can only adhere to the Convention if all the current parties unanimously invite such a state to do so.[54] However, in light of the fact that the high seas pollock fishery in the Doughnut Hole only began in the mid-1980s and that all of the states whose vessels ever participated in that fishery are already parties to the Convention, it is not clear that any other state could claim a 'real interest' in that fishery and legitimately argue for adherence to the Convention on the strength of Article 8 (3) of the Fish Stocks Agreement.

More compelling differences between the two treaties concern the degree of precaution that must be taken in adopting fishing restrictions and the attention to the ecosystem as a whole in which the regulated fishery occurs. The Fish Stocks Agreement outlines a 'precautionary approach' to the conservation and management of ocean fisheries that, among other things, requires regulators to take into account all related species in the relevant ecosystem.[55] The Doughnut Hole Convention adopts an approach to regulating the pollock fishery that might be described as precautionary but which does not expressly provide for the application of 'precautionary reference points' as envisioned in annex II to the Fish Stocks Agreement. Moreover, as discussed above, the Doughnut Hole Convention essentially deals only with pollock, although it does make provision for the possibility to consider related species in the Bering Sea ecosystem if the parties agree to do so.

Finally, Article 12 of the Fish Stocks Agreement calls for transparent procedures to be adopted in regional fishery arrangements that, among other things, give representatives of international and non-governmental organizations a meaningful opportunity to take part in meetings and other proceedings. Article XII (5) of the Doughnut Hole Convention conditions the participation of 'any representative of a non-party' on an invitation from the parties 'by unanimous agreement'. The parties to the Convention have not agreed to date to any set of rules on this subject that would provide for the transparency envisioned by the Fish Stocks Agreement.

6 Conclusion

Is the Convention a model for other regional fishery agreements? The answer to this question may vary in accordance with the old axiom: 'where you stand depends on where you sit.' The Convention clearly represents the successful culmination of the effort by the Bering Sea coastal states to secure an agreement for regulating high seas fishing for the straddling stock of pollock in an effective manner. As such, the Bering Sea coastal states have certainly lauded the Convention as a success.

The states whose vessels participated in that fishery before it collapsed may have a less enthusiastic view of the Convention. From their perspective, the Convention represents the inevitable and unhappy progression of events that began with the establishment of 200-mile fisheries jurisdiction, which forced many of their vessels out of the most lucrative fishing grounds. In the end, though, even the states whose vessels operated in the Doughnut Hole understand that fish are renewable resources and that a properly regulated fishery in the Doughnut Hole for a recovered stock of pollock—on which the Convention is premissed—is in their interest as well.

Notes

1. Joint Statement on the Need for Voluntary Suspension on Fishing in the Central Bering Sea, issued at the Summit Meeting between the United States and the Russian Federation, 17 June 1992.
2. Some descriptions of the Bering Sea include a small area of the North Pacific Ocean just south of the Aleutian Islands. National Research Council, *The Bering Sea Ecosystem* (Washington: National Academy Press, 1996), 28.
3. The Doughnut Hole occurs in an area of the Bering Sea generally referred to as the Aleutian Basin, the region of deeper water beyond the continental shelves adjacent to the coasts. If the Aleutian Basin is defined as the area of the Bering Sea that is seaward of the 1,000-metre isobaths, the Doughnut Hole represents approximately 17.5% of the Aleutian Basin. See Map 5.1.
4. E. Meltzer, 'Global Overview of Straddling and Highly Migratory Fish Stocks: The Nonsustainable Nature of High Seas Fisheries', *Ocean Development and International Law*, 25 (1994), 283–4.
5. Above the continental shelf within the US EEZ in the Bering Sea, most areas are no more than 600 feet (*c*.180 metres) deep. By contrast, most areas of the Aleutian Basin, including the Doughnut Hole, range from 6,500 to 10,000 feet (2,000–3,000 metres) deep.
6. International Convention for the High Seas Fisheries of the North Pacific Ocean, 1952 (4 *UST* 380; *TIAS* 2786). In 1992, the United States, Japan, and Canada, along with the Russian Federation, brought into force a new treaty to replace this agreement, the Convention for the Conservation of Anadromous Stocks in the North Pacific Ocean (hereinafter 'Anadromous Stocks Convention').
7. Meltzer, 'Global Overview of Straddling and Highly Migratory Fish Stocks', 287.
8. See S. Kaye, 'Legal Approaches to Polar Fisheries Regimes: A Comparative Analysis of the Convention for the Conservation of Antarctic Marine Living Resources and the Bering Sea Doughnut Hole Convention', *California Western International Law Journal*, 26 (1995), 100–1. In fact, some of the reported catch from the Doughnut Hole may in fact have been taken by vessels illegally poaching inside the US and Soviet zones adjacent to the Doughnut Hole.
9. Kaye, 'Legal Approaches to Polar Fisheries Regimes', 101; E. D. Miles and W. T. Burke, 'Pressures on the United Nations Convention on the Law of the Sea of 1982 Arising from New Fisheries Conflicts: The Problem of Straddling Stocks', *Ocean Development and International Law*, 20 (1989), 348. By 1991, Japanese scientists concurred that pollock harvested in the Doughnut Hole are part of a larger stock occurring in the Aleutian Basin. Meltzer, 'Global Overview of Straddling and Highly Migratory Fish Stocks', 284.
10. L. Miovski, 'Solutions in the Convention on the Law of the Sea to the Problem of Overfishing in the Central Bering Sea: Analysis of the Convention, Highlighting the Provisions Concerning Fisheries and Enclosed and Semi-enclosed Seas', *San Diego Law Review*, 26 (1989), 529.

11. Ibid. 528–9; Kaye, 'Legal Approaches to Polar Fisheries Regimes', 100; Meltzer, 'Global Overview of Straddling and Highly Migratory Fish Stocks', 286.
12. Meltzer, 'Global Overview of Straddling and Highly Migratory Fish Stocks', 285.
13. In particular, see discussion by Orrego, Ch. 1 above.
14. See generally part V of the LOS Convention, Arts. 55–75.
15. LOS Convention, Arts. 116–19.
16. Ibid., Art. 63 (2) provides:

   Where the same stock or stocks of associated species occur both within the exclusive economic zone and in an area beyond and adjacent to the zone, the coastal State and the States fishing for such stocks in the adjacent area shall seek, either directly or through appropriate subregional or regional organizations, to agree upon the measures necessary for the conservation of these stocks in the adjacent area.

17. Letter of US Congressman John Miller to C. William Verity, Jr., US Secretary of Commerce, 22 Feb. 1988.
18. Miles and Burke, 'Pressures on the United Nations Convention on the Law of the Sea', 348–9.
19. For an additional analysis of the negotiations that led to the Convention, see Kaye, 'Legal Approaches to Polar Fisheries Regimes', 101–2.
20. Art. 122 of the LOS Convention provides: 'For the purposes of this Convention, "enclosed or semi-enclosed sea" means a gulf, basin or sea surrounded by two or more States and connected to another sea or the ocean by a narrow outlet or consisting entirely or primarily of the territorial seas and exclusive economic zones of two or more coastal States.'
21. Art. 123 of the LOS Convention provides:

   States bordering an enclosed or semi-enclosed sea should co-operate with each other in the exercise of their rights and in the performance of their duties under this Convention. To this end they shall endeavour, directly or through an appropriate regional organization:

   (a) to co-ordinate the management, conservation, exploration and exploitation of the living resources of the sea;
   (b) to co-ordinate the implementation of their rights and duties with respect to the protection and preservation of the marine environment;
   (c) to co-ordinate their scientific research policies and undertake where appropriate joint programmes of scientific research in the area;
   (d) to invite, as appropriate, other interested States or international organizations to co-operate with them in furtherance of the provisions of this article.

22. A. N. Vylegzhanin and V. K. Zilanov, 'The Central Bering Sea Problem in International Law', unpublished paper on file with author (1989), 2.
23. Cf. B. Oxman, 'The Third United Nations' Conference on the Law of the Sea: The 1977 New York Session', *American Journal of International Law*, 72 (1978), 80.
24. The withdrawal of vessels from the Doughnut Hole calls to mind an emblematic passage from E. Hemingway, *The Sun Also Rises* (New York: Charles

Scribner's Sons, 1926), 136 (' "How did you go bankrupt?" Bill asked. "Two ways", Mike said. "Gradually and then suddenly" ').

25. Joint Statement on the Need for Voluntary Suspension on Fishing in the Central Bering Sea, issued at the Summit Meeting between the United States and the Russian Federation, 17 June 1992.

26. The Record of Discussions is not formally part of the Convention and is not legally binding. As discussed below, however, the Record of Discussions served as a vehicle to accommodate certain concerns that were not addressed in the text of the Convention itself.

27. Statement by Ambassador David A. Colson, Deputy Assistant Secretary of State for Oceans, at the signing of the Convention on the Conservation and Management of Pollock Resources in the Central Bering Sea, 16 June 1994 (on file with author).

28. Toward the end of 1994, the six nations also agreed to extend the voluntary suspension on pollock fishing in the Doughnut Hole through 1995, recognizing that the pollock stock had not recovered. Thus, the delay in the entry into force of the Convention did not cause fishing in the Doughnut Hole to resume.

29. For another analysis of the Convention, see Message from the President, Convention on the Conservation and Management of Pollock Resources in the Central Bering Sea, 9 Aug. 1994, S. Treaty Doc. 103–27, 103d Cong., 2d Sess.; see also W. V. Dunlap, 'The Donut Hole Agreement', *International Journal of Marine and Coastal Law*, 10 (1995), 114–26.

30. Art. 66 (3) of the LOS Convention generally prohibits directed fishing for anadromous stocks on the high seas, except in cases where the prohibition would result in 'economic dislocation' for a state other than the state of origin. At the time the LOS Convention was concluded, only Japan maintained a high seas fishery for anadromous stocks. The 1992 Anadromous Stocks Convention, to which Japan is party, ended that fishery.

31. Other provisions of the Convention also provide for the possibility that activities concerning species other than pollock can take place under the auspices of the Convention. See e.g. Art. IV (1) (f), envisioning cooperative scientific research on living marine resources other than pollock; Art. IV (1) (i), giving the Annual Conference the authority to consider matters related to the conservation and management of living marine resources other than pollock; Art. IX (1) envisioning work by the Scientific and Technical Committee on 'pollock and other living marine resources covered by this Convention'; and Art. X (1), obligating the parties to cooperate in the conduct of scientific research on 'the pollock resources and, as may be determined by the Annual Conference, on other living marine resources covered by this Convention'.

32. Pursuant to Art. V (2) of the Convention, '[a] matter shall be deemed to be a matter of substance if any Party considers it to be of substance'.

33. Unlike the Record of Discussions, the annex to the Convention is legally binding, constituting an 'integral part of the Convention'; Art. XIV (1).

34. All participants in the negotiations recognized that US domestic law requires the United States government, as part of its management of pollock fishing in the US EEZ, to determine the pollock biomass in this area. The negotiators had confidence that this determination would be made in good faith, on the

basis of the best available scientific data; Dunlap, 'The Donut Hole Agreement', 118.

35. As noted above, the Annual Conference has set AHLs of zero each year since the Convention entered into force.

36. This rough estimate is derived from an analysis of the US regulations pursuant to which harvest levels in the US EEZ for Aleutian Basin pollock are set. Comparable regulations are believed to be in place in the Russian Federation.

37. The negotiators could not reach agreement on a 'pre-set' AHL for any biomass greater than 2.5 million metric tons, but instead left such an issue to be determined 'by consensus' by the Annual Conference. At the time of the negotiations, a biomass of such size unfortunately seemed a remote possibility.

38. Art. IV (1) (c) of the Convention.

39. Dunlap, 'The Donut Hole Agreement', 114.

40. Art. 92 (1) of the LOS Convention.

41. Art. XI (5) (e) of the Convention.

42. Art. V of the 1992 Anadromous Stocks Convention contains comparable provisions on the boarding and inspection of high seas fishing vessels by non-flag states. The primary purpose of that treaty, however, was to prohibit high seas fishing for anadromous stocks entirely; unlike the Doughnut Hole Convention, it was not intended to regulate any ongoing fishery. Accordingly, the parties to the Anadromous Stocks Convention (Canada, Japan, Russia, and the United States) understood that the boarding and inspection provisions of that treaty would be much less likely to be exercised. Those provisions nevertheless provided a recent precedent for Art. XI of the Doughnut Hole Convention, which in turn became a critical precedent for the Fish Stocks Agreement and other regimes. Pursuant to Art. XVIII of the Convention on Future Multilateral Cooperation in the Northwest Atlantic Fisheries, the members of the Northwest Atlantic Fisheries Organization have also established reciprocal boarding and inspection rights.

43. In accordance with Art. XI (7) (c), only the flag state may actually try the vessel, master, or crew for any violation and impose any penalties.

44. The LOS Convention entered into force on 16 Nov. 1994.

45. *Report of the United Nations Conference on Environment and Development*, UN Doc. A/CONF.151/26 (1992), vol. ii, Agenda 21, ch. 17, para. 17.52. The Declaration of Cancun, adopted just before the Rio Conference at a meeting of states concerned with ocean fisheries, had also called for such action.

46. FAO Compliance Agreement, Arts. III (1) (a), III (2), and III (3).

47. The FAO Compliance Agreement is also discussed by Vukas and Vidas, Ch. 2 above, and by Hønneland, Ch. 4 above.

48. Art. 117 of the LOS Convention.

49. See Art. 91 (1) of the LOS Convention in conjunction with Art. 94 (1); see the discussion by Vukas and Vidas, Ch. 2 above.

50. Art. XI (1) and XI (2) (a) of the Convention.

51. Agenda 21, ch. 17, para. 17.49 (e), UN Doc. A/CONF.151/26 (vol. ii).

52. See the analysis of the Peanut Hole situation by Oude Elferink, Ch. 6 below.

53. For a fuller discussion of Arts. 21 and 22 of the Fish Stocks Agreement, see D. A. Balton, 'Strengthening the Law of the Sea: The New Agreement on

Straddling Fish Stocks and Highly Migratory Fish Stocks', *Ocean Development and International Law*, 27 (1996), at 140–1.

54. Art. XVI (4) of the Convention.
55. Art. 6 and annex II of the Fish Stocks Agreement for provisions relating to the precautionary approach, and Art. 5 (d)–(g) for provisions calling for ecosystem-wide management.

6

The Sea of Okhotsk Peanut Hole
De facto Extension of Coastal State Control

ALEX G. OUDE ELFERINK

1 Introduction

The Sea of Okhotsk Peanut Hole is an area of high seas completely surrounded by the 200-nautical-mile zone of the Russian Federation.[1] The Peanut Hole comprises some 3 per cent of the total area of the sea. Alaska pollock, the most important commercial fish stock in this area, straddles the Russian economic zone and the Peanut Hole. After the commencement of fishing in the high seas enclave by distant water fishing nations in 1991, the Russian Federation advanced claims for an extension of coastal state control to the enclave and a moratorium on fishing in it.[2]

The dispute over fisheries in the Sea of Okhotsk has a number of linkages with global and regional regimes regarding straddling stocks. In the Barents and the Bering Seas, the Russian Federation is one of two coastal states whose 200-nautical-mile zones are adjacent to a high seas enclave. In the Barents Sea, the other coastal state is Norway, and in the Bering Sea, this is the United States.[3] At the United Nations Conference on Straddling Fish Stocks and Highly Migratory Fish Stocks (Fish Stocks Conference), the regime of the high seas enclave in the Sea of Okhotsk was of particular concern to the Russian Federation. The Agreement adopted by the Conference contains two provisions with direct relevance for the Sea of Okhotsk.[4]

The following analysis starts with an assessment of the situation and the significance of the Sea of Okhotsk fisheries. It then addresses the unilateral measures taken by the Russian Federation regarding fisheries in the Sea of Okhotsk and the developments involving the Russian Federation and the interested states. The Russian submissions concerning the regime of straddling stocks made during the Fish Stocks Conference are analysed and compared to the subsequent negotiating texts and the Fish Stocks Agreement. The legal arguments of the Russian Federation are then assessed against the relevant rules of international law. Finally, the question will be raised of whether or not internal developments in the Russian Federation, such as the transition to a market economy and the changes in its political system, offer an explanation for the Russian Federation's policy with regard to fisheries in the Sea of Okhotsk. The conclusion identifies the linkages of the regime for fisheries in the Sea of Okhotsk to other regimes and suggests how this regime may further evolve.

2 The situation and significance of the Sea of Okhotsk fisheries

The Sea of Okhotsk is one of the major catch areas for the Russian fishing fleet. For instance, the total catch for the Russian Federation in 1995 was 4.3 million metric tons, while the total allowable catch (TAC) for pollock in the Sea of Okhotsk in the same year was 1.5 million metric tons. According to the Russian Federation, the high seas enclave is of particular importance for managing the pollock stocks because the various sub-populations, which reproduce in other parts of the Sea of Okhotsk, intermingle in this area. It was for this reason that a permanent ban on fishing was introduced in the high seas enclave. The ban was observed by states that traditionally fished in the Sea of Okhotsk and which were accorded access to the Russian economic zone. Pressures on stocks have occurred since 1991 when fishing vessels of mainly China, the Republic of Korea, Poland, and Panama started operating in the high seas enclave following the collapse of fisheries in the Bering Sea Doughnut Hole. These states did not consult with the Russian Federation about conservation measures, and these fishing practices are said to have destroyed the system for conservation and management of Alaska pollock established by the Russian Federation. Because of overfishing, the TAC in the Russian economic zone for the years 1992 and 1993 had to be adjusted downward in order to prevent spawning stocks from being totally eliminated in the ensuing years.[5] States fishing in the high seas area in the Sea of Okhotsk have disputed some of the Russian propositions on the status of pollock stocks.[6]

Two other factors may have contributed to the lesser abundance of pollock stocks. Pressure on pollock stocks in the Sea of Okhotsk may in part be attributed to the Russian fishing effort. Resource exploitation is central to the economy of the Russian Far East and there is a general interest in short-term exploitation.[7] Changes in stock abundance also result from climatic changes in the Sea of Okhotsk. The most important impact on the epipelagic fish community of the Sea of Okhotsk can be illustrated by comparing the 1980s to the period 1993–5, when the pollock stock abundance decreased two to three times and the herring abundance increased four to five times.[8]

The impact of fisheries on stock abundance has been confirmed by Russian scientists, who have indicated that the pollock stock in the Sea of

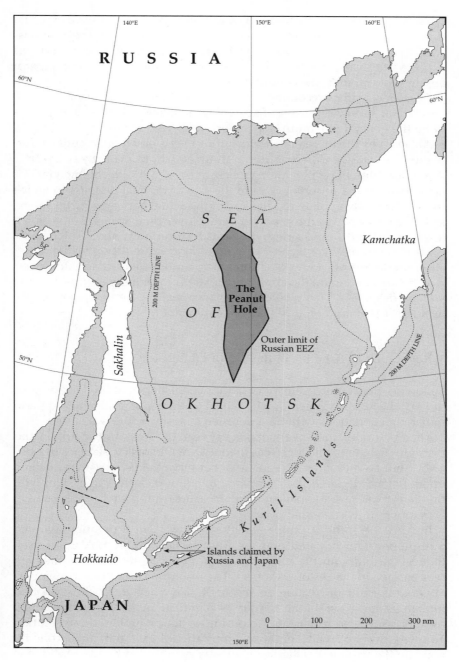

Map 6.1. The Sea of Okhotsk

Okhotsk has been greatly reduced by a combination of excessive exploitation and high by-catches of juvenile pollock.[9] The Sea of Okhotsk biomass was expected to decrease until 1999, when a strong 1995 year class was expected to increase abundance.[10] Recent information does not suggest any improvement in the condition of the pollock.[11]

Russian scientists recommend a TAC based on a 30 per cent exploitation rate of survey estimates of spawning stock levels.[12] This rate appears to be the general maximum for pollock. The TAC for the pollock stocks established by the Russian fisheries authorities is based on scientific information and may be different from recommendations made by scientists.[13] A problem with the exploitation rate used to make TAC recommendations appears to be the uncertainty as to the size of the real biomass to which the TAC actually applies and the size of the actual harvests. Furthermore, lack of consistency in the survey coverage over time has made it difficult to evaluate what a time series represents.[14] Uncertainty about catch levels is also caused by the alleged existence of large-scale illegal fishing operations in the Sea of Okhotsk.[15] These uncertainties concerning catch levels would seem to require the application of a precautionary approach to the pollock fisheries.[16] This would for instance seem to argue against establishing a TAC based on a 30 per cent exploitation rate.

3 Regulation of fisheries in the Sea of Okhotsk

Following the commencement of large-scale fisheries in the Peanut Hole in 1991, the Russian Federation has taken a number of unilateral steps and initiated negotiations with the interested states to address this issue.[17]

The first multilateral negotiations between the Russian Federation and the states fishing on the high seas in the Sea of Okhotsk took place in April 1992,[18] but no measures to regulate or conserve the fisheries were agreed upon. Poland declared itself prepared to adopt measures consistent with the conservation and management measures adopted by the Russian Federation in its economic zone.[19]

In April 1993, the Supreme Soviet of the Russian Federation adopted a resolution which stated that the Russian Federation took upon itself the responsibility for the conservation of the living resources in the high seas enclave in the Sea of Okhotsk.[20] The resolution established a temporary moratorium on fishing in the high seas enclave for Russian and foreign fishing vessels from 15 June 1993 until an international agreement on this issue was reached.[21] According to its preamble, the resolution adopted this approach because international law did not explicitly regulate the regime of fisheries in an area surrounded by the EEZ of one state. Shortly after the adoption of the resolution, a spokesperson of the Russian Federation Ministry of Foreign Affairs indicated that any measures taken to enforce the moratorium would not contradict international law.[22] The Russian Federation Committee on Fisheries stated that it reserved the right to claim damages from foreign fishing vessels that violated the resolution.[23]

Shortly before the moratorium was to enter into force, the Russian Federation, Japan, Poland, the Republic of Korea, and China met in Moscow on 31 May and 1 June 1993 at the initiative of the Russian Federation to discuss the fisheries in the Sea of Okhotsk. The Russian Federation proposed a three-year moratorium on fisheries in the Peanut Hole.[24] Japan agreed to abide by this measure on a voluntary basis but at the same time reportedly questioned the legality of any unilateral steps of the Russian Federation to ban fishing in the Sea of Okhotsk.[25] Japan had already ceased fishing for Alaska pollock in the Sea of Okhotsk from 1 January 1991. Poland, the Republic of Korea, and China were prepared temporarily to diminish their catches in the high seas enclave by 25 per cent in comparison with the same period in 1992.[26] The Russian Federation indicated the total insufficiency of measures aimed at the partial reduction of fishing and declared its intention to take all necessary measures on the basis of international law to promote the conservation of the pollock stock.[27]

At the Conference, there was no agreement over how seriously the pollock stocks in the Sea of Okhotsk had been depleted. To address this issue it was agreed to establish a special scientific committee to prepare a report on the condition of the Alaskan pollock in the Peanut Hole for the second session of the Conference.[28] This second session never materialized.

After the first meeting of the Conference on Fisheries in the Sea of Okhotsk, negotiations between the Russian Federation and the interested states have been conducted on a bilateral basis, an approach reportedly preferred by the Russian Federation. These negotiations did not touch upon legal questions of fishing in the high seas enclave in detail, and differences in this respect continued. For instance, a 1995 Agreement on fisheries between the Russian Federation and Poland[29] suggests that little common ground existed with respect to the legal regime for conservation and management.[30] The Agreement purports to regulate mutual relations in the field of fisheries within the exclusive economic zones (EEZs) of the parties and in areas of the high seas beyond those zones.[31] The clause on fisheries in such high seas areas only provides that the parties shall cooperate directly or through the relevant international organizations to guarantee the conservation and management of marine living resources in areas adjacent to their EEZs and those of third states. The parties can consult on questions of common interest, which can be addressed by the relevant international organizations.[32]

The Russian Federation took a further unilateral step in September 1993. The Russian Government charged the Ministry of Foreign Affairs to examine the expediency of reconsidering or denouncing bilateral fisheries and trade agreements with states whose fishing vessels were engaged in fishing in the Peanut Hole and to look into the possibility of other trade and economic measures. The allotment of catch quotas in the Russian Federation's economic zone to foreign legal or natural persons conducting or having conducted fisheries in the Peanut Hole was prohibited. Furthermore, a number of measures were enacted against foreign fishing vessels that were conducting or had conducted fisheries in the Peanut Hole to discourage their operation in this area.[33]

In November 1995, the Decision was amended, revoking the prohibition to allot catch quotas in the Russian Federation's economic zone to foreign legal or natural persons who formerly conducted fisheries in the enclave. Furthermore, the servicing in Russian ports of ships of such foreign legal or natural persons no longer was prohibited.[34] This amendment was most likely the consequence of the cessation of fishing by all states that previously fished in the high seas enclave in exchange for access to the Russian economic zone.[35] The catch quotas which have been accorded to the interested states since 1995 have been lowered each year.[36] Still, statements by the Governor of the Primorye region indicated opposition to the allocation of these catch quotas.[37]

Reportedly, Poland did not exclude the possibility that Polish fishing vessels would return to the high seas enclave in the Sea of Okhotsk if the Russian Federation showed itself too inflexible in the negotiations over catch quotas in the Russian economic zone.[38] Poland's initial reluctance to suspend its fishing operation in the Peanut Hole may in part be explained by the fact that alternative fishing grounds were not readily available. However, it seems that a number of alternatives have developed, such as Polish shipowners cooperating with Canada, New Zealand, and Mauritania. There are also some fishing opportunities on the high seas in the Antarctic region and the North Atlantic Ocean.

The arrangements between the Russian Federation and the interested states, which give them access to the Russian economic zone in exchange for a suspension of fishing activities in the Peanut Hole, have ramifications for the conservation and management regime in the Sea of Okhotsk. The Russian Federation, as the coastal state, unilaterally establishes the conservation and management regime for its 200-nautical-mile zone. States that formerly fished on the high seas have no influence on the formulation of these conservation and management measures.

The Russian management regime includes on-board inspections of foreign vessels, daily reporting on fishing activities, and a procedure for passing through specially designated areas to enter the Russian economic zone.[39] The 1995 Agreement between Poland and the Russian Federation provides that each state shall guarantee that its nationals and ships observe the measures adopted by the other party in its EEZ. The parties agree to on-board inspections of their fishing vessels in the EEZ of the other party, and if infringements of fisheries legislation are established, enforcement action can be taken, including detention and arrest of the ship and its crew.[40]

Before the interested states agreed to refrain from fishing activities in the Peanut Hole, the Russian Federation conducted military exercises and weapons testing on the high seas in the Sea of Okhotsk. These manœuvres were probably related to the dispute over fisheries.[41] Russian fisheries organizations proposed to close the central part of the Sea of Okhotsk temporarily in order to hold military manœuvres in December 1991, but at that time the proposal was rejected by the Russian Ministry of Foreign Affairs.[42] The areas of the high seas enclave which have been used for military exercises and weapons testing are those in which most fishing activities by third states have taken place.[43]

There do not appear to have been any official protests against the military exercises and weapons testing as such, although Poland has protested against the fact that the Russian Federation in certain instances disseminated information about military activities only through radio messages and at very short notice. Some of the exercises which were announced did not materialize.

Although military exercises and weapons testing are among the freedoms of the high seas, they shall, like any other use compatible with the status of the high seas, not involve an unreasonable interference with the rights of other states.[44] Whether or not military exercises or weapons testing leads to such an unreasonable interference can be assessed by such factors as the duration of the exercises or testing, the size of the areas involved, the other activities normally taking place in these areas, and the availability of alternative areas. The somewhat scant information on the Russian military activities in the Sea of Okhotsk would seem to suggest that these activities may have constituted a case of unreasonable interference.

The Russian Federation has been supported by the United States in its conflict over fisheries resources in the Sea of Okhotsk.[45] In the Bering Sea, both states had been faced with a similar situation of intense fishing efforts by third states in a high seas enclave since the end of the 1980s.[46] The United States did not have a particular interest in the fisheries in the Sea of Okhotsk.[47]

In 1996, the United States and the Russian Federation concluded an agreement on straddling fish stocks in the Sea of Okhotsk. The preamble of the Sea of Okhotsk Agreement indicates that the parties are guided by the Fish Stocks Agreement. The Agreement recognizes that all fishing for straddling stocks in the central part of the Sea of Okhotsk is subject to the rights, duties, and interests of the Russian Federation.[48] A similar provision is contained in Article 16 (1) of the Fish Stocks Agreement, which, however, uses the words *'shall take into account* the rights, duties and interests of the coastal State'.[49] The United States obliges itself to ensure that nationals and vessels subject to its jurisdiction observe the measures adopted by the Russian Federation for the conservation and management of the pollock resources in the entire Sea of Okhotsk, including the high seas area. These measures are compatible throughout the entire biological range of these resources.[50] This arrangement differs from the approach taken in the Fish Stocks Agreement, which provides for the compatibility between the measures of the coastal state in its EEZ and those adopted by the states fishing on the high seas. The Russian Federation may consider this a recognition of the fact that its coastal state rights in the Sea of Okhotsk are of a different nature from those of the coastal state generally in respect of the part of a straddling stock located in the high seas.

Under the Sea of Okhotsk Agreement, each party shall prohibit nationals and vessels subject to its jurisdiction from the fishing of pollock in the enclave until the Russian Federation has determined, on the basis of the best scientific evidence available, that pollock resources have recovered sufficiently to allow a resumption of such fishing. If the Russian Federation considers the possibility of resumption, it shall consult with the United States.[51] The Agreement provides for cooperation concerning scientific data and information regarding the pollock stock and contains steps that the parties shall take to ensure that third states comply with the conservation and management of pollock stocks in the Sea of Okhotsk.[52]

It appears that, in general, international cooperation has hitherto had a limited role in the generation of scientific information about the pollock stocks, although bilateral agreements with the Russian Federation provide for the possibility of cooperation in this field.[53] The North Pacific Marine Science Organization (PICES), which was established in 1992,[54] could become more actively involved in management issues in the future if its member states so decide.[55] At present, however, PICES has no role in stock assessment or in offering management advice, but the organization is mainly focused on establishing area-wide comparative studies of fish–ocean interactions.[56] At present, it does not appear that the Russian Federation and other member states of PICES are interested in a more active role of the organization in fisheries management.

4 The Sea of Okhotsk fishery and the Fish Stocks Agreement[57]

The Fish Stocks Agreement contains two articles that specifically address the regime of fisheries in sea areas such as the Sea of Okhotsk. This concerns Article 15 on enclosed and semi-enclosed seas and Article 16 on areas of high seas surrounded entirely by an area under the national jurisdiction of a single state.[58] Reportedly, much of the strong sentiment at the Fish Stocks Conference over the formulation of the article on enclaves arose from the conflict over fisheries in the Sea of Okhotsk.[59] During the last substantive session of the Conference (from 24 July to 4 August 1995), the draft articles on enclosed and semi-enclosed seas and high seas enclaves were among the remaining contentious issues. One of the arguments of the distant water fishing nations for rejecting a special regime in this case was reportedly that bilateral agreements were already in place.[60] These states questioned the international codification of an article (Article 16) that could be seen to allow coastal state control over areas of the high seas.[61] The final text of Article 16 of the Agreement reportedly was the result of intensive negotiations between the Russian Federation and Poland.[62]

Documents submitted by the Russian Federation to the Conference make it possible to construct in some detail its involvement in the drafting of Articles 15 and 16 of the Fish Stocks Agreement.[63] It seems that the efforts of the Russian Federation were at first only aimed at the inclusion of an article on enclosed and semi-enclosed seas in the document to be adopted by the Conference, and later shifted to the provision on high seas enclaves.[64] This was paralleled by a shift in the relative importance of these two provisions in the subsequent negotiating texts.[65]

The Russian proposals on enclosed and semi-enclosed seas and high seas enclaves confer more extensive obligations on the states engaged in fisheries on the high seas than the subsequent negotiating texts. The subsequent negotiating texts on the Article on enclosed and semi-enclosed seas only entailed an obligation (which underwent some slight modification) for states to take into account the characteristics of such seas and to act in a manner consistent with part IX of the LOS Convention and other relevant provisions thereof.[66] The Russian Federation submitted two proposals on enclosed and semi-enclosed seas, which implied coastal state control over straddling stocks in the EEZ and the adjacent high seas area.[67] A later amendment of the Russian Federation to draft Article 13 on enclosed and semi-enclosed seas, which was not accepted, only proposed to include a reference to the legal circumstances of the conduct of the fisheries and the rights and interests of the coastal states.[68]

The main difference between Russian proposals concerning high seas enclaves and the subsequent negotiating texts of Article 16 of the Fish

Stocks Agreement appears to be that the former contain more far-reaching obligations for states fishing on the high seas pending the absence of provisional arrangements or measures. Article 16 (2) of the Agreement provides that, pending the establishment of provisional arrangements or measures, the states concerned shall take measures in respect of vessels flying their flag in order that they do not engage in fisheries which could undermine the stocks concerned. In the last draft of this Article, such an obligation was not yet included.[69] A proposal of the Russian Federation concerning this latter draft Article would have obliged states to prevent fishing in an enclave in the absence of conservation and management measures.[70] Two proposals for a draft resolution on high seas enclaves submitted by the Russian Federation contained language that gave the coastal state the right unilaterally to undertake interim protection measures.[71] The Russian Federation also reserved its right to take unilateral measures in order to protect its interests in the Sea of Okhotsk.[72] Reportedly, during the debate over draft Article 16 at the fifth substantive session of the Fish Stocks Conference, there were also numerous references to unilateral measures, including the use of force.[73]

It can be questioned whether Articles 15 and 16 contain any obligations which go beyond those of the other provisions of the Fish Stocks Agreement and the LOS Convention. Article 15 only reiterates obligations which already exist under the LOS Convention. Article 16 is mainly based on Articles 7 and 8 of the Fish Stocks Agreement.[74] Elements of Article 16 that do not figure in these articles appear either in Article 5 of the Agreement on general principles or are already contained in the LOS Convention.[75] Nonetheless, it might be argued that, under Articles 15 and 16, greater weight should be given to the position of the coastal state.[76] It has to be assumed that these articles in principle are not intended merely to rephrase other parts of the Fish Stocks Agreement.

Of the states interested in the Sea of Okhotsk fisheries, the Russian Federation and the United States ratified the Fish Stocks Agreement on 21 August 1996 and 4 August 1997 respectively, and China, Japan, and the Republic of Korea have signed it. Poland has not taken any action in respect of the Agreement.[77]

5 A legal assessment of the arguments of the Russian Federation

Central to the Russian Federation's arguments is that the Sea of Okhotsk has certain unique features which distinguish it from most other sea areas. This is considered to justify a legal regime that gives the Russian Federation as a coastal state more extensive control over fisheries in the high seas than is normally the case.[78] To support these contentions, the Russian

Federation has advanced specific interpretations of articles of the LOS Convention concerned with fisheries (especially Articles 61 and 63) and of part IX of the Convention on enclosed and semi-enclosed seas.

At the Fish Stocks Conference, the Russian Federation took a coastal state view on the interpretation of Articles 61 and 63 of the LOS Convention.[79] This view has not prevailed at the Conference, as the Fish Stocks Agreement seeks to strike a balance between this interpretation and that advanced by distant water fishing nations.

The interpretation of the provisions on enclosed and semi-enclosed seas of the LOS Convention advanced by the Russian Federation is controversial.[80] Article 123 of the Convention has been invoked by the Russian Federation as supporting a differentiation between the regime of straddling fish stocks in enclosed and semi-enclosed seas and in other sea areas. However, Article 123 (a) only provides that states bordering such seas shall endeavour to coordinate the management, conservation, exploration, and exploitation of living resources. This Article does not create an independent basis for coastal state rights. The legal basis for specific measures to be taken by coastal states is to be found in the other articles of the LOS Convention, which do not make a differentiation between coastal states' rights over straddling fish stocks in enclosed and semi-enclosed seas and other sea areas.[81] The claim made in Russian legislation that the issue of straddling stocks in enclosed and semi-enclosed seas is not explicitly regulated under international law, justifying unilateral actions by the coastal state, does not seem tenable. International law provides for a number of basic obligations concerning the conservation and management of straddling stocks, and these are also applicable to enclosed and semi-enclosed seas. However, this obligation does not include coastal state enforcement on the high seas of measures adopted unilaterally.

A central element of the regime for enclosed and semi-enclosed seas and high seas enclaves advocated by the Russian Federation seems to be that, as a coastal state of the Sea of Okhotsk, it would be responsible for setting the TAC not only for the Russian economic zone but for the whole sea and also fully utilize the TAC.[82] Even if it is accepted that Article 116 of the LOS Convention authorizes the coastal state to establish conservation measures for a straddling stock as a whole,[83] measures intended to make the right of fishing on the high seas non-existent would not be included. The Fish Stocks Agreement stresses the obligation of the coastal state and the states fishing on the high seas to reach compatible conservation measures, including areas of high seas completely surrounded by an area under the national jurisdiction of one state.[84]

In its submissions to the Fish Stocks Conference, the Russian Federation did not refer to the existence of historic factors of relevance for the determination of the legal regime of the Sea of Okhotsk. This argument was raised in 1993 in a publication by three prominent Russian authors who reviewed the status of high seas enclaves under international law.[85]

6 Domestic factors explaining Russian policies

Among the domestic factors which might explain the policy of the Russian Federation on fisheries in the Sea of Okhotsk are the importance of this sector to the regional economy, a shift in markets, and the changing relation between the Far Eastern region and the central government in Moscow.

The Far Eastern region of the Russian Federation, which borders on the Sea of Okhotsk, plays a leading role in the Russian fisheries industry. In 1996, some 70 per cent of the Russian Federation's overall catch was taken in the Far East. The fisheries industry is among the most important economic sectors of this region. The larger power of the Russian regions in relation to the central government since the demise of the Soviet Union may have been another relevant factor. The central government may consider that support to the Far Eastern region on an issue of major significance for its economy is essential for the continued allegiance of this region to the centre.[86]

Another factor contributing to an explanation of the Russian posture over pollock stocks in the Sea of Okhotsk is the development of Russia's internal market and export markets. Russian domestic prices of fish products are below world market levels and internal shipping costs are high. This has led Russian firms to search for export markets and to compete with firms from other countries. Pollock is among the fish products being exported. The curtailing of fisheries in the Peanut Hole in the Sea of Okhotsk and the Doughnut Hole in the Bering Sea has contributed to a reduction of the abundant supply of pollock in the world market,[87] which would seem to favour Russian exporters.

During the Fish Stocks Conference, the Russian Federation negotiated almost strictly from a coastal state perspective, mostly because of concerns about overfishing in the Sea of Okhotsk, despite the fact that the Russian Federation still has considerable interest in distant water fishing operations.[88] Several factors might explain this approach. The Russian Federation may have felt that other states, such as Japan, China, and the European Union, would be able to ensure that distant water fishing interests were not unduly affected by the Agreement. Furthermore, as distant water fishing became economically less attractive, the Russian fishing industry may have been more interested in securing control over resources closer to base. Finally, the domestic actors interested in the Sea of Okhotsk fisheries seem to have been more organized than Russian distant water fishing interests, and this probably contributed to their comparatively large role in policy formulation.[89]

7 Conclusion

When establishing regime linkages[90] between arrangements on fisheries in the Sea of Okhotsk and other regimes, the LOS Convention, the Fish Stocks Agreement, PICES, the Doughnut Hole Agreement,[91] and the Loophole Agreement[92] can be taken into consideration. The LOS Convention and the Fish Stocks Agreement provide a number of material linkages to arrangements in the Sea of Okhotsk. To a large extent, these linkages appear to have been obstructive, as the interested states did not agree on the interpretation of these global regimes.

The negotiations on the Fish Stocks Agreement, which paid particular attention to the issue of compatibility between measures of the coastal state and states fishing on the high seas and stressed the importance of subregional and regional fisheries management organizations and arrangements, have not patterned the cooperation between the Russian Federation and the states engaged in fishing in the Peanut Hole. Conversely, the situation in the Sea of Okhotsk has significantly influenced the negotiations on Articles 15 and 16 of the Fish Stocks Agreement. The Fish Stocks Agreement has influenced the Sea of Okhotsk Agreement concluded by the Russian Federation and the United States. However, Article 2 of the latter Agreement provides for a different mechanism to establish compatible measures from the Fish Stocks Agreement, giving a larger role to the coastal state in this respect.

The Doughnut Hole Agreement has not led to the adoption of a similar regime in the Sea of Okhotsk.[93] Its provisions on fishing operations by third parties have been included in the Russian–US Sea of Okhotsk Agreement.[94] The bilateral fisheries agreement of 1995 between Poland and the Russian Federation models its provision on fishing in areas adjacent to the EEZ of the other party on Articles 63 and 64 of the LOS Convention, without providing any further elaboration. This Agreement, which was concluded before the final substantive session of the Fish Stocks Conference, does not contain any reference to the work of the Conference.

The impact of the disputes over fisheries in the Bering Sea and the Sea of Okhotsk on the PICES Convention seems to have been limited. PICES has not been given any role in stock assessment or offering management advice, although cooperation in these fields through PICES might have been an element in a regime for the Sea of Okhotsk and the Bering Sea. The International Council for the Exploration of the Sea (ICES), which served as a model for PICES, has a role in stock assessment and offering management advice. Nonetheless, the activities of PICES may result in a weak interactive linkage to the Sea of Okhotsk fisheries.

The Sea of Okhotsk high seas enclave is one of three high seas enclaves that are adjacent to the economic zone of the Russian Federation.[95] In the Barents Sea, the legal regime that has been agreed upon between the interested states is similar to that of the Sea of Okhotsk. One author discussing the Loophole Agreement has classified this as a 'bilateral, or coastal state approach'.[96] In explaining this approach, several factors have been proffered: the possibility that Norway and the Russian Federation may have wished to avoid the consequences stemming from a regional fisheries arrangement under the Fish Stocks Agreement; the perceived weaknesses of the relevant regional fisheries organization; a fear that a regionalist regime would weaken the role and functions of the bilateral Norwegian–Russian management regime; the belief that a regime limiting fishing to the EEZ would be easier to enforce; the fact that a small proportion of stocks are found in the high seas enclave; and more general foreign policy considerations calling for limited third state involvement in this strategically sensitive area.[97] These considerations also apply to a certain extent in the Sea of Okhotsk.

In the Bering Sea, the coastal states and the distant water fishing states did reach agreement on a management regime covering the high seas enclave in 1994.[98] In contrast, negotiations between the Russian Federation and these same distant water fishing states over the Sea of Okhotsk in 1992 and 1993 did not result in a regional arrangement. At first sight, it might have been expected that the experience in the Bering Sea, where negotiations started at an earlier date, would have made a similar agreement for the Sea of Okhotsk a likely outcome. The difference in outcome can be explained by a number of factors. In the Sea of Okhotsk, the high seas enclave is completely surrounded by the economic zone of the Russian Federation. The absence of the Russian Federation's need to coordinate its policy with another coastal state may have contributed to a more inflexible stance. In the Sea of Okhotsk, the Russian Federation seems to have resorted to military exercises as a means of pressurizing states that fish in the high seas enclave. In the Barents and Bering Seas, such a move might have seriously antagonized the other coastal state. The legality of such exercises and testing in the context of the Sea of Okhotsk fisheries dispute can be questioned. Some other measures that the Russian Federation has taken in the Sea of Okhotsk have also been agreed upon with Norway for the Barents Sea.

Another important difference from the Bering Sea situation is that in the Sea of Okhotsk, there was still an alternative available for the distant water fishing states. Fishing activities in the Sea of Okhotsk started after the decline of stocks in the Bering Sea in 1991. For Polish fishing vessels, the Sea of Okhotsk seems to have been of vital importance in the first half of the 1990s.[99] This obviously limited the room for compromise. Moreover, the distant water fishing states active in the Sea of Okhotsk do not seem to have shared the Russian Federation's evaluation of the condition of pollock stocks. A review of some of the available data suggests that there is some room for such doubt.

A further explanation for the difference between the fishery regimes of the Bering Sea and the Sea of Okhotsk may lie in the fact that the Russian Federation at the Fish Stocks Conference attached particular importance to the inclusion of a special regime applicable to the Sea of Okhotsk in a Fish Stocks Agreement. A solution of the dispute over the fisheries regime in the high seas enclave would have seriously limited any chance of success for such a strategy.[100] A final difference regarding the Bering Sea regime is that the United States had a preference for a regional conservation and management regime with the participation of all interested states.[101] The cooperation of the Russian Federation with the United States over the Bering Sea Doughnut Hole has probably been instrumental in securing the latter state's support for the Russian position in the Sea of Okhotsk.

In the Sea of Okhotsk, the conservation and management regime for the high seas enclave consists of a set of bilateral arrangements of the Russian Federation with the United States and the states formerly active in the high seas enclave. The distant water fishing states have been accorded access to the economic zone of the Russian Federation in exchange for an abstention from fishing activities in the high seas enclave, while reserving their position on the legal issues involved.

Compared to the regime envisaged in the Fish Stocks Agreement, the present regime seems to be advantageous to the Russian Federation. Instead of having to agree on the compatibility of the conservation and management measures adopted for its economic zone with the measures adopted by the states fishing on the high seas, the measures adopted by the Russian Federation form the setting in which discussions on catch quotas take place. However, because fisheries on the high seas could be resumed, the Russian Federation must continue, to some extent, to take into account the interests of distant water fishing nations.

Existing arrangements are highly supportive regarding the main tasks of fisheries management.[102] The Russian Federation can take effective measures with respect to all of these tasks. However, the strength of these arrangements (the concentration of decision-making power in the coastal state) is at the same time their weakness. The arrangements entail the cessation of fishing activities on the high seas, whereas the global regime, as contained in the LOS Convention and the Fish Stocks Agreement, recognizes the freedom of fishing on the high seas, albeit with important qualifications. The absence of an interactive linkage to the global regime that validates the arrangements makes them susceptible to challenges on that account.

It remains a possibility that this could occur if the Russian Federation and the distant water fishing states cannot reach agreement over the conditions of access to the Russian economic zone. The outcome of such a conflict is hard to predict, as it depends to a large extent on the willingness of the states involved to reach a mutually acceptable interpretation of the rules of international law applicable to the high seas enclave. The analysis of Articles 15 and 16 of the Fish Stocks Agreement (which has not yet entered into force) shows that these articles leave room for different interpretations. Moreover, it is possible that the Russian Federation would argue for a larger measure of coastal state control over fisheries than what is provided for under the Agreement. This is suggested by the fact that the Russian Ministry of Foreign Affairs hailed the Sea of Okhotsk Agreement as a mutually acceptable long-term solution and an example for those states which had been engaged in fishing in the Peanut Hole.[103] This Agreement provides that the United States shall ensure that nationals and vessels subject to its jurisdiction observe measures adopted by the Russian Federation that are compatible for all of the Sea of Okhotsk.

The fact that the decline of Russia's distant water fishing effort could be reversed may restrain the Russian Federation from making claims for a special regime for the Sea of Okhotsk. Other coastal states might refer to the regime in the Sea of Okhotsk as a precedent against these interests of the Russian Federation, especially as it seems questionable that the Russian argument that the factual situation in the Sea of Okhotsk is unique is completely tenable.[104]

The Russian Federation may also be restrained by the existing global regime. Although the Russian Federation might support an interpretation of this regime in line with its preferred outcome, it is doubtful that such an interpretation would be upheld. This especially concerns the claim of the Russian Federation that it should be accorded the right to adopt unilaterally certain management measures for the entire Sea of Okhotsk. Moreover, as the Russian Federation, through the arrangements with distant water fishing nations, has *de facto* control over the high seas area,[105] there seem to be a number of powerful arguments which suggest that the Russian Federation would be best served by a maintenance of the status quo in the Sea of Okhotsk.[106]

Notes

The author thanks Olav Schram Stokke, the participants in the POLOS workshops, and three anonymous reviewers for their comments on earlier versions of this chapter.

1. Japan, the only other coastal state in the Sea of Okhotsk, has a limited coastal front and its exclusive economic zone (EEZ) does not extend to the high seas enclave. Japan has maintained a low profile on the straddling stocks issue in the Sea of Okhotsk. The Russian Federation considers that it is the only coastal state as regards the conservation and management of fisheries in the Peanut Hole; A. G. Oude Elferink, 'Fisheries in the Sea of Okhotsk High Seas Enclave: The Russian Federation's Attempts at Coastal State Control', *International Journal of Marine and Coastal Law*, 10 (1995), 1, at 4–5.
2. The dispute over the regime for fisheries in the high seas enclave does not concern anadromous stocks that are regulated by the Convention for the Conservation of Anadromous Stocks in the North Pacific Ocean of 11 Feb. 1992; *The Law of the Sea: Current Developments in State Practice*, iv (New York: United Nations, 1995), 188.
3. Management of the Barents Sea Loophole is discussed by Stokke, Ch. 9 below; on the Bering Sea Doughnut Hole, see Balton, Ch. 5 above.
4. Agreement for the Implementation of the Provisions of the United Nations Convention on the Law of the Sea of 10 Dec. 1982 relating to the Conservation and Management of Straddling Fish Stocks and Highly Migratory Fish Stocks of 4 Dec. 1995 (Fish Stocks Agreement), Arts. 15 (enclosed and semi-enclosed seas) and 16 (areas of high seas surrounded entirely by an area under the national jurisdiction of one state); 29 *LOSB* 25.
5. UN Doc. A/CONF.164/L.21, p. 2. According to Shuntov and Dulepova catches in the Russian economic zone in the Sea of Okhotsk remained stable until 1993 when the level declined from a maximum of 2.5 million metric tons to about 2 million metric tons; Vi. P. Shuntov and E. P. Dulepova, 'Biota of the Okhotsk Sea: Structure of Communities, the Interannual Dynamics and Current Status', *PICES Scientific Report*, 6 (1996) (Proceedings of the Workshop on the Sea of Okhotsk and Adjacent Areas), 263, at 265.
6. See below.
7. V. G. Wespestad, *Trends in North Pacific Pollock and Cod Fisheries* (www.wrc.noaa.gov/~jianelli/norfish/norfish.html), Sept. 1997.
8. V. V. Lapko, 'Interannual Dynamics of Epipelagic Ichtyocen Structure in the Okhotsk Sea', *PICES Scientific Report*, 6 (1996), 237, at 237–8.
9. J. N. Ianelli and V. Wespestad, *Trends in North Pacific Cod and Pollock Catch 1991–1998* (31 Oct. 1998) (www.refm.noaa.gov/stocks/Presentations/norfish/gfish98.htm).
10. Wespestad, *Trends in North Pacific Pollock and Cod Fisheries*. Russian fishery authorities are working to establish wider mesh sizes and other measures to protect the 1995 year class; Ianelli and Wespestad, *Trends in North Pacific Cod*

and Pollock Catch. The Pacific Institute of Fisheries and Oceanography (TINRO) in Vladivostok has produced the following estimates (year and spawning biomass in million metric tons): 1985: 6.6; 1986: 8.7; 1987: 9.1; 1988: 8.3; 1989: 6.6; 1990: 3.3; 1991: 4.7; 1992: 4.8; 1993: 3.8; 1994: 6.2; 1995: 5.0; 1996: 3.6; 1997: 3.7 (e-mail of V. Wespestad to the author, 28 July 1997).

11. E-mail of V. Wespestad to the author, 16 Mar. 2000; Press Release on the Briefing of the Chairman of the Committee on Fisheries of 19 Jan. 2000 (Interfax) (in Russian; on file with the author); 'Fish Catch Plunges 8.5 Percent', *Vladivostok News* (20 Aug. 1999) (www.vladnews.ru/).

12. Wespestad, *Trends in North Pacific Pollock and Cod Fisheries*.

13. V. Wespestad, *Trends in North Pacific Pollock and Cod and 1998 Harvest Prognosis* (www.afsc.noaa.gov/refm/norfish/FORUM3.htm).

14. E-mail of V. Wespestad to the author, 28 July 1997.

15. On this illegal fishing see e.g. *BBC Summary of World Broadcasts, Weekly Economic Report Part I, Former USSR* (hereinafter *SWB Economic Report*), SUW/0503 WA/5 [18]; ibid., SUW/0546 WA/9 [37]; ibid., SUW/0549 WA/12 [50].

16. Fish Stocks Agreement, Art. 6.

17. For developments relating to fisheries in the Sea of Okhotsk, E. Meltzer, 'Global Overview of Straddling and Highly Migratory Fish Stocks: The Nonsustainable Nature of High Seas Fisheries', *Ocean Development and International Law*, 25 (1994), 255, at 290–3.

18. Ibid. 292. The level of these contacts is not altogether clear. No report on this conference has appeared in the journal published by the Russian Federation Ministry of Foreign Affairs, and a conference on living resources in the Sea of Okhotsk from 31 May to 1 June 1993 is referred to in this publication as the first to take place, *Diplomaticheskii Vestnik*, 13–14 (1993), 69.

19. Meltzer, 'Global Overview of Straddling and Highly Migratory Fish Stocks', 292.

20. Resolution of the Supreme Soviet of the Russian Federation 'On Measures to Protect the Biological Resources of the Sea of Okhotsk' of 16 Apr. 1993; *Vedomosti Soveta Narodnykh Deputatov Rossiiskoi Federatsii i Verkhovnogo Soveta Rossiiskoi Federatsii*, 18 (1993), Item 638.

21. One of the first reports in the Russian press on alleged overfishing in the Sea of Okhotsk already suggested that the Russian Federation under international law could establish a temporary moratorium on fisheries in the enclave; 'Dostanetsia li Nam 'Dyrka ot Bublika?', *Izvestiia* (23 Nov. 1991), 2. Recently, the Governors of the Primorye and Sakhalin regions reportedly urged the extension of the Russian economic zone beyond 200 nautical miles or the declaration of the Sea of Okhotsk an internal sea; *Vladivostok News*, 186 (26 Mar. 1999) (www.vladnews.ru/); O. Mikhailova, 'Prevratim Okhotskoe More v Ozero!' *Asiainfo*, 5 May 2000 (www.asiainfo.narod.ru/arhiv/mai_2000/09_14/prevratim_see.htm). Influental Duma members questioned the propriety of such a step; Mikhailova, 'Prevratim Okhotskoe More v Ozero!'

22. *Diplomaticheskii Vestnik*, 13–14 (1993), 70; 'MID RF Nastaivaet na Moratorii na Promysel Mintaia', *Segodnia*, 15 (12 May 1993); K. A. Bekiashev and V. F.

Korels'kii, 'Itogi Vtoroi Sessii Konferentsii OON po Transgranichnym Rybnym Zapasam i Zapasam Daleko Migriruiushchikh Ryb', *Moskovsksii Zhurnal Mezhdunarodnogo Prava*, 4 (1994), 70, at 84–5 for a discussion of measures the Russian Federation might take. See further below for the measures actually taken by the Russian Federation.

23. Meltzer, 'Global Overview of Straddling and Highly Migratory Fish Stocks', 293.

24. *Diplomaticheskii Vestnik*, 13–14 (1993), 69. The distant water fishing states had agreed to such a moratorium in the Bering Sea Doughnut Hole in 1992. This moratorium became effective in 1993; Balton, Ch. 5 above.

25. *BBC Summary of World Broadcasts, Part I, Former USSR*, SU/1696 A1/2 [5].

26. UN Doc. A/CONF.164/INF/6, p. 1. The Republic of Korea had voluntarily suspended fishing in the area since 25 Apr. 1993 but indicated that it might resume fishing in Sept. 1993 if no arrangement on access to the Russian economic zone was reached, *Korea Herald* (26 Aug. 1993), 8, as reported in *Foreign Broadcast Information Service* (FBIS-EAS-93-164) (26 Aug. 1993), 19.

27. UN Doc. A/CONF.164/INF/6, pp. 1–2.

28. Ibid. 1.

29. Agreement between the Government of the Republic of Poland and the Government of the Russian Federation on Mutual Relations and Cooperation in the Field of Fisheries (1995) (on file with the author).

30. This is especially the case if this Agreement is compared to the Fish Stocks Agreement and the Agreement between the Government of the United States of America and the Government of the Russian Federation on the Conservation of Straddling Fish Stocks in the Central Part of the Sea of Okhotsk (1996) (hereinafter Sea of Okhotsk Agreement) (text provided by the United States Department of State; on file with the author) (on this latter Agreement, see below).

31. Agreement between the Government of the Republic of Poland and the Government of the Russian Federation on Mutual Relations and Cooperation in the Field of Fisheries, Preamble.

32. Ibid., Art. 6.

33. Decision of the Council of Ministers—Government of the Russian Federation 'On Additional Measures for the Conservation of Living Resources and the Protection of Fisheries Interests of the Russian Federation in the Sea of Okhotsk' of 22 Sept. 1993, No. 962; *Sobranie Aktov Prezidenta i Pravitel'stva Rossiiskoi Federatsii*, 40 (1993), Item 3857, paras. 2, 3, and 5. For a report in English on the Decision, see *SWB Economic Report*, SUW/304 WA/1 [3] and ibid., SUW/0316 WC/4 [19]. The Decision refers to an earlier decision of the Government of the Russian Federation (No. 667-52) of 1 Sept. 1992 (not published).

34. Decision of the Government of the Russian Federation 'On the Amendment of the Decision of the Council of Ministers—Government of the Russian Federation of 22 September 1993 No. 962' of 2 Nov. 1995, No. 1065. *Sobranie Zakonodatel'stva Rossiiskoi Federatsii*, 45 (1995), Item 4327.

35. See further *SWB Economic Report*, SUW/0304 WC/4 [23]; ibid., SUW/0316 WC/4 [19]; and ibid., SUW/0334 WC/5 [22].

36. For instance, in 1993 the Republic of Korea and the Russian Federation initially had agreed on a catch quota in the Russian economic zone of 155,000 metric tons; the *Korea Herald* (26 Aug. 1993), 8 as reported in FBIS-EAS-93-164 (26 Aug. 1993), 19. The Republic of Korea was awarded a catch quota of 30,000 metric tons of Alaska pollock in the Sea of Okhotsk in 1999 (Economic Report, SUW/0565 WA/14 [43]). Poland received quotas of respectively 85,000 and 70,000 metric tons of Alaska pollock for 1998 and 1999 in the 200-nautical-mile zone of the Russian Federation. Of this latter figure, 30,000 metric tons was accorded in the Sea of Okhotsk and 40,000 metric tons in the Bering Sea.

37. As quoted in N. Wadhams, 'Nazdratenko Claims Foreign Fleets Steal Okhotsk Fish', *Vladivostok News*, 165 (17 Apr. 1998) (www.vladnews.ru/).

38. L. Sosnowska-Smogorzewska, 'Poland's Fight for Pollock', *Warsaw Voice*, 3 (21 Jan. 1996), 378.

39. Ordinance No. 86 of 30 May 1994 of the Fisheries Committee of the Russian Federation 'Procedures and Regulations for Granting Permits to Carry out Fishing Operations of the Biological Resources inside the Economic Zone and the Continental Shelf of the Russian Federation for Foreign Legal Entities, Foreign Individuals and Russian Companies with Foreign Investment'.

40. Agreement between the Government of the Republic of Poland and the Government of the Russian Federation on Mutual Relations and Cooperation in the Field of Fisheries, Arts. 2 and 3.

41. See also *SWB Economic Report*, SUW/0337 WC/3 [15].

42. 'Pora Zakryvat' Okhotskoe More', *Izvestiia* (5 Dec. 1991), 7.

43. Exact information on the timing of the exercises and testing is not available. This issue became moot after 1995 when all states involved ceased their fishing activities in the Peanut Hole.

44. Convention on the High Seas (1958), Art. 2 (450 *UNTS* 11); United Nations Convention on the Law of the Sea (1982) (hereinafter LOS Convention), Art. 87 (2); 21 *ILM* 1261. For support for the appropriateness of a 'test of reasonableness' to evaluate whether in a specific case the designation of areas of the high seas for military exercises or weapons testing falls within the freedom of the high seas see e.g. R. R. Churchill and A. V. Lowe, *The Law of the Sea*, 3rd edn. (Manchester University Press, 1999), 206–7; M. S. McDougal and N. A. Schlei, 'The Hydrogen Bomb Tests in Perspective: Lawful Measures for Security', *Yale Law Review*, 64 (1955), 648, at 652–3 and 690–5. For a criticism of the test of reasonableness as being too imprecise or subjective, see D. P. O'Connell, *The International Law of the Sea*, i (Oxford: Clarendon Press, 1982), 58; J. M. Van Dyke, 'Military Exclusion and Warning Zones on the High Seas', in T. A. Clingan, Jr., and A. L. Kolodkin (eds.), *Moscow Symposium on the Law of the Sea* (Honolulu: The Law of the Sea Institute, University of Hawaii, 1991), 75, at 122.

45. See e.g. UN Doc. A/CONF.164/L.33 of 28 July 1993.

46. See e.g. E. L. Miles and W. T. Burke, 'Pressures on the United Nations Convention on the Law of the Sea Arising from New Fisheries Conflicts: The Problem of Straddling Stocks', *Ocean Development and International Law*, 20 (1989), 343, at 348–9.

47. At the time the Sea of Okhotsk Agreement was concluded, the United

States had no fishing presence in the Sea of Okhotsk. Subsequently, several US fishing vessels, possibly reflagged to the Russian Federation, have operated in the Russian economic zone (e-mail of D. Balton to the author of 22 Dec. 1997).

48. Sea of Okhotsk Agreement, Art. 1.

49. Emphasis added.

50. Sea of Okhotsk Agreement, Art. 2. Preceding the conclusion of the Agreement, in Jan. 1995, a bill was introduced in the US House of Representatives which sought to prohibit fishing in the central part of the Sea of Okhotsk by vessels and nationals of the United States (HR 715 RH, 104th cong., 1st Sess. (Report No. 104–42)). The Sea of Okhotsk Fisheries Enforcement Act of 3 Nov. 1995 (US Public Law 104–43, title V) prohibits US fishing vessels from fishing in the Sea of Okhotsk, except in accordance with an agreement between the two states.

51. Ibid., Art. 3.

52. Ibid., Arts. 4 and 5. In case fishing operations of any third state could affect adversely the long-term sustainable use of the pollock resources of the Sea of Okhotsk the parties shall take measures, individually or collectively, in accordance with international law, that they deem necessary and appropriate to deter such operations (ibid., Art. 5 (3)). The United States has lent support to the Russian efforts to control overfishing in the Peanut Hole through diplomatic channels (e-mail of D. Balton to the author of 2 Dec. 1997).

53. Agreement between the Government of the Republic of Poland and the Government of the Russian Federation on Mutual Relations and Cooperation in the Field of Fisheries, Art. IV; Sea of Okhotsk Agreement, Art. 4. The United States and the Russian Federation have carried out such cooperation in a number of ways.

54. Convention for a North Pacific Marine Science Organization (PICES) (1990) (pices.ios.bc.ca/struct/Conventn.htm). Part of the information on PICES is based on information provided to the author by V. Wespestad and W. Wooster.

55. At present, Poland is the only state active in the Sea of Okhotsk that is not a member of PICES. Interested states can accede to the PICES Convention after a notification to the Depository and the absence of a written objection by a contracting party (Art. XIV). Poland attended the first meeting of PICES in 1992 as an observer. It seems that Poland lost interest in PICES when it became evident that it was not to have a role in fisheries management.

56. PICES organized a workshop on the Sea of Okhotsk in 1995, which included scientific papers on fisheries; 'Proceedings of the Workshop on the Okhotsk Sea and Adjacent Sea Areas', *PICES Scientific Report*, 6 (1996). A second workshop on the Sea of Okhotsk, which was held in Nov. 1998, paid much less attention to fisheries; 'Proceedings of the Second PICES Workshop on the Okhotsk Sea and Adjacent Areas', *PICES Scientific Report*, 12 (1999).

57. For an evaluation of the Fish Stocks Agreement see e.g. P. G. G. Davies and C. Redgwell, 'The International Legal Regulation of Straddling Fish Stocks', *British Yearbook of International Law*, 67 (1997), 199, at 257–72; D. Freestone

and Z. Makuch, 'The New International Environmental Law of Fisheries: The United Nations Straddling Stocks Agreement', *Yearbook of International Environmental Law*, 7 (1996), 3; M. Hayashi, 'The 1995 Agreement on the Conservation and Management of Straddling and Highly Migratory Fish Stocks: Significance for the Law of the Sea Convention', *Ocean and Coastal Management*, 29 (1995), 51; E. Hey, 'Global Fisheries Regulations in the First Half of the 1990s', *International Journal of Marine and Coastal Law*, 11 (1996), 459, at 472–82; F. Orrego Vicuña, *The Changing International Law of High Seas Fisheries* (Cambridge University Press, 1999), 137 ff.

58. Art. 15 reads:

Enclosed and semi-enclosed seas

In implementing this Agreement in an enclosed or semi-enclosed sea, States shall take into account the natural characteristics of that sea and shall also act in a manner consistent with Part IX of the Convention and other relevant provisions thereof.

Art. 16 reads:

Areas of high seas surrounded entirely by an area under the national jurisdiction of a single State

1. States fishing for straddling fish stocks and highly migratory fish stocks in an area of the high seas surrounded entirely by an area under the national jurisdiction of a single State and the latter State shall cooperate to establish conservation and management measures in respect of those stocks in the high seas area. Having regard to the natural characteristics of the area, States shall pay special attention to the establishment of compatible conservation and management measures for such stocks pursuant to Article 7. Measures taken in respect of the high seas shall take into account the rights, duties and interests of the coastal State under the Convention, shall be based on the best scientific evidence available and shall also take into account any conservation and management measures adopted and applied in respect of the same stocks in accordance with Article 61 of the Convention by the coastal State in the area under national jurisdiction. States shall also agree on measures for monitoring, control, surveillance and enforcement to ensure compliance with the conservation and management measures in respect of the high seas.

2. Pursuant to Article 8, States shall act in good faith and make every effort to agree without delay on conservation and management measures to be applied in the carrying out of fishing operations in the area referred to in paragraph 1. If, within a reasonable period of time, the fishing States concerned and the coastal State are unable to agree on such measures, they shall, having regard to paragraph 1, apply Article 7, paragraphs 4, 5 and 6, relating to provisional arrangements or measures. Pending the establishment of such provisional arrangements or measures, the States concerned shall take measures in respect of vessels flying their flag in order that they not engage in fisheries which could undermine the stocks concerned.

59. *Earth Negotiations Bulletin*, 7/54 (7 Aug. 1995), 4–5; see also Hayashi, 'The 1995 Agreement', 64. Art. 16 is also of relevance for a high seas area surrounded by the EEZ of Japan and two smaller areas surrounded by the EEZ of New Zealand; see the map '200 Nautical Mile Maritime Claims as of May 1985' (6025 5-85 STATE(INR/GE) (Washington: US State Department, 1985). Japan and New Zealand did not participate actively in the discussions on Art. 16. A number of bilateral fisheries agreements concluded by New Zealand after it established a 200-nautical-mile zone in 1977 addressed fishing activities by the other states involved in the two high seas areas completely surrounded by this zone. The Soviet Union agreed that its vessels would not fish in these high seas areas (Exchange of Letters of 4 Apr. 1978 between the Minister of Fisheries of the Union of Soviet Socialist Republics and the Minister of Foreign Affairs of New Zealand (1151 *UNTS* 283)). The Letter of the Minister of Fisheries of the Soviet Union states that the agreement contained in it 'cannot be considered as prejudicial to the Soviet position regarding freedom of fishing on the high seas'. The Republic of Korea and Japan agreed that only vessels licensed under their bilateral agreements with New Zealand would fish in these areas, complying with the conservation and management measures applicable within the New Zealand 200-nautical-mile zone; Fisheries Agreement between the Government of New Zealand and the Government of the Republic of Korea (1978), Art. VI (2) (1167 *UNTS* 416); Exchange of Letters of 1 Sept. 1978 between the Ambassador of Japan in New Zealand and the Minister of Foreign Affairs of New Zealand (ibid. 446).

60. The Russian Federation and Poland had concluded a new bilateral agreement on fisheries, also addressing fisheries in areas adjacent to the economic zone, on 5 July 1995. Other interested states also had reached agreement with the Russian Federation over their fishing activities in the Sea of Okhotsk (see further above).

61. *Earth Negotiations Bulletin*, 7/54 (7 Aug. 1995), 5.

62. D. Doulman, 'Structure and Process of the 1993–1995 United Nations Conference on Straddling Fish Stocks and Highly Migratory Fish Stocks', *FAO Fisheries Circular*, 898 (1995), 22.

63. This concerns UN Doc. A/CONF.164/L.2 and UN Doc. A/CONF.164/L.2/Corr. 1; UN Doc. A/CONF.164/L.21; UN Doc. A/CONF.164/L.25; UN Doc. A/CONF.164/L.26; UN Doc. A/CONF.164/L.33 (submitted jointly with the United States); and UN Doc. A/CONF.164/INF/6 submitted during the 2nd session of the Conference; UN Doc. A/CONF.164/L.38; UN Doc. A/CONF.164/L.43; and UN Doc. A/CONF.164/L.45 submitted during the 3rd session of the Conference; and UN Doc. A/CONF.164/L.47 and UN Doc. A/CONF.164/L.47/Corr. 1; UN Doc. A/CONF.164/L.48; and UN Doc. A/CONF.164/L.49 submitted during the 5th session of the Conference. The states fishing in the Sea of Okhotsk did not submit documents to the Conference that specifically addressed this issue (for some information on their position, see above para. 3 and this paragraph above).

64. For example UN Doc. A/CONF.164/L.2 and UN Doc. A/CONF.164/L.2/Corr. 1 containing a list of issues for the Fish Stocks Conference include

a point 'specific aspects of the conservation of straddling stocks in the enclaves of enclosed and semi-enclosed seas' and do not contain a specific reference to enclaves surrounded by areas under the national jurisdiction of one state. See also UN Doc. A/CONF.164/L.21, UN Doc. A/CONF.164/L.25, UN Doc. A/CONF.164/L.26, and UN Doc. A/CONF.164/L.38, which all refer to Art. 123 of the LOS Convention on enclosed and semi-enclosed seas. In two proposals of the Russian Federation on a draft resolution relating to areas fully surrounded by the EEZ of one or more states reference to Art. 123 does not appear (UN Doc. A/CONF.164/L.45 and UN Doc. A/CONF.164/L.48).

65. See the relevant articles in UN Doc. A/CONF.164/22; UN Doc. A/CONF.164/22/Rev. 1; and Fish Stocks Agreement. A number of earlier proposals on a draft agreement only included an article on enclosed and semi-enclosed seas and did not contain a precursor to Art. 16. See e.g. UN Doc. A/CONF.164/L.11 (submitted by Argentina, Canada, Chile, Iceland, and New Zealand) and UN Doc. A/CONF.164/L.44 (submitted by Ecuador). The original focus on enclosed and semi-enclosed seas can be explained by the fact that this concept had already received legal validation through its inclusion in part IX of the LOS Convention. The shift in focus might be explained by two circumstances. First, Art. 16 concerns fewer high seas areas than Art. 15, which made it possibly easier to reach agreement. Secondly, the choice for two separate articles made it possible to avoid the formulation of an article on enclosed and semi-enclosed seas going beyond the provisions of part IX of the LOS Convention. For the negotiating history of Arts. 15 and 16 of the Fish Stocks Agreement, see also Orrego, *The Changing International Law of High Seas Fisheries*, 194–7.

66. UN Doc. A/CONF.164/22, Art. 13; UN Doc. A/CONF.164/22/Rev. 1, Art. 13; Fish Stocks Agreement, Art. 15.

67. UN Doc. A/CONF.164/L.25 and UN Doc. A/CONF.164/L.38. The latter document in fact proposed the same coastal state control over: (*a*) straddling stocks, which basically are constituted in and inhabit the EEZ and only at certain periods of their life cycle migrate beyond the limits of the EEZ; and (*b*) stocks in enclosed and semi-enclosed seas, in which there is a high seas enclave through which fish stocks migrate in transit, passing through it at various periods of their life cycle. The only difference that was envisaged was that in the latter case Art. 123 of the LOS Convention would also be applicable. See also below for an assessment of the Russian Federation's interpretation of the articles of the LOS Convention on enclosed and semi-enclosed seas.

68. UN Doc. A/CONF.164/L.47.

69. UN Doc. A/CONF.164/22/Rev. 1 Art. 16 (2).

70. UN Doc. A/CONF.164/L.47, Art. 14 (2) (b).

71. UN Doc. A/CONF.164/L.45, para. 3 and UN Doc. A/CONF.164/L.48, para. 3. The draft resolution as amended contained an additional safeguard for the interest of third states as it provided that such measures can be taken 'in situations where there is a danger of the destruction of stocks . . . on the basis of the precautionary principle and of international law'.

72. UN Doc. A/CONF.164/L.33 (submitted jointly with the United States); UN

Doc. A/CONF.164/L.43; and UN Doc. A/CONF.164/L.49. While the first of these documents indicates that measures will be taken in accordance with international law (para. 9), the second does not contain any qualification (para. 7), and the third provides that the Russian Federation will take all necessary measures in accordance with its national legislation (para. 4). In an earlier submission on compliance, the Russian Federation had indicated that in its view enforcement of conservation and management measures for straddling stocks 'is feasible only if those measures are applied by the coastal State over the stock's entire habitat' (UN Doc. A/CONF.164/L.26, para. 2).

73. *Earth Negotiations Bulletin*, 7/54 (7 Aug. 1995), 5.
74. Hayashi notes that Art. 16 of the Agreement 'was inserted at the very last minute to provide for additional measures on the basis particularly of the compatibility principle laid down in Article 7'. He finds that the duty to reach provisional arrangements under Arts. 7 and 16 is similar; Hayashi, 'The 1995 Agreement', 64–5.
75. See also Freestone and Makuch, 'The New International Environmental Law of Fisheries', 33; Hey, 'Global Fisheries Regulations in the First Half of the 1990s', 475; G. Vigneron, 'Compliance and International Environmental Agreements: A Case Study of the 1995 United Nations Straddling Fish Stocks Agreement', *Georgetown International Environmental Law Review*, 10 (1998), 581, at 602.
76. Vigneron, 'Compliance and International Environmental Agreements', 602; see also Orrego, *The Changing International Law of High Seas Fisheries*, 199.
77. Status of the Agreement for the Implementation of the Provisions of the United Nations Convention on the Law of the Sea of 10 Dec. 1982 relating to the Conservation and Management of Straddling Fish Stocks and Highly Migratory Fish Stocks; as at 1 Mar. 2000 (www.un.org/Depts/los/los164st.htm).
78. The argument of unique characteristics to support a special legal regime has also been advanced by the Russian Federation in relation to the Caspian Sea (see e.g. Joint Russian–Iranian Statement on the Caspian Sea, issued at Teheran on 30 Oct. 1995 (UN Doc A/51/59 of 27 Jan. 1996, annex)).
79. Some authors have maintained that under the LOS Convention the coastal state has special rights over straddling stocks; see e.g. W. T. Burke, *The New International Law of Fisheries: UNCLOS 1982 and Beyond* (Oxford: Clarendon Press, 1994), 133–5; B. Kwiatkowska, 'Creeping Jurisdiction beyond 200 Miles in the Light of the 1982 Law of the Sea Convention and State Practice', *Ocean Development and International Law*, 22 (1991), 153, at 167–73. Another view is that the coastal state is not granted any special rights over straddling stocks, other than the duty to cooperate of the states fishing on the high seas; see e.g. R. Lagoni, 'Principles Applicable to Living Resources Occurring both within and without the Exclusive Economic Zone or in Zones of Overlapping Claims (Report of the International Committee on the EEZ of the International Law Association)', *Report of the Sixty-Fifth Conference* (London: International Law Association, 1993), 254, at 272–4 and 276–7; S. Oda, *International Control of Sea Resources* (Dordrecht: Martinus Nijhoff, 1989), pp. xxi–xxii.
80. See also Balton, Ch. 5 above.

81. See also Burke, *The New International Law of Fisheries*, 141–2; S. N. Nandan and S. Rosenne (eds.), *United Nations Convention on the Law of the Sea, 1982: A Commentary*, iii (Dordrecht: Martinus Nijhoff, 1995), 356 and 366.

82. UN Doc. A/CONF.164/L.33; *Earth Negotiations Bulletin*, 7/39 (29 Aug. 1994), 5; see also V. Zilanov as cited in W. T. Burke, 'UNCED and the Oceans', *Marine Policy*, 17 (1993), 519, at 530.

83. B. Applebaum, *Managing Fishery Resources beyond 200 Miles: Canada's Options to Protect Northwest Atlantic Straddling Stocks* (Halifax: Oceans Institute of Canada, Jan. 1990), 66; Burke, *The New International Law of Fisheries*, 134.

84. Fish Stocks Agreement, Arts. 7 and 16.

85. S. V. Molodtsov, V. K. Zilanov, and A. N. Vylegzhanin, 'Anklavy Otkrytogo Moria i Mezhdunarodnoe Pravo', *Moskovskii Zhurnal Mezhdunarodnogo Prava*, 2 (1993), 39, at 50. Soviet practice and legal doctrine in the past advanced arguments regarding historic rights related to the seas bordering the Soviet Union in order to exclude these seas from the regime generally applicable to the high seas. To this same effect the doctrine of closed seas was espoused (see e.g. the overview in W. E. Butler, *The Soviet Union and the Law of the Sea* (Baltimore: Johns Hopkins University Press, 1971), 111–14 and 116–33.

86. On recent signs of dissatisfaction at the regional level with the Russian policy in respect of the Peanut Hole, see above.

87. Wespestad, 'Trends in North Pacific Pollock and Cod Fisheries'; see also 'Seafood', Report of the American Embassy, Moscow, of 18 Sept. 1995.

88. D. A. Balton, 'Strengthening the Law of the Sea: The New Agreement on Straddling Fish Stocks and Highly Migratory Fish Stocks', *Ocean Development and International Law*, 27 (1996), 125, at 149 n. 74. If figures of 1980 and 1994 are compared, the importance of Russia's economic zone for its fishing effort has increased considerably. In 1980, 51% of the overall catch was taken in this zone while in 1994 this figure was 78%. For this same period, the share of catches in the 200-nautical-mile zones of other states declined from 27% to 17%, and the share of catches on the high seas from 14% to 3% (figures cited in 'Seafood', table 5). A reversal of this trend might be forthcoming. In 1995, there was a sharp increase in Russian distant water fisheries catches; FAO Fisheries Department, *Recent Trends in Global Fishery Production* (www.fao.org/waicent/faoinfo/fishery/trends/catch/distantf.htm). A draft policy document of the Russian Government of 1997 stressed the need of reinforcing fisheries on the high seas and cooperation with other states over access to their EEZ. See *Diplomaticheskii Vestnik*, 2 (1997), 32; see also Press Release on the Briefing of the Chairman of the Committee on Fisheries of 19 Jan. 2000 (Interfax) (in Russian; on file with the author). Economic factors impede that quotas outside of the Russian economic zone are fully employed. In 1999 only 20% of the sea quota were actually caught (Press Conference of the New Chairman of the Committee on Fisheries of 19 Jan. 2000) (in Russian, on file with the author).

89. Distant water fishing only forms a negligible share of fishing activities in the Far Eastern region. Only 2% of catches are taken outside the Russian 200-nautical-mile zone. V. Monakhov, 'The Fishery Industry in the Russian Far East', *Eastfish Fishery Industry Profile*, 19 (Copenhagen: Eastfish/FAO, 1998).

90. For a discussion of the types of regime linkages referred to here, see the Introduction and the Conclusions to this book.

91. Convention on the Conservation and Management of Pollock Resources in the Central Bering Sea (1994); *International Journal of Marine and Coastal Law*, 10 (1995), 127.

92. Agreement between the Government of Iceland, the Government of Norway and the Government of the Russian Federation concerning Certain Aspects of Co-operation in the Area of Fisheries, with Protocols (1999); reproduced in *International Journal of Marine and Coastal Law*, 14 (1999), 484 ff.

93. See further below for a discussion of some possible explanations.

94. Cf. respectively Arts. XII and 5; a more general provision addressing this issue is contained in Arts. 17 (4) and 33 of the Fish Stocks Agreement.

95. On fisheries in the Bering Sea, see e.g. Balton, Ch. 5 above; W. V. Dunlap, 'The Donut Hole Agreement', *International Journal for Marine and Coastal Law*, 10 (1995), 114; on fisheries in the Barents Sea see e.g. R. R. Churchill, 'The Barents Sea Loophole Agreement: A "Coastal State" Solution to a Straddling Stock Problem', *International Journal of Marine and Coastal Law*, 14 (1999), 467; see also Stokke, Ch. 9 below.

96. Churchill, 'The Barents Sea Loophole Agreement', 483.

97. Ibid.

98. Balton, Ch. 5 above.

99. Cf. Sosnowska-Smogorzewska, 'Poland's Fight for Pollock'.

100. It seems that the distant water fishing states already employed the argument that a regime was in place; they referred to their bilateral agreements with the Russian Federation which arguably made a specific provision in the Fish Stocks Agreement superfluous.

101. Balton, Ch. 5 above; Dunlap, 'The Donut Hole Agreement', 124–5.

102. These main tasks are the generation of sufficient information about stock vulnerability to enable informed decisions about conservation measures: the establishment of conservation measures for all vessels operating in the relevant area; and the establishment of an adequate system to enhance compliance with conservation measures agreed to, including surveillance and enforcement.

103. *Diplomaticheskii Vestnik*, 7 (1996), 72.

104. Cf. above n. 67.

105. Cf. C. A. Fleischer, 'Fisheries and Biological Resources', in R. Dupuy and D. Vignes (eds.), *A New Handbook on the Law of the Sea*, ii (Dordrecht: Martinus Nijhoff Publishers, 1991), 989–1125, at 1116, where it is noted that 'Bilateral agreements to fish inside the 200-mile zone may be used by the coastal State to gain a sort of *de facto* control or *quasi-sovereign rights* even in regard to activities which take place and resources which are found in the high seas beyond the 200-mile limit.'

106. As was noted above, there seems to be some resistance in the Far Eastern region against maintaining this status quo.

7

On the Borderline?
Canadian Activism in the Grand Banks

CHRISTOPHER C. JOYNER

1 Introduction

Developments during the last twenty years have called into question two
fundamental principles of ocean law: the freedom to fish on the high seas
and exclusive flag jurisdiction over vessels fishing on the high seas.[1] This
situation became dramatically highlighted in 1995 by tensions that arose
over Spanish vessels fishing just beyond the limits of coastal jurisdiction
claimed by Canada in the north-west Atlantic Ocean.

On 9 March 1995, Canadian fishery authorities boarded and arrested a
Spanish-registered vessel, the *Estai*, on the high seas at least 18 miles
beyond Canada's 200-mile exclusive fisheries zone in the Grand Banks.[2]
This action was taken on grounds that the trawler had allegedly violated
Canada's fishing laws, which had a short time before been amended to
apply to high seas areas. This international incident sparked a six-week-
long diplomatic confrontation between Canada and the European Community (EC)—a dispute deemed so serious that the press termed it the
'Turbot War';[3] turbot is the local name for Greenland halibut, the fish
species targeted. Spain in addition presented a claim against Canada to
the International Court of Justice; the ICJ rejected the claim on 4 December 1998 on grounds that the Court lacked proper jurisdiction to adjudicate the dispute.[4]

Canada's unilateral actions against Spanish fishing vessels in the Grand
Banks challenged the fundamental norms of international law. The
dispute also brought into sharp focus the need for more effective international fisheries laws to regulate so-called straddling, stocks, i.e. fishery
stocks that move in and out of offshore jurisdictional zones of coastal
states and the adjacent high sea areas beyond. Indeed, as Canada argued,
a deep interdependence links fisheries management within waters under
coastal jurisdiction to the superjacent ocean space beyond. No matter how
effective fishing measures are when implemented and enforced within
jurisdictional waters, failure to comply with such measures *outside* those
waters, on the high seas, renders such internal measures futile in the case
of straddling stocks. The converse is also true. If a coastal state does not

properly regulate fishing for straddling stocks within its exclusive economic zone (EEZ), other states whose vessels wish to fish for the stocks
on the high seas will suffer. This special concern of Canada and other
coastal states came into clear perspective during the United Nations
Conference on Straddling Fish Stocks and Highly Migratory Fish Stocks,
which convened in six sessions from 1993 to 1995.[5]

   This study explores why the fisheries conflict erupted between Canada
and the EC and how it was resolved. The legal issues at stake for
both sides are assessed, as are the dispute's political and economic
repercussions and the ways in which these affected the development
of international law. Finally, critical reflection is given to what can be
learned from this episode with respect to the future for international
fisheries law.

2 Fisheries management in the Northwest Atlantic

At the same time as negotiations over fishing rights in the LOS Convention were drawing to a close,[6] the world's fisheries were beginning to
experience crisis conditions symptomatic of the 'tragedy of the commons',
with fishing levels reaching the point of diminishing returns. The principal cause for this fisheries crisis during the late 1970s was (and still is)
chronic overfishing, which was subsidized by governments that were
attempting to prop up an unsustainable industry.[7] Drastic declines in traditional fisheries prompted fishers to cast their nets elsewhere, especially
in the offshore waters of African, Caribbean, and Pacific states. As a result,
overfishing in the early 1990s not only produced drastic declines in fish
populations worldwide but also adversely affected biological diversity
and impinged upon the health of marine ecosystems.

   Compounding this crisis situation in world fisheries was the uncertain
status of international law for regulating the global fishing enterprise. The
fundamental conflict of fishery interests arose during the late 1980s. On
the one hand, certain distant water fishing nations (DWFNs) advocated
the creation of narrow fishing zones offshore because they sought new
fishing grounds and wanted to fish in more ocean space, with fewer
degrees of restriction. On the other hand, most coastal states were concerned about the conservation of fishery stocks within their EEZs, and
were interested principally in maximizing and maintaining harvest
opportunities for their domestic fishermen; hence, coastal states supported the establishment of broad conservation zones offshore, as were
provided for in the 1982 LOS Convention.[8]

   Within the framework under development by the Third United Nations

Conference of the Law of the Sea, Canada had adopted a 200-mile exclusive fisheries zone (EFZ) which was put into effect 1 January 1977.[9] After 1978, only about 20 per cent of the country's total catches were harvested in distant waters, whereas harvests within Canada's fishing zone waters accounted for the remaining 80 per cent.[10] Canadian authorities specified maximum catch levels so as to maintain a sustainable level.[11] Nevertheless, these measures could not offset impacts caused by the increasing harvesting by foreign fishing fleets in the Northwest Atlantic.

The attribution of coastal state jurisdiction through the concept of either an EFZ or EEZ did not eliminate the critical need for international cooperation. Fish stocks moved freely through the ocean unaware of man-made political boundaries. Indeed, it is in this context that modern ocean law emphasizes the necessity of cooperation between coastal states and flag states of fishing vessels. The 1982 LOS Convention clearly assigns the responsibility for managing such cooperation to regional or subregional organizations.[12]

Prior to Canada's extension of coastal state jurisdiction to 200 miles in 1976, fishing in the Northwest Atlantic was administered under the auspices of the International Convention for the Northwest Atlantic Fisheries (ICNAF). The withdrawal of the United States from ICNAF, coupled with Canada's unilateral extension of offshore fisheries jurisdiction, led to the creation of the Convention on Future Multilateral Cooperation in the Northwest Atlantic Fisheries, which was signed in October 1978.[13] This Convention created the Northwest Atlantic Fisheries Organization (NAFO), which became intimately involved in the fisheries dispute between Canada and the EC. Although extending its jurisdiction out to 200 miles, Canada still had salient interests in participating in the regional fisheries management organization, especially given that its extended fisheries zone could not adequately address the need to protect straddling stocks. These persistent interests help to explain Canada's subsequent actions during the mid-1990s to extend national enforcement jurisdiction beyond its 200-mile exclusive fisheries zone.

The chief purpose of NAFO, of which both Canada and the EC are members, is 'to contribute through consultation and cooperation to the optimum utilization, rational management and conservation of the fisheries resources'[14] of the north-west Atlantic Ocean. Put tersely, NAFO is to manage those fishery resources of the Northwest Atlantic found beyond the limits of national jurisdiction, or in the contemporary sense, beyond the limits of 200-nautical-mile EEZs throughout the region. Regarding management of stocks that live within or migrate between EEZ limits and adjacent waters of the high seas, NAFO has the duty to cooperate with any affected coastal states.[15] Importantly, the areas under

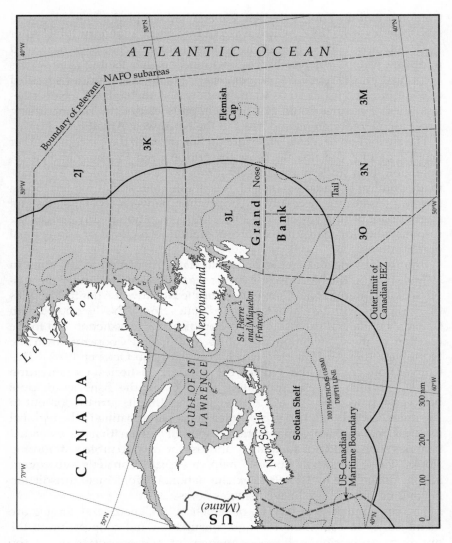

Map 7.1. Relevant parts of the NAFO Convention Area

NAFO management can be classified as two types: the *NAFO Convention Area* that includes the Canadian EEZ and adjacent high seas,[16] and the *NAFO Regulatory Area* that only extends throughout the adjacent high seas.[17] As far as straddling stocks are concerned, measures taken under the NAFO framework 'shall seek to ensure consistency between . . . any proposal that applies to a stock or group of stocks occurring both within the Regulatory Area and within an area under the fisheries jurisdiction of a coastal state'.[18] Under these measures, contracting parties are required to inform NAFO members, through NAFO inspectors, about catches and other facets of fisheries management both within and beyond their national EEZ jurisdictions.[19]

A fundamental principle for regulating relations among NAFO members is the objection procedure.[20] Under this provision, each member retains the right to reject application of any policy adopted by NAFO. Dissatisfied with a 1985 NAFO decision to a moratorium on harvesting of Northern cod on the high seas 'nose' of the Grand Banks, the EC filed an objection and set for itself a unilateral quota. In the following years, EC objections to NAFO conservation measures became regular events not only for cod but for other species as well, including redfish, American plaice, and several flatfishes. While lower water temperatures and Canadian overfishing inside its own national waters should also be mentioned, this management conflict forms part of the explanation for the sweeping groundfish crisis that impacted the Northwest Atlantic at the turn of the decade. By 1992, the cod stock had collapsed, and Canada closed the fishery within its EFZ. Between September 1993 and December 1994, NAFO put moratoria also on other straddling stocks, including American plaice. NAFO also set reductions in total catches for other species and adopted various technical measures for fisheries conservation.[21]

These NAFO decisions also applied to Canada's EFZ since areas where these straddling stocks were located fall within those jurisdictional waters. Thus, while the Regulatory Area of NAFO extends only *beyond* the 200-mile limit, decisions concerning management of turbot stocks (and other species) still affect the entire Convention Area, including ocean space within Canadian waters. Improved management of resources occurred in some areas during the 1980s, but this was not accompanied by equivalent improvements in the management of Canada's fishing fleets. Consequently, overcapacity and inefficiency in the Canadian fleet prevailed, especially off Nova Scotia and Newfoundland in the Atlantic.[22] Indeed, policies permitting uncontrolled expansion of Canada's fishing fleets between 1976 and 1982 fostered a 30 per cent increase in the number of persons employed in the industry. Of the goals articulated for Canadian fisheries policy in the 1980s, fisheries managers highlighted employment as the first priority, even over economic efficiency and conservation.[23] Thus, '[m]ajor groundfish stocks on the Atlantic coast continued to show a marked decline in 1992'.[24] Moreover, between 1986 and 1992, Canadian vessels replaced foreign fleets in fishing the most important straddling stocks beyond Canada's EFZ.[25] As a result, according to reports presented to the NAFO Fisheries Commission by the contracting parties, the Canadian fleet largely depleted swordfish stocks, while other NAFO members actually reduced their catches. Because of considerable declines in the traditionally commercialized groundfish stocks, the Canadian fishing industry during the 1990s increasingly turned to harvesting previously under-utilized species, such as turbot.[26]

To compound the economic situation, a three-year moratorium on harvesting cod left 50,000 Canadian fishers and fish plant workers unemployed. Aggravated by Canada's oversized fishing fleet, moratoria set by NAFO between 1986 and 1995 cost 30,000 jobs in Newfoundland alone. This troublesome economic situation at home became a crucial factor in prompting Canada to take an unusually forceful position in the turbot dispute abroad.[27] Beginning in the 1970s, the Canadian fishing industry had widely demanded that Canada extend its jurisdiction for the industry's harvesting activities. Such action purportedly would not be aimed at establishing a sole claim by Canada to harvest straddling stocks on the high seas but rather at preserving both Canada's and international interests in conservation of these stocks.[28] Regardless of the major objective of the action, such an extension clearly challenged principles in the 1982 UN Law of the Sea Convention. The outcome of Canada's domestic overcapacity to harvest its fisheries was a conservation record that was less than satisfactory with regard to the government's attainment of the stated goal of its fisheries policy.[29]

In sum, heightened pressures to obtain more fish to feed expanding populations, the search for new fishing grounds and potential target species by distant water fishing fleets, and the continued rise in fishing capability by vessels equipped with more sophisticated harvesting technology escalated the tension over compliance with international fishing rules. Economic dislocation caused by deteriorating conditions in domestic fishing industries complicated political solutions at home, bringing the situation to new crisis levels for many governments, including Canada and Spain, in the early 1990s.[30]

Canada's challenge to international norms with the extension of its fisheries jurisdiction occurred more gradually than the events of 1995 might suggest. The Canadian Parliament had already amended the Coastal Fisheries Protection Act of 13 May 1994, largely to protect its depressed fishing industry in the Maritime Provinces. This amending legislation was principally directed at stateless and flag of convenience vessels rather than at EC or Spanish fishing vessels.[31] Canada's decision to amend its national legislation was intended to enable it to take any urgent action necessary to prevent further destruction of stocks straddling its fisheries zone while international efforts to find more effective global solutions were ongoing.[32] The international response to Canada's unilateral extension of offshore fisheries jurisdiction was notable, but muffled. While United States and European diplomats criticized Canada's legislation as contrary to international law, neither sanctions nor official acts condemning the policy were forthcoming.

3 The turbot issue

The dispute between Canada and the European Community arose over who should have access to and control over living resources in waters beyond the limits of national jurisdiction, i.e. on the high seas. In meetings held in Brussels between 30 January and 2 February 1995, NAFO decided by majority vote to allocate the total allowable catch (TAC) for turbot that had been fixed at 27,000 metric tons by its September 1994 annual meeting. Canada received 60 per cent of the TAC, based on that country's traditional catch of turbot stock in the region;[33] however, in more recent years, Spain had recorded the biggest catches.

There was consensus in NAFO regarding both the TAC itself and the need to reduce catches to a sustainable level. But the issue of how the quotas were to be allocated sparked the conflict between Canada and the European Community. As the EC claimed one-half of the total catch,[34] its Council of Ministers unanimously adopted a proposal by the European Commission that invoked the objection procedure to overrule NAFO's decision.[35] It was even more disconcerting when the European Commission then set its own quota at 69 per cent within the overall ceiling of 27,000 metric tons, six times the amount allotted to the EC under its NAFO quota.[36] The European Commission defined its position as a redistributive exchange between the Canadian and the European quotas. The absence of any specific regulation prohibiting this strategy in the 1982 Law of the Sea Convention—apart from a general requirement for international cooperation over straddling stocks[37]—invited the supposition that the EC's rejection of NAFO's TAC decision was not a fundamental breach of international law.[38]

By March 1995, the EC and Canada were on the brink of a fisheries war over NAFO's 1995 allocation of turbot quotas. On 3 March the Canadian Minister of Fisheries announced that Canada's Coastal Fisheries Protection Regulations had again been legislatively amended. Whereas the Coastal Fisheries Protection Regulations had previously applied only to stateless or flag of convenience vessels beyond the 200-mile limit, the new amendment would permit enforcement of that legislation to include fishing vessels from Spain and Portugal beyond Canada's jurisdictional waters,[39] but within the Regulatory Area of NAFO. Canada's basis for this action did not rely on the aspirations of sovereign acquisition of new ocean areas, nor on any preferential right by coastal states to exploit neighbouring high seas resources. Rather it reflected the perception that coastal states held special interests over straddling stocks that affected their exclusive economic or fishery zones.[40] The rationale for these regulations, which applied prescribed conservation and management measures to vessels from distant water fishing nations, was to protect fish stocks beyond Canada's fisheries zone from being over-exploited by fishermen from European Union states.[41]

When accused by the EC of violating international rules, Canada responded that it was protecting an endangered fishery species.[42] The Canadian government sought to defend its policy on grounds of concern for conservation, rather than what appeared to the EC to be creeping extraterritorial jurisdiction into the Northwest Atlantic. Apart from EC threats of trade sanctions against Canada for its legally questionable seizure of the *Estai*,[43] the parties' claims focused fundamentally on two points: Canada's main objective was to secure effective enforcement of NAFO's measures so as to protect the last important groundfish stock in the Northwest Atlantic for its fishermen;[44] the central issue for the EC concerned renegotiation within the NAFO framework of the 1995 turbot quotas.

3.1 The Canadian view

Seen from Canada's vantage point, the legal issues were clear. Ottawa believed that its fisheries service was enforcing national regulations designed to conserve fishery resources offshore. During the 1980s, EC vessels had fished more than seven times the amount of cod, redfish, and flounder allotted to them under NAFO. This situation led to moratoria being put on flatfish and cod in the 'nose' and 'tail' of the Grand Banks. The EC fleet then turned to turbot, which had previously been harvested mainly by Canada. Between 1989 and 1993, the EC's turbot catch rose from 4,000 metric tons to more than 50,000 metric tons. The Spanish factory trawler fleet accounted for most of this increase.

Canada maintained that the turbot stocks, which swam in and out of Canada's 200-mile exclusive fisheries zone, were being excessively exploited by Spanish vessels on the high seas in disregard of the NAFO TAC limits agreed upon. The Canadians were also angered by the fact that the EC had employed the NAFO objection procedure and set for itself a quota of 18,630 metric tons—or 60 per cent of the allowable catch that year. Such extravagant harvesting, the Canadian government asserted, was taking place without regard for the duty to conserve the living resources of the high seas, as mandated by Articles 117, 118, and 119 of the 1982 LOS Convention. Further, Spanish fishermen were reported to be using nets with unlawfully small mesh sizes, thus precluding the opportunity for juvenile fish to escape. Being most severely impacted by this situation, Canada, in an effort aimed at international fishery conservation, resorted to self-help to halt such unregulated taking of straddling stock resources. Under the existing, extreme conditions, Canada asserted that it had both the right and the responsibility to take action to curb overfishing on the high seas by Spanish vessels.

Throughout the *Estai* episode, considerable attention was given in Canada to the perceived reckless nature of EC actions regarding the turbot stocks off the shore of Canada. The EC response at the time to these accusations reveals much about the fundamental nature of the dispute. In unilaterally setting its own quotas, the EC continued to abide by the overall TAC set by the NAFO Commission, and, more importantly, it further advised the Canadian Government that it would abide by the TAC limit, irrespective of who first harvested the allocations.[45] What the EC had effectively vetoed were the decisions made by NAFO at Brussels on 30 January–2 February, 1995, which related to the economic allocation of the TAC, not to the underlying conservation principles. In response, Canada reiterated the fact that each NAFO member state was entitled to fish the quota allocated to it, and moreover, that if all EC members held to their allocations and each state fished its unilateral quota, the fish stocks in the Northwest Atlantic would inevitably be exhausted.[46]

3.2 The European view

Canada's action in the high seas was viewed by the EC as an unlawful unilateral claim of coastal state jurisdiction to portions of ocean space beyond its exclusive economic zone, into areas where high seas rights (inclusive of fishing) under Article 86 of the 1992 Convention apply.[47] Similarly, the EC contended that Canada's imposition of a ban on foreign vessels fishing beyond its 200-mile EFZ violated Articles 87 and 116 of the 1982 Convention, which upheld traditional freedoms of the high seas and granted to all states equal right of access to fishery resources of the high seas. The EC also argued that by applying municipal law to foreign vessels in high seas areas and by enforcing such measures against those vessels and their crews, Canada had breached Article 89 of the 1982 Convention by subjecting parts of the high seas to its sovereign authority. Further, by taking enforcement action against foreign vessels on the high seas, Canada stood accused of superseding the exclusive right of the flag state to exercise legislative and enforcement jurisdiction over its vessels on the high seas (under Article 92 (1) of the 1982 Convention). Finally, the EC held that Canada had failed to engage in cooperation on straddling stocks pursuant to Article 63 (2) of the 1982 LOS Convention. The use of force against Spanish fishing vessels made that irrefutable. Thus, the dispute between Canada and Spain was not merely a bilateral conflict. It was actually a conflict between Canada's national fisheries policy and the EC's common fisheries policy; the 'Turbot War' became a contentious dispute *de facto* and *de jure* between Canada and the European Community.[48]

Economic considerations often drive legal objectives, and this also proved to be the case in the fisheries dispute between the EC and Canada. The EC's market policy aims to maintain stable market prices and to secure incomes for the fishing industry, as well as to safeguard consumer interests. A withdrawal price is set in such a manner as to act as a threshold: if market prices fall below the withdrawal price, excess supply must be removed from the market. This contingency does not act as an incentive to reduce catches, however, because fishermen receive compensation payments for any fish withdrawn. Hence, though this policy might contribute to achieving stability in the market place, it does little to strengthen conservation efforts in the north Atlantic.

The EC's conservation policy aims to 'ensure the protection of fishing grounds, the conservation of biological resources of the sea and their balanced exploitation on a lasting basis and in appropriate economic and social conditions'.[49] The policy set technical measures, specified TACs, and assigned quotas among Community members 'in a manner which assures each Member State's relative stability of fishing activities for each of the stocks considered'.[50] This principle of relative stability remains fundamental to EC fishery policy and underlies the allocation of fishing quotas under the NAFO framework. Enforcement of the conservation policy was lax. As in Canada's case, fisheries policy within the EC generally became complicated by its intimate connection to serious domestic economic pressures and political problems. This is especially true for Spain where unemployment was already extremely high.[51] Generally speaking, western Europe's fishing industry has been burdened in recent years by an overwhelming excess of fishing capacity relative to the actual availability of stocks in the Atlantic for harvest.

4 Dispute resolution: the 1995 Canadian–EC Agreed Minute

By early April, Canada and the EC had agreed to discuss their disputed claims. Despite mounting tension due to Canada's harassment of Spanish fishing vessels and the EC's threats of retaliatory trade sanctions against

Canada, negotiations proved constructive and successful. These discussions focused on improving conservation rules as well as on the need for NAFO to reallocate a more equitable distribution of its TAC among the membership.[52]

Agreement on the need to enforce conservation measures, such as inspection, was reached early on. The quota question remained a critical issue in the negotiations. In order to determine new quota allocations, more exact knowledge was needed about the amount of turbot already being caught by Spain in the Northwest Atlantic. Significant to note is that Canada's estimates of the Spanish catch exceeded the estimates suggested by the EC by 3,000 metric tons.[53] Meanwhile, thousands of Spanish fishermen demonstrated in Madrid, fearing that reallocation of TAC quotas could cost them their jobs.[54]

Following intensive talks between 16 March and 16 April, delegations from the European Commission and the Government of Canada agreed 'to enhance cooperation on management and conservation of fisheries resources in the context of the NAFO Convention, particularly with regard to control and enforcement measures, and to the allocation of the total allowable catch of Greenland halibut in the area'.[55] The EC, moreover, obtained an understanding from Canada that the latter's legislation affecting vessels of Spain and Portugal would be repealed and that all proceedings pending in Canada against the *Estai* would be settled satisfactorily before provisional application of the agreement.[56]

4.1 Implications for Canadian–EC relations

The formal instrument of agreement between Canada and the EC, known as the Agreed Minute,[57] consisted of four types of provisions, tailored to the various issues addressed. First, there are *control and enforcement measures*. The European Community and Canada recognized their mutual commitment to enhance cooperation in the conservation and rational management of fish stocks, as well as in the pivotal role of control and enforcement. They consequently agreed on several measures for amending NAFO conservation and enforcement policies, specifically regarding inspection of vessels, transmission of information from inspections, increasing the inspection presence both in the NAFO Convention area and in the NAFO Regulatory Area, improving the hail system, and establishing a pilot project for observers and satellite tracking, *inter alia*.[58]

The EC and Canada also jointly agreed to seek support from the other NAFO members for adoption of a new protocol on the enforcement of conservation measures.[59] By October 1995, the NAFO Commission had prepared such a protocol instrument and secured agreement of all contracting parties that had adopted the measures in the Minute.

A second accomplishment of the Agreed Minute was the resolution of the critical issue of *total allowable catch* and its allocation. The EC and Canada reaffirmed their commitment to the 27,000 metric tons TAC of turbot for 1995 in subareas 2 and 3 of the NAFO Convention area.[60] Both parties also recognized turbot as a straddling stock and agreed on three new management arrangements:

1. For 1995, Canada's catches would not exceed 10,000 metric tons, inclusive of the 7,000 metric tons caught in its jurisdictional waters within subareas 2 and 3K of NAFO.[61]
2. After 16 April 1995, the EC could catch a maximum of 5,013 metric tons per year.[62]
3. For 1996 and thereafter, the European Community and Canada proposed that NAFO manage the turbot stocks in area 3LMNO. Quotas would be reallocated in a ratio of 10:3 for the EC and Canada, respectively. Canada would manage turbot in Canadian waters in subareas 2 and 3K, under the scientific advice of the NAFO Scientific Council. Finally, the NAFO Scientific Council would provide advice for turbot management and conservation in both the above-mentioned areas.[63]

A third aspect of the agreement pertained to Canada's recent *national legislation* that affected offshore jurisdiction. Canada agreed to repeal provisions of its Regulation of 3 March 1995. The Regulation had amended the Coastal Fisheries Protection Act, extending its provisions to Spanish and Portuguese vessels in NAFO Regulatory Areas, i.e. on the high seas.[64] Both Canada and the EC maintained their positions on the conformity of the prior text of the Act with international law and the NAFO Convention.

A fourth facet of the Canadian–EC agreement concerned its *duration*. The Agreed Minute would be an interim type of measure, terminating on 31 December 1995, or as soon as the measures were adopted by NAFO, if that were to occur earlier.[65] The latter situation prevailed, with NAFO adopting the appropriate measures by September 1995.

4.2 Implications for international fisheries law

Two aspects of the Canada–EC agreement deserve special mention here. First, radical changes were made from the original quota limits set by NAFO. Put simply, the result of the dispute settlement left Canada with only about one-half of its previous quota, whereas the EC quota had gained nearly a fourfold increase. Such a profound shift acknowledged that, as the EC had asserted, the original division had not been fairly representative of more up-to-date catch trends, which constitute the purported basis for NAFO's specification of quotas.

A second legal implication concerns coastal state jurisdiction. The unilateral extension of jurisdiction by a coastal state (i.e. Canada) over superjacent high seas was implicitly rejected as being contrary to the contemporary law of the sea. The EC and Canada both recognized that greater conformity with international law lay in the Canadian Coastal Fisheries Protection Act before the amendment of 3 March 1995 that had authorized Canada's fisheries service to assert a police role on the high seas.[66]

Despite its notable improvements in enforcement and control measures, the Canadian–European Community agreement on the management of fisheries in the Northwest Atlantic could not guarantee long-term international cooperation. The fact is that TACs *per se* are not sufficient to ensure fisheries management. Key questions remain concerning what policy priorities governments seek and what TACs are determined by NAFO for which countries. Relatedly, calculation of TACs is hardly a precise scientific exercise. Determination of TACs for NAFO members remains highly politicized and economically volatile, particularly in states with shaky economies. Indeed, problems of unemployment in the fisheries industry, both in Canada and in EC countries, continue to weigh heavily on fishery policies and will also impinge upon TAC-determination decisions. Further, while maximizing employment stands as an important social objective, maintaining oversized national fishing fleets remains biologically—and therefore also economically—unsustainable. Only economic objectives that adequately take into account species scarcity are environmentally and economically sustainable. If fishery stocks persist in declining in the Northwest Atlantic, the availability of large distant water fishing fleets will be incompatible with intentions to conserve those stocks, and with heightened efforts by Canada (and the United States) to curtail foreign fishing activities that have an adverse impact upon species within their EEZs. These considerations emphasize the need for coastal states to place greater reliance upon multilateral fishery organizations for managing and regulating high seas conservation policies, and for a new international instrument that can establish more suitable standards for straddling stocks and highly migratory species.

5 Implications for international fisheries management

5.1 Regional management under NAFO

The agreement between Canada and the European Community bolstered the role of regional fishery organizations in marine conservation and ocean management. In that regard, the 1995 Agreed Minute contained the following specific declaration:

The European Community and Canada, in recognition of their commitment to enhanced cooperation in the conservation and rational management of fish stocks, and the pivotal role of control and enforcement in ensuring such conservation, agree that the proposals set out in Annex I shall constitute the basis for a submission to be jointly prepared and made to the NAFO Fisheries commission, for its consideration and approval, to establish a Protocol to strengthen the NAFO Conservation and Enforcement Measures.[67]

Such a protocol was adopted by NAFO in September 1995.[68] The overall outcome of this fisheries 'war' may be seen as positive for NAFO in general and for the disputants in particular. The agreement clearly strengthens the management responsibility and role of NAFO. It also confirms the special biological nature of straddling stocks and recognizes the need for particular international legal stipulations to regulate their exploitation. The role of the NAFO Fisheries Commission in managing turbot in area 3LMNO also implies a reduction of Canada's ability to manage fisheries unilaterally within part of its jurisdictional waters.[69]

The NAFO regime was enhanced mostly in terms of enforcement and monitoring of regional fisheries activities. The Canadian–EC conflict stemmed in part from weaknesses and ambiguities in existing regulations. While the Canadian position maintained that enforcement provisions of the previous NAFO regime were inadequate to meet the challenges posed by rogue fishers, the factual position is less clear in cases where the flag state is unwilling to engage in proper enforcement measures against its vessels. This was a view particularly held by the EC. In any event, new provisions contained in annex I of the Protocol appear regulatively sound and more capable of fulfilling—and therefore significantly improving—those shortcomings in the legal regime that had precipitated conflict in the first place. The final agreement increases the range of permissible non-flag state monitoring and enforcement actions, a fact that undoubtedly will permit more able and consistent regulation of fisheries within the NAFO region.

The system for vessel inspection established in the annex to the Agreed Minute provides for an increase in the inspection presence, an improvement of the hail system, the conduct of dockside inspections at each port of call, and other measures.[70] In addition, contracting parties agreed 'to implement a Pilot Project to provide for properly trained and qualified observers on all vessels fishing in the NRA [NAFO Regulatory Area] and satellite-tracking devices on 35% of their respective vessels fishing in the NRA'.[71] These 'impartial and independent observers'[72] will be placed on every vessel by each contracting party (i.e. by the flag state). Should a party fail to do so, 'any other Contracting Party may, subject to the consent of the Contracting Party of the vessel, place an observer on board'.[73] Observers are in charge of conducting ongoing and comprehensive monitoring of the vessel's activities, including the amount of catch, catch composition, gear employed, entries made to logbooks, *inter alia*. When identifying any apparent major infringement, observers are to communicate within forty-eight hours with a NAFO inspection vessel, as well as directly with the NAFO Executive Secretary.[74] Monitoring activities under the NAFO regulatory framework have indeed been strengthened in a notable way, and these improvements can serve as a model for other regional fishery organizations to draw upon.

Regulation of 'major infringements' in fisheries regimes is also stressed in annex I, among them the refusal of crews to cooperate with an inspector or an observer, misreporting of catches, mesh size violations, hail system violations, and interference with the satellite tracking system.[75] In such instances, the conduct of additional inspections is permitted in port, notably to allow NAFO inspectors 'from another Contracting Party [i.e. from a state other than the flag state], subject to the consent of the Contracting Party of the vessel, [to] board the vessel as it proceeds to port and [to] be present during the inspection of the vessel in port'.[76] The agreement suggests that 'a transparent and effective legal process' be established and asserts that penalties in domestic legislation must be such as to provide an effective deterrent. Such punitive measures might include refusal, suspension, and withdrawal of the authorization to fish in the area.[77] While vaguer language is used for penalties than in the rules for monitoring, the role and ability of NAFO to enforce its conservation measures nevertheless appears bolstered, providing useful lessons for other regional fishery organizations.

Improvements in NAFO's general system for inspections and communications were necessary even aside from its conservation and management policies. Definition of a TAC without specifying feasible methods for verifying actual catches would have made enforcement and compliance of the TAC impossible. The new TAC regulations adopted by NAFO constitute a minimum basis upon which an adequate regional conservation and management fisheries policy can be built. While TAC regulations clearly are necessary, whether they will prove sufficient for guaranteeing fisheries conservation remains a question of political, as well as scientific, considerations. In any case, if annex I successfully secures the TACs set by NAFO, its contribution to that organization's goal of regional fisheries management will be substantial.

5.2 Interplay with the Fish Stocks Agreement

The United Nations Conference on Straddling Fish Stocks and Highly Migratory Fish Stocks convened in its sixth session in New York from 24 July to 4 August 1995. The Conference concluded with the adoption through consensus of the Fish Stocks Agreement.[78] In adopting this instrument, the Conference overcame the political fallout from the Canada–EC bilateral conflict and created useful rules and standards that could be applied worldwide. Perhaps not surprisingly, the Canadian–European Community fisheries dispute and adoption of the Fish Stocks Agreement were soon thereafter interrelated.

The timing of the Canada–EC conflict must be appreciated within the context of the timing of the fifth session of the Fish Stocks Conference. It is not mere coincidence that Canada chose to adopt an aggressive stance against Spanish fishermen in early March 1995. Unable to resolve bilaterally its long-standing disputes with European fishermen over straddling stocks in high seas beyond its EFZ, the Canadian government sought to press its case before a world forum—the United Nations—and in the process attract support from other coastal states.[79] The Stocks Conference was scheduled to reconvene in its fifth session on 27 March. This timing suggests that Canada timed its confrontation with Spain in order to pursue its own interests in the Northwest Atlantic, as well as to prompt the UN Conference to come to a satisfactory conclusion on the straddling stocks and migratory species regulatory question. By intensifying the dispute with the EC, Canada hoped to attract diplomatic support from coastal states in the conference. The dispute between Canada and Spain could thus be used by Canada to produce a 'boomerang effect', such that confrontation with the European Community would be generated to demonstrate the dire need for new international fisheries law, which would in turn serve to obviate further conflict in the future. Canada's principal aim was to secure a regulatory system that guaranteed compatibility of conservation measures within and beyond national EEZs. Canada intended to impose such compatibility by pursuing a *de facto* police role on the high seas for coastal states bordering the Northwest Atlantic.

The text of the Fish Stocks Agreement addresses such concerns of jurisdiction and management within the general framework of the law of the sea and contains provisions particularly relevant to the Canadian–European Community fisheries dispute. Even so, neither Canada nor the EC (or its member states) has yet ratified the Fish Stocks Agreement, although both have asserted the intention to do so. That notwithstanding, at least five concerns in this special agreement directly relate to issues explicitly evident during the 'Turbot War', thereby attesting to the dispute's relevance for and impact upon the final agreement.

First, regarding jurisdiction, efforts by Canada to force recognition of extended coastal state jurisdiction for the purpose of protecting (i.e. 'conserving') straddling stocks were set aside. The Fish Stocks Agreement actually confirms a legal framework that renders unlawful any extraterritorial actions such as Canada's seizure of the *Estai*. No less important, the new Agreement establishes a mandatory obligation to settle disputes by peaceful means.[80]

A second concern focused on the compatibility of conservation measures. Like the consistency provision in the NAFO Convention,[81] the Fish Stocks Agreement addresses the issue of conflicts between conservation measures inside the EEZ and those for the high seas. The Agreement sets out factors for governments to consider in order to determine what measures are most appropriate and compatible for conservation and management. Among such factors are existing EEZ and high sea regulations, measures adopted within the framework of a regional fisheries management organization, the 'biological unity and other biological characteristics' of fishery stocks, and even 'the respective dependence of the coastal States and the States fishing on the high seas on the stocks concerned'.[82]

More practically, the Fish Stocks Agreement calls upon coastal and flag states to develop provisional arrangements and to inform each other reciprocally about their respective national regulations and legislation.[83] It also provides that, should no agreement be achieved on compatibility of conservation and management measures, 'any of the States concerned' may bring the issue to binding and compulsory dispute settlement, using procedures set out in part VIII of the Agreement.[84] In sum, Canada's concern over the compatible character of conservation measures for both EEZ and adjacent high seas regions appears satisfactorily and effectively resolved.

A third concern centred on regional fishery organizations. The Agreement promotes in considerable detail fundamental aspects of such organizations, such as their functions,[85] admission of new members,[86] and the need for transparency in their activities.[87] The text also references specific provisions of fishery organizations when regulating general issues such as enforcement and the settlement of disputes.[88] The Fish Stocks Agreement upholds and extends the roles of regional and subregional organizations such as NAFO for resolving conservation and management issues regarding straddling fish stocks. The 1982 LOS Convention serves as a framework agreement. Application and enforcement of that general international law ostensibly can be performed more effectively by regional fishery organizations, because they are able to enforce regulations more strictly over localized fishing areas.

Still a fourth concern centred on control and enforcement of conservation measures. Enforcement provisions in the Fish Stocks Agreement significantly increase legal pressures on fishing vessels of parties to conform to the rules.[89] The Agreement clearly articulates the general principle that coastal and flag states *shall* 'implement and enforce conservation and

management measures through effective monitoring, control and surveillance'.[90] Specific duties of flag states to comply and enforce are established, emphasizing that these governments *shall* 'enforce such measures
irrespective of where violations occur'.[91] The duty for all states to cooperate is affirmed, so as to ensure compliance with and enforcement of
all measures.[92] These provisions are neither suggestions nor exhortations.
They are commands and fiats. Use of the verb 'shall' clearly signifies
deliberate intent and asserts the imperative obligation to comply with
these stipulations. Governments are legally obliged to fulfil these duties.
Further, they are expected to share information and evidence concerning
violations and to assist each other in investigations and vessel-identifica-
tion. Bluntly put, flag states are duty-bound to cooperate, even though
they retain jurisdiction over vessels flying their flag.[93]

The Fish Stocks Agreement, like the Agreed Minute between the EC and
Canada, also allows a range of permissible non-flag state monitoring and
enforcement actions. In fact, prescriptions regarding enforcement in the
Fish Stocks Agreement mirror patterns established in the EC–Canadian
agreement. The enforcement language in both instruments correlates
closely, and the inspection regimes are very similar.

Finally, the Fish Stock Agreement gives due attention to the settlement
of disputes.[94] These provisions were built upon the scheme for dispute
settlement set out in part XV of the 1982 LOS Convention and simply
apply it to contentious issues affecting straddling stocks and migratory
species. Thus, disputes over straddling stock species may become subject
to compulsory, binding settlement.[95] Such a prospect presumably fur-
nishes considerable incentive for governments to uphold their obligations
under the Agreement.[96]

The Fish Stocks Agreement supplies fairly specific rules that reduce
ambiguities in international environmental law over straddling stocks,
and thus decrease—though not eliminate entirely—the potential for conflicts over such species. As with NAFO, such rules for regulating fishery
activities furnish a minimum basis on which to build a regime for adequate living marine resources conservation. Yet, such a regime requires
prudent political decisions and the political will of governments to
enforce these rules over their own nationals engaged in fishing activities.
If the past is prologue, securing those essential perquisites will be neither
easy nor quick to attain.

Finally, notable implications for NAFO are listed. In the wake of the
1995 Canadian–European tensions, NAFO has adopted a more clearly
articulated precautionary approach to fisheries management in the Northwest Atlantic. The precautionary approach acknowledges that scientific
information cannot always provide definitive management. Rather than
exploit fish stocks at excessive levels, the precautionary approach
advocates conservative catch quotas and more restrictive fishing

operations. This approach offers ways to prevent the collapse of stocks managed with imperfect information.

Since 1995, NAFO has provided for the conservation and management of twelve fish stocks, divided into two categories, in its Regulatory Area. First, there are 'straddling' stocks, which are found both within Canada's 200-mile EEZ and on the high seas beyond. The straddling stocks managed by NAFO included 3LNO American plaice, 3LNO yellowtail flounder, 3NO cod, 3NO witch flounder, 3LN redfish, 3 LMNO turbot, and 3NO capelin.[97] Second, there are 'discrete' stocks, which are located entirely outside Canada's 200-mile limit in the Flemish Cap region. Four Flemish Cap stocks are managed by NAFO, 3M cod, 3M American plaice, 3M redfish, and 3M shrimp. Importantly, the forty groundfish stocks found exclusively within Canada's waters are managed by Canada. In line with recommendations submitted by Canada's Fisheries Resource Conservation Council and supported by NAFO's Scientific Council, NAFO has instigated the precautionary approach by putting moratoria on certain stocks, in particular straddling stocks. Included among these stocks are 3LNO American plaice, 3M American plaice, 3LNO yellowtail flounder, 2J and 3KL cod, 3NO cod, 3M cod, 3NO witch flounder, and 3NO capelin.[98]

As provided by the 1995 agreement between Canada and the EC, new conservation and enforcement measures have been implemented in the NAFO Regulatory Area. As requested by Canada, in year 2000 there is full observer coverage on all vessels fishing in the region. These observers, who inspect vessel catch records and fishing gear to ensure compliance with NAFO regulations, are required to report infractions to the nearest NAFO inspection vessel within twenty-four hours. The agreement also provides that 35 per cent of the vessels fishing in the NAFO Regulatory Area must be equipped with satellite transponders that automatically locate vessels on a continual basis. Sanctions have also been strengthened. If a NAFO inspector cites a major infringement, the inspector will stay on board until the vessel's flag state authorities arrive to determine the appropriate course of action, which might include fines, forfeitures, and other penalties. In addition, the 120mm mesh size exemption for polypropylene nets has been eliminated, standardizing all net sizes and thus facilitating enforcement to protect juvenile fish.

To improve conservation and enforcement measures in Northwest Atlantic waters, the members of NAFO (which represent more than thirty states) have also agreed to actions to deter vessels of non-contracting parties from fishing in the NAFO Regulatory Area contrary to NAFO conservation rules. Such actions include Canada's ability to control fishing by flag of convenience vessels on the 'nose' and 'tail' of Newfoundland's Grand Banks and agreement by NAFO members to prohibit the landing, trans-shipment, and sale of fish from non-complying, flag of convenience vessels operating in the region. Taken in concert, these actions have resulted in significantly improved levels of compliance in Northwest Atlantic waters since 1996.[99]

6 Conclusion

The 1982 LOS Convention lacked specific provisions on the legal rights and obligations for harvesting certain species of fish that swim back and forth between coastal states' EEZs and adjacent high seas areas. This dearth of regulation invited the possibility of conflict between coastal states and distant water fishing nations. Even more unfortunate, the situation inhibited effective enforcement and implementation of conservation measures for living marine resources. Hence, during the 1990s, straddling stocks came under increasingly severe pressures from exploitation efforts worldwide.

The politically charged 'Turbot War' between Canada and the European Community became the diplomatic catalyst for producing a positive legal outcome. The agreement negotiated by Canada and the EC strengthened the legal importance of the Northwest Atlantic Fisheries Organization, mainly by increasing recognition of NAFO's competence, but also for clarifying obligations to inspect more often, accept observers on board, and keep inspection vessels within the area when fishing vessels were engaged in harvesting operations. All these activities strengthened NAFO's legal reach and responsibility to monitor and enforce fishery conservation in the Northwest Atlantic. The prospects for regional cooperation, particularly regarding turbot, are much stronger today than in 1995, as the Agreed Minute has secured consensus on the total allowable catch and defined more clearly the specific enforcement and monitoring rules for fishing vessels in the Grand Banks area.

The Canada–EC dispute affirmed the need for new, more resolute international law to regulate straddling and highly migratory fisheries. The Fish Stocks Agreement represents the realization of that need and is a salient step toward fostering international cooperation on ocean law matters. Although this instrument has not yet entered into force, it still contributes to bridging the gap in international law regarding the legal status of and national jurisdiction over those special stocks. It embodies a 'far-sighted, far-reaching, bold and revolutionary' instrument with provisions that 'are detailed, precise and sound and [that] are firmly based on the principles enshrined in the 1982 United Nations Convention on the Law of the Sea'.[100] The Fish Stocks Agreement accordingly lessens the problem of jurisdiction by affirming the regulatory regime established by the 1982 Law of the Sea Convention: the authority of coastal state juris-diction is paramount over resource activities in its EEZ, and all peoples are free to fish in the high seas, albeit they are obligated to conserve living resources. The Fish Stocks Agreement also provides for measures that engender greater consistency of conservation measures for both the EEZ and the high seas, while strengthening the propriety, role, and respon-sibilities of regional fishery organizations. The Agreement's rules for compliance and enforcement, coupled with mandatory dispute settlement provisions, contribute to more comprehensive and effective conservation measures for regulating fishing activities beyond the area of national jurisdiction.

From a legal perspective, the international environmental law for fisheries has been substantially enriched. The 1995 Canadian–European Community fisheries dispute well illustrates how and why confrontations can occur between coastal states and distant water fishing governments in the absence of a more clearly defined regulatory framework. Fortu-nately, the 'Turbot War' compelled governments to seek viable legal solu-tions to complex political and economic problems at home. An even more comprehensive legal framework will, no doubt, remain essential to the efficient conservation of straddling stocks species.

The outcome of the Turbot War illustrates the relevance and evolving character of international environmental law for ocean space. The final agreement between Canada and the EC, coupled with a subsequent instrument produced by a special United Nations conference on strad-dling stocks and highly migratory species, helped clear up legal ambigu-ities and resolve shortcomings of the general regulatory framework for straddling stocks provided by the 1982 Law of the Sea Convention. Yet, while the overall outcome of the Canadian–EC fisheries dispute appears quite positive, economic and political considerations remain the key to thoroughly resolving problems associated with straddling stocks deple-tion. A more adequate legal framework will certainly improve compliance with and enforcement of fisheries management and conservation mea-sures. But regardless of how appropriate the international legal frame-work is, the future sustainability of fisheries ultimately depends on the economic and political decisions that governments make to enforce com-pliance by their nationals with that law. That comes down to a matter of political will and the ability of governments to balance methods of sustaining the welfare of domestic fishermen and their industry with the need to conserve adjacent straddling stocks. Given the trend for the increasing world demand for fishery resources, set against the continued decline of global fisheries, the successful accomplishment of these tasks constitutes daunting challenges for governments in the twenty-first century.

Notes

The author would like to thank David Balton, Donald Rothwell, and especially Michael Sean Sullivan for their helpful comments and suggestions on an earlier draft of this chapter.

1. H. Grotius, *Mare Liberum. The Freedom of the Seas: Or the Right Which Belongs to the Dutch to Take Part in the East Indian Trade* (1633), this edn. trans. and rev. R. van Deman Magoffin (Oxford University Press, 1916), pp. vii–viii.
2. The *Estai* was boarded by Canadian officers and escorted to Newfoundland. Canadian inspectors examined the vessel and discovered a hidden hold allegedly containing about 25 metric tons of flatfish, a type of groundfish under a unanimously agreed upon NAFO moratorium. Moreover, 80% of the stored turbot were allegedly immature fish; see 'EU/Canada; EU Suspends Ties with Canada over Fisheries Dispute', *European Report*, 2,024 (25 Mar. 1995), 8–9. In addition, nets from the *Estai*, found later in the high seas, were illegal under the NAFO rules for mesh size; ibid. 16. Yet, according to the official EC position, the vessel was subsequently examined in a Spanish port by British inspectors, who did not find substantiation for allegations made by Canada; see 'Both Sides Declare Progress in Fish Talks', *European Report*, 2,029 (1 Apr. 1995), 6. Cf. 'EU/Canada: Tensions Ride Again over Fish in North Atlantic', *European Report*, 2,028 (29 Mar. 1995), 3. Canadian authorities decided not to release the vessel and the crew unless the imposed penalty of C$500,000 was paid. The owners of the *Estai* paid that fine, and the vessel was released on 15 Mar.; 'EU/Canada: Release of Spanish Trawler Raises Hope of Settlement of Fish Row', *European Report*, 2,025 (18 Mar. 1995), 11.
3. C. H. Farnsworth, 'Canada and Spain Face off over Fishing Zone', *New York Times* (12 Mar. 1995), 19. For the reaction in Spain, Primitivo Carbajo, 'Canadá apresa al pesquero español "Estai" tras cinco horas del de persecución en aguas internacionales' ('Canada Seizes the Spanish Fishing Vessel "Estai" after Chasing it for Five Hours in International Waters', *El País* (Madrid edn.) (10 Mar. 1995), 55. See also Yann-Huei Song, 'The Canada–European Union Turbot Dispute in the Northwest Atlantic: An Application of the Incident Approach', *Ocean Development and International Law*, 28 (1997), 269, and M. S. Sullivan, 'The Case for Canada's Extension of Fisheries Jurisdiction beyond 200 Miles', *Ocean Development and International Law*, 28 (1997), 203. The fifteen European states in the EC in 1995 that aligned against Canada in the 'Turbot War' included Austria, Belgium, Denmark, Finland, France, Germany, Greece, Ireland, Italy, Luxembourg, the Netherlands, Portugal, Spain, Sweden, and the United Kingdom.
4. The *Fisheries Jurisdiction Case (Spain v. Canada)* ICJ Press Communiqué, 95/12 (2 May 1995); P. H. F. Bekker, 'International Court of Justice Rejects Jurisdiction in Fisheries Jurisdiction Case brought by Spain against Canada', *ASIL Flash Insight* (Dec. 1998). For the text of the decision, see www.icj-cij.org/.
5. Draft Final Act of the United Nations Conference on Straddling Fish

Stocks and Highly Migratory Fish Stocks, UN General Assembly Doc. A/CONF.164.32 (2 Aug. 1995).

6. United Nations Convention on the Law of the Sea, opened for signature 10 Dec. 1982, Arts. 55–7, entered into force 16 Nov. 1994, UN Doc. A/CONF./62/122 (1982), reprinted in *The Law of the Sea: United Nations Convention on the Law of the Sea with Index and Final Act of the Third United Nations Conference on the Law of the Sea*, UN Sales No. E.83.V.5 (hereinafter cited as 1982 LOS Convention).

7. World Wildlife Federation, The Rise and Fall of Modern Fisheries (www.wwf.org/species/marine/fish32.htm), 1–2. Globally more than one million large fishing vessels and two million smaller fishing boats unceasingly exploit the world's oceans, ibid. A Food and Agriculture Organization study has indicated a disparity between annual revenues on the one hand and operating and capital costs on the other of $54 billion; by comparison, the annual revenues in *were* calculated at $70 billion. Moreover, the EC, one of the largest fishers, possesses at least 40% more vessels than it needs to catch fish on a sustainable basis; ibid. 1.

8. B. Kwiatkowska, 'The High Fisheries Regime: At a Point of No Return?', *International Journal of Marine and Coastal Law*, 8 (1993), 327; D. A. Balton, 'Strengthening the Law of the Sea: The New Agreement on Straddling Fish Stocks and Highly Migratory Fish Stocks', *Ocean Development and International Law*, 27 (1996), 125; and F. Orrego Vicuña, 'Toward an Effective Management of High Seas Fisheries and the Settlement of the Pending Issues of the Law of the Sea', *Ocean Development and International Law*, 24 (1993), 81.

9. At the outset, Canada did not claim an exclusive economic zone, but rather an exclusive fisheries zone. The rights and duties involved in the EFZ legal regime are analogous to those in the EEZ, save for the regulation of research and pollution control. In 1996, a full EEZ was claimed.

10. W. G. Doubleday, A. T. Pinhorn, R. G. Halliday, R. D. S. Macdonald, and R. Stein, 'The Impact of Extended Fisheries Jurisdiction in the Northwest Atlantic', in E. Miles (ed.), *Management of World Fisheries* (Seattle: University of Washington Press, 1989), 42–5.

11. Ibid. 52.

12. 1982 LOS Convention, Arts. 63 and 119.

13. Convention on Future Multilateral Co-operation in the Northwest Atlantic Fisheries (1978), *OJ* L378 (1978) (hereinafter the NAFO Convention). This Convention replaced the International Convention for the Northwest Atlantic Fisheries (1949). At present contracting parties to NAFO include Bulgaria, Canada, Cuba, Denmark, Estonia, the European Community, France, Iceland, Korea, Latvia, Lithuania, Poland, Norway, Romania, Russian Federation, and the United States. See the NAFO home page (www.nafo.ca).

14. NAFO Convention, Art. II (1).

15. Ibid., Art. XI (3) (b).

16. Ibid., Art. I (1).

17. Ibid., Art. I (2). The Convention area also includes part of the US EEZ.

18. Ibid., Arts. I (4) and XI (3) (a).

19. Ibid., Arts. VI (3) and XI (3) (b).

20. NAFO Convention, Art. XII (1).
21. Doubleday *et al.*, 'The Impact of Extended Fisheries Jurisdiction', 38.
22. R. Churchill, 'Fisheries Management and the 200-Mile Zone', in *The Regulation of Fisheries: Legal, Economic and Social Aspects* (Strasbourg: Council of Europe, 1987), 3.
23. R. W. Crowley, 'Rights to Fish: The Canadian Experience', in *Property Rights Modifications in Fisheries* (Paris: Organization for Economic Cooperation and Development, 1992), 38.
24. Fisheries Reports and Statistics (Paris: Organization for Economic Cooperation and Development, 1992), 50.
25. C. Emery, 'Overfishing outside the 200-Mile Limit: Atlantic Coast', Canadian Doc. 90-6E (10 Oct. 1990) Research Branch, Library of Parliament, Canada (revised 13 Apr. 1993, with 1995 addendum), 9.
26. Fisheries Reports and Statistics, 50.
27. Farnsworth, 'Canada and Spain Face off over Fishing Zone', 19.
28. Emery, 'Overfishing outside the 200-Mile Limit', 9.
29. European Commission, 'Difference of the European Union with Canada concerning the Fisheries Dispute II', Information Note, 15 (30 Mar. 1995), 3–4.
30. E. L. Miles and W. T. Burke, 'Pressures on the United Nations Convention on the Law of the Sea of 1982 Arising from New Fisheries Conflicts', *Ocean Development and International Law*, 20 (1989), 243; and E. Meltzer, 'Global Overview of Straddling and Highly Migratory Fish Stocks: The Nonsustainable Nature of High Seas Fisheries', *Ocean Development and International Law*, 25 (1994), 255.
31. Canada, Coastal Fisheries Protection Act, RSC ch. C-21, s. 1, as amended 12 May 1994, in *Canada Gazette*, part II, 128/12 (15 June 1994), 2,222–7; *Canada Gazette*, part II, 128 Extra (17 June 1994), 1–4; and *Canada Gazette*, part II, 128/13 (15 June 1994), 2,574–8 (entered into force 25 May 1994), reprinted as 'Canada: Coastal Fisheries Protection Act' (1994); 33 *ILM* 1383, with Implementing Regulations of 3 Mar. 1995, s. 21, table IV, Items 1 and 2 (SOR/95-136), *Canada Gazette*, part II (1995), 650.
32. Coastal Fisheries Protection Act, RSC ch. C-33, s. 5.1 (1985) (Can.), amended by ch. 14, 1994 SC (Can.). For an insightful assessment of the background and implications of this legislation, see Sullivan, 'Canada's Extension of Fisheries Jurisdiction', 220–9.
33. Emery, 'Overfishing outside the 200-Mile Limit', 14. The following allocations were agreed upon: 3,400 metric tons (12.59%) to the EC; 16,300 metric tons (60.37%) to Canada; 3,200 metric tons (11.85%) to Russia; 2,600 metric tons (9.63%) to Japan; and 1,500 metric tons (5.56%) to other NAFO members.
34. But see X. Vidal-Folch and J. Hermida, 'Canadá endurece sus condiciones y exige que la cuota de pesca de la UE sea del 32%' ('Canada Hardens its Position and Demands that the EU's Quota be 32 Percent'), *El País* (Madrid edn.) (1 Apr. 1995), 50.
35. 'Fisheries: EU Formally Objects to NAFO Turbot Quotas as Canada Warns Against', *European Report*, 2,021 (4 Mar. 1995), 1.
36. Emery, 'Overfishing outside the 200-Mile Limit', 15.

37. 1982 LOS Convention, Art. 63 (2).
38. From 1979 to 1986, the EC did not object to any conservation measure taken by the NAFO contracting parties. From 1986 to 1992, the EC resorted to the objection procedure fifty-two times. In this regard, it is noteworthy that Spain and Portugal joined the EC on 1 Jan. 1986. From 1992 to Feb. 1995, no EC veto of a NAFO policy measure took place, even though in this period Spanish and Portuguese catches increased in NAFO's subarea 3J. A. Beesley and M. Rowe, 'International Law Supports our Actions', *Daily Gleaner* (12 May 1995).
39. Emery, 'Overfishing outside the 200-Mile Limit', 15.
40. 1982 LOS Convention, Arts. 63 (2), 87, and 116.
41. Canadian Department of Fisheries and Oceans Press Release, NR-HQ-95-27E (3 Mar. 1995) (Statement of Brian Tobin, Minister of Fisheries and Oceans).
42. 'EU/Canada: Release of Spanish Trawler Raises Hope of Settlement of Fish Row', *European Report*, 2,025 (18 Mar. 1995), 11.
43. 'EU/Canada: EU Suspends Ties with Canada over Fisheries Dispute', *European Report*, 2,024 (15 Mar. 1995), 8.
44. 'EU/Canada: Release of Spanish Trawler Raises Hope of Settlement of Fish Row', *European Report*, 11.
45. See comments of Sir Leon Brittan, in *Globe and Mail* (Toronto, Ontario) (15 Mar. 1995), at A 20.
46. Department of Fisheries and Ocean Press Release NR-HQ-95-34E (27 Mar. 1995). The author is grateful to Michael Sullivan for bringing this point to his attention.
47. The European Commission, which immediately condemned the seizure, accused Canada of 'organized piracy' and claimed that such an action damaged possibilities for finding a diplomatic solution to the quotas; 'Fisheries: Bonino Condemns Canadian Attack as an Act of Piracy', *European Report*, 2,023 (11 Mar. 1995), 1.
48. D. Freestone and A. Fleisch, 'The Common Fisheries Policy', in J. Lodge (ed.), *The Institutions and Policies of the European Community* (New York: St Martin's Press, 1983), 77–84 and R. R. Churchill, 'EC Fisheries and an EEZ: Easy!', *Ocean Development and International Law*, 23 (1992), 145–63.
49. As defined by Regulation 170/83, *OJ* L24 (1983), 30; see also R. R. Churchill, *EEC Fisheries Law* (Dordrecht: Martinus Nijhoff, 1987), 110–11.
50. Art. 4 of Regulation 170/83. Regulation 3760/92 of 20 Dec. 1995 did not modify these essential provisions in the 170/83.
51. At the time of the Canadian–EU dispute during Mar./Apr. 1995, Spain had an unemployment rate of 23.9%; *The Economist* (27 Apr. 1996), 112.
52. 'Both Sides Declare Progress in Fish Talks', 5–6.
53. See 'EU Divided on How to Tackle Fish Row with Canada', *European Report*, 2,031 (1 Apr. 1995), 10, 12.
54. 'La pesca española, al borde del naufragio' ('The Spanish Fishing Industry, on the Brink of Shipwreck'), *ABC* (7 Apr. 1995), cover and 'Negro como el fletan' ('Black as Turbot') *El País* (Madrid edn.), (17 Apr. 1995), 12.
55. 'Communication from the Commission to the Council on the outcome of

negotiations with Canada on fisheries, including a proposal for a Council decision' (Brussels: Commission of the European Communities, 16 Apr. 1995). Greenland halibut is synonymous with turbot.

56. See the diplomatic exchange between Canada and the European Commission (1995); 34 *ILM* 1272.
57. Done at Brussels, 20 Apr. 1995; 34 *ILM* 1260.
58. Ibid., s. A. See also annex I.
59. Ibid., s. A.1. annex I, 'Proposal for Improving Fisheries Control and Enforcement', contains the provisions for that protocol.
60. Ibid., annex II, s. I (a).
61. Ibid., annex II, ss. I and II.
62. Ibid., annex II, s. II (b). Of note here, Spanish vessels had already taken at least 7,000 metric tons before that date; 'EU Divided on How to Tackle Fish Row with Canada', 12.
63. Ibid., annex II, s. III.
64. Agreed Minute, s. C.1.
65. Ibid., s. E.
66. Importantly, in settling the dispute, Canada agreed to repeal that amendment; Agreed Minute, provision C (1).
67. Agreed Minute, para. A.1.
68. 'NAFO Annual Meeting, 12–16 September 1995', Press Release IP/95/988 (Brussels: European Commission, 15 Sept. 1995), 2.
69. See Map 7.1.
70. The Agreed Minute, annex I, s. II.
71. Ibid., annex I, s. II.11.
72. Ibid., annex I, s. II.11, para. A.1 (a).
73. Ibid., annex I, s. II.11, para. A.1 (b).
74. Ibid., annex I, s. II.9 (e) (i) (iii).
75. Ibid., annex I, s. II.9.
76. Ibid., annex I, s. II.9 (iv).
77. Ibid., annex I, s. II.10.
78. Agreement for the Implementation of the Provisions of the United Nations Convention on the Law of the Sea of 10 Dec. 1982 relating to the Conservation and Management of Straddling Fish Stocks and Highly Migratory Fish Stocks; 34 *ILM* 1542. As of 22 Sept. 2000, fifty-nine states are signatories, but only twenty-seven have ratified or acceeded to the Fish Stocks Agreement. See web site (www.un.org/Depts/los/los164st.htm). Thirty parties are required for the Agreement to enter into force; Fish Stocks Agreement, Art. 40 (1).
79. Balton, 'Strengthening the Law of the Sea', 150 n. 80.
80. Fish Stocks Agreement, Art. 27.
81. NAFO Convention, Art. XI (3).
82. Fish Stocks Agreement, Art. 7 (2) (e); see the discussion by Orrego, Ch. 1 above.
83. Fish Stocks Agreement, Art. 7 (6), (7), and (8).
84. Ibid., Art. 7 (4).
85. Ibid., Arts. 8–10.

86. Ibid., Art. 11.
87. Ibid., Art. 12.
88. Ibid., Arts. 19–21, 28, and 30.
89. Balton, 'Strengthening the Law of the Sea', 141.
90. Fish Stocks Agreement, Art. 5 (l). My emphasis.
91. Ibid., Art. 19 (1) (a). My emphasis.
92. Ibid., Art. 20.
93. See the discussion by Vukas and Vidas, Ch. 2 above.
94. Fish Stocks Agreement, Arts. 27–32 (part VIII).
95. For a careful discussion of this matter, see Boyle, Ch. 3 above.
96. Balton, 'Strengthening the Law of the Sea', 142.
97. Fisheries and Oceans Canada, Backgrounder, The Northwest Atlantic Fisheries Organization, B-HQ-97-38E (www.ncr.dfo.ca/communic/backgrou/1997/hq38e1.htm).
98. Fisheries Resource Conservation Council, '4.2.3. Stocks in the NAFO Regulatory Area' (www.ncr.dfo.ca/frcc/fisheries/4/423.html) (Sept. 1997), 2.
99. Fisheries and Oceans Canada, Backgrounder 'New Conservation Measures in the NAFO Regulatory Area (B-HQ-97-38E2)' (www.ncr.dfo.ca/communic/backgrou/1997/hq38e2.htm) (Sept. 1997).
100. 'Statement of the Chairman, Ambassador Satya N. Nandan, on 4 August 1995, upon the Adoption of the Agreement for the Implementation of the Provisions of the United Nations Convention on the Law of the Sea of 10 December 1982 Relating to the Conservation and Management of Straddling Fish Stocks and Highly Migratory Fish Stocks', UN Doc. A/CONF.164/35 (20 Sept. 1995), 1.

8

Managing Straddling Fish Stocks in the North-East Atlantic: A Multiplicity of Instruments and Regime Linkages—but How Effective a Management?

ROBIN R. CHURCHILL

1 Introduction

The North-East Atlantic, as defined for the purposes of this chapter,[1] contains two areas of high seas. The first is an enclave in the Norwegian Sea, often referred to as the Banana Hole, bounded by the 200-mile zones of Greenland, Iceland, the Faroes, and Norway (including Svalbard). The second, which forms part of the general high seas area of the central North Atlantic, lies to the south of Iceland and west of the British Isles and is bordered by the 200-mile zones of Greenland, Iceland, the Faroes, the United Kingdom, Ireland, France, Spain, and Portugal (see Map 8.1).[2] The main straddling stocks of the first high seas area are herring, blue whiting, and capelin; those of the second area are redfish, mackerel, and blue whiting. Of these stocks, herring, redfish, and mackerel have so far been the subject of detailed management arrangements, which accordingly form the subject of this chapter.[3]

Each of these arrangements will be examined in detail in turn. It will be argued that each arrangement now has sufficient substantive and operational components to be regarded as a regime.[4] These regimes are, in part, the product of, and have elements deriving from, a number of pre-existing legal instruments and regimes. These instruments will be out-lined first. This will be followed by a discussion of the herring, redfish, and mackerel regimes in turn. In each case the content and operation of the regime will be explained; the role and influence of these pre-existing instruments on the regime (i.e. regime linkages or interplay, to use the conceptual terminology of the Introduction) explored; and the effectiveness of the regime evaluated.

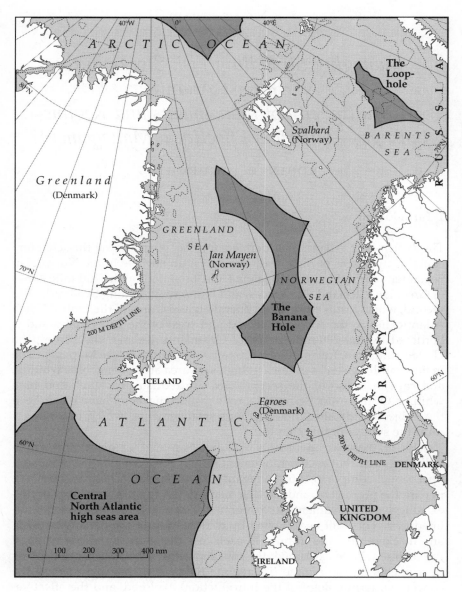

Map 8.1. Areas of high seas in the North-East Atlantic

2 Pre-existing instruments

There are five sets of legal instruments which form the background to, and have influenced and contributed to, the herring, redfish, and mackerel regimes. At the global level there are two instruments, the UN Convention on the Law of the Sea (UNCLOS) and the Fish Stocks Agreement. At the regional level, there are three elements which must be considered: the North-East Atlantic Fisheries Commission (NEAFC), the International Council for the Exploration of the Sea (ICES), and national fisheries management systems applying within 200-mile fishing or economic zones. Each of these instruments will now be sketched: the global regimes briefly, the regional ones in more detail.

The *Law of the Sea Convention*[5] obviously provides the basic framework—in terms of the 200-mile EEZ, the high seas, and the obligation to cooperate over the management of straddling stocks—which underlies the straddling stocks issue, but this is so well known that it needs no further elaboration here and in any case is discussed earlier in this book. All that need be said here is that nearly all states of the North-East Atlantic (as well as the EC) are parties to the Convention. The only exception is Denmark (including therefore the Faroes and Greenland), but this is not of major significance as most of the fisheries provisions of the Convention have passed into customary law.

Equally the *Fish Stocks Agreement*[6] has been discussed in earlier chapters so that nothing further needs to be said here except to mention that three North-East Atlantic states—Iceland, Norway, and Russia—have so far ratified the Agreement. In addition, the EC and all its member states have signed, but not yet ratified, the Agreement.

More needs to be said about the regional instruments, however, as these are less familiar. The *North-East Atlantic Fisheries Commission* was set up by a convention signed in 1980.[7] NEAFC effectively replaced a commission of the same name that had been set up in 1959 to regulate fisheries in both the then 12-mile fishing zones of its member states and the high seas of the North-East Atlantic. The creation of the new NEAFC was prompted by the extension in the late 1970s by all coastal states of the North-East Atlantic of their fisheries jurisdiction to 200 miles. NEAFC's function is to serve as a forum for consultation and exchange of information on the fishery resources of the North-East Atlantic. More specifically, it may adopt management measures, known technically as 'recommendations',[8] such as gear regulations, closed areas and seasons, and TACs and quotas, for fisheries conducted on the high seas. In doing so, NEAFC 'shall seek to ensure consistency' between any of its measures which apply to straddling stocks and measures adopted by coastal states for the same stocks, and NEAFC and the coastal states concerned 'shall accordingly promote the co-ordination' of their respective measures.[9] NEAFC may also adopt measures applicable to fisheries within the 200-mile zone at the request and with the agreement of the relevant coastal state(s). In general, NEAFC is to perform its functions in the interests of the conservation and optimum utilization of the fishery resources of the North-East Atlantic and shall take into account the best scientific evidence available to it. At present, the members of NEAFC are the EC, Denmark (in respect of the Faroes and Greenland),[10] Iceland, Norway, Poland, and Russia.[11]

Already a number of regime linkages, both explicit and implicit, may be pointed out. The Preamble to the NEAFC Convention states that the parties take into account the work of the Third UN Conference on the Law of the Sea in the field of fisheries, and the Convention, by establishing a regional body for cooperation over the conservation of high seas fishery resources which is required to take account of the best scientific evidence, reflects the provisions of the then Draft Convention (and now Convention) on the Law of the Sea that call on states to cooperate in the conservation of high seas fishery resources, *inter alia* through regional organizations.[12] NEAFC is also clearly a regional fisheries organization of the kind referred to in the Fish Stocks Agreement, and the NEAFC Convention's provisions requiring consistency between its measures regulating straddling stocks and those of the relevant coastal state(s) anticipate the Agreement's requirement of compatibility between high seas and coastal state measures. This similarity is not a coincidence. NEAFC is quite closely modelled on the Northwest Atlantic Fisheries Organization (NAFO), which was set up two years before NEAFC and which also has a consistency requirement; NAFO in turn served to a considerable extent as a model for the provisions of the Fish Stocks Agreement dealing with regional fisheries organizations.[13] There is also a direct linkage between NEAFC and one of the other regional instruments. Article 14 of the NEAFC Convention directs NEAFC, 'in the interests of the optimal performance' of its functions, to seek information and advice from the International Council for the Exploration of the Sea on such matters as the biology and population dynamics of the fish stocks concerned, the state of the stocks, the effect of fishing on those stocks, and measures for their conservation and management. In practice NEAFC makes specific requests for advice to ICES at its annual meetings, and ICES prepares a report each year for NEAFC in response to such requests. Since 1996, NEAFC has asked ICES, when giving its advice, to take into account the precautionary approach: such an approach is, of course, called for by the Fish Stocks Agreement. In 1998, NEAFC and ICES put their relations on a more formal basis with the signature of a Memorandum of Understanding.[14]

The way NEAFC has operated in practice presents quite a striking contrast compared to its sister regional fisheries organization in the North Atlantic, NAFO. Whereas NAFO has actively and continuously engaged in managing the straddling and discrete high seas stocks of the Northwest Atlantic since its inception in 1979, NEAFC for much of its existence has been a rather dormant organization. Only in 1996 did NEAFC begin adopting significant management measures (discussed below). There appear to be a number of reasons for this state of affairs. First, there are few high seas or straddling stocks of commercial significance in the North-East Atlantic. Secondly, significant levels of fishing for some of these stocks is rather recent and, indeed, in the case of herring (as will be seen below) its very existence as a straddling stock is a recent phenomenon. Thirdly, the political situation is very different from that of the North-West Atlantic. In the latter region there is effectively a single coastal state (Canada) and some fifteen high seas fishing states, most of which are from outside the region; the activities and agenda of NAFO have been very much driven by the Canadian Government, spurred on by domestic political pressures.[15] In the North-East Atlantic, by contrast, the interests of states are more diverse. There is no clear-cut distinction between coastal states and high seas fishing states. Some coastal states, such as Iceland, Russia, and the EC, fish quite extensively on the high seas, and in fact most high seas fishing in the North-East Atlantic is conducted by coastal states: apart from a few flag of convenience vessels, the only high seas fishing by non-coastal states, and then on a very limited scale, is by states from the Baltic (principally Poland) and Japan. Furthermore, some coastal states have a limited interest in the straddling stocks found in their 200-miles zones, for example the EC in respect of blue whiting. A final reason for NEAFC's lack of activity is that because of the differing interests of its members, it may be difficult to get the two-thirds majority required for the adoption of management measures.

A revitalization of NEAFC appears to be starting to occur, however. As mentioned, NEAFC adopted its first significant management measures in 1996. At its annual meeting that year, NEAFC also established two working groups. The first was to look at NEAFC's future. Its terms of reference required it to 'evaluate the structure and function' of NEAFC 'measured against the provisions' of the NEAFC Convention and 'in the light of the UNCLOS and the development of relevant international law, in particular' the Fish Stocks Agreement and the FAO Code of Conduct for Responsible Fisheries.[16] The second working group was charged with considering the desirability of introducing a control and enforcement scheme for high seas fishing in the North-East Atlantic.[17] An extraordinary meeting of NEAFC was held in June 1998 to consider the reports of these working groups. At this meeting NEAFC adopted a Scheme of Control and Enforcement in respect of vessels fishing on the high seas, which is modelled on the relevant provisions of the Fish Stocks Agreement[18] and the NAFO scheme (itself a model for the Agreement); and, on the basis of the report of the first working group, established an independent secretariat. In addition, at its annual meeting held in November 1998, NEAFC adopted a scheme (similar to that adopted by NAFO in 1997) to promote compliance by the vessels of non-members with NEAFC measures[19] and decided to examine the transparency of the organization at its next meeting; transparency in the decision-making and other activities of regional fisheries organizations is called for by the Fish Stocks Agreement.

The second regional instrument is the *International Council for the Exploration of the Sea.* Founded as long ago as 1902,[20] ICES is probably the foremost intergovernmental organization concerned with marine scientific research, not only on account of its longevity but also because of the quality of its work and the impartiality of its advice. The Council's functions include the promotion, coordination, and publication of research relating to fisheries, and to some extent pollution, in the North Atlantic, the North Sea, and the Baltic Sea; the compilation and publication of statistics relating to fish catches; and, through its Advisory Committee for Fishery Management (ACFM), providing advice and making recommendations on fisheries management to NEAFC, to the International Baltic Sea Fisheries Commission, to the North Atlantic Salmon Conservation Organization, and to the EC.[21] In 1997, the ACFM announced that henceforth its advice would be based on a precautionary approach, as formulated in recent international legal texts including the Fish Stocks Agreement.[22] ICES has eighteen members, including all the coastal states of the North-East Atlantic. As has been seen, there are significant linkages between ICES and NEAFC.

The final legal instrument, or rather set of legal instruments, relating to the management of the straddling stocks of the North-East Atlantic is the fisheries management systems of the coastal states of the region. In terms of numbers, these coastal state management systems are fewer than might initially be supposed. Since the EC is responsible for the management of the fish stocks, including straddling stocks, within the 200-mile zones of its member states, the ten EC coastal states of the North-East Atlantic effectively count as one. Thus, there are in reality only four coastal states (using the term broadly, as the EC is obviously not a state) of the North-East Atlantic—Denmark (in respect of the Faroes and Greenland, which are not part of the EC[23]), the EC, Iceland, and Norway. Arguably Russia should also be included as a coastal state because, although it does not border the North-East Atlantic as defined for the purposes of this chapter, the straddling herring stock of the Norwegian Sea, which is considered in the next section, migrates to Russia's 200-mile zone. Even though there are so few coastal states, it is impossible for reasons of space to give any account of the details of the systems of fisheries management used by these states for their 200-mile zones.[24] Suffice it to say that all are influenced to a greater or lesser extent by the fisheries provisions of the UN Convention on the Law of the Sea and thus have a degree of similarity, although there are also significant differences between them. All the states concerned are members of NEAFC and ICES, and all receive advice on fisheries management from ICES. As mentioned, the EC is effectively a single coastal state as far as management of fish stocks within 200-mile zones is concerned, but a word should also be said about its role on the external plane, i.e. as an actor in relation to third states and international organizations. On the external plane the EC's competence as far as fisheries are concerned is almost wholly exclusive: that is, the EC alone is competent to act to the exclusion of its individual member states.[25] Thus, in external fisheries matters the EC also resembles a single coastal state.

Having now looked at the various instruments which are relevant to the management of straddling stocks in the North-East Atlantic, we can turn to examine the actual arrangements for the management of the straddling stocks of the region which have so far been adopted.

3 The herring arrangement

3.1 Background

Of the various herring stocks found in the North-East Atlantic, the one with which we are concerned in this chapter, and apparently the only one that is a straddling stock, is the Norwegian spring-spawning herring. Before 1970 this stock had a well-established migratory pattern. It wintered off Iceland, then moved eastwards to spawn in the coastal waters of Norway in the late winter and early spring, and then migrated into the central Norwegian Sea and to the waters off Iceland; some juvenile herring also migrated into the Barents Sea. During the 1950s and 1960s, a considerable fishery for this stock developed, mainly by fishermen from Norway, Iceland, and the USSR, with annual catches of between 1 and 2 million metric tons.[26] Fishing at these levels was unsustainable. Efforts by the old NEAFC and trilateral agreements between Iceland, Norway, and the USSR[27] to regulate the fishery were too little and too late to be effective. In 1969 the stock collapsed totally. The spawning stock biomass was reduced to virtually zero from a maximum figure of over 11 million metric tons in 1956.[28] This collapse is thought to have disturbed the ecological balance of large parts of the Norwegian and the Barents Seas.[29]

Thereafter the stock confined itself to Norwegian waters for many years. Thanks to Norwegian conservation measures, the stock was gradually rebuilt and by the early 1990s had begun to resume an extensive migratory pattern, but one rather different from that before the collapse of the stock in 1969. Although the present migratory pattern is currently not fully understood—and appears to vary from year to year depending on various factors such as the age structure of the stock, abundance of zooplankton, and water temperature—the main features of the pattern appear to be as follows.[30] The herring winter off northern Norway and then move south to spawn in the waters off mid-Norway. Juvenile herring drift north into the Barents Sea and the coastal waters of Norway and Russia. The older herring move into the high seas Banana Hole of the Norwegian Sea by May, and by June and July they are in the 200-mile zones of the Faroes and Iceland (and in some years the EC). By late August the fish are returning to Norwegian waters to winter (see Map 8.2). The taking up of such a migratory pattern meant that by the early 1990s the Norwegian spring-spawning herring had become a straddling stock, as NEAFC noted at its annual meeting in November 1995.[31] Since the herring migrates from the Norwegian EEZ into not only the high seas but also into the 200-mile zones of other states, it is a shared stock as well as a straddling stock, and thus falls within the ambit of Article 63 (1) of the Law of the Sea Convention, which calls on the coastal states concerned to seek to agree upon the measures necessary to coordinate and ensure the conservation and development of the stock in question.

Following the regeneration of the stock, fishing for herring began again on a modest scale in Norwegian waters in the mid-1980s. In the summer of 1994, an international fishery began in the high seas enclave of the Norwegian Sea, and in 1995 fishing took place for the first time for many years in the 200-mile zones of the Faroes and Iceland. Catches for the period 1986–95 are shown in Table 8.1. The major part of the catch was taken by Norwegian vessels in Norwegian waters, with smaller catches being taken by the Faroes, Iceland, and Russia.

With fishing taking place on an increasing scale, it was clear that if the herring was not to suffer the same fate as it had done in the 1960s, a proper regulation of the fishery would be necessary. In early 1995 negotiations began between the Faroes, Iceland, Norway, and Russia, but these soon broke down because of differences over the principle of allocation, the Faroes and Iceland being insistent that the principle should be zonal attachment and Russia being opposed to this. Negotiations resumed again in the late summer of 1995 when a scientific working group was set up to evaluate the zonal attachment of the herring to the various 200-mile zones and the high seas.[32] Following the report of the working group, negotiations continued. The main difficulty was still the principle of allocation,

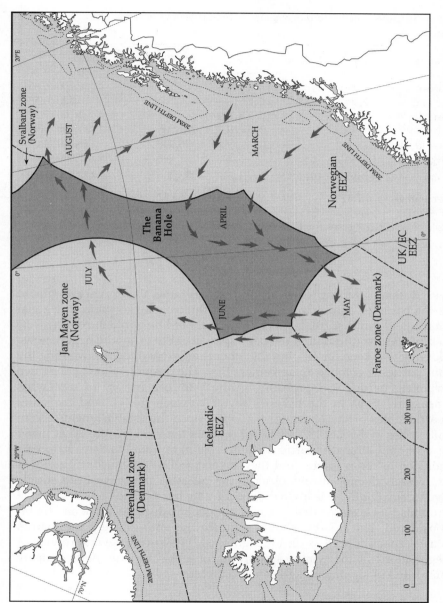

Map 8.2. The general migration pattern of adult Norwegian spring-spawning herring, spring to autumn 1995

Table 8.1 Total catches of Norwegian spring-spawning herring 1986–1995 (metric tons)

Waters	Faroes	Iceland	Norway	USSR/Russia	Total (%)
Faroes	50,000	116,200	—	—	166,200 (6.85)
Iceland	2,500	11,000	—	—	13,500 (0.56)
Jan Mayen	—	—	4,100	—	4,100 (0.17)
Norway	—	—	1,842,100	297,300	2,139,400 (88.15)
Russia	—	—	—	26,000	26,000 (1.07)
High seas	7,900	64,500	5,500	—	77,900 (3.21)
Total	60,400	191,700	1,851,700	323,300	2,427,100 (100)
Percentage	2.47	7.9	76.3	13.32	—

Note: The catch figures for 1993–5 incorporated in this table are provisional.
Source: Report, cited in n. 30, table 9.6.

with Russia preferring to use historic catches rather than zonal attachment as the basis for allocation and the other three countries preferring zonal attachment but disagreeing as to how it should be applied. Another difficulty was the question of the participation of the EC in the negotiations: Norway was keen on this, but the other three were opposed, wanting the four parties to come to an agreement first. The position taken by the three opposing parties was probably attributable to a history of somewhat uneasy relations in the fisheries sector between the EC and the other coastal states of the North-East Atlantic since the establishment of 200-mile zones in the late 1970s. The other states tend to view the EC as using its economic strength (particularly in relation to trade) to drive hard bargains on fisheries issues, and they suspect (with some justification) that EC vessels do not always observe the bargains that have been struck. Eventually the EC was invited to participate but declined to do so on the grounds that it feared that it would not get an adequate quota and that it considered that NEAFC should regulate the entire fishery (i.e. within coastal zones as well as on the high seas).[33] Following several rounds of negotiations in the winter and spring of 1996, the four parties finally succeeded in signing an agreement on 6 May 1996.

3.2 *The initial arrangement: the four-party agreement*

The four-party agreement is entitled Protocol on the Conservation, Rational Utilization and Management of Norwegian Spring Spawning Herring (Atlanto-Scandian Herring) in the North-East Atlantic.[34] The nomenclature is unusual because normally an instrument called a proto-col refers to an agreement supplementary to a pre-existing treaty. In the present case, however, there is no principal treaty to which the Protocol is supplementary.

In paragraph 1 of the Protocol, the parties undertake to cooperate in the conservation, rational utilization, and management of the herring, 'taking into account the best scientific advice available', and to 'establish such measures as will ensure that the spawning stock will be maintained above safe biological limits, where sufficient recruitment is ensured to allow for long-term sustainable exploitation'. The Protocol established a total allowable catch (TAC) for 1996 of 1,107,000 metric tons. This figure relates to the entire fishery, both within 200-mile zones and on the high seas. The TAC is divided into quotas as shown in Table 8.2.[35] The basis for allocating the quotas is a negotiated compromise between various criteria, principally historic catches and zonal attachment (on which, as noted earlier, the parties disagreed as to both the relevance of the principle and its practical application: in any case, zonal attachment will vary over time). Accompanying the Protocol are a series of bilateral agreements between the parties providing for access by the vessels of one party to the 200-mile zone of the other party for the purpose of taking part of its quota.

The Protocol goes on to provide that the parties are to 'initiate work to establish harmonized conservation measures' for the fishery and are to 'facilitate and further co-operation in the field of inspection and control to ensure compliance with conservation measures' (paras. 3.2 and 3.3). The parties are also to cooperate to enhance scientific research relating to the stock. To this end the Protocol provides for the setting up of a scien-tific working group to monitor and assess the development and distribu-tion of the stock according to agreed biological criteria. The work of this group, which is to cooperate with ICES, is to be used as the basis for future negotiations on conservation and management of the stock.

Compared with straddling stocks in other areas, the Norwegian spring-spawning herring presents a number of unusual features as a straddling stock that help explain several aspects of the Protocol that differ from regional agreements elsewhere. In many areas, such as the North-West Atlantic, the South-West Atlantic, and the Bering Sea, straddling stocks straddle the 200-mile zones of one, or at most two, coastal states, whereas the herring straddles the zones of several states and is not only a strad-dling stock but also a shared stock. Secondly, unlike other regions, there is no clear-cut distinction between coastal states and high seas fishing states. Nearly all high seas fishing is by coastal states and all the coastal states fish on the high seas. These factors help to explain why the Protocol relates to all fishing for the stock and not simply to high seas

Table 8.2 TACs, quotas, and catches for herring 1996–2000 (metric tons)

(*a*) *TAC and quotas set for 1996 by Protocol* (actual catches in brackets)

TAC (for whole stock) (high seas and national zones)	1,107,000	(1,027,754)
Quotas		
Faroes and Iceland	256,000	(213,684)
Norway	695,000	(695,000)
Russia	166,000	(119,070)

Note: EC unilateral quota 150,000 (194,912).

(*b*) *TAC and quotas since 1997* (actual catches in brackets)

	1997	1998	1999	2000
TAC for whole stock	1,500,000 (1,429,003)	1,302,000 (1,233,691)	1,302,000 (1,257,255)	1,252,000
Allocated by agreed record				
EC	125,000[a] (127,763)	109,000[d] (91,665)	109,000[d] (94,792)	104,800[d]
Faroes and Iceland	315,000[ab] (280,828)	273,000[def] (268,671)	273,000[def] (259,839)	262,500[dfh]
Norway	854,000[c] (852,126)	741,000[fg] (743,000)	741,000[fg] (744,875)	712,500[fg]
Russia	204,000[c] (168,761)	177,000[g] (128,357)	177,000[g] (157,329)	170,200[g]
Subtotal	1,498,000 (1,429,003)	1,300,000 (1,233,691)	1,300,000 (1,257,255)	1,250,000
Allocated by NEAFC				
Denmark	25,000 (16,355)	20,000 (7,411)	20,000 (14,438)	20,000
EC	25,000 (96,196)	20,000 (37,641)	20,000 (31,887)	20,000
Iceland	25,000 (89,842)	20,000 (22,338)	20,000 (29,787)	20,000
Norway	25,000 (5,062)	20,000 (2,629)	20,000 (5,878)	20,000
Poland	2,000 (0)	2,000 (0)	2,000 (0)	2,000
Russia	25,000 (15,598)	20,000 (4,467)	20,000 (20,544)	20,000
Subtotal	127,000 (223,203)	102,000 (73,346)	102,000 (102,534)	102,000

[a] By bilateral agreement the Faroes transferred 5,000 metric tons of its quota to the EC.
[b] By bilateral agreement the Faroes and Iceland divided their quota between them, the Faroes receiving 82,000 metric tons and Iceland 233,000.
[c] By bilateral agreement Russia transferred 2,500 metric tons of its quota to Norway.
[d] By bilateral agreement the Faroes transferred 4,000 metric tons of its quota to the EC (3,800 metric tons in 2000).
[e] By bilateral agreement the Faroes and Iceland divided their quota between them, the Faroes receiving 71,000 metric tons and Iceland 202,000.
[f] By bilateral agreement Norway transferred 2,000 metric tons of its quota to the Faroes (1,900 metric tons in 2000).
[g] By bilateral agreement Russia transferred 2,000 metric tons of its quota to Norway (1,900 metric tons in 2000).
[h] The Agreed Record itself divides the quota between the Faroes and Iceland allocating 68,270 metric tons to the Faroes and 194,230 metric tons to Iceland.

Source: Various NEAFC documents and Norwegian parliamentary papers *St. meld.* 47 (1997–8), s. 5.1.9, and 49 (1998–9), s. 5.1.9.

fishing (which is the case with other regional arrangements) and why the Protocol is accompanied by a collection of bilateral agreements on access.

As already mentioned, the EC thought that it should have been a party to the negotiations on the management of the stock. At the time of those negotiations, in late 1995 and early 1996, the EC's justification for being included, either because it was a coastal state or a high seas fishing state, seems on the face of it to be fairly tenuous. As regards its claim to be considered as a coastal state, the four-party working group on zonal attachment found the zonal attachment of herring to EC waters up to and including 1995 to be nil.[36] After the negotiations were concluded, herring were found in EC waters in the summer of 1996, but not in 1997.[37] The EC's claim to be considered as a high seas fishing state was perhaps slightly stronger. German vessels caught several thousand tonnes of herring between 1965 and 1969, and British, Danish, Dutch, and German vessels began fishing for herring in the summer of 1995.[38] Excluded from the Protocol but feeling that it was entitled to a share of the fishery, the EC set an autonomous quota for itself for 1996, the regulation[39] doing so being adopted by the Council, whether by design or coincidence, on the same day that the four parties signed the Protocol.

3.3 Subsequent arrangements: the five-party agreements and NEAFC measures

Although the 1996 Protocol was intended to lay down a long-term framework for management of the herring stock, it contained specific management measures only for 1996. There was, therefore, a need for measures for 1997. There was also a need to try to widen the four-party arrangement to include the EC, as the Protocol recognized, paragraph 4.1 providing that 'the parties shall seek to obtain agreement with other relevant parties to bring about a comprehensive management of the stock'. Contacts took place between the four parties during the autumn of 1996, and at the annual meeting of NEAFC held in late November 1996, Norway put forward a proposal for a NEAFC recommendation for the high seas fishery. There was insufficient support for this proposal and no agreement was reached on any NEAFC measure. However, just before and following the NEAFC meeting, further contacts between the four parties and the EC took place. There was insufficient time to negotiate a long-term five-party agreement to replace the Protocol. Instead, the parties agreed on measures for 1997 that were embodied in the Agreed Record of Conclusions of Fisheries Consultations on the Management of the Norwegian Spring-Spawning Herring (Atlanto-Scandian Herring) Stock in the North-East Atlantic for 1997 (hereafter referred to as the 1997 Agreed Record), signed on 14 December 1996. The Agreed Record, which, in spite of its name and rather informal nature, appears to be a treaty and thus legally binding, established a TAC and quotas for 1997 (see Table 8.2) and was accompanied by a series of bilateral agreements on access.

As can be seen from Table 8.2, the combined total of the parties' quotas falls 2,000 metric tons short of the TAC. This was deliberate and was designed to allow NEAFC to establish quotas for high seas fishing. This it did at a special meeting held in March 1997 when it adopted a Recommendation on Regulatory Measures for Norwegian Spring-Spawning Herring (Atlanto-Scandian Herring) Stocks for 1997. In this Recommendation NEAFC (which, it must be remembered, comprises the five parties to the Agreed Record with the addition of Poland and Greenland (represented by Denmark)), after noting that the Agreed Record had set a TAC of 1.5 million metric tons for the total stock, set an allowable catch of 127,000 metric tons for the high seas fishery and divided this into quotas amongst its members (see Table 8.2): the quotas of the five parties to the Agreed Record are included in their quotas under the Agreed Record and are not additional to them. Furthermore, the Recommendation provides that the five parties' quotas under the Agreed Record may be fished on the high seas, thus implying that the five parties are not limited to catching on the high seas the quotas laid down in the NEAFC Recommendation. Poland voted against, and subsequently objected to, the Recommendation on the ground that it was wrong in principle for a majority of members of NEAFC to agree to something outside NEAFC and then present it to a meeting of NEAFC for adoption.

Similar arrangements to those for 1997 have been agreed for 1998, 1999, and 2000.[40] The various TACs and quotas adopted are shown in Table 8.2. In addition, the 1998 Agreed Record set up a working group to study and evaluate 'appropriate harvest strategies for medium- and long-term management of the stock' with the objective of establishing stable catch levels and preventing the stock from reaching critical levels. Based on the labours of this working group, the 2000 Agreed Record includes (in annex II) an arrangement on the long-term management of the herring stock whereby the parties agree to implement a long-term management plan which is 'consistent with a precautionary approach, intended to constrain harvesting within safe biological limits and designed to provide for sustainable fisheries'.

3.4 The herring regime and regime linkages

Arrangements for the management of Norwegian spring-spawning herring have now been in place since 1996. How far is it legitimate to describe these arrangements as constituting a regime? A regime is defined in the Introduction to this book as comprising a substantive component and an operational component. The herring arrangements certainly have a substantive component. This consists of the 1996 Protocol (which remains in force, although its provisions on the TAC and quotas are obviously spent), together with the subsequent annual Agreed Records; and the annual recommendations adopted by NEAFC for the high seas fishery; all of which are underpinned by the Law of the Sea Convention and Fish Stocks Agreement. There is also an operational component. This comprises the meetings of NEAFC, its Scheme of Control and Enforcement, the annual meetings of the five parties to the Agreed Records (which now seem to have a quasi-institutional status), the working groups set up by these meetings, and ICES. It therefore seems legitimate to describe the various arrangements relating to the management of Norwegian spring-spawning herring as a regime. A final and important element of this regime is coastal state management within 200-mile zones, where most fishing for herring in fact takes place. Such management is concerned primarily with the implementation of the Protocol and Agreed Records, mainly to ensure that quotas are complied with. In the case of Norway it could also include additional measures for the protection of spawning and nursery areas.

It may be premature to regard this regime as either static or stable. It is quite possible that the regime will evolve and develop, for example by utilizing other conservation measures in addition to the current catch limitations (as is envisaged by the 1996 Protocol) and by developing control and enforcement mechanisms additional to those currently in existence to improve compliance (as is again envisaged by the Protocol). As regards the regime's stability, a regime that has an ad hoc annual agreement on a TAC and quotas as its central element has an inherent risk of breaking down. The development of any significant fishery by third states would put pressure on the regime. More importantly and more likely, any cuts in exploitation levels which might be deemed necessary in order to conserve the stock, which is a realistic scenario given the predicted fall in spawning stock biomass over the next few years (see below), will put pressure on the regime and make agreement on the TAC more difficult to obtain, particularly as virtually all fishing fleets of the North-East Atlantic suffer from overcapacity, especially the enormous EC fleet.

Turning to regime linkages, two of the instruments outlined in the second section of this chapter, NEAFC and coastal state management, provide, as has been seen, components of the herring regime. Employing the typology of the Introduction, these are intra-regime linkages that seem to be both material (in the sense that the two instruments provide substantive components of the herring regime) and interactive (in the sense that the products of the two instruments have been combined into a further regime). One might also question whether we are really looking at separate regimes at all here or rather at a regime network, given that the participants in all the regimes are virtually identical—the five parties to the Agreed Records are also the coastal states of the regime and comprise five out of the six (or seven, if Greenland is considered separately) members of NEAFC. In other words, we are talking about the same five actors who act collectively, although in two different fora (the annual negotiations on the Agreed Record and NEAFC), and sometimes to a degree individually (coastal state management—although this is generally for the purpose of implementing the collective action).

For a study in regime linkages, it is probably more instructive to examine the relationship between the herring regime and two of the other instruments discussed in the first section, the Fish Stocks Agreement and ICES. These are inter-regime linkages. As regards the Agreement, there appear to be a number of material linkages with the herring regime, both explicit and implicit. The most explicit linkage is paragraph 4.3 of the 1996 Protocol, which states that the parties 'shall co-operate to achieve regulation of the fisheries on the stock in areas beyond fisheries jurisdiction through [NEAFC] in conformity with the provisions laid down in' the Fish Stocks Agreement. Specific provisions of the Agreement also find echoes in the Protocol. Thus, paragraph 4.1 provides that 'the Parties shall seek to obtain agreement with other relevant parties to bring about a comprehensive management of the stock'. This provision reflects Article 8 of the Fish Stocks Agreement which provides that all high seas fishing states and relevant coastal states have the right to participate in regional fisheries arrangements (which the herring regime clearly is). The EC may well have had Article 8 in mind (as well as the provisions of its bilateral agreements with the Faroes, Iceland, and Norway calling for cooperation over straddling stocks[41]) when it demanded to be involved in the negotiations on the management of the herring stock, although no doubt it was motivated primarily by self-interest and the desire to obtain its share of the fishery. Another explicit material linkage between the Agreement and the herring regime is paragraph 4.2 of the Protocol, which provides that 'the Parties shall co-operate to deter in conformity with their international rights and obligations the activities of vessels flying the flag of other States which undermine the effectiveness of conservation and management measures agreed by the Parties'. This provision very closely echoes the language of Article 17 (4) of the Agreement.

As well as these explicit linkages, there are also a number of implicit material linkages between the herring regime and the Agreement. First, the fact that fishing for herring on the high seas is regulated by NEAFC is an application of the Agreement's stipulation that states fishing for straddling stocks on the high seas shall cooperate in their management through regional fisheries organizations (Art. 8 *et seq*.). In addition, as has been seen, the Agreement prompted a review of NEAFC. Secondly, the fact that the coastal states adopt management measures (through the Protocol and the Agreed Records) and that NEAFC adopts measures for the high seas, and that such measures are compatible (the NEAFC recommendations speak of their purpose being to 'ensure consistency and compatibility' with the Agreed Records), could be viewed—and clearly is viewed by some participants in the regime—as an application of Article 7 of the Agreement, which provides that 'conservation and management measures established for the high seas and those adopted for areas under national jurisdiction shall be compatible in order to ensure conservation and management of the straddling fish stocks . . . in their entirety'. Although the herring regime could be regarded as an illustration of the two-stage process of Article 7, the two steps involved (the conclusion of the Agreed Record and the adoption of the NEAFC recommendation) are in some ways a rather artificial division, as the actors involved in both steps are largely identical, the Agreed Records establish the overall TAC for both national zones and high seas, and the parties to the Agreed Record are apparently not limited to catching the quotas laid down by NEAFC when fishing on the high seas. Thirdly, as pointed out above, in the Agreed Record for 2000 the parties undertake to implement a new management strategy from 2001, based on the precautionary approach. As is well known, the Agreement calls on states to make the precautionary approach one of the central principles of fisheries management for straddling stocks (see Articles 5 and 6).

As regards the question of whether the interplay of the herring regime and the Fish Stocks Agreement has been supportive or obstructive, there is no evidence that the interplay has been obstructive and no reason to suppose that it will be. As to whether the interplay has been supportive, the Agreement probably had little effect on the regime's coming into being. The major motive for the regime, negotiations for which in fact began before the adoption of the Agreement, was a desire to avoid the mistakes of the 1960s when the lack of effective regulation caused the herring stock to collapse, with the loss of a major resource to the fishing industries of the North-East Atlantic for over twenty years. It is possible that the Fish Stocks Agreement negotiations had some effect on the timing of the coming into being of the herring regime. The fact that the 1996 Protocol was not adopted until after the conclusion of the Fish Stocks negotiations may indicate either that those negotiations induced caution during the early stages of the herring negotiations or that the adoption of the Fish Stocks Agreement facilitated conclusion of the herring negotiations. Whatever the position, the Agreement has almost certainly influenced the form of the regime—the two-stage process of Protocol/Agreed

Record and NEAFC recommendation—and gave support to the other coastal states to resist the demand of the EC that NEAFC should manage the herring stock in its entirety. The Agreement appears so far, however, to have had little influence on the substantive content of the regime. Few of the principles of fisheries management set out in Articles 5 and 6 of the Agreement have yet been incorporated in the regime, although there is now an undertaking to introduce a precautionary approach from 2001. Furthermore, the Agreement has had no influence on the way in which the TAC is allocated among participants in the herring regime. This is scarcely surprising since the only provisions on allocation in the Agreement relate to allocation between high seas fishing and coastal states and to new members of regional fisheries organizations or arrangements, and in both cases a number of possible principles of allocation are merely listed by way of illustration (see Articles 7 (2) and 11). The most significant influence of the Agreement on the substantive content of the herring regime is probably in relation to control and enforcement, through the new NEAFC scheme adopted in response to the Agreement.

The linkages between the herring regime and the Fish Stocks Agreement relate to regulation and compliance and are primarily material in character. By contrast, the linkages between the herring regime and ICES bear on scientific knowledge and are interactive rather than material in nature. This interplay consists primarily of the feeding of scientific information and advice from ICES into the regime. Thus, for example, the Working Group on Zonal Attachment, whose report helped to pave the way for the adoption of the 1996 Protocol, drew on numerous ICES reports and statistics in preparing its report. The regime did not initially choose to use ICES directly, as, for example, NEAFC does. Thus, the Protocol set up its own Scientific Working Group, which is nevertheless directed to cooperate with ICES, while the Agreed Record for 1998 set up its own Harvest Strategies Working Group, which is directed to draw on specific ICES reports. However, since 1999, the Agreed Records have contained direct requests to ICES for specific advice.[42] As regards the question of whether this operational interplay has been supportive or obstructive, there would seem considerable evidence that it has been supportive.[43] While ICES' advice has not been followed fully in setting the TAC, that advice has been the starting point when annual negotiations on the TAC have taken place and is likely to have been a restraining factor in the setting of the TAC. Ever since TACs were first introduced as a tool of fisheries management in the international fisheries regimes of the North-East Atlantic in the early 1970s, the tendency has been for fisheries managers to set a TAC at a level higher than that recommended by scientists in order to obtain agreement. It is likely, although it cannot be proven, that in the herring regime, and in other regimes, the existence of independent scientific advice from a respected organization like ICES is a restraining factor, and that without such advice the TAC would be set at an even higher level. ICES has also played a supportive role when it comes to allocation of the TAC, since ICES data have helped to establish the zonal attachment of the herring and the levels of past catches—the two principal criteria used in allocating the TAC.

Overall, therefore, there have been a number of linkages, both material and interactive, between the herring regime and other regimes, and these linkages have generally been supportive, although perhaps to a fairly modest degree.

3.5 Evaluation of the herring regime

In evaluating the effectiveness of the herring regime, the framework of analysis used will be that outlined in the Introduction to this book. Thus, we will ask three questions: first, whether the regime generates adequate scientific knowledge for the resource to be properly managed; secondly, whether the regulatory management measures are adequate to conserve the stock on a long-term sustainable basis in the light of the scientific knowledge; and thirdly, whether there is compliance with these measures.

As regards the first of these questions, the knowledge generated directly by the regime through its various working groups, together with the research done under the auspices of ICES, would seem to be as much as could reasonably be expected and required in the circumstances. Certainly the stock does not fall into the 32 per cent of the stocks in the North-East Atlantic of which not sufficient is known in order to determine whether or not the stock is within safe biological limits.[44] The level of knowledge of the herring stock may therefore be presumed to be adequate for management purposes, although no doubt more knowledge would be desirable in order to improve and better evaluate management measures.

Turning to the second question, the main regulatory measure used is the setting of annual TACs. In evaluating the effectiveness of this measure, one may begin by asking how far the TAC actually set corresponds to the scientific advice received. For 1996, ICES recommended that the stock be managed in a cautious way, that the total catch should not exceed 1 million metric tons, and that the spawning stock biomass be maintained above 2.5 million metric tons.[45] In the 1996 Protocol the TAC was set at 1.107 million metric tons: this figure was pushed a little way above the ICES recommended figure of 1 million metric tons in order to secure agreement. In addition, it must be remembered that the EC set an autonomous catch limit of 150,000 metric tons. Thus, the total catch limit set for herring in 1996 was 1.257 million metric tons, 25.7 per cent above the ICES recommended figure. For 1997, the TAC was set at 1.5 million metric tons, even though ICES had advised that a TAC at this level might lead to the spawning stock biomass falling below the recommended minimum level.[46] This level of TAC was severely criticized for giving insufficient weight to ICES advice, and the five parties were accused of taking advantage of uncertainty in the advice to obtain the highest possible short-term yield.[47] Since 1998, the TAC has gradually been reduced to a level that ICES regards as not excessive. In its most recent report, ICES' Advisory Committee for Fishery Management states that the herring stock 'is at present considered to be harvested within safe biological limits' and that current management measures 'comply with the precautionary approach'.[48]

The only kind of management measure used so far in the herring regime is the traditional one of setting a TAC and dividing it into quotas. It is desirable that the parties to the regime should consider the use of other management tools. As has been seen, the parties are committed to introducing a precautionary approach from 2001, and in keeping with this the management plan contained in the 2000 Agreed Record determines precautionary reference points and the action to be taken if such points are exceeded.[49] In addition, it may be necessary for the parties to consider measures to protect juvenile herring such as minimum fish sizes, gear regulations, closed seasons, and closed areas. Finally, in order to reduce pressure on the stock, it may be desirable to consider forms of effort limitation other than catch limits, such as limitations on the number of vessels entitled to participate in the fishery. Such measures, which are notoriously difficult to agree on in international fisheries regimes, are recommended by Article 6 (6) of the Fish Stocks Agreement for new fisheries (which arguably the herring fishery is) and would help to promote compliance with catch level limits. A step in this direction has been taken in NEAFC's Scheme of Control and Enforcement, Article 3 (d) of which requires each NEAFC member to manage the number of its vessels authorized to fish on the high seas and their fishing effort 'commensurate to the fishing opportunities available to' that member.

The final aspect of evaluating the herring regime is the question of compliance. As can be seen from Table 8.2, total catches have not exceeded TACs in any year, although on occasions individual states have exceeded their quotas, but usually only marginally. In theory the prospects for continued compliance should be quite good, as most fishing takes place within 200-mile zones where coastal states have the opportunity and every incentive to enforce the regime, especially against foreign vessels. Enforcement on the high seas is in principle more problematic, but generally less than 10 per cent of the TAC is actually caught there and the possibilities for enforcement have increased since NEAFC's Scheme of Control and Enforcement came into force on 1 July 1999.

The herring regime is in its early years. It is therefore too soon to make any very considered overall evaluation of its effectiveness. Nevertheless, one or two observations may be made. After some initial weaknesses, when the TAC was set too high, the regime currently seems to be functioning reasonably well, with TACs not only being set at levels regarded by ICES as appropriate but also being complied with. In part this has been helped by recruitment to the herring stock from good year classes in the early 1990s. A sterner test for the regime will come when the spawning stock biomass starts to fall significantly below its current high level of over 10 million metric tons, as ICES predicts will inevitably happen because of weaker year classes in recent years, but hopefully by then a proper precautionary approach to management will have been put in place.

4 The redfish arrangement

4.1 Background

There are various stocks of redfish in the North-East Atlantic. The only such stock that is relevant to this chapter is the oceanic redfish (*sebastes mentella*) which is found in the waters between Iceland and Greenland, an area known as the Irminger Sea. This area is part of the second area of high seas in the North-East Atlantic identified at the beginning of this chapter, i.e. the central northern Atlantic. Scientists first became aware of the Irminger Sea redfish in the late 1940s, but more detailed knowledge was not obtained until the 1960s. Scientific knowledge is still somewhat sketchy. Originally it was thought that oceanic redfish were confined to the high seas, but by 1990 the general scientific view was that the stock was no longer so confined. It is thought that oceanic redfish migrate north-east from the high seas into Iceland's 200-mile zone during the autumn and winter. After spawning, the stock migrates south-west, with the major part being in Greenland's 200-mile zone during the summer. Some larvae even drift westward into Canadian waters. In 1982, a fishery for oceanic redfish began on the high seas. Catches for the period 1982–95 inclusive are shown in Table 8.3(*a*). As can be seen, the major states involved were (in order of total catch during the period) USSR/Russia, the EC, Iceland, Bulgaria, and Norway. In 1991 and 1993, respectively, fishing for oceanic redfish began in the 200-mile zones of Iceland and Greenland. Catches up until 1995 are shown in Table 8.3(*b*).[50]

NEAFC began discussing possible management measures for oceanic redfish in 1989.[51] Rather fruitless discussions, made difficult by the lack

Table 8.3 Catches of redfish 1982–1995 (metric tons)

(a) On the high seas

	1982	1983	1984	1985	1986	1987	1988	1989	1990	1991	1992	1993	1994[a]	1995[a]
Bulgaria	—	—	2,961	5,825	11,385	12,270	8,455	4,546	2,690	—	628	3,216	n/a	n/a
EC	—	155	989	5,438	8,574	7,023	16,848	6,797	7,957	244	6,253	18,168	16,593	18,542
Faroes	—	—	—	—	5	382	1,090	226	—	115	3,765	7,121	2,896	3,974
Greenland	—	—	—	—	—	—	—	—	—	—	9	8	—	156
Iceland	—	—	—	—	—	—	—	3,761	4,537	6,933	13,388	20,305	36,246	22,746
Japan	—	—	—	—	—	—	—	307	1,500	5	n/a	n/a	n/a	1,057
Norway	—	—	—	—	—	—	—	—	7,085	6,198	14,654	13,875	7,535	5,428
Poland	581	—	239	135	149	25	—	112	—	—	—	—	—	n/a
Russia[b]	60,000	60,079	60,643	60,273	84,994	71,469	65,026	22,720	9,247	9,289	15,733	24,165	17,814	36,255
Others[c]	—	—	—	—	—	—	—	—	—	—	9,408	23,689	n/a	9,682
Total	60,581	60,234	64,832	71,671	105,107	91,169	91,149							

[a] Figures for 1994 and 1995 are provisional.
[b] USSR 1982–91, Russia 1992–5.
[c] Estonia, Latvia, Lithuania, and Ukraine. Figures for 1995 are for Latvia only.

(b) *In national waters*

	Iceland	Greenland	Norway	Others
Iceland's 200-mile zone				
1982–90	56	—	—	—
1991	1,959	—	—	—
1992	2,090	—	—	—
1993	2,603	—	—	—
1994*	17,716	—	—	—
1995*	1,282	—	—	—
Greenland's 200-mile zone				
1982–92	—	—	—	—
1993	—	—	702	—
1994	—	—	—	—
1995	140	—	—	—

[a] Figures for 1994 and 1995 are provisional.

Source: Report of the Working Group on Oceanic Redfish, cited in n. 50, 11–19.

of adequate scientific knowledge and complicated by the acknowledgement in 1990 that redfish were a straddling stock, continued at NEAFC
annual meetings for several years. It was not until an extraordinary
meeting held in March 1996 that NEAFC, on the basis of recommendations of a Working Group set up at its 1993 annual meeting to recommend
a TAC and the work of a preparatory meeting called for at the 1995
meeting to consider the criteria for allocating a TAC among interested
states,[52] was able to adopt its first management measures for oceanic
redfish.

4.2 *The arrangements*

The Recommendation adopted by NEAFC at its March 1996 meeting
set a TAC of 153,000 metric tons for 1996. This TAC applies to the whole
stock, including therefore that part of the stock found in the EEZs of
Greenland and Iceland as well as that part of the stock found on the high
seas.[53] The TAC was divided into quotas allocated as shown in Table 8.4.
The 'cooperation quota' in the table refers, and is designed to apply,
to non-members of NEAFC fishing for redfish. Such third states, which
come mainly from the Baltic, have been requested to report their catches
to NEAFC and invited to become members of the organization.[54] The
way in which quotas were allocated was a negotiated compromise
between a number of suggested criteria, such as zonal attachment,
past contributions to research, past catches, and the degree of dependence
on the fishery.

The Recommendation was adopted by four votes to two, the two votes
against being those of Poland and Russia. Not surprisingly, these two
states exercised the possibility under the NEAFC Convention to object to
the Recommendation and were accordingly not bound by it. The reason
for their action was dissatisfaction with the size of quotas they had been
allocated. In addition, Russia was also unhappy with the fact that NEAFC
had set a TAC and quotas for the whole stock. It thought that NEAFC
should have limited its Recommendation to the high seas part of the stock,
and that Iceland and Greenland should have adopted national measures
for that part of the stock within 200-mile zones.[55] Russia was also disap-
pointed with the advice from ICES and had doubts as to whether oceanic
redfish really was a straddling stock, and considered that it was probably
a discrete high seas stock. It was also unhappy with the allocation of a
quota to non-NEAFC members.

In spite of the fact that a major fishing state (Russia) had objected to the
March 1996 Recommendation, NEAFC adopted a very similar Recommendation for the 1997 fishery at its annual meeting held in November
1996. Again Poland and Russia voted against, and again they objected. At

Table 8.4 Redfish TACs, quotas, and catches 1996–2000 (tons; actual catch in brackets)

	1996	1997	1998	1999	2000
TAC (for whole stock)	153,000 (130,428)	158,000[a] (98,435)	153,000 (96,606)	153,000 (87,872)	120,000[f]
Denmark[b]	40,000[c] (10,706)	40,000[c] (7,006)	40,000[c] (9,120)	40,000[c] (8,925)	30,573[g]
EC	23,000[c] (19,073)	23,000[c] (15,991)	23,000[c] (15,234)	23,000[c] (17,855)	17,580[g]
Iceland	45,000 (45,466)	45,000 (37,213)	45,000 (45,024)	45,000 (43,094)	—
Norway	6,000 (4,304)	6,000 (2,285)	6,000 (758)	6,000 (4,171)	4,586
Poland	1,000 (0)	1,000 (662)	1,000 (0)	1,000 (6)	1,000
Russia	36,000 (45,748)	41,000[a] (35,136)	36,000 (25,787)	36,000 (13,821)	30,573
'Cooperation' Quota[d]	2,000 (6,526)	2,000 (142[e])	2,000 (683)	2,000 (0)	1,529

[a] The NEAFC Recommendation provided that if Russia objected (which it in fact did), the TAC would be reduced to 153,000 metric tons and Russia's quota to 36,000 metric tons.
[b] i.e. the Faroes and Greenland.
[c] The Faroes transferred 4,000 metric tons of its quota to the EC, thus effectively increasing the latter's quota to 27,000 metric tons.
[d] i.e. quota for non-members of NEAFC.
[e] A number of non-members of NEAFC which reported their catches in 1996 do not appear to have done so in 1997.
[f] The TAC for 2000 does not apply to Iceland's EEZ.
[g] The Faroes transferred 3,200 metric tons of its quota to the EC, thus effectively increasing the latter's quota to 20,780 metric tons.

Source: Information provided by NEAFC.

the 1997 and 1998 annual meetings, the story was virtually the same (see further Table 8.4). At its 1999 annual meeting, NEAFC adopted a Recommendation similar to those of previous years except that it did not apply to Iceland's EEZ because Iceland voted against the Recommendation and under Article 6 (2) of the NEAFC Convention Recommendations do not apply to the waters of coastal states that vote against them. On the other hand, for the first time neither Poland nor Russia voted against the Recommendation.

4.3 *The redfish arrangements and regime linkages*

Following the approach of the Introduction to this book, it would seem possible to regard the redfish arrangements as a regime. The substantive component comprises the annual NEAFC recommendations on TACs and quotas, which, it must be remembered, are legally binding, underpinned by the Law of the Sea Convention and the Fish Stocks Agreement. The latter has a particular role to play here (as explained below) in relation to non-members of NEAFC and those members of NEAFC who objected to its recommendations. The operational component of the regime comprises NEAFC, including its Scheme of Control and Enforcement, and ICES. As with the herring arrangements, national fisheries management systems have an important role to play in securing implementation of and compliance with the regime within 200-mile zones even though only a minority of the fishery takes place within those areas.

Because the core elements of the redfish regime derive from NEAFC, the linkages between the redfish regime and other regimes, in particular ICES and the Fish Stocks Agreement, are largely the same as those between such regimes and NEAFC, which were outlined earlier in section 2. In addition, there are a number of further specific linkages between the redfish regime and the Agreement. The first such linkage concerns the treatment of non-members of NEAFC by the regime. This has two aspects. First, provision is made for some fishing by non-members by means of the 'cooperation quota' referred to earlier. Secondly, the NEAFC Scheme to promote compliance by non-members with NEAFC measures (referred to in section 2 above) provides that non-member vessels fishing for other than the cooperation quota are presumed to be undermining NEAFC measures. Such vessels are to be inspected if they call at the port of a NEAFC member and landings of their catches are prohibited. These provisions are broadly in accord with the Agreement, under which states with an interest in the fishery must be permitted to join the relevant regional fisheries organization or, if they choose not to do so, must comply with its measures if they are to continue to fish for the stock in question.[56] The NEAFC Scheme also broadly reflects Article 23 of the Agreement on port state measures. The second linkage concerns objection to NEAFC measures by its members. Such members, if they are parties to the Agreement, are required not to undermine the effectiveness of those measures.[57] For example, they should not set themselves autonomous quotas significantly in excess of those they would have received under the NEAFC measure (as Poland and Russia did in respect of redfish in 1997).

All of these features of the Agreement are, of course, supportive of the redfish regime.

Finally, some comments may be made about the relationship between the Agreement and the form and content of the redfish arrangements, negotiations for which (it must be recalled) began before the Agreement was concluded. As regards the form of the arrangements, this contrasts with that for herring because the NEAFC recommendations relate to the whole of the stock, not just to the high seas component. When discussing the herring regime, it was suggested that the Agreement envisaged a two-stage process, with the coastal state(s) adopting management measures for the stock within the 200-mile zone and measures being adopted for the high seas, both sets of measures being compatible. While this is the model espoused by the Agreement and the model preferred by Norway and Russia for redfish, there is no reason why the two stages should not be telescoped into one and a single set of measures for the stock adopted by the regional fisheries organization, provided that the coastal state(s) concerned agree. This would not be inconsistent with the Agreement. Such an approach makes particular sense for the Irminger Sea redfish, where nearly all fishing takes place on the high seas. As regards the substantive content of the arrangements and their relationship to the Agreement, the same comments can be made as were made earlier in relation to the herring regime.

4.4 Evaluation of the redfish regime

The same framework of analysis for evaluating the effectiveness of the redfish regime will be used as was used for the herring regime. As regards the adequacy of scientific information, as with all fisheries considered by NEAFC, scientific knowledge is provided by ICES, which established a study group on oceanic redfish in 1989. As already mentioned, there is still considerable scientific uncertainty about many fundamental issues concerning oceanic redfish, including its population size, migratory pattern and range, and zonal distribution. However, so far the regime does not appear to have prompted significantly more research on redfish than would otherwise have occurred as part of ICES' routine activities.

As with the herring regime, the redfish regime has so far used a single management tool, the annual TAC. ICES is of the view that the level of TAC which has so far been set is unsustainable and that there will be a sharp decrease in catches in the early years of this century.[58] The fact that the TAC is very substantially in excess of any previous annual catch is worrying. It suggests that the TAC was arrived at as the lowest generally acceptable figure and is therefore unrelated to biological considerations.

If so, this does not bode well for the future when, if ICES predictions are correct, reductions in current catch levels will be required if the redfish stock is to be sustained. As with herring, there is a need to consider other types of management measures. NEAFC's Working Group on Oceanic Redfish did this when it discussed minimum mesh and fish sizes (which it thought were unnecessary because the fishery was directed at the mature part of the stock), closed seasons (which it thought were unnecessary as the stock was currently within safe biological limits), and effort limitation (as to the desirability of which it offered no view).[59] The Working Group did not, however, consider those kinds of measures that are required for a precautionary approach, which is surely what is needed for this fishery, given the high degree of scientific uncertainty. In 1999 ICES endorsed the need for a precautionary approach and recommended that measures be adopted to protect juvenile redfish and reduce by-catches in the shrimp fishery.[60]

As regards compliance with the TAC and quotas, at least by those four members of NEAFC that are bound by them, the catch figures for 1996–9 (Table 8.4) show that catches by those four members were within their quotas. In 1996 Russia and third states, in particular Estonia, significantly exceeded their quotas, but since then they have kept within their quotas. Overall, however, the total catches have fallen some way short of the TACs.

While it is still premature to make any considered evaluation of the redfish regime, there must be worries that the regime will not provide effective management of oceanic redfish. These worries are increased by the fact that a major fishing nation, Russia, until 1999 chose to stand outside the NEAFC recommendations, and may do so again.

5 The mackerel arrangement

5.1 Background

Mackerel is one of the most numerous fish species of the North-East Atlantic. For many years there was considerable uncertainty and debate about whether there was one mackerel stock or several, and whether mackerel was a straddling stock. It now appears to be widely accepted that there is essentially only one stock, and that the stock migrates between the 200-mile zones of the EC, the Faroes, and Norway, and to a lesser extent onto the high seas. Thus, like the herring discussed earlier, mackerel is both a shared stock and a straddling stock. As a shared stock, mackerel has been managed for many years by the coastal states jointly within the framework of their bilateral fisheries agreements and annual consultations held thereunder.[61] In recent years, joint management by the EC and Norway, who are responsible for most of the stock, has taken the form of a multi-annual management strategy based on the precautionary approach. In November 1999, the three coastal states concluded an agreement putting management on a trilateral basis for the first time.[62]

Fishing for mackerel on the high seas has increased significantly in recent years. In 1996 the high seas catch was 50,000 metric tons, most of which was taken by Russian vessels. In the mid-1990s, ICES began warning that mackerel was in danger of becoming over-exploited and that the level of fishing ought to be reduced.[63] At its 1997 annual meeting, NEAFC therefore established a working group to recommend possible management measures for high seas fishing for mackerel.[64] However, before this working group could complete its task, the three coastal states (the EC, the Faroes, and Norway) put forward a proposal for management at the following NEAFC meeting, in November 1998. There was insufficient support for this proposal, but it was agreed to hold an extraordinary meeting in February 1999 to discuss the issue further.[65] At this meeting, the coastal states put forward a similar proposal for management, which this time was adopted, albeit by four votes to two.[66]

5.2 The arrangements

The NEAFC Recommendation lays down arrangements for fishing for mackerel in the two areas of high seas referred to at the beginning of this chapter for the period 1999–2001 inclusive. The reason for a multi-annual approach was to allow the Russian quota to be adjusted (and reduced) gradually and the coastal states' quotas to be increased. The Recommendation established a TAC for 1999 of 44,000 metric tons to 'ensure compatibility' with the management measures adopted by the three coastal states, which had established a TAC for their fishery of 500,000 metric tons. The high seas TAC is divided into quotas as shown in Table 8.5. The Recommendation also lays down quotas for 2000 and 2001, assuming that the TAC will remain the same; however, the Recommendation does provide that should developments in the stock point to a different TAC in 2000 and 2001, the quotas will be adjusted accordingly. In fact, the stock situation has improved, and at its November 1999 meeting NEAFC increased the TAC to 50,000 metric tons, divided into quotas as shown in Table 8.5.

As mentioned earlier, the NEAFC Recommendation was adopted by four votes to two. The two members voting against were Iceland and Russia. Iceland did so because it had not been recognized as a coastal state: it maintained that it should have been because even if there was no mackerel fishery in its waters, some mackerel were found there. Russia

Table 8.5 Mackerel TACs and quotas 1999–2001 (metric tons)

	1999	2000	2001 (provisional)
TAC (for high seas)	44,000	50,000	50,000
Quotas			
Denmark, EC, Norway	10,000[a]	17,000	22,500
Iceland	2,000	2,500	2,500
Poland	1,000	1,500	1,500
Russia	30,000	28,000	22,500
Cooperation quota	1,000	1,000	1,000
Coastal states' TAC	500,000	560,000	—

[a] The three parties announced that their joint quota would be reserved for conservation purposes and therefore remain unfished.

Source: Information provided by NEAFC.

voted against, and subsequently objected to, the recommendation because it thought that the TAC should have been set higher (at 65,000 metric tons) and that its treatment in relation to quotas was unfair. At the November 1998 meeting, Russia had also expressed the view that any regulation of the high seas mackerel fishery was premature because of a lack of scientific knowledge.

The three coastal states regretted that it had not been possible to adopt the measure by consensus. They pointed out that under the precautionary approach, lack of scientific knowledge was not a reason for delaying taking action. They emphasized the need to adopt regulatory measures both in order to ensure compatibility with coastal state measures and to curtail the activities of non-members of NEAFC, who, as in the case of redfish, are given a 'cooperation quota'. It was pointed out that the Recommendation contained an important element of burden-sharing and had to be seen against a background of restraint exercised by the coastal states in the past.

5.3 The mackerel arrangements and regime linkages

The substantive component of the mackerel regime comprises the bilateral/trilateral agreements between the coastal states (the EC, the Faroes, and Norway) and the NEAFC recommendations, underpinned by the Law of the Sea Convention and the Fish Stocks Agreement. The operational component of the regime comprises NEAFC, including its Scheme of Control and Enforcement and its Scheme to promote compliance by non-members, and ICES, as well as enforcement measures within national zones.

As regards regime linkages, similar comments can be made as were made for the redfish regime, with one significant difference. Whereas the redfish regime has a single element (the annual NEAFC recommendations) applicable to both the high seas and national zones, the mackerel regime has two elements, coastal state measures and high seas measures, which are declared to be compatible. The mackerel regime thus follows much more closely the model found in Article 7 of the Fish Stocks Agreement. In relation to the latter, it is also significant that in the discussion preceding the adoption of the NEAFC recommendation there were frequent references by the coastal states to the precautionary approach (with specific citation of the Agreement and the FAO Code of Conduct on Responsible Fisheries), especially to counter Russian arguments that no measure should be adopted because of a lack of scientific knowledge. The recommendation itself is said to be based on a precautionary approach.

5.4 Evaluation of the mackerel regime

At the time of writing (March 2000), the mackerel regime had been in operation for only just over a year. It is thus premature to attempt any considered evaluation of the regime. However, two preliminary observations may be made at this stage. First, there is clearly a need for more research to increase knowledge of the state of the mackerel stock, its distribution, and migratory pattern, as has been acknowledged both in the discussion preceding adoption of NEAFC's recommendations and in the coastal states' 1999 trilateral agreement. More specifically, it needs to be clearly resolved whether mackerel are found within Iceland's 200-mile zone; resolution of this question would hopefully bring Iceland into the regime. This last point relates to the second observation, which is that the mackerel regime is essentially flawed as long as Russia, the principal high seas fishing state, remains outside the regime. Of course, Russia will be obliged by the Fish Stocks Agreement not to undermine the effectiveness of NEAFC measures. Again more knowledge of the stock, lack of which was a major reason for the Russian objection to the NEAFC recommendation, may help to bring it within the regime.

6 Conclusion

Three straddling stocks in the North-East Atlantic have so far been the subject of regional fisheries management—Norwegian spring-spawning

herring, oceanic redfish, and mackerel. The management arrangements
for these stocks differ quite considerably in form from those of the other
regions discussed in this book, in part because there is no sharp division
between high seas fishing states and coastal states in the North-East
Atlantic and in part because herring and mackerel are shared stocks as
well as straddling stocks. These management arrangements may legitimately be described as regimes. There are significant linkages, both material and interactive, between these regimes and other regimes, especially
NEAFC, ICES, and the Fish Stocks Agreement. NEAFC provides a good
deal of the substantive content of the regimes, while ICES provides a significant input of scientific knowledge. The Agreement has been supportive in a number of ways. First, it appears to have been a catalyst for a
revitalization of NEAFC. Before the adoption of the Agreement, NEAFC
had been bogged down for some years in inconclusive discussions about
the management of straddling stocks. The Agreement, along with the
development of the herring as a straddling stock and the recognition that
redfish and mackerel were also straddling stocks, appears to have stimulated NEAFC into adopting management measures. The Agreement has
also prompted NEAFC to adopt Schemes of Control and Enforcement and
in respect of non-members. Secondly, the Agreement seems to have had
some influence on the form of the herring and mackerel regimes; it also
appears to have influenced their substantive content to some degree in
that the mackerel regime is said to be based on a precautionary approach
and such an approach is to be introduced into the herring regime from
2001. Thirdly, while the Agreement appears so far to have had little direct
impact on the redfish regime, once it comes into force it has the capacity
to benefit that regime, and the other regimes, because of its provisions on
enforcement, the position of non-members of regional fisheries organizations, and the non-undermining of the management measures of such
organizations (which will limit the freedom of action of states objecting
to NEAFC recommendations).

Turning to the effectiveness of the regimes, while it is too soon to make
a considered evaluation, there are some fairly encouraging signs as far as
the herring regime is concerned. The stock currently appears to be in a
fairly healthy state and the parties to the regime have undertaken to introduce a precautionary approach to management from 2001. In the case of
the other two regimes, however, there must be some doubt about their
capacity to provide effective management for the stocks concerned on any
long-term basis. As far as the redfish regime is concerned, the main doubt
concerns the levels at which TACs are being set, which are probably too
high to be sustainable. In order to improve management and increase the
chances of long-term sustainability of the stock, there is a need to move
beyond the use of the simple management tool of annual TACs and

consider other kinds of measures, including those required for a precautionary approach. In the case of the mackerel regime, the main problem is that Russia, the principal high seas fishing state, currently stands outside the regime.

Summing up as regards the management of straddling fish stocks in the North-East Atlantic, at the present time there is a multiplicity of instruments and regime linkages comprising and underpinning the various management regimes. Such a multiplicity has not yet, however, produced optimum, or in some cases even satisfactory, management. The various instruments and regime linkages do, however, have the capacity to improve management, provided that the parties to the various regimes have the political will to utilize them.

Notes

I would like to take this opportunity to thank the following for their help: participants in the POLOS Workshops held in Nov. 1997 and Nov. 1998 (and now my fellow contributors to this book) and a number of anonymous reviewers for their comments on earlier versions of this chapter; NEAFC, Chris Hedley, Alf Håkon Hoel, Olav Schram Stokke, and Geir Ulfstein for providing me with documentation and information; and various government officials who must remain nameless.

1. For fisheries purposes, the North-East Atlantic is normally considered to comprise the waters falling within the area to which the North-East Atlantic Fisheries Convention (see text at n. 7) applies, i.e. the waters north of 36 degrees north and between 42 degrees west and 51 degrees east (but excluding the Baltic and Mediterranean Seas). For the purposes of this chapter this definition of the North-East Atlantic is modified to exclude the Barents Sea, as the straddling stocks of this area are the subject of Ch. 9.

2. This area of high seas became considerably enlarged in 1997 when the United Kingdom gave up measuring its 200-mile zone from Rockall. The absence of agreed boundaries between the 200-mile zones of some of the states mentioned means that it is not possible to be certain that they all border the area of high seas concerned.

3. The other stocks have been the subject of some very limited arrangements. The North-East Atlantic Fisheries Commission has laid down minimum mesh sizes for fishing on the high seas for capelin in 1984 and for blue whiting in 1986, and since 1988 the Commission has suggested a voluntary overall catch limit for high seas fishing for blue whiting. It is quite likely that in the not too distant future blue whiting will become subject to binding NEAFC management measures. The coastal states concerned have also adopted some management measures for these stocks for their national zones.

4. On the concept of international regimes, see the Introduction to this book.

5. United Nations Convention on the Law of the Sea (1982); 21 *ILM* 1261.

6. Agreement for the Implementation of the Provisions of the United Nations Convention on the Law of the Sea of 10 Dec. 1982 relating to the Conservation and Management of Straddling Fish Stocks and Highly Migratory Fish Stocks (1995); 29 *LOSB* 25.

7. Convention on Future Multilateral Co-operation in North-East Atlantic Fisheries (1980); *OJ* L227/22 (1981). The Convention came into force in 1982.

8. In spite of their name, recommendations are legally binding on members unless objected to during a specified period following their adoption.

9. Art. 5 (2) of the Convention.

10. While metropolitan Denmark is obviously part of the EC, both the Faroes and Greenland are outside the EC and are therefore separately represented by Denmark in international fora such as NEAFC and the Law of the Sea Convention.

11. For a somewhat more extended discussion of NEAFC's origins and functions, see R. G. Halliday and A. T. Pinhorn, 'North Atlantic Fishery Management

Systems: A Comparison of Management Methods and Resource Trends', *Journal of Northwest Atlantic Fishery Science*, 20 (1996), 83–4; and S. Sen, 'The Evolution of High-Seas Fisheries Management in the North-East Atlantic', *Ocean and Coastal Management*, 35 (1997), 85.

12. Arts. 118 and 119. On the other hand, the concept of full utilization referred to in the NEAFC Convention is not found in the provisions of the Law of the Sea Convention (or any of the negotiating texts) dealing with high seas fisheries. The concept is, however, referred to in the provisions on the EEZ, which state that one of the duties of the coastal state is to promote the optimum utilization of the living resources of its EEZ (Art. 62 (1)). It is also referred to in the Fish Stocks Agreement where states are required to promote the optimum utilization of straddling stocks both on the high seas and in the EEZ (Arts. 3 (2) and 5 (a)).

13. D. H. Anderson, 'The Straddling Stocks Agreement of 1995: An Initial Assessment', *International and Comparative Law Quarterly*, 45 (1996), 463, 470.

14. The text of the Memorandum is reproduced in NEAFC, *Report of the Seventeenth Annual Meeting* (1999), 44.

15. For illustrations of and support for this point, see *inter alia* D. Day, 'Tending the Achilles' Heel of NAFO', *Marine Policy*, 19 (1995), 257; and C. L. Mitchell, 'Fisheries Management in the Grand Banks, 1980–92 and the Straddling Stock Issue', *Marine Policy*, 21 (1997), 97.

16. NEAFC, *Report of the Fifteenth Annual Meeting* (1997), 5.

17. Ibid. 4.

18. In particular parts of Arts. 18–22 (Vukas and Vidas, Ch. 2, and Hønneland, Ch. 4 above). The Scheme also has a number of additional elements, e.g. there are provisions on the marking of vessels and gear, the carrying of logbooks, the satellite tracking of vessels, and the authorization of vessels to fish. The last of these reflects provisions in the 1993 FAO Compliance Agreement; Hønneland, Ch. 4 above.

19. This scheme is discussed in more detail in s. 3.5. The text of the scheme is published in NEAFC, *Report of the Seventeenth Annual Meeting*, 39.

20. ICES is currently governed by the Convention on the International Council for the Exploration of the Sea (1964), 652 *UNTS* 237.

21. For fuller discussion of the role and functions of ICES, see B. Floistad, 'The International Council for the Exploration of the Sea (ICES) and the Providing of Legitimate Advice in Fisheries Management', FNI Report 3/90 (Lysaker: The Fridtjof Nansen Institute, 1990) and K. Hoydal, 'ICES Procedure in Formulating Management Advice' in FAO, 'Expert Consultation on the Regulation of Fishing Effort', *FAO Fisheries Report*, 289, Supplement 3 (1985), 215. For a more recent exposition of the role of the ACFM, see *ICES Cooperative Research Report*, 223, part I (Copenhagen: ICES, 1999), 5–9.

22. *ICES Cooperative Research Report*, 223, part I, 5–9.

23. Although Denmark is in general responsible for the international relations of the Faroes and Greenland, these territories enjoy a significant degree of autonomy in international fisheries negotiations.

24. For such an account, see Halliday and Pinhorn, 'North Atlantic Fishery Management Systems', 34–71. See also the papers on Iceland (A. Danielson), the

EC (D. Symes), and Norway (B. Hersoug and S. A. Rånes) in the Special Issue of *Ocean and Coastal Management* on 'Fisheries Management in the North Atlantic: National and Regional Perspectives', 35 (1997), 121, 137, 157 respectively.

25. For discussion of the extent of the EC's competence on the external plane as regards fisheries, see R. R. Churchill, 'The EC and its Role in Some Issues of International Fisheries Law', in E. Hey (ed.), *Developments in International Fisheries Law* (The Hague: Kluwer, 1999), 536.

26. For figures see NEAFC, *Report of the Twelfth Annual Meeting* (1994), 27.

27. The first trilateral agreement was signed in 1970; see Norwegian parliamentary paper *St. prp.* 47 (1970–1), which also gives details of what was done by NEAFC. A second trilateral agreement was signed in 1971: *St. prp.* 66 (1971–2). Appropriate scientific advice was also given too late: O. Nakken, 'Past, Present and Future Exploitation and Management of Marine Resources in the Barents Sea and Adjacent Areas', *Fisheries Research*, 37 (1998), 29.

28. NEAFC, *Report of the Twelfth Annual Meeting*, 27.

29. *ICES Cooperative Research Report*, 168, part I (1990), 28.

30. This account is based on H. Vilhjalmsson *et al.*, 'Report on Surveys of the Distribution, Abundance and Migration of the Norwegian Spring-Spawning Herring, Other Pelagic Fish and the Environment of the Norwegian Sea and Adjacent Waters in Late Winter, Spring and Summer of 1997', ICES Document CM 1997/Y:04 (1997), and 'Report of the Scientific Working Group on Zonal Attachment of Norwegian Spring-Spawning Herring' (Nov. 1995).

31. NEAFC, *Report of the Fourteenth Annual Meeting* (1996), 3.

32. For the working group's terms of reference, see 'Report of the Scientific Working Group on Zonal Attachment of Norwegian Spring-Spawning Herring', 1.

33. In fact NEAFC discussed the issue at its annual meeting in Nov. 1995. Norway, with the support of Russia, put forward a proposal for NEAFC measures for the high seas fishery, but there was no agreement on this from the other members. Instead NEAFC, after noting that the stock should be regarded as a straddling one and that the Fish Stocks Agreement gave particular emphasis to the role of regional management organizations, decided to hold a preparatory meeting in Feb. 1996 to discuss management measures. No agreement on such measures was reached at this meeting; see NEAFC, *Report of the Fourteenth Annual Meeting*, 3.

34. As far as I am aware, neither the Protocol nor the agreements for later years have been published. I am very grateful to those people mentioned in the initial footnote for supplying me with copies of the texts.

35. It will be noted that the total of the quotas exceeds the TAC by 10,000 metric tons. The explanation for this is that 10,000 metric tons of the Russian quota is to be reserved 'for conservation purposes'.

36. 'Report of the Scientific Working Group on Zonal Attachment of Norwegian Spring-Spawning Herring', 9. The question of zonal attachment was complicated by the fact that, in the absence of an agreed boundary between the 200-mile zones of the Faroes and the United Kingdom until 1999 (when a

boundary agreement was concluded), the precise extent of EC waters was uncertain.

37. Vilhjalmsson *et al.*, 'Report on Surveys of the Distribution, Abundance and Migration of the Norwegian Spring-Spawning Herring', 12–13.

38. Sen, 'The Evolution of High-Seas Fisheries Management in the North-East Atlantic', 95. These catches are not shown in Table 8.1, but it should be noted that the data given for 1995 are provisional. The catches are shown in later, definitive, ICES statistics; *ICES Cooperative Research Report*, 223, 255. The total EC catch for 1995 was 39,983 metric tons.

39. Reg. 846/96, *OJ* L115/1 (1996). The quota the EC awarded itself was 150,000 metric tons, which represented 15% of the 1 million metric tons which ICES had recommended as the maximum TAC for the stock. The figure of 15% as the EC share was arrived at, according to the Commission, 'under prevailing circumstances and with due regard to all relevant sea areas, where the Community enjoys either exclusive or equal fishing rights'; EC Doc. COM (96) 147, 1–2.

40. Agreed Records and accompanying bilateral agreements signed on 28 Oct. 1997, 7 Oct. 1998, and 20 Oct. 1999; and NEAFC recommendations adopted at its annual meetings held in Nov. 1997, Nov. 1998, and Nov. 1999. At the Nov. 1997 meeting of NEAFC Poland again voted against the Recommendation, but since 1998 the NEAFC recommendations have been adopted unanimously.

41. EEC–Faroes Agreement on Fisheries (1977), *OJ* L226/12 (1980); EEC–Iceland Agreement on Fisheries and the Marine Environment (1992), *OJ* L161/2 (1993); and EEC–Norway Agreement on Fisheries (1980), *OJ* L226/48 (1980).

42. In this connection it is noteworthy that in 1996 ICES decided to increase the level of scientific research being carried out on the herring stock; Vilhjalmsson, 'Report on Surveys of the Distribution, Abundance and Migration of the Norwegian Spring-Spawning Herring', 2.

43. On the concept of operational interplay, see the Introduction and the Conclusions of this book.

44. NEAFC, *Report of the Fifteenth Annual Meeting*, 43.

45. EC Doc. COM (96) 147, 1. ICES has also recommended that in view of the severe ecosystem impact caused by the collapse of the herring stock in 1969, management policy should also take ecological reactions into account; NEAFC, *Report of the Eleventh Annual Meeting* (1993), 20.

46. NEAFC, *Report of the Fifteenth Annual Meeting*, 38.

47. Nakken, 'Past, Present and Future Exploitation and Management', 34; P. Prokosch, 'The Herring Drama: A Key Case for Examining Feasibility of Sustainable Fishery', *WWF Arctic Bulletin*, 2 (1996), 15–16.

48. *ICES Cooperative Research Report*, 236, part I (2000), 64.

49. Cf. Art. 6 and annex II of the Fish Stocks Agreement.

50. The above account is largely based on NEAFC, *Report of the Working Group on Oceanic Redfish* (1995).

51. NEAFC, *Report of the Eighth Annual Meeting* (1990), 3.

52. NEAFC, *Report of the Twelfth Annual Meeting*, 4; and *Report of the Fourteenth Annual Meeting*, 3.

53. This conclusion follows from the fact that the Recommendation states that it is based not only on the provisions of the NEAFC Convention giving NEAFC the power to adopt measures for the high seas but also on those provisions giving it the power to adopt measures for coastal states' 200-mile zones. This conclusion is confirmed by EC Doc. COM (96) 162.

54. NEAFC, *Report of the Fourteenth Annual Meeting*, 3. No third state has yet taken up this invitation.

55. Although it voted in favour of the recommendation, Norway shared this view.

56. Art. 8 of the Agreement. Cf. also Arts. 17 and 18.

57. Art. 18 (1) of the Agreement.

58. NEAFC, *Report of the Fifteenth Annual Meeting*, 33–7. In 1992 ICES advised that a TAC in excess of 50,000 metric tons, which is one-third of the size of the current TAC, would probably lead to a significant decline in stock biomass, NEAFC, *Report of the Fifteenth Annual Meeting*, 24. In 1999 ICES, having pointed out that the stock biomass had declined significantly during the 1990s, recommended a TAC of 60,000 metric tons for 2000—half of that actually set by NEAFC; see *ICES Cooperative Research Report*, 236, part I, 137.

59. *Report of the Working Group on Oceanic Redfish*, 7–8.

60. *ICES Cooperative Research Report*, 236, part I, 137–8.

61. EEC–Norway Agreement on Fisheries (1980), *OJ* L226/48 (1980); EEC–Faroes Agreement on Fisheries (1977), *OJ* L226/12 (1980); and Norway–Faroes Agreement on Mutual Fishery Rights (1979), Norwegian parliamentary paper *St. prp.* 89 (1979–80). For details of recent consultations, see Norwegian parliamentary papers *St. meld.* 47 (1997–8), s. 3 and annex 2, and 49 (1998–9), s. 3 and annex 2.

62. Norwegian Ministry of Fisheries, Press Release No. 67/1999.

63. NEAFC, *Report of the Thirteenth Annual Meeting* (1995), 47 and *Report of the Fourteenth Annual Meeting*, 47–8.

64. NEAFC, *Report of the Sixteenth Annual Meeting* (1998), 12–14.

65. NEAFC, *Report of the Seventeenth Annual Meeting*, 11–12.

66. NEAFC, *Report of the Extraordinary Meeting of the North-East Atlantic Fisheries Commission in Brussels, 8–9 February 1999* (1999), 1–5.

9

The Loophole of the Barents Sea Fisheries Regime

OLAV SCHRAM STOKKE

The Barents Sea Loophole is a high seas pocket located between the exclusive economic zones of Norway and Russia. Throughout most of the 1990s, vessels from a number of states, especially Iceland, targeted cod in this high seas area without having been allocated quotas by the regional management regime. This chapter assesses the *interplay* between efforts to accommodate this straddling stock problem within the existing regional framework and the partially parallel evolvement of the United Nations Fish Stocks Agreement.[1]

After a brief discussion of the regional regime and its adaptation to the Loophole challenge, the extent to which this particular regional dispute influenced state positions and outcomes at the New York negotiations will be assessed, as well as the likely impact of the Fish Stocks Agreement on effective management of the Loophole fishery.

1 Regional management in the Barents Sea: bilateralism challenged

Due to the extension of coastal zones from the mid-1970s, a new and largely bilateral fisheries regime evolved as the most appropriate means for management of Barents Sea fish stocks. The new regime replaced a wider regional regime that had its basis in the North-East Atlantic Fisheries Convention.[2]

Three agreements between Norway and the Soviet Union provided the core of the new regime.[3] The 1975 *Framework Agreement* stresses the need for conservation, rational utilization, and the building of good, neighbourly relations between the two nations.[4] It also provides for the Norwegian–Russian Fisheries Commission as the institutional hub of the regime.[5] The Commission meets annually to make consensual recommendations on total quotas of the three shared stocks—cod, haddock, and capelin, each of which is seen as a single biological unit. It allocates quotas to the parties, decides on the shares to be allocated to third parties, and determines operational restrictions. It also coordinates scientific research among institutions in the two countries.

The *Mutual Access Agreement* supports this framework and paves the procedural ground for reciprocal fishing; this Agreement secures parties' access to the 200-mile zone of the other, i.e. access within agreed-upon quotas, beyond 12 miles, and subject to coastal state rules and licensing.[6] The third agreement, the *Grey Zone Agreement*, provides for a system of enforcement applicable, *inter alia*, to a disputed part of the Barents Sea (see Map 9.1).[7] This Agreement acknowledges parallel jurisdiction in an 'adjacent area' that also covers most of the disputed waters. Russia and Norway have agreed that the enforcement of conservation and management measures in the Grey Zone is to be exercised by the state that has issued the licence to operate there—and both coastal states may issue licences within agreed quotas. The purpose of this arrangement is to avoid situations where Norwegian fishermen are subject to Russian inspections in waters claimed by Norway, and vice versa, as this would be seen as jeopardizing the respective claims of these countries to sovereignty over the disputed area.

In addition to these agreements between Russia and Norway, a set of other agreements between these two coastal states and non-coastal user states forms part of the basis for the Barents Sea fisheries regime. In essence, the latter agreements imply that certain non-coastal states obtain access to the Barents Sea fisheries within the overall regulatory framework set up by the coastal states.[8] Such an arrangement, centred on one bilateral decision-making body but supported by a cluster of external bilateral accords, can be termed bilateralist.[9]

1.1 The emergence of high seas operations

Because of changes in temperature and salinity, the availability of cod in the Barents Sea Loophole, which spans some 62,400 square kilometres, increased markedly around 1990. Cod thus became a straddling as well as a shared stock, and despite the short season due to ice conditions, this new fishing opportunity soon attracted the attention of distant water vessel operators. In 1991 the fishery began cautiously, with vessels from the European Community, Greenland, and the Faroes; but two years later it accelerated when Iceland turned its attention vigorously to this fishery. A drop in the total cod quota in domestic waters to a historic low—combined with a rapid growth in the harvesting capacity of Iceland's fleet—prompted the Icelandic interest. Illustrating the interdependence of regional management efforts, this growth in capacity had occurred in part by purchases of very inexpensive trawlers from the Canadian offshore fleet following the closure of the Northern cod fishery in the North-West Atlantic. By 1995, as many as eighty Icelandic trawlers had operated in the Loophole,[10] and the Icelandic press reported very good catches: when the factory trawler *Akureyrin* returned to Iceland in the late autumn of 1995, after sixty-seven

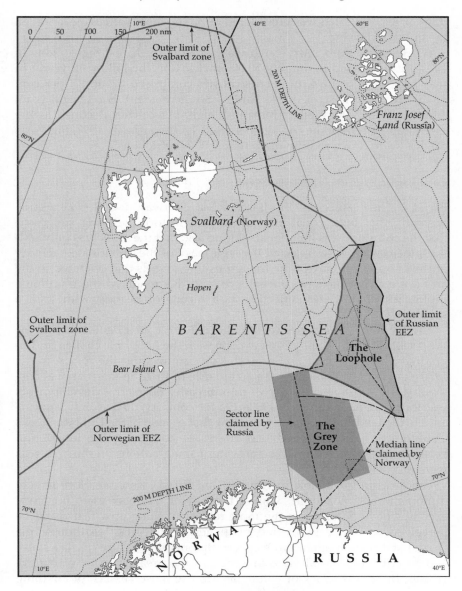

Map 9.1. The Barents Sea

days at sea, the catch was considered to be the most valuable ever taken by an Icelandic ship.[11]

Whereas the third party catch was a moderate 12,000 metric tons in 1993, this increased to roughly 50,000 metric tons the following year.[12] In that peak year of 1994, high seas catches comprised around 7 per cent of the total cod harvest in the Barents Sea ecosystem. For several years afterward the fishing effort remained high, but catches declined as the migration pattern of the cod again shifted southwards. By 1998, high seas catches were down to little more than 2,000 metric tons.

1.2 Dealing with the challenge: coastal state strategies

Faced by newcomers in the Barents Sea, Norway and Russia argued fervently that both zonal attachment and historical fishing suggested that the cod stock was binational. Noting also that the stock was fully utilized, the coastal states rejected the legitimacy of the unregulated activity in the Loophole. Many of the foreign fishing vessels that operated in the area were flying flags of convenience, and this rendered the traditional diplomatic channel less effective as a means of dealing with such a problem.[13]

The Barents Sea fisheries regime did not serve as an effective tool for the coastal states in their efforts to cope with the Loophole challenge. The gradual phasing out of non-coastal state fishing from the region in the 1970s had been validated by the acceptance of EEZs in international customary law, but no such support from broader normative developments was forthcoming in the early 1990s. On the contrary, the Icelandic appearance in the Loophole coincided with the first session of the UN Fish Stocks Conference, which implied that the rules governing the interaction between coastal states and distant water fishing nations on the high seas were in a state of flux.

The measures available to Norway and Russia were therefore largely diplomatic and economic. Unlike the Sea of Okhotsk case, no naval exercises have occurred in the most relevant fishing area that could be perceived as partly motivated by fisheries concerns.[14] Although the coastal states soon agreed to step up diplomatic pressure on flag states and to enhance coastal state presence in the area in terms of control vessels, there was a lack of willingness to use those vessels for anything more drastic than observing the unregulated harvesting activity in the region.[15] Instead, what may be coined the 'quota card' became the most powerful means to dissuade newcomers from engaging in unregulated harvesting. Coordinated allocation of parts of the total quota to third parties was provided for in the annual bilateral protocols drawn up by the coastal states. After bilateral negotiations with Norway in 1991–2,

Greenland and the European Community decided to limit activities in the Loophole and keep total harvests in the Barents Sea within the overall quotas allotted under reciprocal access agreements.[16] The Faroes agreed in 1996 to prohibit landings of fish that had been taken without quotas in international waters.[17]

Not surprisingly, the coastal states had been eager to avoid the impression that quotas in national waters would subsequently be awarded to any state engaging in the Barents Sea fishery. Regarding the agreement with Greenland, Norway insisted that there was no relationship whatsoever between ongoing Greenlandic harvesting in the Loophole and the allocation of quotas,[18] and the Agreement itself stressed the reciprocal nature of this allocation. Nevertheless, few were in doubt that obtaining Greenland's acceptance of a coastal state role beyond the EEZ had come at a price for Norway—for Greenland for the first time had been granted a Barents Sea cod quota.[19]

The coastal state diplomatic strategy versus Iceland, the remaining challenger, proved much less effective. When the Icelanders first appeared in the area, Norway and Russia argued that Iceland had no historic record of harvesting in the region and refused to negotiate Icelandic demands for a Barents Sea cod quota.[20] As a result, although their vessels fished on the same stock, coastal and non-coastal user states remained unable to achieve compatible measures through coordination of their management policies. Formal negotiations began in 1995, partly because the Icelanders, refusing to yield to political pressure, had rapidly acquired some 75 per cent of the unregulated harvests in the Loophole, and partly because the coastal states were reluctant to stretch international law regarding unilateral enforcement measures beyond 200 miles, an issue that at the time was under negotiation in the UN. The coastal states sought to establish an arrangement that would give Iceland a share of a separate Loophole quota; the size of the total Loophole quota would correspond with the zonal attachment of the cod stock to the high seas area, estimated at 2 per cent.[21] After years of negotiations, however, no agreement had been reached, despite various economic sanctions launched by the coastal states to render unregulated harvesting more costly. In Norway, domestic legislation was introduced in 1994 prohibiting the landing of high seas catches taken without a quota;[22] in practice, even port calls were rejected.[23] On one occasion, Iceland complained to the EFTA Surveillance Authority that Norway's refusal to render repair services to an Icelandic vessel that had been engaged in Loophole fishery was a violation of the Agreement on the European Economic Area.[24] The Authority's response was cautious; it acknowledged the occurrence of such a violation, but no further action was taken because 'the underlying conflict concerned a dispute between Norway and Iceland over Icelandic fishing rights in the Barents Sea'.[25]

Another significant coastal state measure to deter unregulated high seas activities was the practice of *blacklisting* Loophole vessels from subsequent access to the Norwegian EEZ, even if the vessel had changed ownership in the meantime.[26] In 1998, such blacklisting was extended to port calls and the result was to reduce the second-hand value of vessels with a history of contravention of rules created by the Norwegian–Russian Fisheries Commission, especially on the European Community market.[27] Like blacklisting of vessels, industry-level sanctions cannot be challenged on the basis of international trade rules, and during the peak years of the Loophole fishery, a series of private *boycott* actions were introduced that aimed at strangling Norwegian supplies of provisions, fuels, and services to Loophole vessels,[28] as well as punishing domestic companies that failed to adhere to such boycotts.[29] The Russian Fisheries Committee exerted similar pressure even in Icelandic ports by encouraging the Murmansk-based industry to discontinue landings of cod from Russian vessels at ports in Iceland.[30] Because of the cod crisis in Icelandic waters, supply contracts with Russian companies were important to the processing industry of that country during the 1990s.[31] The public and private sanctions did not deter unregulated harvesting activities, mainly for two reasons: the fleets operating in the Loophole were able to operate independently of the Russian and Norwegian fishing industries, and the Icelanders were determined to establish a sizeable fishery in the Loophole. In the long run, however, reliance on Icelandic ports, some four day-trips away, would add considerably to the overall costs of fishing in the Barents Sea. This is especially true for new, efficient trawlers, the profitability of which tends to be highly sensitive to reductions in the number of annual fishing days.

To *summarize*, the Loophole problem emerged in the early 1990s because the existing bilateralist regime, centred on the Norwegian–Russian Commission but including reciprocal access agreements with non-coastal states, was no longer perceived as legitimate by all significant user states. The Loophole issue differs from the Doughnut Hole situation on the other side of the Russian Arctic in that the proportion of the cod stock found in the Loophole is very small compared to that in the EEZs—and the stock was in fairly good shape in the period when unregulated fishing occurred on a large scale.[32] Moreover, while there has been some activity by flags of convenience vessels in the Loophole, the dispute has been largely trilateral, involving two coastal states and one newcomer. All considered, the bilateralist regime played a minor role in the efforts to cope with unregulated harvesting in the region. The regime helped to harmonize coastal state measures on the issue, the most powerful of which was regulation of access to national waters and ports.[33] Except with regard to the disputed area, however, both the allocation of quotas to those who would follow the coastal state rules and the blacklisting of vessels that engaged in unregulated Loophole harvesting would have been perfectly feasible even without the Norwegian–Russian Fisheries Commission.

1.3 The trilateral Loophole Agreement

In 1999, four years after all the parties involved in the Loophole dispute had signed the UN Fish Stocks Agreement, a regional accord was finally reached.[34] The terms of the Agreement are similar to those previously drawn up bilaterally between Norway and Greenland and the Faroes. In exchange for cod quotas in the EEZs of the Barents Sea, Iceland must refrain from harvesting cod or seeking new fishing rights for the cod stock beyond the coastal zones; Iceland must also open its national waters to vessels from the other two countries.[35] Other provisions oblige the parties to discourage their nationals from operating vessels under flags of convenience in the Barents Sea, to prohibit landing of catches that are taken without a quota, and, subject to other obligations under international law, to deny port access to vessels that engage in these activities.[36] As a result of the Agreement, Icelandic vessels were removed from the 'blacklist' of vessels that are banned from the Norwegian EEZ.[37] The steep decline of the Loophole fisheries in the years preceding the signing of the Agreement had served to reduce the distance between coastal state quota offers and Icelandic demands,[38] and the Agreement provides for a stable Icelandic share of a little less than 2 per cent of the TAC. Industry groups both in Iceland and in the coastal states were highly critical of the Agreement. The Chairman of the Federation of Icelandic Fishing Vessel Owners complained that the quota was 'simply too small', whereas the Chairman of the Norwegian Fishermen's Association told the press he was 'nearly shocked' at how much the Icelanders had achieved in the negotiations.[39]

As the Loophole dispute partially overlapped in time with the UN Fish Stocks Conference, it is significant to consider the possible influences of the Loophole dispute on the negotiation of the Fish Stocks Agreement and thus on the specification of the global high seas fisheries regime; it is also relevant to consider whether the Fish Stocks Agreement is likely to facilitate or impede high seas management in the Loophole in the future.

2 The effect of the Loophole dispute on the Fish Stocks Conference

When regional management disputes and global negotiations are addressing similar issues, there are generally at least two ways in which the politics of the former can influence the course and outcome of the latter. By

a process that may be termed diffusive interplay, the substantive or operational solutions to difficult problems that regional negotiations may
provide can be adapted for use at the global level; and through political
interplay, regional disputes may influence the relative bargaining power
of competing blocs or encourage or facilitate various types of leadership
activities at global negotiations.[40]

2.1 Diffusive interplay

In the one and a half years it took to negotiate the Fish Stocks Agreement,
regional efforts to manage the Loophole fishery moved from disappointment to disillusion. Several rounds of negotiations, bilateral and trilateral,
were held without the emergence of any substantial improvements. The
only allocative 'solution' discernible in the Loophole case was the usage
by the coastal state of the quota card to dissuade long-distance fishing
operations; and apart from the ineffectiveness of this measure against
Iceland, the quota card solution hardly corresponded with the emphasis
in the Fish Stocks Agreement on a multilateral approach to regional management. Rather tangential to the Loophole discussion, Norway and
Canada agreed in 1995 to grant each other inspection and enforcement
rights in the international waters adjacent to their respective EEZs;[41] but
the model for those particular provisions was the Agreed Minute between
Canada and the European Community, which in turn reflected draft
material of what were later to become Articles 20–2 of the Fish Stocks
Agreement.[42]

2.2 Bargaining power

Rather atypically, the three main antagonists in the Loophole dispute all
belonged to the *coastal state bloc* during the negotiation of the Fish Stocks
Agreement; but each of these also had a tradition of distant water fishing
operations. True to tradition, Iceland was among the original members of
the so-called 'core group', the group of coastal state parties that played
an active role in the process that led up to the Fish Stocks Conference.
Throughout the negotiations, the core group remained a salient forum for
joint action, including the drafting of proposals on controversial issues.[43]
When a large fleet of Icelandic vessels became engaged in controversial
high seas activities in the Barents Sea, however, Iceland's participation in
the core group became more problematic.

Because of its distant water fishing interest, and also with a view to
upcoming membership negotiations with the European Union,[44] Norway
responded with caution to the idea of convening a straddling stocks
conference under the UN and did not support the so-called 'Santiago

Document' at the fourth preparatory committee meeting to the UN Conference on Environment and Development in 1991.[45] The fisheries bureaucracy had entered the process at a fairly late stage and it was only in the months prior to the first substantial session of the Fish Stocks Conference (July 1993) that a broader assessment was made of the various interests involved. Influenced partly by the Loophole situation but also by the expected resumption of high seas fisheries for Norwegian spring-spawning herring by non-coastal states in the North-East Atlantic, Norway landed firmly on the coastal state side of the straddling stocks issue.

Russia, for its part, has traditionally loomed large in the global distant water fishing league. However, a decade of phase-outs from coastal zones had prompted a partial return to domestic waters that was accelerated by the economic decline of the 1990s and the rapid privatization of the fishing industry, both of which implied greater attention to the fleet's operational costs. Whereas an estimated half of the Russian catch was taken in waters beyond its jurisdiction in 1980, the share had fallen to 22 per cent in 1994.[46] However, the Barents Sea situation was hardly decisive for Russia's position as being 'like-minded' with the coastal state core group on key issues at the Fish Stocks Conference. This position preceded the escalation of the Loophole issue in 1993 and was largely shaped by the already well-established high seas dispute in the Far East, a region where today no more than 2 per cent of the harvest is taken outside the EEZ.[47]

Thus, the relative bargaining power of coastal states and distant water fishing nations was scarcely affected by the Barents Sea situation. Russia's position was already firm, whereas Norway's movement toward the coastal state core group position was balanced out by Iceland's adjustment in the opposite direction.

2.3 Leadership

Whereas several forms of leadership were exercised by the parties to the Loophole dispute during the Fish Stocks Conference, on closer inspection none of these leadership roles appears to have been triggered by the Barents Sea situation.[48] Historically, *Iceland*'s dependence on fisheries and overall reliance on proximate fishing grounds that traditionally had also been exploited by others largely explains the structural leadership this country was able to provide in the early 1970s. Structural leadership implies the ability to bring material capabilities to bear on the negotiation of particular issues. Iceland's establishment and stubborn enforcement of first a 50-mile and then a 200-mile exclusive fishery zone placed Iceland among the coastal state front-runners in the law of the sea context.[49] In the pre-negotiation stage of the UN Fish Stocks Conference, Iceland had again actively promoted coastal state interests. The emergence of the Loophole fishery, however, blended these interests with a concern for the rights of newcomers on the high seas and a corresponding reluctance to extend coastal state enforcement rights in such waters.

Having one foot in each camp can sometimes be expedient in producing another type of leadership—entrepreneurial brokerage rallying support for compromise solutions.[50] There are, however, few indications that Iceland assumed such a role. On the contrary, after a change in the leadership of Iceland's delegation to the Fish Stocks Conference in 1994, when the Loophole fishery was at its most rewarding, Iceland's visibility at the negotiations faded markedly. Toward the end of the Conference, however, Iceland championed, with only partial success, the inclusion of an allocative principle that would give preferential treatment to newcomer states whose economies are overwhelmingly dependent on the exploitation of living marine resources. This proposal, apparently motivated by Iceland's interests in the Barents Sea as well as in the North-East Atlantic herring fisheries, was strongly opposed by Norway, and it was included in the Fish Stocks Agreement with the important qualification that it applied only to coastal states.[51] As, elsewhere in the Agreement, and also in the Law of the Sea Convention, the term 'coastal state' refers restrictively to states having jurisdiction over parts of the area where the stock in question occurs, this criterion would not be relevant in the Loophole.[52]

The Barents Sea situation was not conducive to motivating the *coastal* states to take coercive measures and thus provide the type of structural leadership that had been provided by Iceland in the 1970s and more recently by Canada in the high seas detention of the Spanish trawler *Estai*.[53] As unregulated fishing in the Loophole continued to grow, fishery organizations in Norway and Russia called for emergency measures and demanded a more activist approach to unregulated harvesting, including intrusive enforcement measures towards foreign vessels. In 1997, a centre-liberal coalition government was formed in Norway on a political platform that included 'consideration of . . . a Norwegian–Russian initiative to extend the Norwegian and Russian exclusive economic zones to 250 nautical miles'.[54] Once in position, however, the new Prime Minister assured that no unilateral measure was contemplated and that any initiative would occur within the framework of international law.[55] The tactical wisdom of any type of unilateral measures in this case would indeed have been highly questionable. Such measures, were they to contribute to the making of international law, would require consent or acquiescence on the part of those subject to them as well as third parties. Dealing with a much more threatened fish stock, a leading scholar, W. T. Burke, has argued that even for a stock that occurs mainly within the EEZs, customary international law does not authorize unilateral measures from the coastal states unless bona fide efforts to reach an agreement with the high seas fishery nations have failed; and even then only if no scientific doubt remains that the unregulated fishery will jeopardize the health of the stock.[56] Partly for this reason the United States and Russia have abstained from unilateral or bilateral regulation of high seas activities in the Bering Sea Doughnut Hole, even when the level of overfishing was known to be utterly destructive to the pollock.[57] Compared to the Bering Sea situation, or Canada's high seas problem in the North-West Atlantic, the Loophole case would be an unlikely candidate for yielding such consent. Even in the record year of 1994, the unregulated cod catch was no more than one-third of the *increase* in the total quotas from the preceding year. While certainly a nuisance, such a level of unregulated fishing could hardly be said to create a state of emergency. This, combined with the fact that Iceland repeatedly declared its willingness to negotiate with the coastal states, implied that unilateralism on the part of Norway or Russia would have been very hard to justify.[58]

Instead of structural leadership, *Russia* resorted primarily to ideational leadership during the Fish Stocks negotiations, that is, sustained argument in favour of certain clearly defined solutions. The period in which the UN negotiations were held was marked by economic disruption, political tension, and administrative reshuffling in Russia, with strong reverberations in the fisheries sector; but the Russian delegation remained stable and was among the most active parties in the negotiations.[59] Documents submitted by Russia in the course of the negotiations, all with a very marked coastal state slant, contained suggestions for the definition of key principles and concepts in the instrument under negotiation and also proposed schemes for compliance control.[60] However, the main thrust of Russian contributions focused on provisions pertaining to enclosed and semi-enclosed seas, spurred not by the Loophole issue but by the management problems in the Sea of Okhotsk.[61]

Norway for its part had maintained a very high profile during the Third Law of the Sea Conference, not least because its delegation head had the role of leader of the informal 'group of legal experts' which hammered out compromises on some of the more controversial issues.[62] Also at the Fish Stocks Conference, Norway sought an influential position by assuming a high level of activity and seeking out powerful allies. After clarification of its position during the preliminary stages, Norway first joined forces with the group referred to as 'like-minded' with the coastal state core group before being admitted as a new member of the core group in 1994. Among the issues given particular attention by the delegation was that of improved means of non-flag state enforcement. Norway eagerly supported proposals for port state measures, including prohibition of

landings, which affected vessels engaged in unregulated fishing operations on the high seas.[63] During the fourth session, moreover, Norway
came forward with a formula for the division of duties and responsibilities between inspecting state and flag state, a formula that advanced the
negotiation of one of the most controversial aspects of the Fish Stocks
Agreement.[64] The Norwegian proposal also contained the idea that the
enforcement procedures agreed to would be applicable even to parties of
the Agreement that were not members of the relevant regional management body, thus laying down global minimum standards on enforcement
applicable in all regions.[65]

In *summary*, compared to some of the other regional straddling stocks
issues, such as that of the North-West Atlantic and in a more restricted
sense that of the Sea of Okhotsk, the high seas problem in the Barents Sea
had scant impact on the Fish Stocks Conference.[66] The failure to reach
agreement at regional levels before 1999 implied that there was no material linkage to be drawn from the Loophole dispute to the evolving UN
Fish Stocks Agreement. The relative strength of the major bargaining blocs
was largely unaffected. Nor did the Loophole issue provide sufficient
urgency to prompt structural leadership in the form of unilateral measures on the outer edge of international law. And finally, most of the rather
moderate entrepreneurial and ideational leadership provided by the
parties to the Barents Sea dispute was only loosely related to the specifics
of the Loophole case.

3 The Fish Stocks Agreement and governance of the Loophole fisheries

When discussing whether and how the Fish Stocks Agreement influences
the management situation in the Barents Sea, the three main tasks of fisheries management come into focus: science, regulation, and compliance
enhancement.[67]

3.1 Scientific practices

The science problem of fisheries management is to generate high-quality,
consensual assessment of stock dynamics and translate such knowledge
into practical regulatory advice. Today, Norwegian–Russian scientific
cooperation, nested within the broader cooperation under the International Council for the Exploration of the Sea (ICES), ensures that the
Barents Sea stocks are comparatively well covered with respect to scientific investigation.[68] An elaborate reporting system has traditionally
formed the backbone of the data input, but as the incentive to under-

report catches has gradually grown, fisheries-independent analysis has gained in importance. Cooperative Norwegian–Russian survey programmes are elaborated and implemented each year, ensuring inter-calibration of measurement and data processing for the entire ecosystem.[69] Regarding the Loophole, coastguard vessels from the two coastal states, and at times even from Iceland, maintained a presence in the area throughout the years of large-scale fishing, allowing rough estimates of the amounts taken by foreign vessels. In addition, Iceland published data concerning domestic landings from the Loophole. Icelandic catch statistics have also included the harvest from vessels under Icelandic ownership but which were flying flags of convenience, presumably an attempt to accumulate some track level of fishing in the area.

If implemented in the Barents Sea, the Fish Stocks Agreement will only moderately affect the scientific aspect of fisheries management. First, the general provision that high seas conservation measures shall be based 'on the best scientific evidence available to the States concerned' is already found in the Law of the Sea Convention,[70]although also specified somewhat in the Fish Stocks Agreement.[71] Secondly, the 1975 Agreement that underpins the Norwegian–Russian Commission already emphasized that decisions were to be based on the best available scientific knowledge,[72] and in this respect the Icelandic regulatory process is no different. The generation and sharing of data required by the Fish Stocks Agreement is already met by all the states engaged in the Barents Sea fisheries through their cooperation in ICES, or, in the Norwegian–Russian case, through their even more elaborate bilateral scientific linkages. The compilation instructions of annex I of the Agreement make some procedural adjustments necessary, but in the Norwegian context the additional work associated with this compilation of data is not expected to exceed two man-years.[73]

Another relevant component of the Agreement is the elaboration of the precautionary approach to management.[74] Since 1998, the scientific component of the Barents Sea management regime has established precautionary reference points for the shared stocks, including cod, as called for by the Agreement.[75] Such reference points, corresponding to the state of the stock and of the fishery, are intended to guide fisheries management decisions.[76] Whereas defining precautionary reference points is an extension of, rather than a deviation from, existing scientific practices in the Barents Sea, the additional research implied by implementing this provision for all commercial stocks in the region has not been estimated.[77]

In short, the substantive and operational elements of the Fish Stocks Agreement concerning generation of scientific knowledge broadly confirm the existing provisions in the bilateral regime. While some minor adjustments in the compilation of data and the setting of precautionary reference points imply some additional work for the scientific organizations, the scientific aspect of Loophole management will be scarcely affected by the Fish Stocks Agreement.

3.2 Means of regulation

Potentially far more influential than the science provisions are the substantive and operational provisions in the Fish Stocks Agreement that considerably strengthen the duty of user states to cooperate on the establishment of conservation and management measures regarding straddling stocks. At a general level, the framework for this obligation was already provided for in the 1982 Law of the Sea Convention.[78] The Fish Stocks Agreement specifies this obligation by stipulating that where a regional management regime has the competence to regulate harvesting of straddling stocks, only states that join the regime or adhere to its conservation and management measures shall have access to the fishery.[79] The application of this rule to the Loophole situation has proved to be a matter of contention. Whereas the coastal states argued that the Norwegian–Russian Commission with its allocation of coordinated third party quotas is the appropriate mechanism for ensuring such cooperation, Iceland held that other users also have a right to be included in decision-making regarding the size and division of the Loophole harvest. The Fish Stocks Agreement provides that the terms for participation in a regional management regime shall not preclude states with a 'real interest' in the fisheries concerned.[80] The relative openness to new participants implied here was among the victories achieved by the distant water fishing nations during the Fish Stocks Conference.[81]

It would be a simplification to argue, as some authors do, that it follows from the Fish Stocks Agreement that after cod became available in the Loophole, the Norwegian–Russian Commission was no longer appropriate as a body for management of this stock and that regulative decisions should be transferred to the North-East Atlantic Fisheries Commission.[82] First, it was very important to the Norwegian delegation during the Conference that the Fish Stocks Agreement directed states to pursue cooperation '*either directly* or through appropriate subregional or regional fisheries management organizations or *arrangements*'.[83] The bilateralist Barents Sea regime, with its Norwegian–Russian Commission and cluster of external agreements with other user states, is clearly such an 'arrangement': in conjunction, these regime components provide a decision-making mechanism (the bilateral Commission) that generates overall regulative measures that (1) pertain throughout the stock's migratory range, including the high seas, and (2) are recognized by third parties (confirmed in annual agreements).[84] Secondly, an assessment of the relative appropriateness of this arrangement and a broader decision-making system would require careful attention to the question of which regime would provide the most powerful means to realize the broader objectives of the Fish Stocks Agreement. In practical terms, this latter question can be dealt with by investigating the relative strength of the present bilateralist regime and the North-East Atlantic Fisheries Commission in meeting the three tasks of management: science, regulation, and compliance control. While a thorough comparative exercise is beyond the scope of this chapter, some parameters can be specified without difficulty.

The centrality of ICES in both regimes suggests that the level of *scientific* problem solving would be roughly similar. The *regulatory* task, however, would clearly be more complicated if placed within the NEAFC framework, by the participation of a larger number of states and the fact that binding Recommendations would require a two-thirds majority.[85] NEAFC's record in seeking to overcome this difficulty in the case of oceanic redfish, the only straddling stock managed largely by that organization, is not reassuring. Only in 1996 did the Commission agree on quantitative restrictions for this species, despite considerably higher fishery pressure than what was recommended by ICES during the preceding five years. And when the Commission did finally agree on quantitative restrictions, the TAC was set higher than any previous annual harvesting.[86] In addition, states that do not approve of the Recommendation may file an objection and thus avoid being bound by it.[87] On the other hand, broadening participation in decision-making would be one way of accommodating determined newcomers in a less conflictual manner than demonstrated in the Loophole case throughout the 1990s. In terms of high seas *enforcement*, NEAFC has recently established a Scheme of Control and Enforcement that mirrors the relevant provisions of the Fish Stocks Agreement, as well as a Scheme to promote compliance by non-members.[88] Port state measures, especially the prohibition of landings of fish taken without a quota, have been used under the bilateralist Barents Sea regime as well, accompanied by the blacklisting of vessels with a history of unregulated fishing. The main approach, however, is to direct non-coastal state vessels to national waters where the full range of coastal state enforcement measures are permitted, including inspection, detention, and legal prosecution. Whereas this latter approach is quite powerful today, it works only as long as access to national zones is more attractive than exploitation of high seas resources.

This brief discussion shows that there is little to suggest that NEAFC would have been able to address more effectively the high seas management of cod in the region throughout the 1990s than the arrangement centred on the Norwegian–Russian Fisheries Commission.[89] Science would have been unaffected; regulation would probably have been complicated by more participants, several of whom do not engage in the Barents Sea cod fishery; and while NEAFC's enforcement scheme provides for inspection and detention on the high seas, these provisions were not in place before the Loophole fishery had been curbed by the declining availability of fish and the inclusion of Iceland in the Barents Sea regime. Two circumstances will determine the stability of this conclusion: first, the share of the stock that is fishable on the high seas; and secondly, the number of states that are not prepared to accept the primacy of the coastal states inherent in the bilateralist regime. At present, both of those circumstances are favourable to the status quo.

On the whole, the normative influence of the Fish Stocks Agreement on the operational side of the Barents Sea fisheries regime has been to increase pressure on all user states to find cooperative solutions on conservation and management. With the passing of time, Iceland's acquirement of a catch record in the region made it steadily harder for the coastal states to maintain that this country had no legitimate place at the negotiating table regarding Loophole management. At the same time, the operational requirements laid down by the Fish Stocks Agreement are broad enough also to embrace the bilateralist arrangement of the present Barents Sea fisheries regime, as long as the regime provides an opening for states with a real interest in regional harvesting.

3.3 Norms of management

The typical regulatory task of fisheries management regimes is twofold; measures shall ensure long-term conservation of stocks and allocate the benefits derived from resource use in an agreed manner. Regarding the first aspect, an important substantive component of the Fish Stocks Agreement is the principle of *compatibility* between conservation and management measures adopted for areas under national jurisdiction and for high seas areas adjacent to these areas.[90] In the Barents Sea context, it was decisive to the coastal states that this matter was resolved by echoing the differentiation made in the Law of the Sea Convention between highly migratory stocks on the one hand and straddling stocks on the other. For highly migratory fish stocks, measures taken internationally would apply also in waters under national jurisdiction; for straddling stocks, international measures would apply to the high seas area only.[91]

Another salient component of the Fish Stocks Agreement is the detailed elaboration of the *precautionary* approach, i.e. that preventive measures be taken when threats of serious or irreversible damage exist, even in the absence of full scientific certainty.[92] In the past, scientific uncertainty has often been used as a reason for postponing or failing to take conservation measures. Whereas the Norwegian–Russian agreements, which form the core of the Barents Sea regime, make no explicit mention of a precautionary approach, the concept had made its way into regional management practice well before the adoption of the Fish Stocks Agreement. The principle of erring on the side of the fish stock whenever there is scientific uncertainty about its ability to replenish itself has to a considerable extent been followed since the 1989 near-collapse of the Barents Sea cod stock. Throughout most of the 1990s, the Norwegian–Russian Commission tended to opt for quota levels toward the lower end of the ranges recommended by ICES.[93] Iceland, the main challenger to the legitimacy of the bilateral Commission in managing the Loophole fishery, has similarly been careful to emphasize that its own harvesting behaviour in the region has indeed been responsible. When the advisory body of ICES in 1997 recommended substantial reductions in the Barents Sea cod quotas, the Icelandic Minister of Fisheries stated that Iceland would consider a reduction of harvesting in the area and that Iceland had always been ready to take the overall condition of the fish stock into consideration.[94] In both 1995 and 1996, an Icelandic Coast Guard vessel was sent to assist and monitor the activities of Icelandic fishing vessels.[95]

This is not to argue that the elaboration of the precautionary approach in the Fish Stocks Agreement has had no impact on regional management practices. In response to the Agreement, ICES established a Study Group on the Precautionary Approach to Fisheries Management; and in 1997, a report was issued that elaborated upon the implications of this approach for the technical and advisory work of the ICES.[96] The following year, this procedure was implemented in the recommendation offered on cod by the application of a safety margin larger than that of earlier years.[97] Despite this development, the health of the cod stock has deteriorated in recent years.[98]

The precautionary approach is part of a broader set of principles of responsible fishing that includes science-based decisions, biodiversity protection, and ecosystem awareness.[99] Like compatibility and precaution, these general principles are applicable not only on the high seas but also within national zones.[100] The *ecosystem* approach is reflected in the long-standing bilateral multispecies modelling effort that focuses on cod–capelin interactions and is based on an extensive stomach analysis programme covering the entire ecosystem.[101] The simplicity of the Barents Sea ecosystem, where there are few species at each level of the food chain, make the plankton-eating herring and capelin particularly vital as links between the primary production in the region and species at higher trophic levels. Despite the rapid recovery first of capelin and then of herring in the early 1990s, low-end quotas were agreed to for the pelagic fisheries in those years; this reflected the multispecies premiss that these species comprise an important part of the diet for cod, which economically is the most significant fish in the Barents Sea.[102] Efforts to implement an ecosystem approach in the management of marine living resources are influenced not only by international fisheries agreements but also by work under the UN Convention on Biological Diversity, the UN Commission on Sustainable Development, and a series of regional environmental agreements.[103]

To sum it up, the general management principles elaborated upon by the Fish Stocks Agreement have largely confirmed management practices that were already well under way in the Barents Sea region. For straddling stocks, the compatibility principle laid down by the Agreement retained the asymmetry between EEZs and high seas areas established by the 1982 Law of the Sea Convention. Furthermore, parties to the Loophole dispute regarded the provisions for a precautionary approach and ecosystem management as unproblematic because stricter domestic provisions were already in place.[104] The more recent precautionary quotas for cod suggest that the potential of this concept to influence management was somewhat larger than anticipated.

3.4 Allocation of quotas

The matter of quota allocation tends to be a highly controversial aspect of fisheries management, and the Loophole dispute is no exception in this regard. Whereas in 1995 the coastal states bowed to the principle of an Icelandic quota, the three parties went through four years of on-and-off negotiations before agreement could be reached on the appropriate size of the quota. Among the main assets held by the coastal states was access to their EEZs, and as catches in the Loophole declined, the value of that asset rose.

The most relevant part of the Fish Stocks Agreement in this context is Article 11, which lays down criteria to be considered when states determine the extent of participatory rights for newcomers to a fishery. Arguably, there is a fairly good fit between some of these criteria and the leitmotif of the coastal state argument that the stock is already fully utilized and belongs to states that have historical track records in the area, manage the stock throughout its migration area, and govern the predominant part of the stock's migratory range.[105] The Agreement highlights 'the status of the straddling fish stocks . . . and the existing level of fishing effort in the fishery', as well as 'the respective interests, fishing patterns and fishing practices of new and existing members or participants'.[106] Furthermore, Article 7 obliges states negotiating high seas measures that are compatible with those of the coastal states to take into account not only the 'biological unity and other biological characteristics of the stocks . . .

including the extent to which the stocks occur and are fished in areas under national jurisdiction' but also the 'respective dependence . . . on the stock concerned'.[107]

On the other hand, the criterion emphasizing 'the needs of coastal fishing communities which are dependent mainly on fishing for the stocks' could play into several hands in the Loophole dispute.[108] And we noted in section 3.3 that the provision that negotiators should take into account 'the needs of coastal States whose economies are overwhelmingly dependent on the exploitation of living marine resources' is the final version of a proposal that would have favoured Iceland in the Loophole dispute had it not been modified by the insertion of the word 'coastal'.[109] All things considered, by providing a list of six criteria without internal priority, Article 11 is too vague to close discussions on allocation and the Fish Stocks Agreement only slightly affected the allocative negotiations over Loophole cod.

3.5 Compliance control

It is the the third task of regional management, that of enforcing compliance with conservation measures in the Barents Sea, that has the greatest potential for being affected by the Fish Stocks Agreement. In this discussion, the elaboration of port state measures and the rules for non-flag state inspection and detention on the high seas are especially relevant.

The *port state measures* provided for in the Fish Stocks Agreement were strongly supported by Norway during the negotiation of that Agreement. These include the right to inspect vessels that are voluntarily in port and, if violations are revealed, to prohibit landing and trans-shipment.[110] Already by 1994, Norway had banned the landing of unregulated Loophole catches, a measure that highlights an interesting type of interplay between international resource management regimes and those aiming at liberal trade practices among states.[111] It has been argued, for instance, that the port state provisions of the Fish Stocks Agreement may conflict with rules under the General Agreement on Tariffs and Trade,[112] and in the Barents Sea context, the regional regime that is based on the Agreement on an European Economic Area may also may be relevant. At both global and regional levels, trade agreements typically require that restrictive measures are applied in a non-discriminatory manner. As long as these circumstances are met, the Fish Stocks Agreement undoubtedly provides normative confirmation to the port state measures that have been taken in the region because parties to the Agreement have explicitly accepted landing prohibitions whenever inspections by the port state have 'established that the catch has been taken in a manner which undermines the effectiveness of subregional, regional or global conservation and management measures on the high seas'.[113]

In terms of *inspection* and *detention*, the Fish Stocks Agreement significantly modifies the traditional high seas compliance regime under international law, which is centred on flag state enforcement. Drawing largely upon a previous FAO instrument, the Agreement strengthens the responsibility of the flag state to monitor and enforce conservation measures.[114] In addition, the Agreement provides procedures for involvement of non-flag states in enforcement activities. The regional enforcement scheme that is envisaged by the Agreement includes reciprocal inspection rights on the high seas and, in cases where the flag state is unable or unwilling to act on severe violations, ultimately the right to bring the vessel to port.[115] So far, such provisions have not been incorporated into the agreements that Norway and Russia have drawn up with non-coastal user states to manage the Loophole fisheries. Instead, other user states are largely obliged to conduct their harvesting inside the EEZs.[116] This solution might become unstable, as noted earlier, if the share of the stock that is fishable on the high seas were to grow significantly, as it did in the early 1990s. A resumption of unregulated harvesting on a large scale in the Loophole would call for either an elaboration of procedures for high seas boarding and inspection within the bilateralist regime or an application of the already existing Scheme of Control and Enforcement under NEAFC. The latter option would imply that NEAFC also be involved to a greater extent in the regulatory process;[117] and both options would draw heavily on the enforcement provisions of the Fish Stocks Agreement.

In *summary*, if the bilateralist regime were again to be challenged by considerable high seas harvesting, the Fish Stocks Agreement would provide a broader and more powerful set of compliance mechanisms than has hitherto been available. Regional port state measures, such as the prohibition of landings of catches taken in defiance of international regulations, is validated by the Agreement, and the legal and political basis for elaboration of an intrusive enforcement system involving action by non-flag states is much stronger than was the case prior to adoption of the Agreement.

4 Conclusion

Six years of significant, unregulated harvesting took place before the Loophole dispute was settled by a trilateral agreement involving the two coastal states, Norway and Russia, and the main distant water challenger, Iceland. During the negotiation of the Fish Stocks Agreement, the Loophole challenge galvanized Norway's and Russia's allegiance to the coastal state bloc, whereas Iceland's engagement in this fishery motivated this state to move from active participation in the coastal state core group to a more mixed position.

The bilateralist Barents Sea fisheries regime, centred on the Norwegian–Russian Fisheries Commission, has had only moderate impact on efforts to cope with the Loophole problem. Some harmonization of coastal state measures has occurred. Coordinated diplomatic pressure has been exerted on relevant distant water fishing states, and requirements to limit activities in high seas areas have been included in their accords with other user states.

The potential influence of the Fish Stocks Agreement on the high seas fisheries problem in the Barents Sea differs from one aspect of management to another. The generation of scientific knowledge will be little affected. Regarding regulation and compliance control, however, the Fish Stocks Agreement places much greater pressure on all the user states to reach agreement on coordination of adequate measures. On the question of allocation, the provisions in the Fish Stocks Agreement which lay out criteria for newcomers' access to a regulated high seas fishery lend themselves to regional application, but they fail to clarify the balance among the criteria involved. A regional solution could only be achieved through negotiations that were shaped largely by the relative need of the parties to reach an agreement; when the availability of cod in the Loophole diminished in the second half of the 1990s, the bargaining position of the coastal states improved. Finally, the provisions in the Fish Stocks Agreement that sets global standards for compliance control schemes under regional management regimes strengthen considerably the basis for effective enforcement of high seas conservation and management measures in the Barents Sea.

Notes

Very helpful comments are appreciated from David Balton, Kjell Olav Gammel-
sæter, Alf Håkon Hoel, Tore Henriksen, Geir Hønneland, Geir Ulfstein, Davor
Vidas, and Johán Williams.

1. Agreement for the Implementation of the Provisions of the United Nations
   Convention on the Law of the Sea of 10 Dec. 1982 relating to the Conservation and Management of Straddling Fish Stocks and Highly Migratory Fish
   Stocks (1995); 34 *ILM* 1547.
2. The North-East Atlantic Fisheries Convention (1959) was superseded by
   the Convention on Future Multilateral Cooperation in North-East Atlantic
   Fisheries (1980); *OJ* L227 (1981) (hereinafter NEAFC Convention), covering
   the remaining high seas areas in the region.
3. Russia is the legal successor of the Soviet Union in these agreements.
   According to Russia, the Treaty concerning Spitsbergen (1920) (2 *LNTS* 7) is
   also a part of the Barents Sea fisheries regime, but this is denied by Norway.
   This Treaty gives sovereignty over Svalbard to Norway with some specified
   limitations. The Norwegian view, shared only by Canada and Finland in
   principle but widely accepted in practice as regards fisheries, is that these
   limitations, including an obligation not to discriminate against foreigners in
   certain issue areas, are restricted to the onshore areas and territorial waters
   and do not concern the EEZ; R. R. Churchill and G. Ulfstein, *Marine Management in Disputed Areas: The Case of the Barents Sea* (London: Routledge,
   1992).
4. 'Overenkomst mellom Regjeringen i Kongeriket Norge og Regjeringen i
   Unionen av Sovjetiske Sosialistiske Republikker om samarbeid innen fiskeri-
   næringen' (1975), *OMFM* (1995), 546.
5. Ibid., Art. III.
6. 'Overenskomst mellom Regjeringen i Kongeriket Norge og Regjeringen i
   Unionen av Sovjetiske Sosialistiske Republikker om gjensidige fiskeri-
   forbindelser' (1976), *OMFM* (1977), 974.
7. The disputed maritime area is located between a median line drawn from
   the territorial boundary (and favoured by Norway) and the sector line
   (favoured by Russia). The 'adjacent area', which is considerably larger than
   the disputed area, is usually referred to as the Grey Zone; 'Avtale mellom
   Norge og Sovjetunionen om en midlertidig praktisk ordning for fisket i et
   tilstøtende område i Barentshavet' (1977), *OMFM* (1977), 436.
8. Based on reciprocal access agreements, the European Community, the Faroes,
   Greenland, and Iceland at present have fishing rights in specified national
   zones in the Barents Sea. In addition, and based on historical fishing, Poland
   has certain quotas in Norway's EEZ and in the Svalbard zone; and on similar
   grounds, Canada, Estonia, and Lithuania are granted access to the shrimp
   fishery in the Svalbard zone; Report to the Storting, Norway, *St. meld.* 11
   (1997–8), s. 3; a broader discussion is found in *St. meld.* 49 (1994–5).

9. On the distinction between bilateralism and regionalism, see the Conclusions.
10. *Daily News of Iceland* (online at www.icenews.is/) (3 Nov. 1995).
11. The catch had been around 1,100 metric tons; *Daily News of Iceland* (17 Nov. 1995).
12. Materials of the Norwegian Coast Guard, on file with the author. As the Coast Guard cannot require catch reports or on-board inspections in international waters, estimations of catches are largely based on visual observation from Coast Guard vessels operating in the area and are therefore somewhat imprecise.
13. See the discussion by Vukas and Vidas, Ch. 2 above.
14. A proposal for such exercises as a means of dealing with unregulated fishing in the Loophole was put forward in *Krasnaya Zvezda*, the newspaper of the Russian Ministry of Defence, in June 1996, but the proposal was subsequently rejected by a spokesman for the Russian Navy; *Aftenposten* (Oslo; online at www.aftenposten.no) (20 June 1996), 9. In the Sea of Okhotsk Peanut Hole, Russian military exercises and weapons testing were conducted prior to negotiating with a group of distant water fishing nations on the terms for their abstention from high seas fisheries outside Russia's EEZ; Oude Elferink, Ch. 6 above.
15. 'Protokoll fra den 22. sesjon i Den blandete norsk-russiske fiskerikommisjon' (1993), 14–15, available from Ministry of Fisheries, Oslo.
16. 'Avtale mellom Norge og Grønland/Danmark om gjensidige fiskeri-forbindelser' (1992), *OMFM* (1994), 1500. In the EC case, high seas activities are not mentioned explicitly in the relevant bilateral agreements; Agreement on Fisheries between the European Economic Community and the Kingdom of Norway (1980), *OJ* L226/48 (1980); and Agreement in the Form of an Exchange of Letters between the European Community and the Kingdom of Norway relating to the Agreement on Fisheries between the European Com-munities and the Kingdom of Norway (1992), Proposition to the Storting, Norway, *St. prp.* 102 (1991–2).
17. Norway, Ministry of Fisheries, 'Felles norsk-færøysk pressekommuniké om kvoteavtalen for 1996', Press Release, 23 Feb. 1996.
18. In 1991, after reaching agreement on the contents of the Framework agree-ment that was adopted the following year, negotiations between Norway and Greenland on an annual quota broke down, allegedly over Greenlandic linkage of Loophole engagement and quotas from Norway; Bjarne Myrstad of the Norwegian Ministry of Fisheries cited in *Fiskaren* (Bergen), (23 Aug. 1991).
19. Criticism from Norwegian industry on this account is cited in *Fiskeribladet* (Harstad) (5 Aug. 1992), 4.
20. Norway's Foreign Minister, Johan Jørgen Holst, cited in *Aftenposten* (25 Aug. 1993), 4, after the collapse of informal talks on the matter.
21. *St. prp.* 74 (1998–9), s. 4.
22. Ibid., s. 2.2; on parallel developments under the Northwest Fisheries Organ-ization, see Joyner, Ch. 7 above.

23. *Daily News of Iceland* (13 and 14 July 1995) (the vessel *Már*) and (22 July 1996) (the vessel *Klakkur*).

24. The incident involved the vessel *Már*; the Agreement on the European Economic Area (1992) was adopted by the European Community and its member states and the members of the European Free Trade Association (EFTA); (www.efta.int/docs/EFTA/LegalTexts/EEAAgr&RelAgr/TABLE%20OF%20CONT.AF.pdf). See in particular Art. 20 in conjunction with Protocol 9, and more generally Art. 36 of the Agreement.

25. 'Freedom to Provide Services', *EFTA Surveillance Authority: Annual Report 1998* (http://www.efta.int/structure/SURV/efta-srv.cfm). Art. 5 of Protocol 9 to the EEA Agreement provides for access to ports and associated facilities but exemption is made for landings of fish from stocks the management of which is subject to severe disagreement among the parties.

26. *St. prp.* 73 (1998–9), s. 2.2; legislation providing for such blacklisting was introduced in 1994 but not used in practice until 'around 1997'; ibid.

27. The European Community is granted considerable quotas of several species in the Norwegian EEZ.

28. *Aftenposten* (9 June 1994), 4, reports that two Icelandic vessels were rejected at Norwegian shipyards on such grounds.

29. Robert Hansen, leader of a regional County Fishermen's Association, maintains that shipyards accepting Loophole vessels will be blacklisted; *Nordlys* (8 June 1994), 12. When it became known that the Faroese branch of the Norwegian oil company Statoil had served Loophole vessels, representatives of several County Fishermen's Associations threatened to boycott this company; *Nordlys* (17 June 1994), 15.

30. *Fiskaren* (6 May 1994), 5, notes that the Russian Fisheries Minister threatened to sever cooperative relations with Iceland; and, in the 1 July 1994 issue, that the Russian party, encouraged by the Russian Fisheries Committee, had broken off industry-level negotiations on direct deliveries to Iceland. According to Icelandic newspapers, Russian authorities again in 1996 suggested to Russian fish companies that they should not sell fish to Iceland if Icelandic vessels reappeared in the Loophole; *Daily News of Iceland* (18 July 1996).

31. According to Icelandic imports statistics, Russian landings were somewhat reduced in 1994 compared to the two preceding years, but they still reached almost 11,000 metric tons; figure reported in *Fiskaren* (7 Mar. 1995), 15.

32. For an analysis of the Doughnut Hole case, see Balton, Ch. 5 above.

33. In annual protocols since the 1992 Commission meeting, Norway and Russia pledged to include Loophole activities in the scope of any quota agreements drawn up with non-coastal states; 'Protokoll fra den 22. sesjon i Den blandete norsk-russiske fiskerikommisjon', 13.

34. Agreement between the Government of Iceland, the Government of Norway and the Government of the Russian Federation concerning Certain Aspects of Co-operation in the Area of Fisheries, with Protocols; reproduced in *International Journal of Marine and Coastal Law*, 14 (1999), 484.

35. Ibid., Art. 4 in conjunction with Arts. 2 and 3; an important implication of this is that Iceland may not require fishing rights in the Svalbard zone, which it has in the past.

36. Ibid., Arts. 6 and 7.
37. *St. prp.* 74 (1998–9), s. 2.2.
38. *Daily News of Iceland* (22 Oct. 1998).
39. See, respectively, Kristján Ragnarsson, ibid. (14 Apr. 1999) and Oddmund Bye in *Aftenposten* (14 Apr. 1999).
40. On those two types of interplay, see the Introduction and the Conclusions.
41. Agreement between the Government of Canada and the Government of the Kingdom of Norway on Fisheries Conservation and Enforcement (1995; not in force); Proposition to the Odelsting, Norway, *Ot. prp.* 3 (1995–6); also Joint Communiqué on Canada–Norway Reciprocal Enforcement Agreement (*Pressemelding fra Fiskeridepartementet* (9 Jan. 1995), Oslo: Ministry of Fisheries).
42. Joyner, Ch. 7 above.
43. On the role of Iceland as a coastal state protagonist in international fisheries law and politics, see the Introduction.
44. The conspicuous management dispute over Northwest Atlantic groundfish implied that, at an early stage, the European Community was the most sharply profiled champion of distant water fishing interests; A. C. de Fontaubert, 'The Politics of Negotiation at the United Nations Conference on Straddling Fish Stocks and Highly Migratory Fish Stocks', *Ocean and Coastal Management*, 29 (1995), 79, at 85. Norway's application for European Union membership was sent in 1992; the negotiated agreement was rejected by the Norwegian Storting after a referendum in 1994.
45. The 'Santiago Document', drawn up at the initiative of a group of Latin American states prior to the third preparatory committee meeting in Aug. 1991, argued strongly in favour of the coastal states having a greater say in the management of high seas fisheries.
46. The estimate is made in 'Seafood', Report of the American Embassy, Moscow, cited in Oude Elferink, Ch. 6 above. More recently, Russian attention to distant water fisheries is reportedly again on the rise.
47. V. Monakhov, 'The Fishery Industry in the Russian Far East', *Eastfish Fishery Industry Profile*, 19 (Copenhagen: Eastfish, Food and Agriculture Organization, 1998), 16.
48. For an interesting discussion of three types of leadership in multilateral negotiations, see O. R. Young, 'Political Leadership and Regime Formation: On the Development of Institutions in International Society', *International Organization*, 45 (1992), 281.
49. For an overview, see J. T. Thór, *British Trawlers and Iceland 1919–1976* (Gothenburg: Department of Economic History of the University of Göteborg, 1995).
50. Young, 'Political Leadership and Regime Formation', 293–8.
51. Fish Stocks Agreement, Art. 11 (d).
52. Law of the Sea Convention, Art. 63; see discussion in T. Henriksen, 'FN-avtalen om fiske på vandrende fiskebestander: nye bidrag til havretten?' (Tromsø: University of Tromsø, Department of Law, Draft, Aug. 1998).
53. Details of the 1995 *Estai* incident are given by Joyner, Ch. 7 above.
54. *Sentrumsalternativet—Vilje til ansvar* (www.aftenposten.no/spesial/valg97/sentrum.htm), s. 2.2.2.8; my translation.

55. Kjell Magne Bondevik to *Aftenposten* (17 Oct. 1997).
56. W. T. Burke, 'Fishing in the Bering Sea Donut: Straddling Stocks and the New International Law of Fisheries', *Ecology Law Quarterly*, 16 (1989), 285.
57. Balton, Ch. 5 above.
58. The Chairman of the Fish Stocks Conference, Satya Nandan, had told the international media that 'unilateral enforcement could be fatal to the agreed regime of the Law of the Sea'; *Newsweek* (25 Apr. 1994), 31.
59. Russia submitted, alone or with other states, eight working documents and one information paper; for an overview, see J.-P. Lévy and G. G. Schram, *United Nations Conference on Straddling Fish Stocks and Highly Migratory Fish Stocks: Selected Documents* (The Hague: Martinus Nijhoff, 1996), 813–29.
60. UN Doc. A/CONF./164/L.25, UN Doc. A/CONF./164/L.26, UN Doc. A/CONF./164/L.27, UN Doc. A/CONF./164/L.32, and UN Doc. A/CONF./164/L.38.
61. UN Doc. A/CONF./164/L.21, UN Doc. A/CONF./164/L.25, UN Doc. A/CONF./164/L.33, and UN Doc. A/CONF./164/L.38.
62. This group, widely known as the Evensen Group, was in operation from the very first (organizational) session in New York in Dec. 1973, and the group played a significant role *inter alia* by drafting negotiating texts.
63. Fish Stocks Agreement, Art. 23.
64. Fish Stocks Agreement, Art. 21; on Norway's role, see M. Hayashi, 'Enforcement by Non-flag States on the High Seas under the 1995 Agreement on Straddling and Highly Migratory Fish Stocks', *Georgetown International Environmental Law Review*, 9 (1996), 1, at 16, citing an Informal Paper of the Chairman of the Conference, 'Issue Raised by Norway' (25 Aug. 1994). Compare in this context (then) Art. 20 of the Draft Agreement prepared for the 4th session (UN Doc. A/CONF.164/21) with the corresponding article in the Draft Agreement presented to the 5th session (UN Doc. A/CONF.164/22/Rev. 1).
65. Fish Stocks Agreement, Art. 21 (1–3); Hayashi, 'Enforcement by Non-flag States', 16.
66. On the significance of the situation off Canada for the convening of the Conference as well as some of the key issues discussed there, including new measures for enforcement, see e.g. D. H. Anderson, 'The Straddling Stocks Agreement of 1995: An Initial Assessment', *International and Comparative Law Quarterly*, 45 (1996), 463.
67. On this trisection of the resource management task, see the Introduction.
68. G. Børsting and O. S. Stokke, 'International Cooperation in Fisheries Science: Research Effectiveness and the Barents Sea Fisheries Regime', *FNI Reports* (Lysaker: The Fridtjof Nansen Institute, 1995).
69. Since 1997, however, despite efforts of Russian fisheries authorities, Norwegian research vessels have either been denied access to the Russian zone or been severely limited in their operations, a policy widely perceived as originating in naval quarters. This impediment of long-standing cooperation is believed to have arisen from dissatisfaction in the Northern Fleet with a parallel set of joint Norwegian–Russian investigations—the measurement programme on nuclear contamination; O. S. Stokke, 'Nuclear Dumping in

Arctic Seas: Russian Implementation of the London Convention', in D. G. Victor, K. Raustiala, and E. B. Skolnikoff (eds.), *The Implementation and Effectiveness of International Environmental Commitments: Theory and Practice* (Cambridge, Mass.: MIT Press, 1998), 475.
70. Law of the Sea Convention, Art. 119.
71. Fish Stocks Agreement, Arts. 5 and 14; also annex I.
72. The Framework Agreement, Preamble.
73. *St. prp.* 43 (1995–6), 11.
74. Fish Stocks Agreement, Art. 6 and annex II; for a more extensive discussion, see Orrego, Ch. 1 above, and the Conclusions.
75. *ICES Cooperative Research Report*, 229, part 1 (Copenhagen: International Council for the Exploration of the Sea, 1999), 17–39 and 79–84.
76. Fish Stocks Agreement, annex II.
77. The Norwegian Government, when submitting the Fish Stocks Agreement to the Storting (parliament), notes that compliance with Art. 6 may require additional resources for scientific purposes; Norway, *St. prp.* 43 (1995–6), 11.
78. For straddling stocks, see Art. 63; on the duty to cooperate, see Arts. 116–20.
79. Fish Stocks Agreement, Art. 8 (4).
80. Fish Stocks Agreement, Art. 8 (3); Art. 8 (1) obliges states, pending establishment of such an arrangement, to act in good faith and with due regard to the rights and interests of other states.
81. Note that 'openness' refers to participation in decision-making and not to access to the resources. The degree of openness required by the Agreement, defined by what constitutes a 'real interest', is debatable. See, on the one hand, Orrego, Ch. 1 above, and on the other, A. Tahindro, 'Conservation and Management of Transboundary Fish Stocks: Comments in Light of the Adoption of the 1995 Agreement for the Conservation and Management of Straddling Fish Stocks and Highly Migratory Fish Stocks', *Ocean Development and International Law*, 28 (1997), 1, at 20.
82. P. Örebech, K. Sigurjonsson, and T. L. McDorman, 'The 1995 United Nations Straddling and Highly Migratory Fish Stocks Agreement: Management, Enforcement and Dispute Settlement', *International Journal of Marine and Coastal Law*, 13 (1998), 119, at 124.
83. Fish Stocks Agreement, Art. 8 (1); emphasis added.
84. R. R. Churchill finds the claim that the Barents regime is an arrangement 'debatable'; 'The Barents Sea Loophole Agreement: A "Coastal State" Solution to a Straddling Stock Problem', *International Journal of Marine and Coastal Law*, 14 (1999), 467, at n. 26. His argument is that neither the Norwegian–Russian Fisheries Commission nor the agreements with non-coastal states qualify as 'arrangements' under the Fish Stocks Agreement; the latter because there is no decision-making mechanism and the former because it 'was not established for the purpose of high seas management of straddling stocks nor does it have such a role'. However, this does not seem to acknowledge the relationship between these regime components (see also s. 1 above). Norway was among the states pushing for inclusion of the 'arrangement' term in the Fish Stocks Agreement. After the adoption of the Agreement, Norway's Minister of Fisheries went further than the

view submitted here by holding that the Norwegian–Russian Fisheries Commission itself is an 'arrangement' as defined by Art. 1 of the Fish Stocks Agreement; J. H. T. Olsen, 'Fiske på det åpne hav', *Fiskeribladet* (21 Sept. 1995), 6.

85. NEAFC Convention, Arts. 5 and 12 in conjunction with Art. 2.
86. *ICES Cooperative Research Report*, 221, part 1 (1997), 50–1.
87. NEAFC Convention, Art. 12 (2).
88. On NEAFC's schemes, see Churchill, Ch. 8 above; on enforcement provisions in the Fish Stocks Agreement, see Hønnand, Ch. 4 above; on port state measures, see Vukas and Vidas, Ch. 2 above.
89. See also Churchill, 'The Barents Sea Loophole Agreement', 479–80.
90. Fish Stocks Agreement, Art. 7.
91. Ibid., Art. 7 (1) (a) and (1) (b) respectively; Orrego, Ch. 1 above. For the significance of this matter for Norway's acceptance of the Fish Stocks Agreement, see Recommendation of a Standing Committee of the Storting, Norway, *Innst.* 29 (1995–6), annex I. Here, attention is also drawn to the procedural safety valve regarding matters pertaining to coastal state jurisdiction in that Art. 32 ensures that the compulsory dispute settlement procedure laid out in Arts. 27–31 does not apply to coastal state measures taken within the EEZ; see the discussion of this view by Boyle, Ch. 3 above.
92. Fish Stocks Agreement, Art. 6 and annex II.
93. *ICES Cooperative Research Report*, vol. 229, part 1 (1999), 27–32; for an extensive discussion, see O. S. Stokke, L. G. Anderson, and N. Mirovitskaya, 'The Barents Sea Fisheries', in O. R. Young (ed.), *The Effectiveness of International Environmental Regimes: Causal Connections and Behavioral Mechanisms* (Cambridge, Mass.: MIT Press, 1999), 91.
94. *Daily News of Iceland* (5 Nov. 1997).
95. Ibid. (3 Aug. 1995) and (14 Aug. 1996).
96. G. L. Lugten, 'A Review of Measures Taken by Regional Marine Fishery Bodies to Address Contemporary Fishery Issues', *FAO Fisheries Circular*, 940 (1998), 85.
97. *ICES Cooperative Research Report*, 229, part 1 (1999), 27.
98. *St. meld.* 44 (1999–2000), s. 1; in 2000 the agreed cod quota was 390,000 metric tons, down from 850,000 tonnes in 1997; *St. meld.* 11 (1997–8), s. 1.
99. Ibid., Art. 5.
100. Ibid., Art. 3; Orrego, Ch. 1 above.
101. The project began in 1985; Børsting and Stokke, 'International Cooperation in Fisheries Science', 20.
102. A. H. Hoel, 'The Barents Sea: Fisheries Resources for Europe and Russia', in O. S. Stokke and O. Tunander (eds.), *The Barents Region: Cooperation in Arctic Europe* (London: Sage, 1994), at 122.
103. *St. meld.* 43 (1998–9), s. 3.3, and *Fiskeridepartementets miljøhandlingsplan 2000–2004* (Oslo: Ministry of Fisheries, 2000), s. 4.1.1.
104. See, for instance, *Innst. S.* 228 (1995–96), annex 1, 5, referring to Arts. 5 and 6 of the Fish Stocks Agreement.
105. The latter, zonal attachment, criterion has been used explicitly *inter alia* in the trilateral agreement between Iceland, Norway, and Greenland regarding

sharing of the joint capelin stock in the Norwegian Sea and between Norway and the European Community regarding the North Sea Herring; S. Engesæter, 'Scientific Input to International Fishery Agreements', *International Challenges*, 13 (1993), 85.

106. Fish Stocks Agreement, Art. 11 (a) (b).
107. Ibid., Arts. 7 (2) (e) and 2 (d) respectively.
108. Ibid., Art. 11 (d).
109. Ibid., Art. 11 (e).
110. Ibid., Art. 23; also Food and Agriculture Organization, Agreement to Promote Compliance with International Conservation and Management Measures by Fishing Vessels on the High Seas (1993), Art. V (2); 33 *ILM* 368.
111. s. 1.2 above.
112. General Agreement on Tarriffs and Trade (1947), 55 *UNTS* 194, as updated by the Final Act Embodying the Results of the Uruguay Round of Multilateral Trade Agreements (1994), 33 *ILM* 1125; for a discussion, see D. Freestone and Z. Makuch, 'The New International Environmental Law of Fisheries: The 1995 Straddling Stocks Convention', *Yearbook of International Environmental Law*, 7 (1996), 3, at 38–41; also the Conclusions.
113. Fish Stocks Agreement, Art. 23 (2).
114. Ibid., Art. 20; Hønneland, Ch. 4 above, offers a compliance-oriented comparison between the Fish Stocks Agreement and the FAO Compliance Agreement.
115. Fish Stocks Agreement, Arts. 20–2; see s. 2.3 above. For a detailed account of the contents and evolution of those provisions, as well as their interplay with regional regimes, see Vukas and Vidas, Ch. 2 above; also Hayashi, 'Enforcement by Non-flag States', esp. 15–26.
116. The Norwegian–Canadian 1995 agreement on compliance mentioned above, which does include provisions reflecting the Fish Stocks Agreement, is only symbolic in this context as Canadian vessels do not operate in the Barents Sea.
117. Whereas the scope of the NEAFC Scheme of Control and Enforcement is 'all fishing vessels' engaged in the harvesting of 'all fishery resources of the Convention area' except sea mammals, sedentary species, and highly migratory species (Scheme, Arts. 1–2 in conjunction with NEAFC Convention, Art. 1 (2)), NEAFC inspectors are authorized to board and inspect vessels only to the extent that this is deemed 'necessary to verify compliance with the measures established by NEAFC'; Scheme, Art. 17 (2); see also Arts. 18–20.

The International Regulation of Patagonian Toothfish: CCAMLR and High Seas Fisheries Management

RICHARD HERR

There can be few more unlikely candidates for international notoriety than the Patagonian toothfish. It is not an especially attractive fish; little known in the public circles, it lacks the mass emotional appeal of baby seals and cannot equal the great whales in being an icon of ecological protection. Nor does its value as a fish, while at the upper end of the retail market, give it the global gourmet status that the bluefin tuna enjoys. Yet, in the few short years that the Patagonian toothfish has been an exploited Antarctic resource, it has absorbed an extraordinary amount of official and public energy. Indeed, over recent years, it has reached an unusually high level of political saliency. At the 1997 Antarctic Treaty Consultative Meeting (ATCM) in Christchurch and in January 1999 through a 'Ministerial Meeting on Ice' at Scott Base, Antarctica, New Zealand attempted to make the management of the fish a significant public issue. Australia responded similarly with an abortive attempt to hold a ministerial level review at the 1999 meeting of CCAMLR in Hobart. The explanation for this apparently unusual situation can be related to the changing post-Cold War priorities for Antarctica as well as to the changing global approaches to resource regulation. Adding public spice to the toothfish controversy has been a liberal sprinkling of 'p' words in the media—piracy, poaching, and plundering[1]—now more prosaically known as illegal, unreported, and unregulated (IUU) fishing.

Whether the Patagonian toothfish issue deserves a place in Antarctic policy's centre stage depends very much on the extent to which it can be seen as a test case for the strength of the entire Antarctic Treaty system (ATS).[2] Charges that the fishery is being exploited at unsustainable levels and thus undermining the environmental protection values of the ATS are to be regarded as serious. So too are the complaints that some of the putative gamekeepers appear to be amongst the main poachers. The primary aim of the Convention on the Conservation of Antarctic Marine Living Resources (CCAMLR) is to secure sustainable fisheries management in the Southern Ocean.[3] If the parties to the Convention are the principal malefactors, how much faith can the international community put in this region's regulatory arrangements? The geographical location of the fishery is a further significant complication to the concerns over CCAMLR's role in managing this fishery. On the one hand, most of the areas being fished are remote, and therefore surveillance and enforcement are physically difficult and costly for both national and regional authorities. On the other hand, these areas lie at the margins of CCAMLR's regulatory ambit, thus opening the possibility of using non-ATS mechanisms either as a means of reinforcing CCAMLR measures or as alternatives to the CCAMLR instruments.

This chapter explores CCAMLR's management of the Patagonian toothfish fishery, including the difficulties posed by sovereignty and the opportunities offered by inter-regime relations. CCAMLR is undeniably the leading regime for dealing with the toothfish issue, but more recent developments have ensured that it is not the sole regime concerned. Both national regulatory arrangements and other global regimes are factors that may have greater or lesser impact as the difficulties confronting a satisfactory resolution of sustainable exploitation of this fish are addressed. Amongst the global regimes likely to be influential in this process is the UN Fish Stocks Agreement,[4] since this treaty has the potential politically to reinforce the rule-making relevance of CCAMLR or to undermine it substantially. Thus far, the application of the Fish Stocks Agreement has only attracted partial support within CCAMLR, but the logic of the Fish Stocks Agreement has had an impact in broadening CCAMLR's regulatory horizons. Nevertheless, the grounds for resistance to utilizing the Fish Stocks Agreement have raised serious questions for an increasingly beleaguered CCAMLR about its own regional approach to fisheries management in a world where global mechanisms are providing a continuously more general framework for regional structures and processes.

1 Emergence of the Patagonian problem

The Patagonian toothfish (*Dissostichus eleginoides*) is mainly a sub-Antarctic demersal fish that occurs at depths between 70 and 2,500 metres. Being some 2 metres in length and weighing up to 100 kilograms, it is one of the largest of the Antarctic fishes.[5] Its precise range has yet to be verified, but it seems to follow cold-water isotherms at its preferred depths perhaps even where these extend well northward from the sub-Antarctic. Significantly, this toothfish tends to be concentrated along the continental shelves associated with sub-Antarctic islands, thus placing its major grounds within the EEZs of the states controlling these islands.[6] Like other cold-water fish, the Patagonian toothfish appears to be slow in maturing

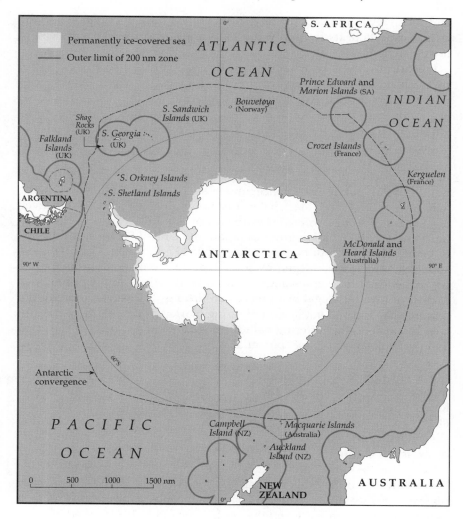

Map 10.1. The Southern Ocean

and relatively long-lived. Its life cycle is not yet fully understood and the critical aspects of its fecundity, mortality rates, and the like still need to be researched.

Historically, the oily, white-fleshed fish was initially taken as a useful by-catch and later for a number of years as a targeted commercial species in the waters around Argentina and Chile and adjacent CCAMLR areas at the southern end of South America.[7] It appears that, when the stocks within the accessible lower latitude maritime zones were unable to sustain rising economic interest, the fleets moved more fully into the CCAMLR Convention Area in pursuit of new stocks in the late 1980s. In the international market place, the toothfish has come to command high prices with general public acceptance under such market names as 'mero', 'Chilean sea bass', and 'black hake'. Just how valuable the fish is, however, is a source of some confusion. Estimates of the dollar value of the catch has varied from '$5 a kilogram in Japan, the United States and Europe'[8] to being 'almost worth bars of gold . . . [at] $17 a kilogram'[9] in Japanese supermarkets. It was alleged by some that this confusion was entirely a consequence of market instability caused by the over-supply of toothfish caused in turn by illegal or unregulated fishing.[10] However, more recent research has focused not just on differing market prices in different countries but also on the differing values from different products of the catch and particularly on the lost potential value from mishandling of 'pirated' fish.[11]

The emergence of a significant Antarctic *Dissostichus* fishery has created management problems for the CCAMLR community at a number of levels—from basic fisheries regulation regarding the total allowable catch (TAC) and access, through the level of environmental impacts regarding sustainability and effects on non-target species, and on to the highest level of policy including even the effectiveness of the ATS itself. Indeed, because the toothfish occurs most accessibly and productively in the lower latitudes of its range around the sub-Antarctic islands, deepwater plateaux and seamounts, these management concerns are related more to issues such as sovereignty and the application of the 1982 United Nations Convention on the Law of the Sea than would be the case were the fishing grounds located only within the ATS area. And reciprocally, because these other complications are present, the management issues have taken on a public urgency that has not often characterized other CCAMLR measures.

As is true for most other widely dispersed species, there is no single, uniform regulatory framework for Patagonian toothfish at present. This situation arises largely because of the differences in jurisdiction over the areas where the fish is taken. National controls apply in the case of the older but diminished resources of Argentina and Chile as well as in the newer fisheries located outside the CCAMLR area, such as those being developed around the Falklands and Macquarie Island.[12] In the case of Kerguelen and Crozet Islands, coastal state jurisdiction has applied since the outset of CCAMLR because at that time the Government of France reserved its rights over this area.[13] However, the issue of regulating the harvesting of *Dissostichus* has taken on an increasingly regional flavour since its inception. CCAMLR and FAO statistics for 1993/4 showed less than 20 per cent of the total catch being taken in Antarctic waters that are subject to CCAMLR regulations, with most of the declared catch coming from national and international waters off Chile and Argentina.[14] However, in subsequent years the balance shifted strongly to reverse these ratios (although the extent of unreported catch makes certainty on this point a significant part of the Patagonian toothfish problem) so that a much greater share of the perceived management responsibility fell increasingly on CCAMLR and its members.[15] For a variety of reasons, which included a shared political will, the absence of institutional competitors, and international expectations that it was the logical and appropriate mechanism, CCAMLR has accepted the responsibility for providing the core management for this disparate and difficult fishery.

The CCAMLR management arrangements are set by the twenty-three-member Commission that meets annually in Hobart, Tasmania, the location for the organization's permanent headquarters.[16] The decisions of the Commission are formally reported as Conservation Measures and Resolutions, the former being the principal mechanism by which the Commission regulates the access of its members to the marine living resources of the Southern Ocean within its jurisdiction. Conservation Measures are used to set TAC limits, season limits, gear type restrictions, and the like as well as to prescribe enforcement and compliance requirements. The measures may be in force on an annual basis or for an indefinite period. Unlike other arrangements, the CCAMLR Convention mandates an ecological approach to fisheries management and, in order to evaluate claims on marine living resources in keeping with this nearly unique environmental constraint, the Commission is assisted in its determinations by a Scientific Committee. This Committee has extraordinary influence within the regional body both by the high level of expertise made available to staff it and its relative autonomy within the organizational structure of CCAMLR. Two specialist 'working groups' within the Scientific Committee undertake the detailed assessments of fish stocks and ecosystem impacts that provide the basis for the Committee's management advice to the Commission.

When the Commission acts on the advice of the Scientific Committee by passing a Conservation Measure, the effect that such a regulation has in the form of compliance is not entirely unambiguous regardless of how precisely the Measure is framed.[17] A member of the Commission can object to a Conservation Measure or seek exemption from the Measure if that member feels the measure should not apply to it.[18] Even when there is no objection, a measure may not have the impact desired. Member state compliance with a Conservation Measure depends not just on the political will of the member but very much also on such factors as the domestic legal status of treaty obligations, internal judicial processes, administrative and political infrastructures, and related factors. Thus, not all CCAMLR members are able to guarantee the same level of domestic enforcement.[19] Partially in recognition of the important national differences in members' capacity to secure compliance, all members of CCAMLR are required under Article XXI (2) of the Convention to provide information on national steps to ensure compliance with CCAMLR regulations. As a consequence, 'Compliance with Conservation Measures in Force' is a standard agenda item for the annual meetings and includes reports from members on actions that both deal with violations by nationals and promote governmental enforcement of new measures.

There are other constraints that further limit the extent of the impact of CCAMLR's Conservation Measures. CCAMLR is essentially a regional organization with a limited breadth of membership. Not even all the parties to the Antarctic Treaty are members of CCAMLR. More importantly, not all states or countries with a capacity for fishing in the Southern Ocean are parties to the CCAMLR Convention. Technically, non-members are not bound by CCAMLR regulations even though they are encouraged to follow CCAMLR guidelines voluntarily.[20] In addition, although the geographic scope of CCAMLR is essentially defined by a physical boundary, the Antarctic Convergence, this is scarcely an impermeable membrane. Many components of the ecology of the Southern Ocean, including seals, whales, seabirds, and fish, cross the Convergence habitually. In the case of the species protected by CCAMLR regulations, this migrating can undermine the effectiveness of the regulations, as is the case with seabirds, or create serious regulatory ambiguities, as is the case with the Patagonian toothfish.

Despite the constraints and limitations of CCAMLR, its essential problem is the issue of illegal, unreported, and unregulated fishing for the Patagonian toothfish. This has been accepted by CCAMLR members individually and collectively. There are no real alternatives in terms of available and usable international mechanisms.[21] Whereas CCAMLR may be unable to handle all aspects of *Dissostichus* management, its powers within the Southern Ocean and the role played by its members in fishing, processing, and/or purchasing toothfish make this organization the most appropriate instrument for assembling and coordinating a coherent response to a fishery under threat.

2 CCAMLR's toothfish conservation measures

Recognition of the toothfish management issue within CCAMLR and acceptance that this regional agency might play an active role has evolved in a short space of time. As noted above, the problem of management has had to be fast-tracked due to the rapid development of the fishery. The rapid pace of developments is partly due to the heightened public awareness of the issue (promoted by environmental NGOs but strongly supported by CCAMLR members who shared the NGO concerns). Moreover, the international environment has changed significantly, as is also the case with elements that have been added to the regulatory armoury of global fishing such as the Fish Stocks Agreement, the FAO Compliance Agreement, and wider acceptance of port state responsibilities. It is also important to note that because CCAMLR is both an environmental regime and a fisheries body, its management approach has necessarily required two strands—establishing sustainable catch limits and minimizing ecological damage. This section will canvass CCAMLR's response to toothfish management over the past decade by considering three areas of CCAMLR activity with regard to toothfish: generating knowledge for management purposes, regulating catch and effort, and pursuing compliance. Progress in the first two areas in fisheries management have proceeded more or less simultaneously (indeed both are important) but concern for the lack of compliance has shifted the CCAMLR emphasis to the third area in recent years.

2.1 Knowledge of the fishery

In keeping with its twin mandates, CCAMLR's requirements for management knowledge falls broadly into two categories—fisheries regulation and environmental protection. While CCAMLR has a Scientific Committee that advises on management and environmental issues, this Committee does not have an autonomous work programme budget and must therefore rely predominantly on national research programmes for the information on which it acts. This is not to say that CCAMLR lacks the capacity to pursue information for management in its own right. The Scientific Committee can identify areas of need in which individual party states or other research bodies can perform research on behalf of the Committee. CCAMLR at present coordinates broad multilateral research efforts such as the current CCAMLR Ecosystem Monitoring Program (CEMP) and maintains a Scheme of International Scientific Observation. Both these endeavours seek to gather a much wider range of management data than would be possible through the efforts of the participating states individually. Nevertheless, the fieldwork related to national research programmes is carried out by participating states as often also is the analysis of data, although at times CCAMLR's Secretariat performs these analyses in-house.

In general, CCAMLR's role in terms of knowledge for fisheries management has been to regulate takers of commercial (and research) catches so that their data are supplied to CCAMLR for assessment. In the case of the *Dissostichus* fishery, both the environmental and management priorities were pursued with the onset of specific conservations for this fishery from the 1990/1 season. Conservation Measure 25/IX required the reporting of catch and effort data as well as biological information from the *Dissostichus* fishery, including data on seabird by-catch particularly in longline fisheries such as the toothfish fishery.[22] In later years, methods for securing better knowledge of the fishery and its impacts have been refined in order to increase awareness of and better manage the potential threats to both the fishery resources and the wider environment.

Initially, regulation to monitor catch and effort followed a fairly standard course for CCAMLR, that is, obtaining reasonable management information without impacting the industry or commercial confidentiality too heavily. The Commission moved to strengthen its monitoring role in the 1991/2 season by imposing more rigorous requirements for reporting catches on a finer scale, and it included the sanction of closing the fishery to the vessels of the contracting party if the required data were not supplied within a specified period (essentially fifteen days).[23] The importance of accurate and timely catch and effort data was emphasized in 1992 when the phrase 'or until the TAC is reached' was added to Conservation Measure 55/XI in 1992 to enable the season to be closed as soon as the TAC was reached.[24] Later meetings added further refinements, especially regarding by-catch, to ensure timeliness and greater detail.[25] However, as concern for the sustainability of the fishery grew during the 1990s, this area of the CCAMLR effort tended to focus more on the key problem of unreported catch.

As early as 1993, unreported (and illegal) catch emerged as a significant issue when the Scientific Committee observed that the Patagonian toothfish stocks in the South Georgia area 'may have been depleted to around 30% of its unfished abundance'.[26] Evidence of contracting parties' failure to report substantial quantities of catch contributed in part to the decision by CCAMLR in 1993 to investigate the issue of 'management in uncertainty' in greater depth and detail.[27] However, Patagonian toothfish probably became an established issue on the CCAMLR agenda when the Commission's Scientific Committee, through its Working Group on Fish Stock Assessment, confirmed officially in 1995 an estimate that the unreported catch 'was either of the same order or higher than the reported catch'.[28] The Scientific Committee found in 1996 that the incidence of high levels of unreported catches had extended to previously unfished areas.[29] When the Committee also estimated that the reported catch from the CCAMLR Area may have only comprised 40 per cent of the total taken,[30] the matter was well and truly in the public domain, where it remained through the turn of the century.

To deal with unreported catch from within Antarctic waters subject to CCAMLR regulation, two basic approaches have been pursued—the presence of authorized international observers on vessels and the development of a vessel monitoring system (VMS) to report vessel location routinely and more accurately. The first was achieved in 1992 through what has been designated as the 'CCAMLR Scheme of International Scientific Observation'.[31] This scheme strengthened the System of Inspection, which, inaugurated in 1988, allowed member states to designate 'inspectors' to board vessels of other contracting parties operating within the CCAMLR Area to determine whether they were complying generally with CCAMLR requirements.[32] As with similar schemes elsewhere, observers are placed on vessels to monitor the proper recording of data and forwarding of this information to the designated authority. Given the broader interests of CCAMLR and its mandate, the scheme also includes a heavy scientific component as indicated by its title; however, some suggest privately this was the 'sugar coating' to make the scheme acceptable to industry and the affected contracting parties. The VMS system has fared less well. Despite nearly a decade of effort by some states within CCAMLR, it was only in 1998 that acceptance of a somewhat limited VMS agreement was achieved contingent on individual members partially setting their own pace for implementation.[33]

Development of the *Dissostichus* fishery has also generated a need to regulate information on its ecological impact. All CCAMLR fisheries have the same obligation to minimize their ecological impacts. The technology associated with harvesting toothfish did raise a specific issue. The decline of several species of Southern Ocean albatross in recent years has been blamed to a substantial degree on incidental mortality due to the birds taking the baited hooks of the bluefin tuna longlines in the waters north of the Antarctic Convergence before the hooks sank below the birds' diving depth.[34] However, the application of bottom longline technology to the harvesting of Patagonian toothfish extended this very significant problem to the fishing grounds within the CCAMLR Area and thus brought the matter directly under the responsibility of CCAMLR.[35] In addition to the requirements imposed for reporting by-catch noted above, member states routinely advise the Commission or its committees in *Reports of Members' Activities* and in *Reports on the Avoidance and Assessment of Incidental Mortality* of information on by-catch, whether by commercial fishing or through scientific research.

2.2 Regulation of the catch

Regulation of the Patagonian toothfish fishery has grown rapidly to occupy a particularly critical position on the CCAMLR agenda throughout the 1990s. A primary reason, if not the only reason, for this regulatory preoccupation has been the decreasing availability of alternative foci. Remarkably, by the 1992/3 season, *Dissostichus eleginoides* was the only reported catch of a targeted commercial finfish out of the thirteen species of finfish taken in significant quantities in the preceding half-decade;[36] by 1996, Patagonian toothfish accounted for 99 per cent of the reported catch of finfish in the CCAMLR Area and the krill catch had dropped below 100,000 metric tons.[37] This unfortunate regional circumstance was the consequence of a number of factors such as the contraction in fish stocks harvested in previous years and a reduction in total fishing effort due to the break-up of the Soviet Union in 1991 and the subsequent shake-out of its extensive fishing fleets. The concentration of Antarctic finfish effort on the Patagonian toothfish remained to the end of the decade with virtually no significant commercial interest in other species in the seasons since 1992/3.[38]

CCAMLR's direct regulatory effort regarding Patagonian toothfish has involved a twofold approach—setting catch limits and, to a lesser extent, controlling effort. Both approaches evolved from the organization's ecological mandate which has increasingly paid formal obeisance to the precautionary principle. Throughout the decade, TACs have been created for ever more statistical subareas, moving generally eastward from the initial grounds to the south and east of Chile and Argentina. Broadly, these limits have been increased or held steady throughout the 1990s despite deepening concerns for the overall sustainability of these fisheries.[39] On rare occasions, as in the 1993/4 season around the sensitive South Georgia area, TACs have been decreased. Whereas the creation of TACs may appear to have promoted fishing for the Patagonian toothfish to those unfamiliar with CCAMLR procedures, the TACs were actually intended to contain fishing because, except where a blanket ban was in place, there would be no cap on the amount of catch to be taken. The TACs were also generally small in absolute terms, being in hundreds of metric tons rather than thousands.

Acceptance of the precautionary principle in setting constraints on the Patagonian toothfish catch has been a feature of the debate within CCAMLR, in part, at least, because the majority of the toothfish debate has occurred after the Rio Earth Summit. The application of the precautionary principle has recurred at several stages in CCAMLR's regulatory process. TACs have been set to allow for a considerable margin of uncertainty, especially with regard to new areas of activity. For example, when

Australia opened a trawl fishery around its sub-Antarctic possessions of Heard and McDonald Islands for Patagonian toothfish, a 'precautionary TAC' of 297 metric tons was set on the advice to the Scientific Committee (significantly, from Australia itself).[40] The Special Area for Protection and Scientific Study that was declared around South Georgia by Conservation Measure 69/XII was another device designed to protect *Dissostichus* against over-exploitation through ignorance of its biology. While more due to pressure to deal with a nascent crab fishery than with the protection of *Dissostichus*, the Commission temporized on how to cope with the demand to open a fishery on which the Commission had insufficient data 'to fulfil its function under Article IX [of the Convention]'.[41] The Commission created the category of 'new fishery' to cover three circumstances: (1) areas where research or exploratory fisheries data had not been submitted to CCAMLR; (2) areas where catch and effort had never been supplied; and (3) areas where catch and effort had not been supplied for the two most recent actual fishing seasons. Member states involved in a new fishery were obligated to submit as much data as possible on proposed fishing techniques, on catch levels, and on likely environmental impacts.[42]

Significant regulatory effort has been devoted to limiting the environmental impacts of *Dissostichus* fishing. CCAMLR's 1991 meeting began to address some of the concerns of the previous two years on the incidental mortality of seabirds from longline fisheries that minimized such losses. Both commercial and research longliners were compelled to sink baited hooks as quickly as possible, to reduce lights during night operations, to ban the dumping of trash and offal while fishing so as not to attract birds, and to deploy lines with streamers in order to discourage birds during daylight operations.[43] In addition to renewing this measure in subsequent years and amending it to strengthen its effect, CCAMLR has adopted other measures better to protect Southern Ocean albatrosses. The longline toothfish fisheries in the South Atlantic had their opening dates held back to 1 March (from the usual early/mid-November) in order to reduce the risk to breeding seabirds. In addition, the Commission has taken the further step of offering direct advice to fishermen on how to implement the intention of Conservation Measure 29/XV entitled 'Fish the Sea Not the Sky'.[44]

While the protection of albatross undoubtedly has been the key focus of the ecological dimension of the Patagonian toothfish management within CCAMLR, this has not been the only area of attention. Fairly stringent by-catch measures were also imposed by the Commission to deal with non-targeted fish species in the *Dissostichus* trawl fisheries. For example, CCAMLR imposed a total limit of 50 metric tons by-catch of all other species in the new Australian fishery in the subarea to the south of

Heard Island and a requirement that the fishing effort for the two targeted *Dissostichus* species be dispersed across the zone.[45]

2.3 *Pursuit of compliance*

The issue of compliance within CCAMLR is limited formally to CCAMLR's contracting parties. Nonetheless, as this regime is placed within the broader Antarctic Treaty system, significant constraints apply with regard to the preferred course to securing member state compliance with Conservation Measures and other recommendations. Traditionally CCAMLR has depended on flag state authority as the primary mechanism by which its measures are enforced. In keeping with the practice of the ATS in other areas, this avoids the sovereignty issues raised by coastal state enforcement. However, coastal state jurisdiction and port state authority have emerged as particularly significant elements in the toothfish issue. Yet, even with a wider range of powers available to member states, the problem of non-member compliance has proven to be a bedevilling concern for CCAMLR's regulation of the *Dissostichus* fishery.

Flag state authority might be deemed to have worked reasonably well for CCAMLR with fisheries located south of 60 degrees south latitude where coastal state possibilities were felt to be precluded by the Antarctic Treaty. The widespread occurrence of toothfish in lower latitudes changed the regulatory equation. Although there are variations in the way that CCAMLR parties treat their sub-Antarctic islands in relation to Conservation Measures, undisputed sovereignty has enabled Australian, French, Norwegian, and South African authorities to claim coastal state prerogatives over their offshore resources.[46] These states argue that the exercise of coastal state jurisdiction 'is a most useful additional way of seeking to ensure compliance' even by non-member states.[47] Nevertheless, it should be noted that even the greater certainty of coastal state jurisdiction is complicated by the 'Antarctic factor'. The remoteness of these fishing grounds makes the practicalities of enforcement especially arduous. The distances involved, the rigours of climate, and the absence of nearby populated settlements make it difficult and costly to insert national surveillance and enforcement assets into these isolated marine zones.

Coastal state authority naturally remains highly problematic in the South Atlantic area where territorial claims are generally challenged. Although the British Government has therefore attempted for the most part to rely on flag state responsibility to enforce fisheries management objectives, this approach has been undermined by a number of problems; this is especially true when the flag state was also in dispute with the UK over claims to sovereignty in Antarctica (namely, Chile or Argentina). Thus, Britain, partially because of its disappointment with the efficacy of some flag state enforcement of violations of CCAMLR,[48] has been tempted to pursue further some coastal state-based enforcement mechanisms despite the recognized political risks within the ATS. For example, Britain declared a 200-mile zone around South Georgia and the South Sandwich Islands (SGSSI) to strengthen its authority for enforcement. The UK regards this zone as consistent with the CCAMLR regime through the exemption provisions of the 1980 Convention Chairman's Statement.[49] The Government of SGSSI exercises responsibility for this zone and charters patrol boats to maintain civilian control of the fisheries protection process. The strengthening of its coastal state control appeared to improve the situation significantly at the time and the UK pointed to the fact 'that since December 1995, when the last heavy fine was imposed, [to late 1997] only two vessels have been sighted fishing illegally in SGSSI waters'.[50]

The need to regulate for compliance with regard to the Patagonian toothfish began with the complaints against the 'poor record' of the USSR for failing to provide CCAMLR with the required information. It was clear from the outset that compliance with CCAMLR's toothfish Conservation Measures could be problematic.[51] A growing anxiety amongst some members over the effectiveness of these measures for regulating the toothfish fishery began to come to a head at the Commission's thirteenth meeting in 1994. The Standing Committee on Observation and Inspection (SCOI), the primary means by which the Commission monitors the level of activities in the CCAMLR Area, lent considerable legitimacy to the claims of significant cheating within the CCAMLR system. It even went so far as to recommend that the Commission 'express its deep concern regarding the strong indication that large-scale fishing in contravention of the Conservation Measures in force is taking place in the CCAMLR Convention Area' and took the unusual step of reminding members of their obligations under the Convention to enforce CCAMLR measures against their nationals.[52]

Throughout the remainder of the 1990s, CCAMLR found itself embroiled in an escalating debate over the extent of the illegal and unreported fishing for toothfish and how to better contracting party compliance with its catch and conservation recommendations. The chief avenues to emerge include the observer scheme and the VMS system noted above as well as strengthening the powers of the Commission to deal with vessel access to the CCAMLR Area, particularly by compulsory licensing[53] and, most recently, a catch documentation scheme. The licensing scheme, which requires vessels to carry a CCAMLR licence to fish in any part of the CCAMLR Area, is essentially part of the regulatory effort in terms of its formal intent. Nevertheless, it also has significant potential compliance effect since the withdrawal of a valid licence, if enforced by the flag state, can impose a substantial loss of income from legal fishing. However, most of these developments progressed with a weather eye out for the un-regulated fishing of third parties as well as for the illegal and unreported catches of CCAMLR members. Thus, the following analysis looks to the further evolution of more effective compliance measures in the context of CCAMLR's relations with non-party fishing interests.

3 Unregulated fishing, the high seas, and inter-regime relations

The regional limitations of CCAMLR have been particularly exposed by the toothfish issue although the Antarctic body is not alone amongst regional fisheries agencies in having to deal with third party fishing.[54] Technically, vessels flagged in states that are not parties to the CCAMLR Convention are not 'poachers' of toothfish in areas regulated solely by CCAMLR measures but generally are engaged in what CCAMLR regards as unregulated fishing. Nevertheless, these vessels may be 'pirates', 'plun-derers', or 'poachers' by being in breach of other national or international regulations. However, it appears that many of the non-CCAMLR states that fish in the CCAMLR Area do comply with other international obli-gations such as the FAO reporting requirements; this, indeed, is often how their activities come to the notice of CCAMLR. Nevertheless, although not formally obliged to comply with CCAMLR regulations, third party vessels may voluntarily comply with the proclaimed Conservation Measures. It is in hope of securing just such voluntary compliance that CCAMLR members and the CCAMLR Secretariat regularly advise the governments of non-member states of the applicable regulations and invite them to join the Commission (or to comply with these measures from outside CCAMLR if necessary).[55]

As alarm over IUU fishing for the Patagonian toothfish deepened during the 1990s, the need to deal with the activities of vessels operating under flags of countries not party to CCAMLR also grew. Initially CCAMLR's interest focused on vessels owned by firms in CCAMLR member states but flagged in non-member states or, more contentiously, on vessels reflagged to such states in order to circumvent CCAMLR mea-sures. In such cases, the motivation of the firms of the involved vessels is significant because it is presumed that they will not report catches fully, if at all, even to the FAO, nor will they observe the basic environmental protection regulations of CCAMLR. While many within CCAMLR regard such companies and vessels as violating the spirit of the CCAMLR Con-vention, a recent attempt by New Zealand to obligate CCAMLR members to enforce compliance on 'nationals' was defeated through the reassertion of a preference for flag state authority in conformity with part 7 of the UN Law of the Sea Convention (1982).[56]

Countries such as Norway (which was particularly identified as involved with nationals operating out of third party states)[57] have apparently attempted to do something through national legislation,[58] but for CCAMLR collectively, the primary concern has been with reflagging. The principal countries providing flags of convenience for participation in the Patagonian toothfish fishery have been identified as Belize, Namibia, Panama, and Vanuatu, with another half-dozen or so countries involved at a lesser level.[59] Reflagging, however, is a global issue and thus beyond any regional solution that CCAMLR might propose. As a consequence, CCAMLR's primary focus has been on cooperation with another international organization with which it has had a long and fairly cooperative relationship—the FAO. CCAMLR recognizes the primacy of the FAO in this area and views FAO efforts to develop a register to monitor reflagged vessels as compatible with its own ultimate aim of securing effective control through the country of ownership or origin.[60]

The problem of a 'moral' default by nationals of CCAMLR members who use the protection of third parties is real enough, but this has been far from the only problem CCAMLR has sought to address regarding third parties and the Patagonian toothfish. The unregulated fishing of third parties, while permitted under the Law of the Sea Convention 1982, has posed significant difficulties for CCAMLR's ecological management approach. This would have been bad enough if the Patagonian toothfish had been confined to the CCAMLR Area, which it is not. From the moment the toothfish became a significant object of CCAMLR interest, the effects of fishing outside the CCAMLR Area on stocks within the Area was noted as a matter of management concern by the Scientific Committee.[61] Over the following years something closer to scientific evidence of the *Dissostichus eleginoides* being a straddling fish stock was presented. The 1992 meeting of the Scientific Committee raised the possibility that much of the stock from the South Atlantic across to the Indian Ocean shelves could be related, if not perhaps be a single stock.[62] Further research has produced some contradictory evidence on the degree to which the Patagonian toothfish stock might be singular, but separate stocks that clearly extend over wide areas have been identified.[63]

Nevertheless, despite some scientific evidence of significant relationships between the stocks of toothfish within the CCAMLR Area and those outside it, the fourteenth meeting of the Commission (1995) baulked at describing these as 'straddling stocks' and instead adopted the more cumbersome phrase 'stocks occurring both inside and outside the Convention Area'.[64] The Commission's difficulties were more than a problem of scientific fact or of semantic exactitude. Some members of the Commission preferred to avoid the political implications of a phrase that had recently acquired some potentially high-risk connotations for CCAMLR. Several months before the fourteenth Commission meeting, the UN Fish Stocks Agreement was opened for signature. This treaty, along with the 1993 FAO Compliance Agreement, raised both challenges and opportunities for CCAMLR by broadening coastal, flag, and port state jurisdiction in ways that could extend its influence beyond the formal regional boundaries and to non-party interests. While some CCAMLR members saw in these global developments an opportunity to improve toothfish management at the regional level, others feared an erosion of their own national positions.

The Fish Stocks Agreement included provisions for greater coastal state influence over adjacent high seas in consultation with other interested parties by imposing a duty on states fishing on the high seas to cooperate either directly or through regional management regimes. Parties to the Agreement that fail to become members of an existing regional regime and refuse to apply the conservation and management measures taken by that regime are denied access to the relevant fishery.[65] The Agreement also strengthens flag state responsibilities in ensuring compliance with regional conservation and management measures, and whether or not parties to the Agreement are members of a regional regime, they must accept boarding and inspection of their vessels in accordance with the procedures of that regime.[66] Article 23 includes port states in this duty to cooperate as well. Davor Vidas argues that this duty to cooperate strengthened CCAMLR's resolve to seek the direct involvement of states such as Mauritius and Namibia in CCAMLR activities.[67] Mauritius and Namibia were invited to attend the 1998 meeting in light of use of their ports by 'vessels implicated in illegal and unregulated fishing in the Convention Area'.[68] Both attended in 1998 and returned again in 1999. Namibia even went so far at the 1999 meeting as to announce its intention to accede to the CCAMLR Agreement and to seek full membership in the Commission.[69]

The relevance of the Fish Stocks Agreement to CCAMLR was pursued with considerable vigour by some members, in particular by Australia at several levels, as early as the fourteenth meeting (1995). The Standing Committee on Observation and Inspection discussed the possibilities of the Agreement's advancing CCAMLR enforcement aims, especially with regard to flag state duties and to building more effective observation and inspection schemes.[70] Japan and other members disagreed on the relevance of the Fish Stocks Agreement to the CCAMLR System of Inspection while other members raised concerns that the Fish Stocks Agreement extended coastal state influence over high seas areas.[71] The USA supported Australia in the SCOI on the latter point by referring back to the earlier occasions when CCAMLR had considered the harvesting of toothfish in terms very close to those of the Fish Stocks Agreement. In the end, Australia succeeded in having the text of the Fish Stocks Agreement circulated to all the members for consideration of its relevance to, and compatibility with, CCAMLR.[72]

When the SCOI Report was presented to the Commission plenum, the issues of the Fish Stocks Agreement and Antarctic straddling stocks took a dramatic new turn. The question of whether CCAMLR's System of Inspection was adequate without tying it to global agreements led Chile to complain that the issue of illegal fishing had been blown out of proportion. The real issue, Chile argued, was not to pursue more international regulatory possibilities but to secure a closer correspondence between national regulatory regimes and that of CCAMLR.[73] Argentina, in supporting Chile's views, went further to challenge the capacity of CCAMLR to act as an appropriate regional body for implementing the Fish Stocks Agreement arrangements when that agreement came into force. It asserted that CCAMLR was *not* a fisheries organization or commission but rather a conservation instrument.[74] The Argentine démarche caused considerable consternation amongst the bulk of the CCAMLR membership which accepted that CCAMLR was a conservation body but held that this was a broader inclusive term that incorporated its fisheries management responsibilities rather than an exclusive, parallel term that denied management activities. Throughout what appears to have been a fairly acrimonious debate, there was general consensus that the matter of effective enforcement of CCAMLR regulations was a genuine test of the value of CCAMLR as a regulating instrument and perhaps even of the ATS itself.[75]

This debate highlighted the reciprocal, if not always openly expressed, relationship between the question of sovereignty and the relevance of the Fish Stocks Agreement to CCAMLR. Many CCAMLR members take the view that a straddling stock is defined by both coastal state jurisdiction and adjacent high seas areas. According to the argument, without straddling stocks, there would be no question of applying the provisions of the Fish Stocks Agreement to the Southern Ocean or of CCAMLR being designated as an 'appropriate subregional or regional fisheries management organization' to assist in the implementation of the Agreement. Thus, it is held, without a coastal state there could be no straddling stock in the meaning of the Fish Stocks Agreement. However, the Fish Stocks Agreement itself does not define the term 'straddling stock' but rather relies on an implied definition in Article 63 of the 1982 Law of the Sea Convention. A commentary on this article maintains that the drafting of it did, indeed, revolve around a distinction between 'transboundary stocks' and 'straddling stocks', the latter involving both one or more exclusive economic zones and an adjacent high seas area.[76]

The implicit problem of sovereignty that some CCAMLR members read into pursuing the Fish Stocks Agreement option beset much of the organization's debates on securing effective compliance at its 1996 and 1997 meetings. The sovereignty problem was addressed directly under the rubric 'Consideration of the Implementation of the Objective of the Convention'. A paper by Chile served to open the 1996 debate and, by careful drafting, managed to canvass many of the key issues without seriously dividing the Commission. Chile's paper accepted the reality and the validity of sovereignty in meeting the objectives of CCAMLR but warned of the risks if national interests were to dominate at the expense of cooperation through CCAMLR.[77] The solution was to reconcile national laws with the objectives of CCAMLR, including the fractious vessel monitoring system issue that had so riven the 1995 meeting.[78] The European Community delegate agreed with many aspects of the paper but felt the new international legal order required CCAMLR 'to address urgently complex issues, *inter alia*, the possible harmonization of approach on straddling stocks, be they within or overlapping the Convention Area'.[79] Many defended the broader, inter-regime approach on the grounds of the risks to CCAMLR and the ATS if IUU fishing was not adequately policed.[80]

Despite the controversy over how relevant the Fish Stocks Agreement might prove to be formally once it entered into force, the sixteenth (1997) and seventeenth (1998) meetings worked within its spirit in pursuing more effective compliance measures. The sixteenth meeting approved one innovative Conservation Measure (118/XVI), which sought to use members' port state authority to monitor toothfish catches and enforce regulations against ships flying the flags of non-contracting parties. The same Measure also sought to use the same authority to monitor and limit trans-shipments. The 1998 CCAMLR Meeting had to amend this Measure to deal with some difficulties with non-contracting parties, but the port state approach to compliance remained salient at the 1999 meeting.[81] As noted above, this approach included seeking to associate more directly some important non-contracting port states with the objectives of CCAMLR and so to extend the reach of this measure.

The growing weight of the IUU fishing issue continued to erode opposition to regulation for more effective compliance within CCAMLR. The seventeenth meeting (1998) achieved a major breakthrough on one of the most contentious compliance issues within the organization—that of requiring all licensed fishing vessels to carry a VMS tracking device. The sustained resistance to this measure (148/XVII) was evident in the monitoring system's limitations. Members were allowed considerable latitude in setting their own pace for implementation (from 1 March 1999 to 31 December 2000), and vessels taking only krill were exempted.[82] Nevertheless, an effective VMS system would not only hugely strengthen CCAMLR's capacity to surveil its own ambit of operations but would also open the door to monitoring fishing in areas adjacent to the Convention Area. After considering this prospect, the Commission offered a recommendation that members pursue the possibility.[83] The value of the VMS scheme would be enhanced by the establishment of a CCAMLR vessel register as proposed by Australia at the same meeting, but the prospect of being able to impose sanctions on vessels through the mechanism of de-listing from such a register was deemed to require further examination.[84]

The concern over the sustainability of the toothfish, indeed, reached such an intense level by the 1998 meeting that CCAMLR was willing to explore even fairly novel measures to secure compliance. Perhaps the most important will prove to be the proposal for adding economic sanctions to the CCAMLR armoury through adoption of a catch documentation scheme which would track the landings and trade flows of *Dissostichus* from the Convention Area.[85] The possibilities were so exciting that an increasingly budget-conscious CCAMLR agreed to an intersessional meeting to progress the prospect as a matter of urgency. The intersessional meeting blended offerings from the USA, Australia, and the European Community to craft a practical and effective scheme that would allow member states to deny access to their markets to fish that had not been caught in compliance with CCAMLR conservation measures. The path-breaking measure (170/XVIII) was passed speedily by the eighteenth meeting despite concern in some quarters that this measure might breach WTO trade discrimination guidelines. The catch documentation scheme provides, *inter alia*, that a contracting party take steps to determine the origin of imported or exported *Dissostichus* and, if the fish is taken inside the Convention Area, to determine whether this has occurred in conformity with CCAMLR conservation measures. A contracting party should also require that vessels flying its flag, and any other vessel landing *Dissostichus* in its ports or trans-shipping it to its vessels, submit a completed *Dissostichus* catch document upon landing or trans-shipment. Moreover, such catch documents, certified by a responsible official of the exporting state, should be required for every shipment of *Dissostichus* imported into the territory of a contracting party.[86]

Given that the primary destination for *Dissostichus* is the markets of CCAMLR members, a properly enforced catch documentation scheme offers a substantial, albeit negative, economic incentive for compliance even by non-contracting parties. Yet the scheme also seeks to encourage non-contracting parties positively by allowing cooperating states to issue catch documents to its flag vessels to enable their catches to enter member state markets if properly harvested. Significantly, the scheme does not raise the issue of sovereignty, which has caused so much consternation with the remedy offered by the Fish Stocks Agreement.

4 CCAMLR and the future of toothfish management

There can be little doubt that the Patagonian toothfish issue is as real as it is obdurate. Indeed, the problems of effective toothfish management have in a few short years pushed CCAMLR to the edge of a rather significant institutional precipice. However, the substantive importance of this fishery alone cannot explain the gravity of CCAMLR's situation at the threshold of the twenty-first century. In different circumstances, it is unlikely that this fishery would have raised such strong passions. Had other fisheries within the CCAMLR Area remained viable at historic levels, the issues raised by *Dissostichus* fisheries might have assumed a less relative importance within CCAMLR. The main reason why the Patagonian toothfish issue has reached such proportions in recent years is that it exposes unpleasant problems with regard to CCAMLR's primary mechanism for compliance—flag state enforcement—at a rather unpropitious time in global fisheries management. The collapse of fisheries elsewhere in the world, the loss of previously established fisheries in the Southern Ocean, greater global regulation of fisheries and the environment, and new post-Cold War order priorities, *inter alia*, have focused extraordinary attention on this fishery. Unfortunately for CCAMLR, such intense scrutiny has been given to one of the most geographically marginal of CCAMLR's fisheries. Because the toothfish is widely dispersed along the entire periphery of the Convention Area, the possibility of national regimes as well as the regional regime of CCAMLR is opened to at least some fisheries managers. In addition, since 1995, coastal states have the Fish Stocks Agreement looming on their immediate diplomatic horizon as a basis for strengthening their claims to protect the stocks of *Dissostichus* in the waters adjacent to their EEZs. To date, no coastal state member of CCAMLR has officially foreshadowed that it will proclaim the Patagonian toothfish a straddling stock, but two members, Australia and South Africa, are known to be investigating this option. Thus all three levels of regime management of fisheries—national, regional, and global—have come into the political arena with regard to the toothfish.

At the regional level, the prospect of the Fish Stocks Agreement has posed new and awkward questions in inter-regime relations for CCAMLR. Certain factors have created special concern in various quarters of CCAMLR: uncertainties as to its implications for tipping the balance between flag and coastal state influence over the toothfish fishery; the application of 'high seas' principles below 60 degrees south latitude; and the designation of CCAMLR as an appropriate regional fisheries organization. Since those most in favour of the relevance of the Fish Stocks Agreement to CCAMLR come from the ranks of coastal states, there may be grounds for the natural suspicion of other members that the Fish Stocks Agreement enhances the position of coastal states. However, events have moved far more quickly for toothfish management than for the Fish Stocks Agreement. The urgency of developing and enforcing an effective management regime for the toothfish has served to reduce the significance of the Fish Stocks Agreement in regional management. The Agreement has yet to enter into force and many supporters within CCAMLR now appear to feel that, even if the problems of coastal state jurisdiction could be surmounted, the rate of ratification is too slow.

It is nevertheless arguable that the Fish Stocks Agreement has already helped to progress the efforts for effective toothfish management across the Southern Ocean and in relevant, adjacent high seas areas outside the CCAMLR Area. If nothing else, exploration of the benefits of the Fish Stocks Agreement has worked to advance the promotion of port state responsibilities within CCAMLR despite the strong preference for maintaining flag state authority amongst many of CCAMLR's members. This development has in turn assisted the rapid acceptance of the catch documentation scheme upon which so many hopes now rest for securing both contracting party and non-contracting party compliance with CCAMLR's management objectives. When the Fish Stocks Agreement comes into force, it may yet also prove useful as a direct mechanism for some members with undisputed coastal state jurisdiction. However, despite the potential benefits for CCAMLR in dealing with third parties, the complexities of applying the Agreement in CCAMLR's high seas areas seem likely to defeat its wider usage.

As circumstances now stand, any effective management of the Patagonian toothfish will be located essentially within CCAMLR; however, it will be a CCAMLR that has learned greatly from past experiences and profited from recent international fisheries developments such as the adoption of the Fish Stocks Agreement and the FAO Compliance Agreement. It will also be a CCAMLR that is less naive regarding the problems of securing compliance from its own members and its dependence on national authorities for implementation. Perhaps the ultimate lesson of the CCAMLR's toothfish conundrum is that the increasingly regional processes for managing far-flung fisheries will require integration into the broader global framework to be truly effective.

Notes

While sole responsibility rests with the author, thanks for comments on earlier drafts of this chapter are due to David Agnew, John Croxall, Robert Hall, Eve Richards, Eugene Sabourenkov, Olav Schram Stokke, and Davor Vidas.

1. For examples: see 'Antarctic Treaty Meeting Aims to Protect Toothfish Stocks', *Canberra Times* (30 May 1997), 5; 'British, French Warships on Alert to Net Toothfish Poachers', *Sydney Morning Herald* (2 May 1997), 12; and A. Darby, 'Pirates Plundering Southern Fisheries', *Sydney Morning Herald* (3 May 1997), 15.
2. While this point is routinely made by NGOs, it has increasingly been made by ATS members themselves; see, for example, CCAMLR, *Report of the Seventeenth Meeting of the Commission* (Hobart, 1998), 81.
3. The Convention was adopted in 1980; 19 *ILM* 837; the acronym CCAMLR is used both for the Convention and for the Commission set up by it. Context should make clear whether this acronym is referring to the Convention or to the Commission.
4. Agreement for the Implementation of the Provisions of the United Nations Convention on the Law of the Sea of 10 December 1982 relating to the Conservation and Management of Straddling Fish Stocks and Highly Migratory Fish Stocks (1995); 34 *ILM* 1547.
5. V. V. Zhivov and V. M. Krivoruchko, 'On the Biology of the Patagonian Toothfish, *Dissostichus eleginoides*, of the Antarctic Part of the Atlantic', *Journal of Ichthyology*, 30/7 (1990), 142–5; and T. Stone and D. Johnson, 'Fishing in the Freezer . . . Australia's sub-Antarctic fisheries', *Professional Fisherman* (20 June 1997), 19.
6. For more on the commercially relevant biology of the toothfish, G. Album, 'The Patagonian Toothfish and Norwegian Interests', *Norges Naturvernforbund Report*, 3 (Oslo: Norwegian Society for the Conservation of Nature/Friends of the Earth Norway, 1997).
7. CCAMLR, *Report of the Ninth Meeting of the Scientific Committee* (Hobart, 1990), 180 and CCAMLR, *Report of the Tenth Meeting of the Scientific Committee* (1990), 218.
8. A. Darby, 'War in a Cold Climate', *Sydney Morning Herald* (10 June 1997), 15.
9. Associated Press, 'British, French Warships on Alert to Net Toothfish Poachers', *Sydney Morning Herald* (2 May 1997), 12.
10. 'Antarctic Treaty Meeting Aims to Protect Toothfish Stocks', *Canberra Times* (30 May 1997), 5.
11. 'The Involvement of Mauritius in the Trade in Patagonian Toothfish from Illegal and Unregulated Longline Fishing in the Southern Ocean', *Occasional Report*, 1, 3rd edn. (Hobart: ISOFISH, 1998).
12. Despite the fact that Macquarie Island is an Australian possession under the jurisdiction of the state of Tasmania, it is commonly depicted in the national media as being subject to CCAMLR regulations, a confusion undoubtedly fostered by the presence of an Antarctic research station on the island.

13. B. W. Davis, 'The Legitimacy of CCAMLR', in O. S. Stokke and D. Vidas (eds.), *Governing the Antarctic* (Cambridge University Press, 1996), 238–9; see also the discussion below on the 1980 CCAMLR Chairman's Statement.

14. CCAMLR, *Statistical Bulletin*, 9 [1987–96] (Hobart: CCAMLR, 1997), 19; and *FAO Yearbook: Fishery Statistics; Catches and Landings*, 80 (1995), 124.

15. CCAMLR, *Statistical Bulletin*, 9 [1987–96], 19.

16. The twenty-three members of CCAMLR's Commission are: Argentina, Australia, Belgium, Brazil, Chile, European Union, France, Germany, India, Italy, Japan, Korea (South), New Zealand, Norway, Poland, Russia, South Africa, Spain, Sweden, Ukraine, UK, USA, and Uruguay. Bulgaria, Canada, Finland, Greece, the Netherlands, and Peru are parties to the CCAMLR Convention but not members of the Commission.

17. For a general discussion of compliance in CCAMLR, see O. S. Stokke, 'The Effectiveness of CCAMLR', in Stokke and Vidas (eds.), *Governing the Antarctic*, 148–50.

18. This consensual aspect of the Commission's decision-making is regarded by some of its members as a particularly useful mechanism for circumventing the tendency of consensus politics to produce lowest common denominator outcomes. The opt-out clause enables states to allow policies that they will not apply to their own vessels or waters to be carried by the majority. On the other hand, states that do not object presumably have fewer grounds subsequently for complaint since they could have used the opt-out provision if they were unwilling to accept the measure.

19. For an example, see Chile's explanation for its own internal difficulties in this regard in CCAMLR, *Report of the Thirteenth Meeting of the Commission* (1994), 15–16.

20. CCAMLR routinely seeks non-member information on fishing in the CCAMLR Area and/or for support of its regulations. For examples, see: CCAMLR, *Report of the Tenth Meeting of the Commission* (1991), 35–6; and CCAMLR, *Report of the Fourteenth Meeting of the Commission* (1995), 8.

21. There are many reasons for CCAMLR leadership but, in global fishing terms, the Patagonian toothfish fishery could be counted a very small issue. Even allowing for the unreported harvests, it accounts for a minuscule fraction of 1% of the global catch. United Nations, Food and Agriculture Organization, *FAO Yearbook: Fishery Statistics; Catches and Landings*, 80 (1995), 89 and 124 suggested a figure of about 0.05 of 1% of the global marine catch well after the start of the toothfish 'rush'.

22. CCAMLR, *Report of the Eleventh Meeting of the Commission* (1992), 16–17 and 43–4. The details of the incidental mortality of albatrosses caused by longlining in the Southern Ocean can be found in G. C. Robertson and R. P. Gales (eds.), *Albatross Biology and Conservation* (Chipping Norton, New South Wales: Surrey Beatty, 1998).

23. CCAMLR, *Report of the Eleventh Meeting of the Commission*, 32.

24. Ibid. 37.

25. Conservation Measures 40/X, 51/XII, 61/XII, and 122/XVI.

26. CCAMLR, *Report of the Twelfth Meeting of the Scientific Committee* (1993), 26.

27. CCAMLR, *Report of the Thirteenth Meeting of the Commission*, 48; CCAMLR, *Report of the Fourteenth Meeting of the Commission*, 57–8; and CCAMLR, *Report of the Fifteenth Meeting of the Commission* (1996), 70–2.

28. CCAMLR, *Report of the Fourteenth Meeting of the Commission*, 11.

29. Ibid. There was a feeling in some South African quarters that the continuing and rapid extension of the toothfish effort to the east may well have been encouraged, in part, by South Africa's public expressions of interest in developing its southern EEZ and, concomitantly, more effectively enforcing its coastal state jurisdiction.

30. CCAMLR, *Report of the Fifteenth Meeting of the Scientific Committee* (1996), 313.

31. The current details for this scheme are given in CCAMLR, *Schedule of Conservation Measures in Force 1999/2000* (Hobart: Nov. 1999), 97–9. Although basically intended to gather scientific data, the presence of scientific observers added additional eyes to CCAMLR's enforcement capacity, especially from 1998 when these observers were allowed to report vessel sightings as well as their scientific observations.

32. For details of this system see CCAMLR, *Schedule of Conservation Measures in Force 1999/2000*, 91–4.

33. CCAMLR, *Report of the Seventeenth Meeting of the Commission*, 19.

34. See in general Robertson and Gales, *Albatross Biology and Conservation*.

35. J. R. Ashford, J. P. Croxall, P. S. Rubilar, and C. A. Moreno, 'Seabird Interactions with Longlining Operations for *Dissostichus eleginoides* around the South Sandwich Islands and South Georgia', *CCAMLR Science*, 1 (1994), 143–54; and J. R. Ashford, J. P. Croxall, P. S. Rubilar, and C. A. Moreno, 'Seabird Interactions with Longlining Operations for *Dissostichus eleginoides* around South Georgia, April to May 1994', *CCAMLR Science*, 2 (1995), 111–22.

36. CCAMLR, *Report of the Twelfth Meeting of the Commission* (1993), 8; and CCAMLR, *Statistical Bulletin*, 9 [1987–96], 19–20.

37. CCAMLR, *Report of the Fifteenth Meeting of the Commission*, 7.

38. CCAMLR, *Statistical Bulletin*, 9 [1987–96], 19–20.

39. New and expanded quotas were a particularly noteworthy feature of the Commission's 15th meeting coming a year after the spectacular revelations of non-compliance the previous year; see CCAMLR, *Report of the Fifteenth Meeting of the Commission*, 53, 61, and 66–9.

40. CCAMLR, *Report of the Thirteenth Meeting of the Commission*, 40–1. Interestingly, however, this was not declared to be a 'new fishery' and thus not subject to all the preliminary (and thus, precautionary) research that otherwise would have been required. Moreover, Australia did not seek a further precautionary limit the next year.

41. CCAMLR, *Report of the Tenth Meeting of the Commission*, 27.

42. Ibid. 27–8.

43. Ibid. 25–6.

44. CCAMLR, *Fish the Sea Not the Sky: How to Avoid By-catch of Seabirds When Fishing with Bottom Longlines* (Hobart: CCAMLR, 1996).

45. Ibid. 41–2.

46. Norway has not yet taken steps to declare exclusive economic zones around Bouvetøya, however.

47. CCAMLR, *Report of the Fourteenth Meeting of the Commission*, 71–4.
48. For example, of the sixteen sightings by the UK of vessels believed to be in violation of CCAMLR regulations from Dec. 1994 to Feb. 1996, nine were of Argentine and Chilean vessels. Personal communication, United Kingdom, Foreign and Commonwealth Office (2 Oct. 1997).
49. Ibid. The 1980 Chairman's Statement is the same mechanism used by France from the beginning to exempt the Crozet and Kerguelen Islands from automatic application of CCAMLR's Conservation Measures and employed more recently by South Africa to claim exemption for Prince Edward and Marion Islands. The Chairman's Statement is reproduced in the *Handbook of the Antarctic Treaty System*, 8th edn. (Washington: US Department of State, 1994), 176.
50. Personal communication, United Kingdom, Foreign and Commonwealth Office (2 Oct. 1997).
51. Although not specified as an overt concern, CCAMLR records indicated that the Soviet Union may have exceeded the quota in Statistical Subarea 48.3 in this year by more than 1,000 metric tons. Compare Conservation Measure 24/IX with the reported catch in CCAMLR, *Statistical Bulletin*, 9 [1987–96], 53.
52. CCAMLR, *Report of the Thirteenth Meeting of the Commission*, 107.
53. The introduction of a licensing measure in 1998 (Conservation Measure 119/XVII) was intended to ensure that CCAMLR had its own regulations in order to fortify the hand of contracting flag states in controlling their own vessels operating in the CCAMLR Area.
54. D. Vidas, 'Emerging Law of the Sea Issues in the Antarctic Marine Area: A Heritage for the New Century?', *Ocean Development and International Law*, 31 (2000), 201.
55. For a recent example of this interaction between SCOI and the Commission on the activities of non-members in the CCAMLR Area, see CCAMLR, *Report of the Fourteenth Meeting of the Commission*, 125–6.
56. CCAMLR, *Report of the Seventeenth Meeting of the Commission*, 22.
57. G. Album, 'The Patagonian Toothfish and Norwegian Interests' and 'The Vikings: The Involvement of Norway in Illegal and Unregulated Longline Fishing for Patagonian Toothfish in the Southern Ocean', *ISOFISH Occasional Report*, 3 (1998).
58. Some of Norway's efforts to deal with IUU fishing at a national level are given in CCAMLR, *Report of the Eighteenth Meeting of the Commission* (1999), 15.
59. Vidas, 'Emerging Law of the Sea Issues in the Antarctic Marine Area', 201.
60. CCAMLR's cooperative inter-regime relationship with the FAO includes *inter alia* support for the FAO's 'Code of Responsible Fishing' and working toward more compatible statistics.
61. CCAMLR, *Report of the Ninth Meeting of the Scientific Committee*, 26.
62. CCAMLR, *Report of the Eleventh Meeting of the Scientific Committee* (1992), 218–20.
63. CCAMLR, *Report of the Thirteenth Meeting of the Scientific Committee* (1994), 143.
64. CCAMLR, *Report of the Fourteenth Meeting of the Commission*, 57–8.
65. Fish Stocks Agreement, Art. 8 (3) and (4).
66. Ibid., Arts. 17–22. A more detailed discussion is given by Vukas and Vidas, Ch. 2, and Hønneland, Ch. 4 above.

67. Vidas, 'Emerging Law of the Sea Issues in the Antarctic Marine Area', 203.
68. Ibid. 12.
69. CCAMLR, *Report of the Eighteenth Meeting of the Commission*, para. 2.8. It should be noted that the participation of the two non-contracting states at the 1998 meeting encouraged CCAMLR to invite virtually all the states providing flags of convenience for *Dissostichus* fishing to attend the 1999 meeting. While only Denmark attended on behalf of the Faroe Islands, Vanuatu sent advice that it too would be acceding to the Convention. Ibid., paras. 2.4 and 2.10.
70. CCAMLR, *Report of the Fourteenth Meeting of the Commission*, 126.
71. Ibid. 126–7.
72. Ibid. 127.
73. Ibid. 22–3.
74. Ibid. 23.
75. Ibid. 21–4. NGO criticism along this line has persisted to the present as a lever against CCAMLR inaction on effective toothfish management; see, for example, 'Time to Get Real', *ECO* 138/4 (Hobart: Friends of the Earth Australia, 5 Nov. 1998).
76. S. N. Nandan and S. Rosenne (eds.), *The United Nations Convention on the Law of the Sea 1982: A Commentary*, ii (Dordecht: Martinus Nijhoff, 1993), 640.
77. Private comments on Chile's paper, however, criticized its failure to emphasize and reinforce the obligations of the organization's members to meet fully their flag state commitments to and through CCAMLR; commitments which would minimize coastal state concerns on compliance, it was felt.
78. CCAMLR, *Report of the Fifteenth Meeting of the Commission*, 78–9.
79. Ibid. 79.
80. Ibid. 79–81.
81. CCAMLR, *Schedule of Conservation Measures in Force 1999/2000*, 19.
82. CCAMLR, *Report of the Seventeenth Meeting of the Commission*, 47.
83. Ibid. 19–20.
84. The vessel register proposal was still under active review in 2000. CCAMLR, *Report of the Eighteenth Meeting of the Commission*, 21.
85. CCAMLR, *Report of the Seventeenth Meeting of the Commission*, 17–18.
86. CCAMLR, *Report of the Eighteenth Meeting of the Commission*, 129–34 sets out the details of this scheme.

Conclusions

OLAV SCHRAM STOKKE

The challenge facing high seas fisheries management is a familiar one: governance without government. Despite the introduction of exclusive economic zones, fish stocks of considerable commercial value straddle beyond national waters and into the high seas. Because of rising over-capacity in the world's fisheries, such stocks are followed with great interest by operators of distant water fishing fleets. In many cases, however, the high seas harvesting of straddling stocks has been perceived by coastal states as illegitimate and also as undermining of conservation efforts in national zones. Distant water fishing nations counter that governance of high seas fisheries is not an exclusive coastal state concern. In the absence of clear rules about who should participate in straddling stocks management and how it should be conducted, accommodation of such opposing views has been attempted through a host of regional negotiation processes during the 1990s. The level of conflict has been very high in some of these processes, and there have been fears that the problems of straddling stocks would yield unilateral coastal state action of a nature that might even undermine the legitimacy of the Law of the Sea Convention.[1] A particularly interesting feature of those regional processes is the way they influenced, and were shaped by, the parallel negotiation of a UN Fish Stocks Agreement.[2]

This concluding chapter has two ambitions. First, framed by the changes in the global high seas fisheries regime recorded in Part I of this book, it comparatively reviews the six regional efforts to govern straddling stocks fisheries canvassed in Part II. Special attention is paid to identifying the conditions that have furthered effective management. Second, and based on this regional review, the concept of regime interplay is elaborated and used to explain whether and how such interplay effects the operation and effectiveness of resource management regimes.

1 Providing governance of high seas fisheries

Throughout this book, the governance problem confronted in straddling stock issues is laid out as providing adequate means for handling three major management problems: (1) the generation of adequate and reasonably consensual scientific knowledge that will provide the basis for informed judgements on whether the exploitation of resources shall be conducted, and if so, in what manner; (2) the need for managers to adopt legitimate and adequate regulatory measures for governing the economic activity in question while taking heed of such knowledge (in the case of living resources, this includes effort or capacity controls as well as operational restrictions such as catch quotas and closed areas); and (3) the maintenance of a system that can elicit compliance with existing conservation and management measures among users of the resource.

A prominent feature of the Fish Stocks Agreement is an emphasis on regional or subregional management regimes that involve both coastal and other user states as the preferred means for dealing with cases of straddling stocks.[3] The broad obligation to cooperate on management of straddling stocks laid down in the 1982 Convention is considerably strengthened by the provision that only states that are members of such a regime or agree to apply the conservation and management measures taken under the regime shall have access to the relevant fishery.[4] The Agreement does, however, allow substantial leeway regarding the exact form of cooperation—namely the requirement to cooperate 'either directly or through appropriate subregional or regional fisheries management organizations or arrangements'.[5] The permissiveness of this formulation should come as no surprise, as the operational structure of fisheries management regimes is often hotly contested. Two broad approaches can be distinguished, based on whether decision-making is bilateral or multilateral.

In *bilateralist* regimes, overall conservation and management measures are taken by the coastal states; examples are the arrangements for cod in the Barents Sea Loophole and pollock in the Sea of Okhotsk Peanut Hole, the coastal states being Norway and Russia. Other user states, or some of them, are tied to these measures by means of bilateral agreements drawn up in annual negotiations. This implies a measure of influence on at least one aspect of management—the allocation of quotas. Thus, bilateralist regimes are not only dyadic in their mode of coordination but more importantly they differentiate participants on a case-by-case basis depending on their strategic position towards a dominant player.[6] The glue of this type of arrangements is typically the preparedness of the coastal state to grant non-littoral state access to its own exclusive economic zone as remuneration for keeping high seas activities within the agreed bounds.

Under *regionalist* regimes, broader decision-making fora are established that involve most or all user states.[7] It can be useful to distinguish between two versions: restricted fora where participation is deliberately limited to a rather small number of states and fora that are conditionally open to any state prepared to accept certain prescribed commitments.[8] The Fish Stocks Agreement provides that the terms for participation in a regional management regime shall not exclude states that have a real interest in the fisheries concerned.[9] This corresponds to the strengthened duty of flag states to cooperate with the coastal state and other user states. The question remains, however, of what constitutes a 'real interest'. Some commentators have interpreted this restrictively as the conduct of actual and significant fishing operations in the region, whereas others see in this provision a clear instruction that coastal states cannot exclude interested newcomers from participation in regional management regimes.[10] It seems to support the former interpretation that the formulation was more restrictive in the Agreement than in the penultimate April 1995 draft; the latter provided that the management regime shall be open to all states 'having an interest' in the fisheries concerned.[11]

Among the multilateral regimes discussed in this book, three have restrictive terms for entry, but all involve the full range of present users. New accessions to the convention that established the 1980 North-East Atlantic Fisheries Commission (NEAFC), which is central to the management of oceanic redfish in the region, can only occur with the approval of three-quarters of the existing contracting parties, whereas unanimous approval is required by the 1994 Doughnut Hole Convention.[12] While not formalized, a similar barrier to entry exists in the 1996 North-East Atlantic herring arrangement in that access to annual multilateral negotiations on overall quota divisions is in practice limited to coastal states governing zones that are straddled by this stock. Note that the annual multilateral quota agreement, which is subsequently endorsed by NEAFC, is also accompanied by a cluster of bilateral accords that ensure reciprocal access to national waters.[13]

For its part, the Convention on the Conservation of Antarctic Marine Living Resources (CCAMLR), nested in the broader Antarctic cooperation, is open to any state prepared to accept requirements that are somewhat lenient. Membership in CCAMLR only requires that the party be interested in harvesting or scientific investigations in the region.[14] Also conditionally open is the regime centred on the Northwest Atlantic Fisheries Organization (NAFO), which allows accession to the decision-making body by any state interested in conducting fisheries in the region.[15]

The interplay of these regional management regimes and the global high seas regime is examined below by posing the question: do prominent substantive and operational provisions of the Fish Stocks Agreement enable more effective regional management of high seas fisheries?

2 Implementing the Fish Stocks Agreement

The three major tasks of fisheries management are closely interrelated. There is much to suggest, for instance, that agreed regulative measures well based in consensual scientific assessment stand a higher chance of being loyally enforced by the governments involved. For analytical purposes, however, it can be useful to deal with these tasks separately when discussing the extent to which the Fish Stocks Agreement and the operational structure of regional regimes serve to facilitate effective management of straddling stocks.

2.1 The science problem

There are two sides to the science aspect of management: the generation of high-quality, consensual assessment of stock dynamics and the translation of such knowledge to practical management advice that is incorporated into the decision-making process. The Law of the Sea Convention provides that high seas conservation measures shall be based 'on the best scientific evidence available to the States concerned' (Article 119). This provision is reiterated in the Fish Stocks Agreement, which adds more specific obligations regarding the collection and exchange of scientific data, including cooperative specification of format, compilation techniques, and assessment methodologies.[16]

Provisions to this effect are also found in most regional management regimes that address straddling stocks, whatever their differences in openness or mode of decision-making. Some regimes, like the one centred on NAFO in the Northwest Atlantic, have established separate scientific advisory bodies. Such bodies are generally meant to provide stable fora for scientific exchange and network building and to facilitate the credible imputation of advice into the decision-making process.[17] For instance, when intra-NAFO relations, especially between Canada and the European Community, soured in the mid-1980s, the parties looked to the NAFO Scientific Council to shed light on the parameters of disagreement; advice was in particular sought on the appropriateness of managing the various Northern cod components as a single unit and the proportion of the biomass found on average and seasonally within and beyond Canada's EEZ.[18]

While NAFO as well as the regional regimes that are based on the CCAMLR and the Doughnut Hole Convention are furnished with separate scientific advisory bodies, this is not the only effective way of meeting the scientific tasks of management. The NEAFC, for instance, relies on an external organization, the International Council for the Exploration of the Sea (ICES), to coordinate relevant scientific investigations and provide management advice. ICES also provides scientific input to the Norwegian–Russian Fisheries Commission and the arrangements for management of herring, redfish, and mackerel in the North-East Atlantic.[19] In some cases, such reliance on external coordination can help guard scientific problem-solving against difficult political issues among regime members. For instance, because Russia does not acknowledge Norwegian management authority in the zone around Svalbard, Russian fishermen are instructed not to report their catches in that zone to the Norwegian Coast Guard.[20] This is not an obstacle to scientific cooperation, however, as data on Russian catches in the Svalbard zone are made readily available through the multilateral ICES framework. Similarly, data on Icelandic Loophole harvests were available for scientific purposes through ICES even before this state became part of the Loophole arrangement.

Consider in contrast the way the scientific challenge has been dealt with in the Sea of Okhotsk, where harvesting is governed by Russian regulations, in tandem with bilateral accords between the coastal state and the various distant water fishing nations, including Japan, Poland, China, and the Republic of Korea. No institutionalized multilateral scientific cooperation similar to the arrangements found in NAFO or CCAMLR is built into this arrangement. Nor are there firm linkages to regional bodies for scientific cooperation that are comparable to ICES. The North Pacific Marine Science Organization (PICES), established in 1992, has so far not been assigned advisory tasks by any of the fisheries management bodies in the region.[21] From an effectiveness point of view, a non-inclusive scientific process makes recommendations vulnerable to criticism by states not taking part in their provision. In 1993, Poland, the Republic of Korea, and China rejected proposals for a three-year moratorium in the Peanut Hole; they argued that such a measure would be insufficiently grounded in scientific evidence.[22]

To summarize, the Fish Stocks Agreement confirms the duty to base regulation on scientific advice—and this requirement can be met effectively in several ways. There is scanty support for concluding that it is better to approach the scientific problem by organizing it within the regional regime than by relying on external or wider frameworks, as has been done in the North-East Atlantic region. Indeed, as shown in the Barents Sea Loophole, such linkages to broader institutions can even serve to insulate scientific cooperation from conflicts among regime members or ensure scientific inputs from newcomers that are not integrated in a regional regime. Of the management regimes discussed here, only the Sea of Okhotsk case lacks multilateral cooperation in the science area, and it was noted that for a period this impeded regional management efforts.

2.2 *Compatible conservation measures*

A major requirement for obtaining compatibility between conservation measures that regulate harvesting inside national waters and those that address adjacent high seas areas is that all significant user states acknowledge the high seas measures that are agreed to. One might expect that the operational structure of management regimes is relevant to the regime's ability to attract broad membership. The argument would be that multilateral regimes provide greater incentives for participation than bilateralist regimes and thus make it more difficult to justify unregulated harvesting; this is specifically the case when multilateral regimes invite a broader set of users to participate in the rule-making.[23]

It is certainly true that the bilateralist regimes' achievement of adequate user coverage has proved both cumbersome and time-consuming. In the case of the Sea of Okhotsk, it required four years from the commencement of international negotiations until all bilateral agreements were in place, and Iceland's entry to the Barents Sea Loophole arrangement in 1999 followed six years of unsuccessful negotiations. In both instances, the factor that ensured non-coastal state acceptance of bilateralism was greater attractiveness of quotas inside national waters. Yet reaching high user coverage for conservation measures has proven just as difficult in regionalist regimes. In the Southern Ocean, harvesting by vessels that fail to acknowledge the conservation measures that have been agreed to under the multilateral regional regime makes compatibility unreachable. During the 1996–7 season, more than a hundred vessels were reportedly engaged in unregulated fishing for toothfish inside the CCAMLR area with an estimated catch of some ten times the harvest reported by CCAMLR members.[24] In addition, significant harvesting occurs beyond the CCAMLR area. The same situation has pertained in the Northwest Atlantic. In 1985, the European Community made use of NAFO's objection procedure regarding a moratorium on high seas harvesting of cod and set its own unilateral quota—a practice reiterated in subsequent years and extended to other stocks as well. Such unilateral quotas form part of the explanation for the sweeping resource crisis that struck the region by the turn of the decade.[25]

It would be a mistake, moreover, to focus only on distant water fishing nations when addressing barriers to compatible conservation measures. Whereas national regulations can be undermined by inadequate high seas rules, the opposite is also true. The coastal state's preparedness to accept stricter commitments regarding their management of the same stock inside the EEZ is often a political requirement for reaching agreement on high seas measures. Such acceptance of international premisses in the management of national waters can be difficult to obtain because coastal states tend to perceive extensive foreign participation as encroaching upon their sovereign rights in the EEZ. Fortunately, there are ways to overcome this sovereignty barrier to compatible measures. Whereas the convention regulating pollock fisheries in the Doughnut Hole applies only to international waters, a legally non-binding but politically compelling Record of Discussions ensures an acceptable level of compatibility with measures taken inside the EEZs of the coastal states.[26] In response to requests by the distant water fishing nations, the United States and Russia recognized the need for compatible measures inside their zones, including a prohibition on harvesting on the Aleutian Basin stock as long as the Doughnut Hole moratorium is in place. Should the agreed moratorium be lifted, the coastal states have agreed to limit harvesting within their zones on the Aleutian Basin stock 'to an appropriate level'.[27]

The sovereignty challenge to compatibility is even more complex in the management of Southern Ocean toothfish; the CCAMLR area includes not only high seas areas and undisputed national waters but also areas where national claims are either disputed or non-recognized beyond the small group of Antarctic claimants, or both. This delicate legal situation has made regime members particularly concerned about ensuring that the procedure of reaching agreement on conservation measures, and the applicability of these rules in the various jurisdictional zones in the Southern Ocean, do not affect the balance between claimants and non-claimants in Antarctic politics.[28] As in the case of the Doughnut Hole, a solution had to be sought outside of the legal instrument that underpins the regime. The so-called 'Chairman's Statement' to the Conference that adopted the Convention stipulates that as long as states with non-disputed possessions, such as Kerguelen, Crozet, and other sub-Antarctic islands, do not object to the applicability of CCAMLR measures in their national waters adjacent to those possessions, they are bound by these measures but also free to adopt and enforce stricter measures.[29]

In summary, the regional cases reviewed in this book do not confirm the expectation that open regimes are better placed than restricted regimes with respect to ensuring adequate user coverage of high seas conservation measures, which is a first requirement for compatibility. Instead, as evidenced in both of the bilateralist cases and also regarding the North-East Atlantic herring arrangement, the decisive factor for realizing compatibility appears to be preparedness on the part of the coastal states to grant quotas in national waters in return for user state concessions regarding high seas measures. The only regime discussed here where compatibility has been realized without quotas being granted in national waters is the Doughnut Hole case, and this occurred only after the complete collapse of the pollock stock. A further impediment to compatibility is the coastal states' insistence on complete management authority inside national waters, which can sometimes be circumvented by informal and diversionary exercises that aim to establish politically credible commitments relating to the management of national waters without affecting legal positions on sovereignty.

2.3 The precautionary approach

The precautionary approach to fisheries management calls for particular care when information about the stock in question is uncertain, unreliable, or inadequate;[30] the risk of fishing mortality exceeding the level that can produce maximum sustainable yield must be very low.[31] The restraint required here is highly demanding in terms of decision-making strength—and presumably particularly difficult to achieve at the international level. It would not be surprising, therefore, if the bilateralist regimes with their strong coastal state influence proved to be more effective than multilateral regimes in implementing this principle at the regional level.[32]

Differentiating levels of precaution is difficult because we lack a standard tenable across cases for judging the extent to which conservation and management measures are conservative in circumstances of uncertainty. Nevertheless, an examination of regional conservation measures through the prism of scientific recommendations can throw light on this situation. While the state of the Sea of Okhotsk pollock stock has evidenced a downward slope for several years, Russian scientists have recommended total allowable harvests based on a 30 per cent exploitation rate of survey estimates of spawning stock abundance.[33] This is regarded as the general maximum for pollock, and a number of uncertainties regarding the underlying estimate lead one observer to conclude that this decision rule cannot be deemed precautionary.[34] The most drastic Russian measure taken so far is the 1993 moratorium on harvesting of pollock in the region. The measure applied only to the high seas area and not to the adjacent Russian zone in which the same stock was being exploited by domestic vessels.

Barents Sea cod, like herring, redfish, and mackerel in the North-East Atlantic, is to a large extent managed on the basis of scientific advice by ICES. Since 1998, ICES advice has been based on the precautionary approach as laid out in the Fish Stocks Agreement; precautionary reference points are estimated for the shared stocks in the Barents Sea and reflected in the recommendations offered.[35] The cod stock has been healthy throughout much of the 1990s, and the Norwegian–Russian Fisheries Commission was largely loyal to the ICES quota advice in this period. Despite this, a sharp decline has set in during recent years and quotas for 2000 are less than half of those for 1997.[36]

The case of the straddling herring stock in the North-East Atlantic is diametrically opposite: the stock has recovered and remains fairly stable although quotas have been set consistently and substantially higher than recommended by ICES throughout most of the 1990s, even to an extent believed by ICES to imply spawning stock biomass falling below the recommended minimum.[37] Since 1998, quotas have been set more in line with scientific advice and the most recent ICES report holds the stock to be within safe biological limits and current management practices to comply with the precautionary approach.[38] Oceanic redfish, largely managed by NEAFC, is also believed to be within safe biological limits; however, after half a decade of notably bigger harvests than recommended, ICES warned in 1996 that knowledge about stock distribution and size is inadequate to provide advice on catch levels.[39] That was the first year that NEAFC managed to set quantitative restrictions, and considering that even then the total quota was set much higher than any previous annual harvesting, it would be difficult indeed to judge NEAFC management of this stock as precautionary.[40] As for mackerel, the stock is considered to be outside safe biological limits, but ICES noted in its report for 1998 that the total fishing mortality agreed between the major user states, Norway and the EC, is consistent with the precautionary approach.[41] On the other hand, Russia is the biggest harvester of mackerel on the high seas, and it is therefore problematic that Russia objected to the first attempt by NEAFC to set a quota for the high seas.[42]

As regards the Northwest Atlantic, the Scientific Council of NAFO responded to the Fish Stocks Agreement by establishing a working group on regional implementation of the precautionary approach; the principle itself was formally endorsed in 1997.[43] Traditionally, NAFO groundfish regulations have been relatively cautious. Indeed, among the complaints launched by the European Community beginning in the mid-1980s was the conservative management strategy applied by the Scientific Council. The EC demanded that the latter instead provide a range of options, including one corresponding to the stock's maximum sustainable yield.[44] Similarly, the introduction of management measures for the straddling Greenland halibut stock that reopened the EC–Canadian controversy in this region occurred in response to scientific concern that the growing pressure, especially by Spanish vessels, was in excess of what the stock would sustain.[45] According to the Scientific Council, the halibut stock is now recovering because of good recruitment and low fishing mortality.[46]

For its part, the Doughnut Hole Convention stabilized a moratorium on pollock fisheries in this region. The ability of this regime to withstand pressure for quota allocations is yet to be tested, as the stock remains depleted. As long as the moratorium is in place, however, it would be difficult to argue that management is not precautionary.[47]

Finally, the CCAMLR regime for management of Antarctic marine living resources is the one that has implemented the precautionary approach most loyally; this is also borne out in the management of Patagonian toothfish. Quantitative restrictions recommended by the Scientific Committee have been translated into binding conservation measures; a Special Area for Protection and Scientific Study around South Georgia is especially relevant to toothfish conservation, as is also the category of 'new fisheries' introduced in 1991, which commits harvesting nations to particularly strict notification, reporting, and assessment procedures.[48]

Hence, whereas the precautionary approach urged by the Fish Stocks Agreement has generated considerable activity at the regional level, actual performance is rather mixed. There does not seem be any clear relationship between the level of precaution and operational structure—both bilateralist and regionalist regimes vary considerably in this regard. Nor is attendance to the precautionary approach related to successful implementation of another management principle that is vital to adequate conservation, namely compatibility. On the contrary, two regimes that are particularly advanced in implementing the precautionary approach, namely NAFO and CCAMLR, are also the regimes where the overall effectiveness of conservation measures has been jeopardized the most by non-party harvesting activities.

2.4 Ecosystem management

At the level of general principles, the Fish Stocks Agreement confirms a broad trend in global environmental accords by emphasizing the need for ecosystem management.[49] The spatial aspect of this is primarily addressed by the careful balance struck in the Agreement between the rights of coastal states and other user states when establishing compatible management measures for individual straddling stocks. In contrast to compatibility, however, which is underpinned by the operational guidelines for establishment of conservation and management measures, the multi-species side of the ecosystem approach is scarcely elaborated in the Fish Stocks Agreement.[50]

At the regional level, the situation is no better. Few of the regional regimes scrutinized in this book are well equipped to handle salient stock interactions in a systematic way; and there is little to suggest that the operational structure of these regimes is weighty here. One reason is simply that efforts to model species interaction have nowhere reached a stage where findings can be applied with any precision in detailed management strategies. Another factor is the limited target scope of many regional fisheries regimes. The regime based in CCAMLR is credited as the first regional fisheries regime to have explicitly highlighted species interaction when defining its management objectives.[51] The permanent Environmental Monitoring and Management group under the Scientific Committee institutionalizes this concern. Regarding toothfish management, ecosystem considerations are borne out in a series of conservation measures that seek to reduce the by-catch of seabirds, for example by mandating rapid sinking of baits when longline equipment is applied, by resorting to reduced light during night operations, and by the deployment of streamers on the line to keep birds away.[52]

In contrast, due to strong resistance among distant water fishing nations to extending pollock restrictions to other potential fisheries in the Central Bering Sea, the Doughnut Hole regime is explicitly single-species in orientation. Somewhere in between those two extremes, NAFO is rather well placed to incorporate multispecies considerations, covering as it does 'all fishery resources of the Convention Area' with the exception of certain species subject to separate regimes under the Law of the Sea Convention.[53] While a corresponding formulation defines the target scope of NEAFC as well, it is much more difficult to apply an ecosystem approach to management within the herring, redfish, and mackerel regimes in the North-East Atlantic. First, especially for herring, NEAFC plays a very moderate role as it merely endorses solutions already reached in more narrowly staged coastal state bargaining. Second, even if NEAFC were to gain more of an independent role in herring management, the two stocks that interact the most strongly with herring, namely North-East Arctic cod and Barents Sea capelin, are clearly beyond NEAFC's ambit as both stocks are managed by the Norwegian–Russian Fisheries Commission. Conversely, the biological interactions between cod, capelin, and herring in the North-East Atlantic also pose severe limits on the potential of ecosystem management under the bilateralist Barents Sea regime. In addition, none of the straddling stocks regimes for the North-East Atlantic has any say on the management of whales, an important predator for cod, herring, and capelin, which are largely managed by the International Whaling Commission (IWC).[54]

The situation is different in the Sea of Okhotsk Peanut Hole; the privileged role of Russia in this arrangement and the fact that the area in question is completely surrounded by Russia's EEZ would seem to provide the jurisdictional means for multispecies management, should this be desired by the coastal state. Indeed, Russia complained during the Fish Stocks Agreement that unregulated harvesting in the Peanut Hole had detrimental effects on stocks of other commercial species such as herring, halibut, and salmon.[55]

To summarize, regardless of whether they are bilateralist or multilateral, regional fisheries regimes typically find it difficult to implement seriously the inter-species side of ecosystem management. This is partly because the science of modelling stock interactions with respect to the generation of practical management advice is still in its infancy; but even if the scientific basis were to improve, the limited stock portfolio of regional regimes implies that serious attempts at multispecies management would require considerable coordination across regimes.

2.5 Allocation between various users

In an ideal world, conservation and allocation of fish resources would be addressed sequentially. On the basis of the best available knowledge, parties would decide on the appropriate level and mode of fisheries pressure before they addressed the question of how catches should be allocated among various users. The reality, however, is often that problems of allocation permeate the regulatory process and encourage states to compromise on conservation needs. Those who drew up the Fish Stocks Agreement were mindful of the allocative barriers to sustainable management; one of the operational tasks of regional management regimes is to enable states to 'agree, as appropriate, on participatory rights such as allocations of allowable catch' and also on 'decision-making procedures which facilitate the adoption of conservation and management measures in a timely and effective manner'.[56] Beyond this, the Agreement lays down relevant considerations for determining the level of participation by new entrants to a fishery.[57] The latter set of provisions is hardly designed to resolve the matter, however, as it is essentially a listing of criteria previously applied in regional accords, including historic catch and the distribution of the stock, plus some new criteria.

Most of the regional regimes reviewed here do indeed allocate national quotas, and many of them have developed substantive or procedural means to make annual negotiations over allocation more tractable. For instance, the bilateralist Loophole regime has extended to non-coastal states a *fixed division-key* approach that for more than two decades has formed the allocative backbone of the Norwegian–Russian Fisheries Commission;[58] the 1999 agreement between Norway, Russia, and Iceland states that future Icelandic cod quotas are to be calculated on the basis of a fixed share of the TAC.[59] Similarly, the allocative dispute over Greenland halibut that triggered Canada's high seas arrest of the Spanish trawler *Estai* was addressed by provisions in the bilateral 1995 Agreed Minute that created a fixed division key between Canada and the European Community regarding halibut taken on the Grand Banks; such keys had been in use for other species managed by NAFO.[60]

In general, however, the rigidity introduced by fixed allocative keys makes the keys vulnerable to substantial variation in, *inter alia*, the zonal attachment of a stock—another criterion often invoked when decisions are made on the allocation of stocks. Such variation is not uncommon for pelagic species such as herring and capelin because their migratory patterns often fluctuate considerably with stock size. Hence, the respective European Community and Norwegian shares of the North Sea herring stock have been adjustable on the basis of scientific models of zonal attachment; and the same is true for a North-East Atlantic capelin agreement involving Iceland, Norway, and Greenland/Denmark.[61] This allocative mechanism is also applied to the North-East Atlantic herring arrangement in the provision that future allocative adjustments shall be linked primarily to findings by a Scientific Working Group concerning changes in the distribution of the stock.[62]

In some cases, the allocative challenge is complicated by regional particularities. For instance, the CCAMLR Commission has abstained from national allocations, primarily because the issue is seen to interfere potentially with the disputed and carefully avoided sovereignty concerns in Antarctic politics. Similarly, efforts to include in the Doughnut Hole Convention specific provisions on future quotas allocation failed due to disagreement on which criteria to apply. Historic catches were rejected by the coastal states as a basis for allocation on grounds that the largely non-coastal state dominance of this fishery throughout the 1980s had been utterly non-sustainable.[63] Instead, the Convention leaves the task of setting national quotas to the Annual Conference of the parties should the fishery be reopened. Absent of consensus here, an olympic fishery would ensue where vessels from all parties would compete for the catches within an overall ceiling.

Hence, the allocative capacity of straddling stock management regimes, whether bilateralist or multilateral, appears to turn primarily on whether they have established default rules that facilitate annual negotiations. Such default rules may be fixed, as in the case of the division keys in the Barents Sea and the North-West Atlantic; but they can also be dynamic and procedural, as are the model-based zonal attachment rules agreed to in the North-East Atlantic arrangements. The Doughnut Hole regime and the regime based in CCAMLR illustrate that provisions for an olympic fishery may serve to de-link the conservation problem from the allocative problem whenever the latter proves impossible to solve.

2.6 *The compliance problem*

The issue of encouraging adherence to regulatory measures agreed to within fisheries management regimes can be approached from two angles—one discursive and one coercive.[64] A high degree of involvement of target groups in decision-making, with a view to strengthening their responsibility for regulative outcomes, is among the more common discursive compliance mechanisms in fisheries management.[65] Another mechanism is to assign a rather prominent role to scientific advice in the regulatory process.[66] Such investigations often involve, or at least are open to, scientists from all member states.

For their part, coercive compliance activities comprise surveillance, detention, and legal prosecution. An important contribution of the Fish Stocks Agreement, in conjunction with some other global and regional agreements, is to broaden the jurisdictional basis for some of these activities and thus reduce the traditional primacy in international law of the flag state in high seas control and enforcement.[67]

One element is strengthened *flag state* responsibilities. Here the negotiators of the Fish Stocks Agreement were able to incorporate the substantive solutions codified globally in the 1993 FAO Compliance Agreement.[68] This agreement specifies the duty of parties to exercise effective jurisdiction over high seas fishing operations by vessels flying their flags. Accordingly, the Fish Stocks Conference could focus on the second and more controversial element of establishing a framework procedure that permits *non-flag states* to inspect and detain fishing vessels on the high seas in a way acceptable to both coastal and distant water fishing nations.[69] Parties to the Fish Stocks Agreement have given advance consent to their vessels being boarded and inspected on the high seas by personnel authorized under a regional management regime, even if these states are not parties to the regional regime.[70] If the inspection reveals evidence that implies that the vessel has violated regional conservation measures, the flag state must either begin its own investigation and prosecution or authorize the inspecting state to proceed with its investigation and, in case of serious violation, even detain the vessel and bring it to the nearest appropriate port.[71] Yet another compliance control element highlighted by the Fish Stocks Agreement is *port state* measures.[72] It is debated whether the rights to inspect vessels voluntarily in port and, if violations are revealed, to prohibit landing and trans-shipments are new rights in the fisheries context or simply emanations from sovereignty over the port.[73]

However, few of the regional straddling stock regimes discussed in this book have been significantly affected by this global-level circumscription of the traditional flag state prominence in the compliance area. As almost all the harvesting activities undertaken under the bilateralist regimes in the Barents and Okhotsk Seas occur in national waters, those regimes rely primarily on coastal state jurisdiction that permits the full range of compliance measures, including inspection, detention, and legal prosecution. To a somewhat lesser extent, coastal state enforcement also predominates in the North-East Atlantic herring arrangement as some 90 per cent of the harvest occurs inside the EEZs of regime members. In the period when these restricted regimes were still challenged by outsiders, port state jurisdiction provided complementary means. Even before the adoption of the Fish Stocks Agreement, Russia and Norway had introduced legislation prohibiting landings of catches taken on the high seas in defiance of international fisheries regulations, and the coastal states persuaded states that received quotas in their EEZs to do the same.[74] A more indirect way of using economic sanctions to induce compliance with high seas management measures, one that does not depend upon voluntary port calls, is expressed in the Norwegian practice of blacklisting vessels engaged in unregulated high seas harvesting from subsequent access to the Norwegian EEZ—even if the vessel has changed ownership in the meantime. Similarly, from 1993 until agreements had been reached with all user states two years later, Russia prohibited the allotment of catch quotas in the Russian zone to foreign vessels that had been engaged in harvesting in the Peanut Hole.[75]

In the Northwest Atlantic, rules for non-flag state inspection and detention preceded their global emergence in the Fish Stocks Agreement; also in place were several provisions designed to facilitate control activities, such as an observer system and gradual phasing in of compulsory satellite tracking devices. Similarly, one year before the adoption of the Fish Stocks Agreement, the Doughnut Hole Convention provided for both non-flag state inspection and detention of vessels in cases where the flag state fails to act on serious violations. Indeed, there is much to suggest that the detention provisions of the Fish Stocks Agreement were substantially inspired by those of NAFO and the Doughnut Hole regime.[76]

Among the compliance mechanisms globalized by the Fish Stocks Agreement, the provisions for port state measures have had the most visible impact on the regional regimes discussed in this book. A 'Scheme to Promote Compliance by Non-contracting Party Vessels with the Conservation and Enforcement Measures Established by NAFO' was adopted in 1997. This was rapidly copied by CCAMLR and NEAFC. The scheme provides that non-member vessels that have been sighted engaging in harvesting in the NAFO Regulatory Area are presumed to be undermining this regime and shall not be permitted to land or trans-ship any fish in a NAFO member port until they have been inspected. In cases where such inspection exposes species regulated by NAFO, landings and trans-shipment will be prohibited unless the vessel can prove that the taking of this fish has not contravened NAFO rules.

In short, the Fish Stocks Agreement provides a comprehensive package of fairly advanced provisions relevant to compliance control. The regional regimes reviewed in this book have either been front-runners in the compliance area, such as the Doughnut Hole Convention and NAFO with regard to non-flag state detention, or they have been able to rely on the more extensive coastal state jurisdiction. Therefore, except for the elaboration of port state measures, these global developments have had limited effect on the range of compliance instruments available to them.

2.7 Summary: conditions for effective high seas management

One conclusion that can be drawn from the above is that the *operational profile* of regional straddling stocks management regimes fails to explain much of the variance among them in terms of effectiveness. No clear pattern appears which identifies either bilateralist or regionalist approaches as generally superior in meeting the three tasks of management. For instance, any expectations that bilateralist regimes, where decision-making is heavily influenced by coastal states, would be more effective in producing precautionary management measures are not confirmed in the analysis. An obvious reason is that decision-making capacity is only one of several conditions for regulatory caution in the face of uncertainty. Equally non-supported is the hypothesis that compatibility, in terms of the spatial scope of regulations and their user coverage, would be easier to realize in regionalist regimes because of broader participation and greater equality in decision-making. On the contrary, the two management regimes that are the most inclusive, CCAMLR and NAFO, are also the regimes most marred by non-party harvesting activities.

Moreover, in the few cases where systematic differences do appear between bilateralist and regionalist regimes, they tend to be based on circumstances other than operational structure. The bilateralist regimes reviewed here are particularly well equipped to ensure adequate compliance control, but this is largely because non-coastal state harvesting activities are successfully directed inside national waters. However, this option is available not because of the operational structure, but rather because of the migratory pattern of the stocks in question, which renders quotas in national waters highly attractive to non-coastal user states.

Whereas operational structure seems scarcely related to regime effectiveness, the analysis above has exposed a set of other factors that seem highly supportive of high seas management. (1) The quality and legitimacy of scientific advice appear to be closely connected with the level of *inclusiveness* of interested parties in the generation of the advice and with the ability to insulate scientific cooperation from inter-state rivalries. (2) Adequate user coverage for high seas conservation measures is very difficult to achieve unless the coastal states in question are prepared to

remunerate acknowledgement of such measures, often by giving concessions regarding their management of the EEZ. The most powerful instrument in this regard is to grant quotas in national waters to user states that
agree to comply with the rules established for the adjacent high seas area.
Another coastal state concession that appears to promote compliance with
high seas measures is to introduce equally strict regulations on its domestic vessels that harvest the same stock in national waters. (3) Efforts to
establish adequate conservation measures are more likely to be successful if regime members are able to agree on *criteria* for allocation of the
catches, either by fixed division keys or by more flexible means such as
scientific models of zonal attachment. Finally, (4) *compliance control* can be
strengthened either by provisions that harvesting be limited to national
waters, by intrusive port state controls, or by reaching agreement on
regional procedures for high seas inspection and detention.

The next section will examine the significance of interplay with other
institutions for the ability of regional regimes to meet these conditions for
effective management of high seas fisheries.

3 Regime interplay and effective governance

Up to now, the focus has been on regional implications of changes under
way in the global regime for high seas fisheries. One purpose has been to
move beyond the tendency in much of the regime literature to analyse a
particular regime without sustained attention to its relationships to
broader or functionally adjacent regimes.[77] In this section, the enquiry into
regime interplay is developed further by elaborating four ways in which
an international regime may modify the effectiveness of another regime.
These four types of regime interaction are termed diffusive, political,
normative, and operational interplay.[78]

3.1 Diffusive interplay

Diffusive interplay refers to situations when the substantive or operational rules of one regime serve as models for those negotiating another
regime. A striking instance of diffusion in the straddling stock context
is the rapid spread of general normative principles such as precaution,
ecosystem management, and compatibility. The precautionary principle,
which received global recognition in the 1985 Ozone Convention, was
subsequently endorsed in the 1992 Rio Declaration and elaborated in the
fisheries context by the Fish Stocks Agreement as part of the UNCED
legacy. For its part, the principle of ecosystem management was increasingly included in regional environmental agreements after its formal

introduction in the 1980 CCAMLR agreement.[79] In the Fish Stocks Agreement the ecosystem approach appears both among the general principles upheld by the agreement and as part of the precautionary approach to management.[80] Similarly, a 'consistency' requirement was elaborated already in the 1978 NAFO Convention and emulated in the NEAFC treaty; since then, the phrase has been upheld in a range of other regional and global high seas fisheries instruments before its elaboration as 'compatibility' in the Fish Stocks Agreement.

As to diffusion of operational regime components, the system for dispute settlement set forth in the Fish Stocks Agreement is a complete incorporation of the apparatus provided in part XV of the 1982 Law of the Sea Convention and thus extends this structure to non-parties to the Convention.[81] The potential impact of this for regional management is enhanced further by the fact that this system can be invoked not only in disputes over provisions in the Fish Stocks Agreement but in 'any dispute between States Parties to this Agreement concerning interpretation or application of a subregional, regional or global fisheries agreement relating to straddling stocks or highly migratory fish stocks'. A plausible implication of this is that the Fish Stocks Agreement amends existing fishery treaties by adding the UNCLOS dispute settlement apparatus, including the conditions of the latter for binding compulsory settlement.[82] The operational structure for enhancing compliance with regional conservation and management measures is another area where emulation has influenced the basis for effective management. The provisions in two regional treaties that address tuna fisheries in the South Pacific and introduce and strengthen the notion of 'flag state responsibilities' over vessels engaged in high seas fisheries provided essential material for the 1993 FAO Compliance Agreement.[83] In turn, the latter shaped the contents of several regional regimes as well as provisions on flag state duties in the Fish Stocks Agreement. Similarly, the port state measures envisaged in the Fish Stocks Agreement that rapidly shaped the compliance control agenda of several regional regimes, including NAFO, CCAMLR, and NEAFC, had a precedent in the vessel-source pollution area already in the 1982 Law of the Sea Convention.[84]

Diffusive interplay promotes the effectiveness of high seas fisheries management when solutions that have been reached in one regime are perceived as applicable to problems that have frustrated cooperation under another regime. An interesting type of leadership in international negotiations is to draw attention exactly to such 'salient solutions' that become prominent because they have been tried in other contexts.[85] But diffusion is not always a straightforward process. The precautionary principle was strongly resisted during the early stages of the Fish Stocks Conference, until agreement was reached that application would not create a moratorium on fishing in cases of scientific uncertainty.[86] Distant water fishing nations that were eager to minimize the scope of the constraints imposed by the Doughnut Hole Convention remained unimpressed by the merits of ecosystem management; they thus insisted that the latter be largely confined to pollock. Opposition to diffusive interplay has been even stronger regarding the compatibility principle—relating as it does to allocative matters and thus inherently much more controversial. In the Northwest Atlantic, the European Community has complained that NAFO's consistency phrase has been used by Canada as an instrument for achieving 'creeping jurisdiction' over high seas areas adjacent to its coasts.[87] It is not surprising that distant water fishing states, while sub-scribing to the notion of compatible measures, were eager to avoid a simi-larly clear coastal state bias in the definition of compatibility worked out in the Fish Stocks Agreement. The issue of whether and under what con-ditions compatibility was to imply the projection of high seas rules into national waters and vice versa was among the most difficult matters for the Conference to resolve.[88]

Accordingly, diffusibility is likely to be lower if the regime feature in question, such as compatibility, lends itself to allocative usage or touches on contested matters such as disputed sovereignty. There is much to suggest that proximity between the regime processes in time, space, and membership is another factor that affects diffusibility. Consider for instance the relationship between the management bodies for the North-West and the North-East Atlantic fisheries. There is considerable overlap in the membership of NAFO and NEAFC, and two decades ago the con-sistency principle and several other regime features spread from the former to the latter. Moreover, the enhanced role of non-flag states regard-ing high seas detention of vessels that have seriously violated agreed con-servation measures was established within a compressed period of time, centred on the parallel negotiation of three legal instruments—the Dough-nut Hole Convention, the Agreed Minute, and the Fish Stocks Agreement. An additional feature of the diffusive path regarding non-flag state enforcement measures was the representative manner in which the two regional front-runners involved the most salient players in the political battle over straddling stocks management. The Doughnut Hole Conven-tion pitted the largest Asian distant water fishing nations against a coastal state hard-liner, Russia, and the United States with its more balanced interests. The Agreed Minute involved, on the one hand, another coastal state front-runner, Canada, and on the other hand the biggest European distant water fishing actor. Regime features that had proved their feasi-bility in these rather representative contexts stand a good chance of also being accepted in other straddling stock situations; this is evidenced by their subsequent endorsement in the Fish Stocks Agreement.

Consider in contrast the 1995 Canadian–Norwegian agreement pertaining to the NAFO area, the Barents Sea Loophole, and the North-East Atlantic Banana Hole.[89] Under this agreement, each party is authorized not only to inspect each other's vessels on the high seas and bring a violator to port, but also to institute proceedings seeking penalties against the vessel. The significance of this particular agreement in diffusive terms was reduced by the fact that the agreement is not representative in membership of most high seas fisheries regimes, involving as it does two members of the coastal state core group during the Fish Stocks Conference.

In *summary*, the emulation of substantive or operational solutions that have been tried out successfully in other contexts is a pervasive practice among negotiators of international regimes. Vague, general principles tend to flow easily, but from an effectiveness point of view, diffusive interplay is particularly interesting if it can facilitate agreement on specific matters that have impeded problem-solving under an international regime. Whenever the substantive or operational regime feature in question has considerable distributive impacts, as do the compatibility principle and the intrusive compliance mechanisms that were developed in the Doughnut Hole Convention, diffusive interplay requires greater efforts on the part of those who favour emulation and usually also that the set of interests represented in the regimes involved are comparable.

3.2 *Political interplay*

Whereas diffusion is a process by which features of a given regime affect the contents of another, political interplay occurs when actor interests or capabilities associated with one regime significantly shape the operation or impacts of another. It will come as no surprise, for instance, that the bargaining roles assumed by the most active states during the Fish Stocks Conference tended to reflect the particular circumstances of the regional management regimes that were closest to their interests. Had NAFO been an effective and successful organization, Canada would hardly have assumed a leadership role in the coastal state core group before and during the UN negotiations. Russia, with its special concerns in the Sea of Okhotsk situation, took a leadership role at the Conference with respect to the parts of the prospective treaty that are particularly relevant for high seas enclaves.[90] In both of these cases, political interplay with other regime processes provided incentives for states to come up with proposals for new management instruments and try to rally sufficiently broad support for them. But political interplay could also constrain international negotiations. For instance, there is much to suggest that multilateral talks on the Peanut Hole were impeded by the fact that success here would have undercut the Russian argument, which was pressed during the Fish Stocks Conference, that high seas enclaves require a special global regime.[91]

Issue linkage, which implies that states mobilize resources from one set of regime negotiations to another, is another type of political interplay. It has been argued, for instance, that during the Doughnut Hole negotiations the United States credibly indicated to its non-coastal state opponents that failure to reach a regional accord could elicit a shift on the part of that country from an intermediate position during the Fish Stocks Conference to a position more favourable to the coastal state bloc.[92] Another instance is the playing of the quota card by coastal states that are seeking to reach and enforce international agreements on high seas management. Here, the privileged position within the 200-mile limit accorded to coastal states by the 1982 Law of the Sea Convention is deliberately drawn upon to shape measures pertaining to the adjacent ocean space. Similarly, we have seen earlier that several coastal states have banned vessels that have a history of unregulated high seas harvesting from trans-shipments, landings, and other port services.

Hence, political interplay occurs when the political logic of one regime spills over into another. Such interplay can be supportive of regime effectiveness when it provides incentives to assume leadership roles during international negotiations or when it implies that capabilities under one regime are used to induce compliance under another. Linkage of issues across functional areas, for instance between resource management and matters related to trade in goods and services, can be difficult to achieve because it tends to require considerable inter-agency coordination on the part of the state making the linkage, and this is unlikely unless the matter is highly politicized.

3.3 Normative interplay

Normative interplay refers to situations when the substantive or operational norms of one regime either contradict or validate those of another regime. Such interplay can be relevant to regime effectiveness because the legitimacy, or compelling force, of a rule or an institution depends on its level of coherence with other rules that are relevant to the subject matter— or its adherence to broader normative principles and rules of right process.[93]

During the 1990s, there has been growing attention to possible conflict between certain trade-related measures authorized by international environmental regimes and global or regional rules of free trade.[94] Some multilateral environmental agreements require that parties impose trade restrictions on certain products, either generally as in the case of the

Convention on International Trade in Endangered Species of Wild Fauna and Flora (CITES) or directed at non-members of environmental regimes or non-compliers as in the 1987 Montreal Protocol to the Ozone Convention.[95] Other instances are the landing and trans-shipment bans agreed upon under NAFO, CCAMLR, and NEAFC regarding fish taken in violation of high seas conservation measures. In addition, some states have passed domestic legislation that authorizes trade sanctions on states that contravene international conservation rules even in the absence of explicit regime provisions to this effect. A well-known instance is the United States' threat to impose import restrictions on seafood products from states contravening the moratorium on whaling that was established by the IWC.[96]

Whereas those concerned with the effectiveness of international environmental regimes tend to look favourably at economic sanctions that seek to enhance compliance with conservation rules, at least two competing concerns are of issue:[97] the free trade communities worry that trade measures for environmental purposes may slide into protectionism; and states relying on certain major markets, such as the United States, perceive threats of trade sanctions as illegitimate intrusions into their sovereignty that commit them in practice to standards established by others.

Normative interplay arising from commitments that the sanctioning state has assumed in the trade area may provide a counter-strategy for states that are subject to conservation-related trade measures. Mexico brought the US embargo on tuna that had not been harvested in conformity with US by-catch rules for the protection of dolphin before a dispute settlement panel under the General Agreement on Tariffs and Trade (GATT).[98] Similarly, in 1995 Iceland filed complaints to the relevant surveillance body that Norway's refusal of port services to Icelandic vessels that had conducted unregulated Loophole harvesting was illegal under the Agreement on the European Economic Area.[99]

Such apparently conflictual normative interplay between different regimes can be addressed in several ways. Sometimes, the legal instruments themselves provide rules of pre-eminence. This is illustrated by Article 4 of the Fish Stocks Agreement which states that 'This Agreement shall be interpreted and applied in the context of and in a manner consistent with the Convention.' In other cases, customary rules of pre-eminence may be relevant: unless otherwise stated, more recent rules generally take precedence over older rules that address the same subject matter and the same is true for specialized rules over more general ones.[100] Those customary rules could be relevant to the discussion of whether prohibitions on landings and trans-shipments of fish taken in violation of high seas conservation rules contravene GATT rules, because parties to the more recent and arguably more specialized Fish Stocks Agreement have explicitly agreed to accept such prohibitions whenever port state inspections have 'established that the catch has been taken in a manner which undermines the effectiveness of . . . conservation and management measures on the high seas'.[101] In the most conflictual cases, as noted, the dispute settlement apparatus that is found in some international regimes can be resorted to. Under WTO/GATT, the legality of conservation-related trade measures has been addressed on the basis of several exemptions in GATT from the general ban on quotas and embargoes. Requiring first that 'arbitrary or unjustifiable discrimination between countries' shall not occur, these exemptions permit trade measures that are *'necessary to* protect human, animal or plant life or health' or *'relating to* the conservation of exhaustible natural resource if such measures are made effective in conjunction with restrictions on domestic production or consumption'.[102] The questions of whether specific trade measures, including those related to US imports of tuna, can be said to be 'necessary to' or primarily 'relating to' conservation goals have been subject to controversy within the scholarly community and different interpretation by dispute settlement panels under WTO/GATT.[103] Such exemptions to the general free trade rule also came into focus when the EFTA Surveillance Authority stated that although in its opinion Norway's refusal of port services to an Icelandic vessel constituted a violation of the regional trade regime, no further action would be taken because 'the underlying conflict concerned a dispute between Norway and Iceland over Icelandic fishing rights in the Barents Sea'.[104] Such abstention under one regime (on trade) on grounds that the issue sorts primarily under another regime (on regional fisheries management) highlights the significance of operational components of regimes as a means for coping with inter-regime tension.

In summary, normative interplay with other regimes, including international trade commitments, may constrain the use of economic compliance mechanisms that are authorized by international fisheries regimes. The priority of such potentially competing measures is sometimes set explicitly in the instruments themselves or by customary rules of pre-eminence; in other cases it can be settled by decisions under one regime to abstain from pursuing a violation. To be successful, therefore, economic measures aimed at promoting compliance with international conservation measures must either be carefully tailored to comply with the substantive exemptions that are provided in global and regional liberal trade agreements, including even-handed treatment of domestic and foreign entities, or be supported by a strong position in the operational apparatus that decides whether or not an alleged contravention shall be pursued.

3.4 Operational interplay

Operational interplay refers to the coordination of activities, whether regulative or programmatic, undertaken within separate regime processes. Such coordination is sometimes envisaged by those who create an international regime, but this type of interplay may also emerge over time as ruling bodies discover that their regulatory work or programmes interact. One purpose of operational interplay is to avoid duplication by pooling available resources for problem-solving activities such as scientific research. The convention that established the fisheries regime for the Southern Ocean, for instance, names the FAO among the external organizations that would be natural cooperation partners.[105] This has been followed up in practice by the regime members, first by granting FAO observer status to Commission meetings and inviting this organization to take part in the work of the Scientific Committee. Another important example is the role of ICES in laying a scientific basis for management decisions not only in NEAFC but also the Norwegian–Russian Fisheries Commission, the North Atlantic Salmon Conservation Organization, and the International Baltic Sea Fishery Commission. The inclusiveness of such broader-based scientific organizations also enhances the legitimacy of scientific advice. The Antarctic experience provides also an instance of obstructive programmatic interplay. An ambitious plan by the FAO to launch a ten-year Southern Ocean research programme was dropped in 1979, most likely because of pressure from Antarctic Treaty parties towards the end of the negotiations that created CCAMLR.[106]

Another purpose of such coordination can be to maximize coherence between norms promulgated in different regime processes that address the same or similar issues. Consider the coordination conducted between the FAO and the UNCED Secretariat in the preparation of chapter 17 of Agenda 21, which led to the subsequent negotiation of the Fish Stocks Agreement. Prior to this, the FAO had already been vital in several other major concerted norm-building efforts in this area, including the Cancun Declaration, a series of technical consultations on high seas fishing, and the 1993 Compliance Agreement.[107] We noted earlier that the predator–prey interactions of many straddling stocks with species that are managed under other regimes imply that ecosystem management will require considerable operational interplay.

In *summary*, operational interplay can promote the effectiveness of adjacent regimes by enhancing the cost-efficiency of programme activities, by enhancing the inclusiveness of scientific assessments and advice, and by ensuring a higher level of coherence among principles or conservation measures. Although such coordination is costly and usually time-consuming, the growing number of international agreements and regime

processes in the environmental management area and the rising awareness of interdependencies between the issues they address suggest that
operational interplay is likely to become increasingly significant in international management of natural resources.

4 Concluding remarks

The past decade has been highly dynamic with respect to the politics and
law of high seas fisheries. A number of regional straddling stock rivalries
escalated to bitter disputes among some of the world's foremost fishing
nations. Partly in consequence, fisheries management increasingly
became part of the broader discourse of environmental affairs. The 1992
Rio Conference triggered a United Nations Fish Stocks Conference that
addressed these concerns, and the Agreement that was negotiated
strengthened and specified the duty under international law to cooperate
on all aspects of high seas fisheries management. The overall effect of the
Agreement is typically to globalize features that have hitherto been confined to the most advanced regional management regimes. In the science
area, this concerns in particular the detailed procedures established for
the cooperative collection and exchange of data. In the regulatory domain,
the provision that only states that are members of, or adhere to, regional
regimes shall have access to the fishery is important. The elaboration of
basic conservation principles, such as precaution, compatibility, and
ecosystem management, has also generated considerable activity at the
regional level. Yet it is especially in the compliance control area that the
Fish Stocks Agreement breaks new ground by creating global minimum
standards that mobilize a broader range of compliance mechanisms than
has usually been the case in regional high seas management regimes. This
includes strengthened flag state responsibilities, procedures for non-flag
state inspection and detention on the high seas, and elaboration of certain
port state measures to enhance adherence to regional conservation and
management measures.

This concluding chapter has examined the interplay of global and
regional high seas management regimes. There is considerable variance
in the operational structure of the regional regimes that are reviewed in
this book. In regionalist regimes, decision-making is multilateral and
usually inclusive, whereas bilateralist regimes are based on a set of bilateral agreements that accord the coastal states a prominent position in high
seas management in return for granting other user states quotas
in national waters. Both types comply with the obligation under the
Fish Stocks Agreement to cooperate 'either directly or through appropriate subregional or regional fisheries management organizations or

arrangements', and there is little to suggest that one of these structures is generally superior in the management of high seas fisheries. Instead, other factors seem decisive for effective management: (1) scientific inclusiveness, (2) ability to induce non-coastal state acceptance of high seas rules, (3) practical criteria for allocation, and (4) agreed provisions for sufficiently intrusive compliance control. In these Conclusions, particular attention has been paid to how these factors are affected by various pathways of regime interplay.

Regarding the scientific aspect of management, we have shown how inclusiveness in stock assessments and recommendations has been enhanced by operational interplay between North-East Atlantic management regimes and the International Council for the Exploration of the Sea. Operational interplay, or the coordination of regulatory and programmatic activities, can also be a way of avoiding wasteful duplication or of maximizing normative coherence between regimes that impinge upon similar or connected activities. Such gains must always be balanced against the costs of cross-regime coordination.

Attaining sufficiently broad user coverage of high seas conservation measures usually requires that non-coastal states are induced, either by reward or by threats of sanction, to acknowledge such measures. Political interplay, which implies that interests or capabilities defined under one regime context spill over into another, is relevant here: the most effective way for coastal states to obtain acceptance from non-user states of rules that restrict high seas operations is to establish a linkage between such acceptance and access to quotas in national waters. A more demanding type of conservation-oriented issue linkage is to impose trade sanctions on states or individual vessels that engage in uregulated harvesting on the high seas. Such linkage across issue-areas typically requires a high degree of politicization and conflict, and those conditions have marked many of the straddling stock disputes discussed in this book. However, the effectiveness of trade-related compliance measures may be reduced if they can be challenged as violating rules upheld by other regimes that address the free flow of goods and services, including GATT. The extent and significance of such normative interplay is typically conditioned on the design of the economic measures taken or the ability to influence the operation of decision-making bodies under the regimes involved. For example, GATT has specific exemptions to the general ban on embargoes; and measures that are applied equally to domestic and foreign entities generally stand a better chance of avoiding being judged as disguised protectionism.

Allocative capacity is another important requirement for effective management: in the absence of agreed criteria on how to divide harvests among the user states, annual negotiations are complicated. The similarity between regional management regimes in how they have approached this matter suggests that a level of emulation across regimes, or diffusive interplay, has occurred. Where the migratory patterns of the fish stocks in question imply a rather stable zonal attachment, management regimes tend to have fixed division keys; pelagic species, whose migratory pattern depends on the size of the stock, often require more flexible keys which correspond to variations in zonal attachment. The existence of regime features that have worked in other regime contexts can facilitate international resource management by offering models for emulation. Factors that appear to promote diffusion of regime features are proximity between the regime processes in time and space and the extent to which such regimes are similar in terms of interest structure. Those factors were present when, in the first half of the 1990s, innovative provisions for compliance control such as port state measures and procedures for high seas inspection and control emerged first in the most conflict-laden regional contexts and then spread by way of the Fish Stocks Agreement to other regional management regimes.

The four pathways of interplay discussed in this book have been relevant to the effectiveness of regional management regimes, and we have identified certain conditions that seem to initiate or constrain such interplay. The practical challenge for fisheries managers is to reinforce regime interplay that is conducive and impede interplay that is obstructive to governance of high seas fisheries.

Notes

I would like to thank Steinar Andresen, David Balton, Robin Churchill, Alex Oude Elferink, Ed Miles, Ron Mitchell, Arild Underdal, Davor Vidas, Johán Williams, Oran Young, and Michael Zürn for very helpful comments. Some of the findings on which this concluding chapter is based, are also reported in O. S. Stokke, 'Managing Straddling Stocks: The Interplay of Global and Regional Regimes', *Ocean and Coastal Management*, 43 (2000), 205.

1. See the discussion in E. L. Miles and W. T. Burke, 'Pressures on the United Nations Convention on the Law of the Sea of 1982 Arising from New Fisheries Conflicts: The Problem of Straddling Stocks', *Ocean Development and International Law*, 20 (1989), 343.
2. Agreement for the Implementation of the Provisions of the United Nations Convention on the Law of the Sea of 10 Dec. 1982 relating to the Conservation and Management of Straddling Fish Stocks and Highly Migratory Fish Stocks (1995); 34 *ILM* 1547.
3. Fish Stocks Agreement, Arts. 8–13. On the notion of international regimes, see the Introduction.
4. Ibid., Art. 8 (4). The duty to cooperate on straddling stocks is laid out in the Law of the Sea Convention, Arts. 63 and 116–20.
5. Fish Stocks Agreement, Art. 8 (1).
6. On this notion of bilateralism, see J. G. Ruggie, 'Multilateralism: The Anatomy of an Institution', *International Organization*, 46 (1992), 561.
7. The term 'regionalist', rather than 'regional', is used to highlight the multilateral decision-making mode of such regimes; as seen above, bilateralist regimes are also regional but the interactive mode is different.
8. On the distinction between restricted and conditionally open regimes, see R. O. Keohane, 'Multilateralism: An Agenda for Research', *International Journal*, 45 (1990), 731, at 750.
9. Fish Stocks Agreement, Art. 8 (3).
10. See, on the one hand, the discussion by Orrego, Ch. 1 above, and on the other, A. Tahindro, 'Conservation and Management of Transboundary Fish Stocks: Comments in Light of the Adoption of the 1995 Agreement for the Conservation and Management of Straddling Fish Stocks and Highly Migratory Fish Stocks', *Ocean Development and International Law*, 28 (1997), 1, at 20.
11. UN Doc. A/CONF.164/22/Rev. 1, Art. 8. The term 'real interest' is undefined by the Agreement and likely to be interpreted differently in various regional settings.
12. Convention on Future Multilateral Cooperation in North-East Atlantic Fisheries (1980); *OJ* L227 (1981), Art. 20, paras. (1), (3), and (4); Convention on the Conservation and Management of Pollock Resources in the Bering Sea (1994), Art. XVI, paras. (1) and (4); 34 *ILM* 67.
13. Churchill, Ch. 8 above.
14. Convention on the Conservation of Antarctic Marine Living Resources (1980), Art. XXIX (1) (accession) and Art. VII (2) (membership in the Commission); 19 *ILM* 837.

15. Convention on Future Multilateral Cooperation in the Northwest Atlantic Fisheries (1978), Art. XXII (4) (accession) and Art. XIII (1) (membership in the Commission); *OJ* L378 (1978).
16. Fish Stocks Agreement, Arts. 5 and 14 respectively; also annex I.
17. S. Andresen and W. Østreng (eds.), *International Resource Management: The Role of Science and Politics* (London: Belhaven, 1989); cf. NAFO Convention, Art. 6.
18. K. M. Sullivan, 'Conflict in the Management of a Northwest Atlantic Transboundary Cod Stock', *Marine Policy*, 13 (1989), 118, at 129–30.
19. See, respectively, O. S. Stokke, L. G. Anderson, and N. Mirovitskaya, 'The Barents Sea Fisheries', in O. R. Young (ed.), *The Effectiveness of International Regimes: Causal Connections and Behavioral Mechanisms* (Cambridge, Mass.: MIT Press), 181, and Churchill, Ch. 8 above.
20. Stokke, Ch. 9 above.
21. S. H. Marashi, 'Summary Information on the Role of International Fishery and Other Bodies with Regard to the Conservation and Management of Living Resources of the High Seas', *FAO Fisheries Circular*, 908 (1996), 60.
22. E. Meltzer, 'Global Overview of Straddling and Highly Migratory Fish Stocks: The Nonsuitable Nature of High Seas Fisheries', *Ocean Development and International Law*, 25 (1994), 255, at 293.
23. For a general argument to this effect, see Ruggie, 'Multilateralism'.
24. Vukas and Vidas, Ch. 2 above; also Herr, Ch. 10 above.
25. Joyner, Ch. 7 above. Other reasons for the collapse are that the agreed NAFO quotas were set too high and that considerable harvesting occurred by vessels flying flags of convenience.
26. Balton, Ch. 5 above.
27. Ibid.
28. O. S. Stokke and D. Vidas, 'Conclusions', in O. S. Stokke and D. Vidas (eds.), *Governing the Antarctic: The Effectiveness and Legitimacy of the Antarctic Treaty System* (Cambridge University Press, 1996), 432.
29. Herr, Ch. 10 above.
30. Fish Stocks Agreement, Art. 6 and annex II. On the emergence of the precautionary principle in international fisheries law and policy, see G. J. Hewison, 'The Precautionary Approach to Fisheries Management: An Environmental Perspective', *International Journal of Marine and Coastal Law*, 11 (1996), 301.
31. On the challenges for fisheries science implied by this approach, see L. J. Richards and J.-J. Maguire, 'Recent International Agreements and the Precautionary Approach: New Directions for Fisheries Management Science', *Canadian Journal of Fisheries and Aquatic Sciences*, 55 (1998), 1545.
32. L. L. Martin, 'Interests, Power, and Multilateralism', *International Organization*, 46 (1992), 765. On regional implementation of the precautionary approach, see G. L. Lugten, 'A Review of Measures Taken by Regional Marine Fishery Bodies to Address Contemporary Fishery Issues', *FAO Fisheries Circular*, 940 (1998), 85.
33. Oude Elferink, Ch. 6 above.
34. Ibid.

35. *ICES Cooperative Research Report*, 229, part I (1999), 27–32.
36. Stokke, Ch. 9 above.
37. *ICES Cooperative Research Report*, 221, part I (1997), 30–1.
38. Churchill, Ch. 8 above.
39. *ICES Cooperative Research Report*, 221, part 1, 50–1.
40. Churchill, Ch. 8 above.
41. *ICES Cooperative Research Report*, 229, part II (1999), 160.
42. Churchill, Ch. 8 above.
43. Lugten, 'A Review of Measures Taken', 87–8.
44. Sullivan, 'Conflict in the Management'.
45. M. S. Sullivan, 'The Case in International Law for Canada's Extension of Fisheries Jurisdiction beyond 200 Miles', *Ocean Development and International Law*, 28 (1997), 203.
46. See the scientific advice for 2000 (www.nafo.ca/science/advice/2000/ghl2+3.pdf).
47. On the scientific basis for the agreed threshold for allowing resumption of high seas fishing, see Balton, Ch. 5 above.
48. Herr, Ch. 10 above.
49. Fish Stocks Agreement, Art. 5, paras. (e), (f), and (g).
50. Ibid., Arts. 8–12; only Art. 10 (d) deals explicitly with multispecies management—and in a context limited to scientific assessment.
51. CCAMLR Convention, Art. II.
52. Herr, Ch. 10 above.
53. NAFO Convention, Art. I (4); the exceptions are salmon (anadromous), tunas and marlins (highly migratory), cetecian stocks managed by the International Whaling Commission, as well as sedentary species.
54. On the interrelations of various regimes addressing whales and whaling, see S. Andresen, 'The International Whaling Regime: Order at the Turn of the Century?', in D. Vidas and W. Østreng (eds.), *Order for the Oceans at the Turn of the Century* (The Hague: Kluwer Law International, 1999), 215.
55. Oude Elferink, Ch. 6 above.
56. Fish Stocks Agreement, Art. 10, paras. (b) and (j).
57. Ibid., Art. 11.
58. Stokke *et al.*, 'The Barents Sea Fisheries'.
59. Stokke, Ch. 9 above.
60. Joyner, Ch. 7 above. Pre-agreed division keys between coastal and non-coastal states are also found in the Bering Sea Doughnut Hole Convention, referring, however, not directly to national allocation but to the share of the pollock stock to be taken in international waters as opposed to the Russian and United States EEZs; Balton, Ch. 5 above.
61. S. Engesæter, 'Scientific Input to International Fishery Agreements', *International Challenges*, 13 (1993), 85.
62. Protocol on the Conservation, Rational Utilization and Management of Norwegian Spring Spawning Herring (Atlanto-Scandian Herring) in the Northeast Atlantic (1996), Art. 6.2; on file with the author.
63. Balton, Ch. 5 above.
64. Hønneland, Ch. 4 above.

65. See, e.g., S. Jentoft, B. J. McCay, and D. C. Wilson, 'Social Theory and Fisheries Co-management', *Marine Policy*, 22 (1998), 423, who also evaluate counter-arguments such as the risks of regulative capture.
66. Fish Stocks Agreement, Art. 14.
67. Vukas and Vidas, Ch. 2 above.
68. Agreement to Promote Compliance with International Conservation and Management Measures by Fishing Vessels on the High Seas (1993); 33 *ILM* 368.
69. M. Hayashi, 'Enforcement by Non-flag States on the High Seas under the 1995 Agreement on Straddling and Highly Migratory Fish Stocks', *Georgetown International Environmental Law Review*, 9 (1996), 1.
70. Fish Stocks Agreement, Art. 21 (1).
71. Ibid., Art. 21 (5)–(8).
72. Ibid., Art. 23; see also FAO Compliance Agreement, Art. V (2).
73. Vukas and Vidas, Ch. 2 above.
74. Stokke, Ch. 9 above.
75. Oude Elferink, Ch. 6 above.
76. Balton, Ch. 5 above.
77. O. R. Young, 'Institutional Linkages in International Society: Polar Perspectives', *Global Governance*, 2 (1996), 1, at 2.
78. See also the Introduction.
79. P. Birnie and A. E. Boyle, *International Law and the Environment* (Oxford: Clarendon Press, 1992), 444.
80. Fish Stocks Agreement, Art. 5 (d), (e), and (f), and Art. 6 (3) (c) and (d) and 6 (5).
81. Ibid., Art. 30.
82. Boyle, Ch. 3 above.
83. A detailed account of this diffusive interplay is given by Vukas and Vidas, Ch. 2 above.
84. Compare Fish Stocks Agreement, Art. 23, and the Convention of the Law of the Sea, Art. 218; the latter goes somewhat further in that the port state may also institute proceedings.
85. O. R. Young, 'Political Leadership and Regime Formation: On the Development of Institutions in International Society', *International Organization*, 45 (1991), 281; A. Underdal, 'Leadership Theory: Rediscovering the Art of Management', in I. W. Zartman (ed.), *International Multilateral Negotiation* (San Francisco: Jossey-Bass, 1994), 178.
86. D. H. Anderson, 'The Straddling Stocks Agreement of 1995: An Initial Assessment', *International and Comparative Law Quarterly*, 45 (1996), 463–75, at 469.
87. For an extensive discussion, and rejection, of this argument, see S. S. Gezelius, 'Limits to Externalization: The EU NAFO Policy 1979–97', *Marine Policy*, 23 (1999), 147.
88. R. Barston, 'United Nations Conference on Straddling and Highly Migratory Fish Stocks', *Marine Policy*, 19 (1995), 159, at 163–4.
89. Stokke, Ch. 9 above.
90. See, e.g. Anderson, 'The Straddling Stocks Agreement', 467.
91. Oude Elferink, Ch. 6 above.

92. Balton, Ch. 5 above.
93. T. M. Franck, *The Power of Legitimacy among Nations* (New York: Oxford University Press, 1990).
94. C. F. Runge, *Freer Trade, Protected Environment: Balancing Trade Liberalization and Environmental Interests* (New York: Council on Foreign Relations Press, 1994).
95. O. S. Stokke and O. B. Thommesen (eds.), *Yearbook of International Cooperation on Environment and Development 2001–2002* (London: Earthscan, 2001).
96. Andresen, 'The International Whaling Regime'.
97. Runge, *Freer Trade, Protected Environment*.
98. General Agreement on Tariffs and Trade (1947); 55 *UNTS* 194. After the Uruguay round of negotiations, this agreement was incorporated into the General Agreement on Tariffs and Trade (1994) and linked to the World Trade Organization; see Final Act Embodying the Results of the Uruguay Round of Multilateral Trade Negotiations; 33 *ILM* 1145. On the tuna–dolphin issue, see T. J. Schoenbaum, 'International Trade and Protection of the Environment: The Continuing Search for Reconciliation', *American Journal of International Law*, 91 (1997), 268.
99. Stokke, Ch. 9 above.
100. The *lex posterior* rule is codified in Art. 30 of the Vienna Convention on the Law of Treaties, Vienna (1969); 1155 *UNTS* 654; for a discussion of this rule as well as the *lex specialis*, see K. Wolfke, *Custom in Present International Law*, 2nd rev. edn. (The Hague: Martinus Nijhoff, 1993), 94–5.
101. Fish Stocks Agreement, Art. 23 (2).
102. General Agreement on Tariffs and Trade (1947), Art. XX (b) and (g); emphasis added.
103. See Panel Reports on US Restrictions on Imports of Tuna (1991), 30 *ILM* 1598 (USA–Mexico), and (1994), 33 *ILM* 839 (USA–EC and the Netherlands); Appellate Body Report on US Import Prohibition of Shrimp and Certain Shrimp Products (1998), 37 *ILM* 832; also the discussion in Schoenbaum, 'International Trade and Protection of the Environment'.
104. 'Freedom to Provide Services', *EFTA Surveillance Authority: Annual Report 1998* (www.efta.int/structure/SURV/efta-srv.cfm). Art. 5 of Protocol 9 to the European Economic Area Agreement provides for access to ports and associated facilities but exemption is made for landings of fish from stocks, the management of which is subject to severe disagreement among the parties.
105. CCAMLR; Art. XXIII (1)–(3).
106. P. J. Beck, *The International Politics of Antarctica* (London: Croom Helm, 1986), 276.
107. See the Introduction.

Index